Bangladesh – showing the island of Bhola

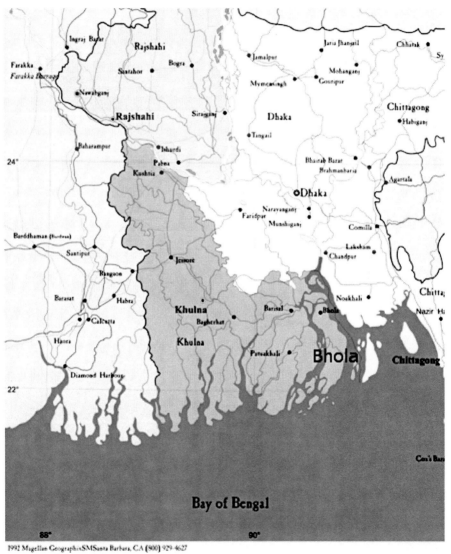

1992 Magellan GeographixSMSanta Barbara, CA (800) 929-4627

Map Credit: Corel Corporation

A BLONDE BENGALI WIFE

By

Anne Hamilton

To Margaret –
   Hope you enjoy this!
   With Best Wishes –
      Anne (H).

A BLONDE BENGALI WIFE

ISBN: 978-1905091-47-8
Paperback version
© 2010 Anne Hamilton. All Rights Reserved
Published by LL-Publication
www.ll-publications.com
57 Blair Avenue
Hurlford
Scotland
KA1 5AZ

Edited by Zetta Brown
Proofreading by Leslie Brown
Book layout and typesetting by jimandzetta.com
Cover Design by Helen E. H. Madden pixelarcana.com © LL-
Publications 2010
Photo Credits: Jacqui Dunbar
Map credit: Corel Corporation

Printed in the UK and the USA
Published in paperback and digital formats

Contents

Dedication

This book is for my ever-growing
Bangladeshi family, both then and now.

And for Ger who has always been there.

Preface

Bhola Island, Bangladesh

Getting There

The road to Bhola has been—is—long and winding. It's the story of a travel diary that evolved into *A Blonde Bengali Wife* and became instrumental in forming the charity Bhola's Children.

It began with my first (of eight and counting) visit to Bangladesh when I fell utterly in love with the country. Starry-eyed, all I wanted to do was talk non-stop about my beloved: the beautiful people and places, the laughter, the tears, the stories. I was running the risk of becoming a complete Bangla-bore.

So, I wrote it all down and ended up with a book so huge it made *The Complete Works of Shakespeare* look like a pamphlet. It needed ruthless editing. Feeling slightly indulgent, I enlisted the help of professional editor Hilary Johnson. Hilary assured me it was worth the price of all the red ink sloshed over it, and then proved it by sending the book to literary agent Dinah Wiener.

Months passed. I went back to Bangladesh. Meanwhile, something had made Dinah fish the manuscript out of that place bigger and more mysterious than *Narnia*, the agent's bottom drawer.

Reading the manuscript made Dinah want to visit Bangladesh. Even as I pointed out the challenges, coincidence or destiny was already at work. By chance, Dinah met an Italian woman, Bruna Colombo-Otten, who knew Bangladesh and had been introduced to Howlader Akkel Ali on one of her visits there. Ali, orphaned at the age of eight and with forty years experience of caring for disabled children, had a dream, a dream of a home and a school where children and young people with different disabilities could live, learn, and work together. Everyone else said it wouldn't—couldn't—possibly work. Everyone, that is, except Bruna. She was so inspired by Ali that she suggested he find accommodation for this home and she would finance it.

Ali comes from the Barisal district of Southern Bangladesh in which lies the island of Bhola jutting out to the Bay of Bengal. In Bengali, *bhola* means "forgotten" and it was on this "forgotten island" that Ali found the property that is now called Bhola Garden. Together with some orphaned and disabled children and staff, he carried out basic renovations, and then began encouraging families all over the island to send their disabled children to daily lessons.

When Bruna made her first trip to Bhola, Dinah went with her. They discovered that Bhola Garden took the traditionally grim notions of orphanages, third-world poverty and disability and simply knocked them on their heads. Bhola Garden was full of life, love, colour, and the word Dinah used to describe it was "magical."

Being There

In November 2007, with enough money and holiday time finally saved, Dinah and I flew to Dhaka and straight into the total blackout that was Cyclone Sidr. The news from Bhola was reassuring: everyone was safe. A massive tree had fallen on the flimsy accommodation where the girls usually slept, but they had been moved into the classroom. Other trees had landed on the roof of the makeshift workshop, but compared with so much of the country, they were unscathed.

A crowded overnight launch, a speedboat across the Bay of Bengal, a motor rickshaw through the once more peaceful dawn, and there were the big, blue and yellow gates marking the entrance to Bhola Garden. I quickly understood exactly why Dinah had called it magical.

Bhola Garden is now home to about forty children and school for another fifteen, with many more waiting in the wings. Mamun and Sofia are blind, so they make clay figures of the pictures the others are colouring in. Little Sonia, the youngest, is deaf, as is Monira, the beautiful and skilled carpenter. This doesn't stop either of them having a sense of rhythm that makes them great dancers. And just because Farouk the caretaker and twelve-year-old Putul have cerebral palsy doesn't mean they aren't a crack badminton double. One minute, there is virtual silence whilst everyone is signing, the next, the harmonium is out and everyone belts out a raucous and enthusiastic verse of "We Shall Overcome." They also learn woodwork, simple farming and sewing. They take turns gardening and cooking, all vital trades which will offer some chance of future independence. In Bhola Garden, I hear the echo of my own father's oh-so-irritating words as I grew up: *"There is no such word as 'can't'!"*

Bhola's Children is a family like any other. They aren't perfect, they fight, they argue, they cry, but there's little a good cuddle doesn't put right. In practical terms, Ali and the children live in very basic conditions. They bathe, swim, do their laundry and breed fish all in the same pond. Their staple food is rice, with meat or fish a couple of times a week; milky, sugary sweets are a rare treat. They grow most of their own vegetables. When they receive gifts, they are delighted with toothbrushes, plastic combs, and hair oil. There is little to spare for visits to the doctor, the dentist, or anything unexpected.

Outreach work, that is teaching the community about disability, is part of daily life. Ali oversees hospital arrangements in Dhaka for the many infants whose frightened parents agonise over cleft palates and club feet. Better, he says, that these are prevented—and educating people about the need to reduce inter-marriage and avoiding very young pregnancies—is the best way forward. Better too, that families learn there is no stigma in their child being blind or deaf and that sending them to school rather than hiding them away will significantly improve their life chances. Imagine how Bhola Garden changed the life of one little girl from a remote village who had no idea—until she met Khaleda and Prionka, children her own age—that other people were deaf too.

Leaving There

Ali is a remarkable man with a remarkable dream, and Bhola Garden is living proof of it. Dinah is a remarkable woman with a remarkable dream, and Bhola's Children, a charity established by Dinah and registered in March 2007, is living proof of that. The charity is a commitment from all of the Trustees—there are now eight of us—to nurture and progress everything that makes Bhola Garden what it is today and what we hope it will be tomorrow.

As well as the day-to-day financial support, Bhola's Children's first purchase was a Toyota microbus so that, for the first time, outings and picnics and trips to appointments don't rely on public buses or rickshaws. For Lailey, the young cook who is an amputee, it means no longer staying at home alone. For Rezia and Rosina, two of the blind girls, it will always be the memory of being led across the muddy beach for their first-ever paddle in the river.

The initial major project was to complete a properly-built, two-storey hostel for the children, staff, and Ali to live in year-round safety and far greater comfort than the tin shacks that barely protected them from the elements. Two years later, the current scheme involves updating the equally primitive sheds in which carpentry and tailoring are taught; proper workshops mean these will grow into businesses creating much needed income. Over the long term, the grand plan is for a dispensary and health clinic that will meet the needs of not just Bhola's Children, but the surrounding community too. Ultimately, of course, it relies on successful fundraising and charitable donation.

All money earned from *A Blonde Bengali Wife* goes direct to Bhola's Children. Not because we're particularly generous or kind people, but because once you've been to Bhola, you just can't *not* be involved. For Ali, though, it's so much more than the money. It's the knowledge that way beyond Bhola Garden, his international "family" is looking out for him and the children. As he so often says, "Thank you for keeping your nice eye on us."

As for the travel diary turned book, *A Blonde Bengali Wife* isn't about Bhola, but it is a tribute to my journeys into Bangladesh and all the friends I have made there. Most of all, the story that follows is the story—the country—that inspired Bhola's Children.

Anne Hamilton
August 2010
www. bholaschildren. org
http://anne-ablondebengaliwife.blogspot.com

Prologue

I fell in love on the sixteenth of February 2002. It was unexpected, a strangeness growing familiar, breeding contentment, and settling with a knowing certainty like a warm cloak around my shoulders. Quietly simmering over days and weeks, it probably began in a makeshift kitchen in Rajoir, developed on a bus in Jessore, reached the point of acknowledgement in front of the television in Dhaka, and was cemented in Chittagong. The honeymoon led me through Cox's Bazaar and finally into the Sunderbans.

Like the best love stories, it was the product of serendipity: a faded picture from my 1970's childhood. When, in the Lenten prelude to Easter, my classmates and I were each handed a small, cardboard money box. We made sincere vows to "feed all the poor children in the world." The grainy, monochromatic photographs on each side of the boxes always showed a tiny, black baby with a protruding stomach being cradled by a jolly nun or a smiling Salvation Army lady. Virtuously, we would vie with one other to poke pennies and tuppences into the narrow slit. Smugly, we identified those with the Sellotaped boxes, evidence that the craving for cola bottles and sherbet lemons had led to a secret plunder. In my shining moment, aged eight, I broke the class record with a grand total of £2. 19½ and for the rest of the year I sat complacent.

I, single-handedly, was saving countless starving babies in a far-off place called Bangladesh.

1

Day 1 - Far and Away

Caught up in the frenzied momentum of the Hall of Arrivings in Zia International Airport, I dodge swarthy policemen whose packed holsters rest on nonchalant hips and join a bedraggled queue for passport control. Drowning in an all-encompassing staccato of foreign language, rendered self-conscious by a thousand stares, I expect delays and confusion, but the bored official takes my landing card, curls his lip and pronounces, "Foreigners not needing this paper." He rips it in half, in quarters, and tosses the pieces high in the air like homemade confetti.

"Lugs? Have lugs?" another uniform barks.

We stare at each other for a long minute. My ears twitch.

"Lugs. Lugs?" he shouts, pointing to a pile of suitcases opportunely passing by on the elderly head of a lone porter. "Wait lugs. Lugs go," he orders through a mist of miscomprehension.

I wait. And I wait a bit more. Luggage grinds around a carousel that breaks down with hypnotising regularity. I see the stuff other passengers load onto their convoys of trolleys, and congratulate myself on a single, if vast, rucksack that shudders into view just as I am confronting the possibility of a night without clean knickers. I hoist it onto an enormous, compartmentalised cart where it resembles the last egg in a two-dozen box, and then dawdle towards the glass doors.

The final threads of my security net snap as I emerge onto a film set of that standard, tele-visual depiction of the Third World. A heavy cloak of heat settles on my shoulders and a celestial glare belies the sky's blanket whiteness. Flying in and descending over the empty, muddy riverbeds slicing through the mustard-coloured bog lands of the well-advanced dry season, I pondered the whereabouts of Bangladesh's 140 million inhabitants.

The answer was in front of me.

Anne Hamilton

On the other side of grey and functional prison gates manned by blue-bereted guards sporting sand-coloured trousers and large rifles, a watchful and abundant crowd pushes forward, eagerly, volubly scanning the emerging passengers. Men in traditional and Western clothing predominate. They are ten, fifteen rows deep, a swarming carpet of locusts grasping the railings, clambering atop one another's shoulders and shaking the clattering metal barriers. Without embarrassment, they are hugging new arrivals, holding hands, weeping with joy. The women, their sleek, dark hair knotted up and shielded by long scarves—*dupattas*—are a rainbow of colours. Saris and *salwar kameezes, the loose tunics worn over baggy trousers,* come in clashing and contrasting shades: reds and golds, bright oranges, and purples. Black burkhas equalise spangled finery and threadbare poverty.

I do note that amongst this heaving, lively, mixed bag of humanity, there appears to be a surprising scarcity of smiling Salvation Army ladies and plump, jolly nuns cradling pot-bellied, huge-eyed babies.

The noise is deafening, everyone is shouting. My problem is that nobody appears to be shouting for me.

"What the hell am I doing here, anyway?" I mutter to myself. "First, my very patient husband drives me through hours of snow to an all-but-closed airport, and then the check-in staff has no record of my reservation. Sensible people would take this as a warning. Me? Oh no, I have to be clever, travel thousands of miles across the world whilst everyone else I know is sitting around in a post-Christmas lethargy, guzzling New Year champagne and canapés..."

Leaning on my trolley, trying to look blasé whilst scanning the crowd and waiting to be found—in this crowd, a pale-faced, blonde-haired Westerner is a beacon—a frowning policeman accosts me.

"Bangla, *na,*" I apologise, bemoaning my half-hearted efforts with Bengali tapes and a phrasebook. We attempt to communicate in sign language since the only English phrase the policeman can repeat frequently and with a serious smile is unconstructive in the circumstances:

"I love you," he announces, arms akimbo. "I love you."

"Thank you," I say. "But do you love me enough to take me home with you? You see, I don't know where I'm going, where I am staying, who is going to meet me, what I will be doing, or indeed, with whom I will be doing it."

Gently, he moves me to a quieter spot where more people can easily watch me. Minutes grind past. Then...

I spy a beige anorak jumping up and down amidst the crowd, a torn cardboard sign hoist above his head. He is pushing through the throng, and then arguing with a security guard, and then braving the concrete no-man's land before me. Is this my saviour in nylon slacks and Jesus sandals? Sure enough, I decipher a faint biro scribble on the back of the cereal packet dangling from his arm.

His mouth is moving. "Hey you, *salaam walekum*. Hello." I think I lip read. "*Salaam.*"

"*Walekum es-salaam,*" I croak, my voice lost in the universal clamour.

"Come." The man motions.

I follow him.

The policeman follows me.

Like the Red Sea, the staring crowd parts for our relay passage.

"Stay," my new escort commands and dashes into the road.

The policeman erects a protective cordon around me. "I love you," he confirms.

"Then, soon you must let me go," I tell him. "It's all right, honestly. That man is from SCI—did you see his sign? SCI: *Service Civil International*. Do you know it?" I raise my eyebrows in hope. "It's an international charity that arranges cultural exchange visits for...Oh, never mind."

"I love you?" he asks.

"I love you too," I echo, almost truthfully.

The constipated traffic is an aural torture chamber with the tinkle of rickshaw bells, squealing brakes, and honking hooters. Battered buses and ponderous, primrose-coloured trucks painted with faded hieroglyphics chug off in a stream of dust. The occasional shiny limo purrs past, and taxicabs are in transit. All have some prang or bump. Worse than the centre of Rome, the congestion of Cairo, or the craziness around the Arc de Triomphe, impotent vehicles strain to speed in every direction. Drivers are oblivious to the whistles of the traffic police. All appear to be ranting and gesticulating their right to a piece—any piece—of the road.

While absent-mindedly cuffing a couple of people around the ear, my policeman helps the SCI representative jam me into a smoky, rattling, three-wheeler auto-rickshaw, and only then does he mooch back to his station. This so-called "baby taxi" has proportions suitable for seating one chubby toddler. My escort and I look like premature twins in the last remaining incubator. There are no doors, just rolled up plastic covers. Our driver jolts us headlong into the throng, bouncing along a road akin to an unpaved quarry, and swerves onto the pavement, pausing for petrol to be poured into a hole just under the steering wheel. Both the driver and the pump attendant lean over cheerfully, the cigarettes dangling from their mouths by no means impede their abuse of a limbless beggar who is surprisingly fleet of foot and a gang of children selling dirty bottles of tap water.

Soon we race down the road until everything blurs. I have one hand on my flight bag—since my companion mimed it worthy of a possible smash-and-grab routine—the other is gripping the seat to delay my inevitable slide to the floor. My knee is wedged against my rucksack, my hair is all over my face, and I am practically sitting on the knee of a Bangladeshi man whose name I cannot fathom. He starts several conversations with a lopsided and incredulous grin:

"Nam?"

"Er, say that again?"

"Nam? Nam? You nam?"

"Oh, I see. Anne. My name is Anne."

He has a good laugh, and then jabs himself violently in the chest. "Me nam: Shadow."

Well, that's what it sounds like anyway. I smile. There is a long pause.

"Your country—where?" he shouts valiantly, proud of his grasp of English.

Encouraged by his enthusiastic and totally incomprehensible hand gestures, I focus carefully.

"It's Ireland. I'm from Ireland. My country is Ireland," I respond, like an English tutor.

"Ireland?" he repeats. "Hmm." He smiles again. "Ahh, England," he says, nodding.

It reminds me of all the people back home who said: "You're going where? Bangladesh? Isn't that in India?"

I open my mouth, choke on a mouthful of hair, and close it again, thus failing my first test of cultural exchange. Instead, I concentrate on not falling out of the auto-rickshaw. I assure myself that the driver knows exactly what he is doing as he scrapes the back of a red and green double-decker and leans out to push a line of bicycle rickshaws from his path. We squeeze through minute spaces until I feel like a cartoon that can morph at will. Equally-optimistic pedestrians hold up warning fists as they thrust through available gaps. Most emerge unscathed on the other side.

Men, women, and children saunter along the grimy, dusty pavement heading home to higgledy-piggledy rows of lean-to shacks where cast-iron cooking pots smoulder on open fires tended by indiscernible figures huddled beneath old blankets and eye their resting braces of scraggy cattle. Simple homes sit shoulder-to-shoulder with large apartment buildings, fancy restaurants, and the grand, policed entrance to the military cantonment.

Mr Shadow clears his throat loudly, turns, and spits generously into the road. "You. Bangladesh. First time." He chuckles, folds his arms, and changes position all the better to watch me.

"Yes," I say chattily and rack my brains for something else. "Do you work in the SCI office?"

His grin widens.

"What is your job?" I try again. Louder.

He wiggles his head.

"You. SCI. Volunteer?" I screech above the sounds of the city.

He claps his hands and laughs harder. "Yes. Me, volunteer. SCI Bangladesh. Shadow. Age twenty-three. Six sister. Three brother...You?"

"Er... Anne. Volunteer. SCI Ireland. Age thirty-two. One brother."

We mutually compute the data.

"You thirty-two? You? Thirty-two? You age? Age *thirty-two*?"

I nod, and he collapses with mirth. "Thirty-two." I hear at intervals. Then another thought strikes him. "One brother. One brother only? No sister?"

I nod again, timidly this time. Pityingly, he shakes his head. I attempt to recover lost ground.

"Husband," I say, pointing to myself. "I have husband."

He scrunches up his brow. "Husband," he says, and then he looks alarmed. "You husband. Where?"

He twists backwards, peers behind the hurtling baby taxi as if we have inadvertently forgotten my other half at the airport and will see him chasing behind us in a rusty Toyota Starlet shouting, "Follow that three wheeler scooter thing!" in fluent Bangla.

"Not here," I yell at his back. "Home. In Ireland."

He turns slowly to me. "Husband Ireland. Wife Bangladesh," he verifies. He shakes his head in disbelief. "Husband Ireland. Wife Bangladesh."

After a long gaze he slaps his leg and laughs, and laughs again. I refuse headroom to a pang of homesickness.

Throughout the journey, he pokes speculatively at my corpse-sized black rucksack. Just as I begin to assume that the crowds never cease, we sidestep a line of stalls selling hot snacks and tea and grind to a halt in a quieter, more residential area. After several minutes of boisterously negotiating the fare (Mr Shadow), trying to blend into the scenery (me), and heaving my bag from what is almost its final resting place (me, Shadow, the rickshaw-*wallah*, plus several onlookers and a cow), I face the SCI office, a narrow, three-storey building behind iron railings.

The second floor reveals a frugal office made of a couple of rooms dwarfed by a conference table from around which a group of men nod in welcome. Overhead spins a lethargic fan. All the furnishings are cracked, stained, and worn. Green paint is peeling from the walls, and the copious shelves of paper files appear to have been stacked circa 1946 and left to rot. Even with the almost-modern computer, the office resembles an unimportant military command post of the Second World War. In the farthest recess, two men are reading newspapers. Mr Shadow formally introduces me.

"She is Anne," he tells them. To me he helpfully adds: "Bonny shoes. Cup cha."

"Hello. I am Bonny," explains the younger of the two men who is plump and has a military moustache. He stands to shake my hand.

"And my name is Suez," says the other, removing thick-rimmed reading glasses and smoothing down a blue and red striped woolly sweater, the style of which only an adoring mother could have knitted. "For SCI, I welcome you to Bangladesh. Shahardot (Ah! Mr "Shadow," I presume!) brings us tea. Please sit down."

Despite their fluent English, I have a poor ear and am reluctant to suggest they repeat themselves more than three times so our chitchat is desultory. We drink the tea, a milky, sweet liquid in small glasses, and I become uncomfortably aware that they, whilst clearly expecting me, are a bit puzzled about what to do with me.

"We have minimum lone female visitors," Bonny says.

"But we are most pleased that you join us," adds Suez. "Also we have word of a lady from Australia coming. She is older."

Suez and Bonny talk amongst themselves for a moment.

"Do you like to stay with a host family? Or you prefer a dormitory?" asks Suez. "You have freedom to be alone in a dormitory, but a host family looks after you. We think host family is best," he adds.

"I would like that." I agree, and they both look relieved. "Are the family expecting me?"

"It is fine," assures Bonny.

"All fine." Suez repeats, standing up. "Come. Now you meet our volunteer colleagues. Meet Bachchu who is Assistant National Secretary, and Moni who…"

I am introduced to eight men, yet it feels like a football crowd, and if a million Euros depended on it, I could not match names to faces.

There are many moments of bewildering, shouted conversation, good-natured banter, and brief argument during which I sit quietly. I have no idea what is going on, and I suspect that this is going to be a familiar feeling. Still, there is some liberation in being so deskilled. I know that today and tomorrow, at least, I can confidently look hopeless and thus pass the buck. On the other hand, I fear that this is something at which I might well excel.

"Anne? Perhaps you send email messages home now?" Suez leads me gently by the elbow to the computer. All the volunteers watch as it cranks to life.

"Tell your family how you like Bangladesh," Suez encourages me.

"Say about SCI," suggests Bachchu the secretary who has, he tells me, just bought the shiny brown leather jacket he is wearing, zipped up to the neck. He is clearly besotted and can't stop stroking it. Periodically, the others ask about it: was it imported specially; could he get them one; can they try it on...? Bachchu looks as scandalised as if someone had offered to buy his new born baby.

"You can tell your country what is good in our country," adds his friend, the very good-looking Moni. He is taller than the average Bangladeshi man, verging on six feet, his styled hair almost touches his collar and his cheek bones are model quality. He clearly prides himself on being "cool." Whilst the others almost trip over in their efforts to charm, Moni is polite but distant.

The team of enthusiastic SCI members hanging over my shoulders is sufficient to give even the most prolific writer a block. I strive for one sharp and witty sentence and eventually, to the delight of all concerned, Bonny reads out my sparkling prose:

"Arrived safely. Love Anne." Bonny is surprised. "Will not your husband want more? If my wife leaves me for many months, I expect many words."

"Your wife is Bangladeshi; she does not leave." Suez points out. "It is the husband in our country who leaves to work or study. In the West, overseas travel is more common for wives too, yes, Anne?"

"Um, sometimes." I hesitate because I'm not really sure that it is. Were it my husband working, that would definitely be "normal," particularly in a rural Irish community where mass emigration remains a recent memory. As a woman though, even (or especially) without children, I do hear unwarranted speculation about my absence: "Things not going well in that household then...?" It's a puzzle to explain to assorted male Bangladeshis that my being away from home is okay. It works for us. Our fifteen-year relationship has thrived around (or because of?) absences for travel or study.

Anne Hamilton

As work resumes, Shahardot is summoned to escort me to my host family. At this stage, I'm like a friendly mongrel tagging along behind anyone who pats him on the head and says, "Come." This time it is a nerve-jangling journey by bicycle rickshaw, and already I wonder if two months will be long enough to master the art of riding. Masses of people cease their eating, talking, walking, and squatting to watch this pallid foreigner sail past houses and shops of all varieties: grocers, bathroom outfitters, outlets touting nothing but loud hailers, tea stalls, and restaurants where the food is prepared on large pavement griddles with piles and piles of eggs stacked up beside them. In untidy terraces, some stores are sturdy, squat buildings, others are impermanent wooden structures; more still comprise a ragged tarpaulin secured between bamboo canes.

The rickshaw halts outside a tall, once-white apartment building; an anonymous entity in a sea of others, entangled with the shanty dwellings of the city's poorest. We climb stairs rising from behind a metal grille to the top floor where Shahardot collapses into a small, square flat. Inside is fourteen-year-old Farabia, slim in her long Western-style skirt, with plaited hair so long she can sit on it, who welcomes me without curiosity and watches Shahardot without comment as he immediately rifles through unpacked groceries and helps himself to oranges from a large, brown packet. He departs, satisfied, leaving the door swinging open behind him.

The entrance of the flat leads directly into a combined sitting and eating area, off which is a small, laundry-draped veranda. A thin curtain shades a room either side. The stone sink, a large hole in the ground beneath it, dominates the rudimentary galley kitchen; two gas burners and an array of blackened cooking pots are piled on the floor. Foodstuffs—vegetables mainly—are heaped beside them, the shelf given over to a meagre assortment of dishes and drinking glasses.

"Here lives me, my mother and father, my brother Alvi, and Mamun, the young brother of my mother," Farabia says.

Gratefully, guiltily, I appreciate her schoolgirl English, and when her little brother arrives a few minutes later, he adds his few words. Having foreigners appear on their doorstep is nothing out of the ordinary.

"Very many SCI visitors stay. We enjoy. You can take your bath now," Farabia tells me in one breath. "Then take rest, and I serve your food."

She shows me where to stow my bag and change my clothes. Alvi, who must be about ten and is as unlike Farabia as it is possible for siblings to be, given he is short and squat with his shirt hanging out and his glasses all lopsided, leans at the door and watches with interest as I root into my bag for toothbrush and a towel. Unlocking the bolt on the outside of the bathroom door, I step over a mat of assorted flip-flops and plastic shoes, lock the door behind me, and take stock.

My new-girl-itis is acute. I hazard a guess at how to use the lavatory since it is of the squat variety and situated on a slightly-raised platform with enamel footprints either side of the bowl. Clearly you hover over it, do your thing and...At this point, I realise why the rubber shoes are outside the door. By process of elimination, I gather that the tap low on the ground and jug beside it are for washing—with the left hand, naturally—and for manual toilet flushing. The shower is an erratic nozzle jutting from the wall with a tap at knee-height below it. But just what is the purpose of the huge, red bucket? Gingerly, I edge it to one side, fearful it is brimful of holy water that I will inadvertently contaminate. I open my mouth to call Farabia, but quickly close it again as I realise that such a question is akin to admitting that I do not know how to wash myself.

Briskly, I peel off my clothes, hook them awkwardly on a rail above the cistern, and turn on the shower to the barest lukewarm trickle. Two seconds later, I am dressing again. My clothes are wetter than I am.

Back in the bedroom, I obediently lie down to drowse but sleep is elusive. My mind is on overdrive. Sunlight and intriguing sounds and smells waft through the open window. The still-giggling Alvi is peeking around the doorframe, and Farabia tiptoes in and out to collect her schoolbooks...her make-up...her magazines. Hours later it is only mid-afternoon, so I get up and Farabia pushes me toward the dining-table. She piles a shallow dish with a mountain of rice that I'll be unable to eat in a lifetime, let alone one sitting, and then spoons out a hard-boiled egg and some sauce. Farabia sits one side of me, with Alvi the other, and both watch carefully as I thrust my right hand into the food, grab a handful, get some of it into my mouth and chew enthusiastically on the cold egg. Farabia offers me a spoon, but gamely I shake my head.

Farabia is intent on looking after me, and although we swap stories with fewer misinterpretations than my earlier discussions with Shahardot, there are still long pauses.

"What would you be doing if I was not here?" I ask her.

Her eyes light up. "I show you," she says, leading me into the second curtained room and gesturing I should recline on the large, low bed. She pulls the blinds until the room is dim and faint strips of light dapple the ceiling. On this, my first afternoon in a strange country, I look forward to a taste of teenage Bangladeshi culture and, smiling beatifically, Farabia indulges me. She switches on the television, fiddles with the remote control, and finds her choice.

"MTV," she sighs happily as loud music and Britney Spears fill the screen.

When the electricity fails the first time, she just shrugs. When it happens again and is gone for a while, Farabia groans and reluctantly turns off the set.

"Come. We go to the roof."

She unlocks the door to the flat roof, which is hung with an array of colourful laundry and dotted with large, green pot plants still dripping water from a neighbour's careful tending. The warmth of the sun belies the haziness of the day, and I realise that the fog is smog and not a heat haze and remember that Dhaka is one of the most polluted cities in the world.

There are tall and short apartment blocks, some partially constructed, others appearing much the worse for wear with bars on their windows and crumbling paintwork. Squashed between them are wooden, jerry-built shacks, reminiscent of the garden shed at the bottom of an old council allotment. The fact they are inhabited is obvious from the women and children on haunches before them, washing pots, themselves, their animals. Brown roads, sandy and dusty, resemble country tracks. Down, far below, sauntering young girls in blue and white uniforms look like child-nurses.

"My school." Farabia is glum. "That is uniform." She runs a complacent hand over her current outfit, a long, loose skirt and thick jumper.

Old and young men casually shoulder huge baskets of cauliflowers, oranges, sacks of rice, even a brace of barely-live chickens. On street corners, they share a glass of tea, a cigarette. Two boys pull an oxen cart piled precariously with metal filing cabinets; a nomadic tailor cuts his cheap cloth on the dusty sidewalk. A shiny, white car roars down the street and tests its brakes in front of our apartment building. The occupants, cool and laid-back in sunglasses, climb out languidly and cannot hide their glee as an admiring throng gathers around the restored bodywork. One of them takes a handkerchief from his pocket, spits extravagantly and wipes an imaginary smudge from the bonnet.

"Name of this area is Mohammadpur," Farabia says. "SCI also in Mohammadpur area. Suez lives in Kallyanpur, next neighbourhood. Bonny also. Moni—do you already meet Moni ?—I do not know where he lives. Moni is maximum handsome," she confides. "But do not tell I say this."

We go back into the flat, sit down in the seating area inside the door, and, joined by Alvi, we all look at each other. As daylight fades, Farabia finds candles and instructs her disinclined brother (sibling rivalry is identical in any language) to dot them around the room. They drag out my pocket photo album, pore over family snaps, marvel over real snow, at the colour-painted houses in my hometown, and at the emptiness of the wild landscape. Farabia is inclined to find a frame for the single shot of my husband ("You put beside bed and not feel lonely"), but knowing how the man is virtually allergic to having his picture taken and would recoil at a public display, I manage to dissuade her.

Before Farabia and Alvi can produce their family photograph albums, the room is filled with artificial birdsong of the doorbell heralding the homecoming of their parents. I stand up, nervous once more, but my trepidation is unwarranted. Pavel and his wife Rehana greet me at the door. Both are chatty and communicative as far as the language barrier allows. In fact, Pavel's English is excellent, if highly accented. Rehana, plump, dark haired and beautiful, finds it a struggle.

"*Amra khai,*" Rehana says, her modicum of English exhausted. She looks helplessly at me, smoothing her hands over her tight *salwar kameez.*

I trawl the fuzzy recesses of my mind. "Eat?" I ask hopefully. "You are going to eat?"

"Ha, ha! Yes, yes." Rehana joins her hands with pleasure.

I begin to refuse more food for fear of bursting, but their combined disappointment is so vast that I help myself to another bucket of rice. Fleetingly, I think of my mother who is convinced I will be living on emergency Red Cross maize. Luckily, the family is distracted from my conservative consumption by the arrival of Mamun, Rehana's brother, exquisitely dressed in casual Western clothes, and his hair teased into gelled scruffiness.

"Hello, you," he nods at me. "Ireland, yes? How much money is kilo rice in Ireland? In Bangladesh, is nothing. I get very good deal. Potatoes? You want? Very good price in Bangladesh."

Mamun is clearly the entrepreneur of the family.

"The Australian woman comes maybe today, maybe tomorrow," Pavel announces. "Friend for you, Anne. She stays here also."

Anne Hamilton

Adding the three thousand mosquitoes that have decided to move in with me, the apartment is beginning to resemble that of the old woman who lives in the shoe.

By now, I am drooping, and I'm glad when Rehana makes a move to bed. Farabia and Alvi take their essentials from the bedroom (school books, moisturiser, and a large toy furry spider, respectively) and clear the bed of cushions.

"Where will you sleep?" I ask Farabia.

"We have many mattresses," she says, gesturing vaguely towards the floor. She ignores my argument.

Alone in the bedroom, I give up trying to put my thoughts in order and instead press all the switches on the wall: I turn on the fan, cause some kind of bell to ring, start up some implement that sounds like an angry waste disposal unit, and finally manage my original intention, to put out the light. I grope my way back to the bed. The blessedly welcome, hard-as-concrete, bed.

Naturally, all my demons erupt in a taunting mass. Of course, I want to be here in Bangladesh, but that doesn't mean I am confident, well-prepared, or calm about it. In fact, I've probably never been confident, well-prepared, or calm about anything, but I do have a well-developed stubborn streak that frequently makes me choose the hardest option.

A fond, probably skewed memory is a facile reason for choosing a travel destination perhaps, but it seemed perfectly logical last July when vague possibility became curious probability. After rejecting India (everyone goes there), Sri Lanka (too much of a holiday destination), and Nepal (the Crown Prince went berserk and wiped out half his family thus closing international ports of entry), I hit on Bangladesh for no better reason other than I knew—know—little about it, and understand even less what to expect, but I desperately want to learn.

"Great help you'll be to a struggling NGO," observed a doubtful friend.

"Is it better that I go with a truck load of misconceptions?" was my response. "Anyway, tell me all you know about Bangladesh?"

"I'm not the one with the crazy notions," she sidestepped.

Still, I feel vindicated. Like me, most people have not a clue about the country.

"Bangladesh?" they say vaguely. "That's interesting. Isn't that in Pakistan?"

Or:

"Bangladesh? Are you crazy? You'll have diarrhoea and...," they whisper, "those places don't have toilet paper."

I am suddenly, thankfully distracted when the harsh bedroom light is snapped on. Rehana is ushering in a tall, thin woman with short, greying hair and a friendly if bemused smile; the same look I have had on my face all day.

"Christine from Australia," Rehana says by way of introduction. "Anne from Ireland. You sleep here." She points to the bed in which I lie, and I obligingly move over to one side. Before Christine or I can say anything, my friend Shahardot, who is lugging two suitcases, launches a huge square canvas bag into the room. He points at me in recognition, laughs for old time's sake, and demands money from Christine.

With Rehana watching avidly, Christine changes into the long johns that contrast nicely with my oversized purple T-shirt. She opens her canvas bag and from its depths, and like a Mary Poppins, she shakes out a full-sized duvet and pillow. We lie down side by side and make the desultory small talk of strangers who have just climbed into bed together.

"Must be a bit like an arranged marriage, this," says Christine.

"Well, they said Bangladesh would be an experience," I add. "I don't know about you, but this is the first time I've slept with someone three minutes after meeting them."

2

Week 1 - Welcome to Dhaka

It is a testing night, less to do with the presence of a stranger beside me or the barely muted city noises than the mummification properties of my brand-new sleeping bag. I think nostalgically of the shiny, oblong version I was forced into on interminable childhood caravan holidays, the bulk of which would never squeeze into this contemporary pocket-sized pouch, but did leave room to stretch.

"What—or who—were you fighting during the night?" Christine asks, on waking.

"Just trying to turn over. I brought medication for most ailments, but unguent for bedsores is not amongst it." I launch into the trials of the sleeping bag.

"Didn't you try it before you bought it?" she sounds surprised.

I shrug. Picture me on a day trip to pre-Christmas-rush Dublin:

"A sleeping bag, Madam? Certainly. Where will you be sleeping? Inside or out? Alone or with a companion? Average ambient temperature at nightfall? All season rating?"

"Er...I don't really know. That blue one is a pretty colour. I'll take that. Oh, and I'd like a rucksack too, please."

"Very well, Madam. Travelling by plane, train, bus, car, or foot? City or country? Sun proof, sand proof, wind proof, or water proof?"

"Yes, thanks. That should just about cover it."

"Then I assume madam would also like a first-aid kit?"

"Ooh, definitely. What kind...?"

"No doubt Madam will be suited by our industrial-sized, one-stop, cure-all bumperkit with household, desert, and mountain survival components, and the latest George Clooney-endorsed edition of *Teach Yourself Emergency Surgery*."

"Including those shiny tinfoil wrappings for warding off hypothermia?"

Christine pokes me and I jump back to reality. "Earth calling Anne...Better tell me about yourself, just in case there's something I should know. History of narcolepsy maybe?"

"I'm perfectly ordinary," I admit. "Too ordinary to want to talk about myself."

"Pooh. This place'll learn you. Your knicker size, annual income, and most embarrassing bowel habits will be broadcast to the nation by next week."

So, as the sky lightens, and the muezzin calls the faithful to prayer, we swap potted life histories. Like me, Christine has not travelled to Bangladesh before, but, unlike me for whom South East Asia is completely undiscovered, she is a veteran of India. Here for four weeks, she plans to participate in one of the SCI-run rural community projects, whereas I should be able to do two or three of them. Christine speedily gathers that my surviving the duration is dependent on an intelligent and sensible sidekick. I am pathetically thrilled with my ready-made best friend.

The suave Mamun, strutting his stuff in tight shorts, interrupts our bonding session. He takes his time retrieving clean clothes from the wardrobe, and then stands in front of our bed, hands on his hips.

"Blue shirt is good, yes? Or, how you say—yellow? How much these fabrics in Australia? In Dhaka, I get for twenty *taka* only. You like?"

"Very nice," I say. "Lovely. But I don't really need any more clothes."

"Okay. You want jewellery? I get bargains from many men."

"Not now, thanks," says Christine, more firmly.

"Okay. Then I go to work. Unless you like to admire my body some more? I am giving free view. Tomorrow you pay only five *taka* to see my shining manhood."

Aiming to be good and polite guests, we don't burst out laughing until he leaves the room.

The tiny house comes alive. Farabia heads off to school, Pavel to work, Mamun to his office. Alvi remains fast asleep on the daybed in the living area, and Rehana prepares breakfast in shifts.

"My servant," she introduces a young girl, bare-footed in a torn and dirty sari on whose skinny hip is balanced a sickly baby. Whilst she washes clothes, scours pots, scrubs vegetables and floors, the child is dumped screaming on the floor. He crouches, whining and snivelling, like an injured animal.

I play with the shower, the bucket, and the jug, squat knowledgeably over the toilet, and join Christine at the table. Rehana, aware of the anxieties of newly arrived volunteers and their tender, un-acclimatised stomachs, proudly demonstrates the boiling and purification of our drinking water. She goes on to describe the food in one-word Bengali. *Padji,* the spicy, green vegetables with potato are scooped up with thin, circular discs of *roti*, literally flat bread. We finish with the first of many, many *kohla*, or bananas.

"And *cha'*," Rehana says, as we drink sweetened tea. "In my country drink much *cha'*."

"Any idea what we do today?" Christine asks me.

"SCI orientation. Someone is coming to collect us at..." I consult my watch. "Well, about two hours ago, actually."

"Can't come soon enough. Coming here was a bit of a last minute thing, so I'm in the dark. You too, by the sounds of it," she adds. "What say we stay together for the first camp?"

Midday comes and goes before the door bursts open.

"Hey, hey. You. You funnies. I come." Shahardot arrives, kicking off his shoes to enter the flat and choose a banana from our breakfast remains. He inspects it, peels and eats it, and places another in his pocket for later. We run around, collecting bags jammed with water bottles, notebooks, guidebooks, tissues, traveller's cheques, sun screen, mosquito repellent, scarves, waterproofs, and socks.

"Have we got everything?" Christine gives a squawk of dismay, disappears momentarily back into the bedroom. "Herbal hay fever remedies," she calls, brandishing them.

"Well, we will be gone all day," I explain to the marvelling Rehana.

Shahardot loads Christine and me into one rickshaw, signals another for his own use, and we ride through the vaguely-familiar streets.

Once in the office, introductions are made to Christine, and Bonny and Suez invite us to sit around the long conference table to begin our Orientation. Do we have any preliminary questions? they ask. We pipe up in chorus:

"When do we leave for the community projects?"

"Do we travel together or individually?"

"What work will we be doing exactly?"

"Where can we get money? I must change my traveller's cheques."

The queries come thick and fast. Bonny holds up a hand and looks pained.

"These are incorrect questions," he explains. "These matters we discuss later. We ask if you have any questions about the forthcoming orientation." He hands around photocopied brochures about the international organisation of SCI and a dual-language booklet about the Bangladesh group in particular. We skim through the information, and then listen whilst Bonny painstakingly reads it out loud to us:

"Service Civil International is a non-government voluntary organisation which started work in Bangladesh in 1958. It is a global peace movement, established in the aftermath of the First World War to promote peace, sustainable development, and social justice throughout the world. It brings together volunteers from all nations to facilitate Work Camps in local communities..."

The room is warm even with the door to the screened veranda open to circulate the breeze. We are back in school on a rare summer's day, and I struggle to keep my eyes open, desperate to pass the test, but wishing it a more creative process. Finally:

"Now we take food, and then," Bonny pauses for the denouement, "we discuss Work Camps."

Alert as meerkats, we refocus.

"I am mostly vegetarian," says Christine.

"Me too. And I don't really eat fish," I add.

It is Suez's turn to look aggrieved. He turns to Bonny. Why do we get stuck with awkward volunteers? his expression complains.

Maybe their countries send them here to get rid of them? counters Bonny with a shrug.

Shahardot emerges from the scullery carrying steaming dishes heaped with beef, chicken legs, and a rice mountain. *Dhal* and salad, the traditional accompaniments, follow. The table is cleared of papers and plates, glasses, and hands are rinsed.

"Is okay to eat with your hand?" Suez asks. Of course, we say. We try to do everything the Bangladeshi way.

"Including to eat meat?" he adds slyly.

"But only bottled water," Christine compromises for both of us. I feel like a recalcitrant and ungrateful guest.

"Is okay. You are new here. You get sick. In two, three weeks, you eat and drink everything." Suez is supremely confident. He serves us generously and laughs aloud at my left-handed attempts to switch to the right.

"No, no. Eat like this, and you stay hungry." He mimics my use of right thumb and forefinger between which I have managed to trap three grains of rice, two of which fall before reaching my mouth. "This, like this."

Extravagantly he pulls up one shirtsleeve and thrusts his hand into the bowl of food, mixing the meat and rice, rolling it into a ball, squeezing the moisture from it, and then munching with relish. He licks his fingers, slurps on them, gulps a tumbler of water and bangs down the empty glass. "See? Use the whole hand."

If I crane my neck so that my forehead is almost touching the bowl, I avoid spilling most of it down my front. So what if I resemble a horse dipping into its nosebag? Suez nods approvingly. Wildly, I imagine going to an upmarket Dublin restaurant, waving the cutlery away and tucking in. I begin to giggle and marginally avoid choking.

We get to the real business once the dishes are cleared.

"There are minor changes to our Work Camp programme," Bonny advises as we look at the scant lists.

"I am interested in the eye and dental project," I remind Bonny.

"That Camp is cancelled," he says benevolently. "We think you would like to go to Rajoir instead." He points to it on the map.

"Wait a second. What do you mean, 'cancelled?'" I'd been looking forward to the medical work and understood from VSI in Ireland (Voluntary Service International is the name of the Irish branch of SCI) that my experience would have been useful there.

"Cancelled," is all Bonny says again. "But Rajoir is a good place that needs your help."

As I wonder how to argue the case, I remember I am equally supposed to be adaptable and go where I am of most use. "Okay," I give in far too quickly. "Where is Rajoir and what happens there?"

"It is in the district of Madaripur," Bonny says. "One hundred and eighty kilometres from Dhaka. See?" He traces a jagged line south from the city. "First you take a bus, then a ferry across the Padma River, then another bus, then a rickshaw-van. Four hours journey maximum."

"Four hours to travel 200k?" Christine whistles. "We could crawl faster."

"And what happens there?" I repeat.

"Rajoir is the home of the local SCI Unit. It is a big town in the locality. I am not yet advised about the type of work."

"Digging..." begins Suez, but is silenced by a frown from his colleague.

"We discuss details later," Bonny advises me smoothly.

"But what about my box of glasses?" I object. "And the drugs?"

"The what?" Christine raises her eyebrows. "You've been holding out on me, girl."

32

"My husband is a pharmacist." I tell her. "And his father is an optician. They always collect old specs and out of date drugs and send them overseas. They've sent a parcel on ahead for the projects here."

"The box is safe at the Post Office," soothes Suez. "It will be delivered appropriately. Please not to worry."

"But I wanted to take them…" I hear the whine in my voice and check myself. As long as they get to the projects, who dispenses them is immaterial. It doesn't stop my feeling tearful for the link with a home now a million miles away. Christine squeezes my arm. It's her turn next.

"I chose the music camp in Mymensingh."

"No Mymensingh this time," Bonny says. "You wait one month."

"But I go home in a month," she complains.

"Then maybe you go to Rajoir Camp also." He stabs the map again.

"I'm a music teacher. Will that be useful there?"

"Of course. Do not worry."

So, in the true spirit of democracy, we are given choice after choice until we make the right one. Travel plans are loosely fixed for the next day.

"Rajoir is the home region of Bachchu. So he goes with you." Suez says. "Also, Moni. Anne? You remember Bachchu and Moni? You meet them yesterday." He lowers his voice. "Also, Rajoir is better for ladies. The sleeping place is best."

"Should I bring a mosquito net?" I ask.

Suez waves the question away. "No need. Mosquito net provided. Also, blankets and pillows."

"Big beds," assures Bonny.

"Is one final point," Suez says seriously. "The people you meet are curious about your countries and the way you are living there. They have many questions about social and political issues, about industry, environment, education, and community services. You prepare yourselves."

Oh my God, I think. I'm not a UN ambassador or running for political office, yet I'll be expected to know as much about Ireland as if I've a degree in politics and history and a penchant for the minutiae of current affairs. I haven't any of those things. The horror must show on my face because Christine nudges me. "Don't worry," she whispers. "They'll be far more interested in how many televisions you have, if you wear mini-skirts, and if you'll marry them for a visa."

"So," Suez says formally. "The Orientation is deceased. Now we walk to National Assembly. The buildings of our Parliament, yes? In Bengali, called *Sangshad Bhaban*."

The parliament buildings are set at the apex of an expanse of wide stone steps, which, together with the park at the foot, are thronged with people free for the evening. We gaze at the concrete cylindrical structures interspersed with rectangular boxes, the ordinary windows replaced by circular and triangular apertures: a Bangladeshi tribute to modernism. Bonny lectures us on the local architecture and history.

"Is designed by American. Louis Kahn. Commissioned by Pakistan in 1963 to be regional capital building for East Pakistan. Because of liberation movement and war of independence, has taken twenty years for finishing."

"Bangladesh is now parliamentary democracy," Suez explains. "You know our government? Power is held by Bangladesh Nationalist Party, by Prime Minister Khaleda Zia. There is maximum rivalry with opposition who are Aswami League." He shakes his head. "Much political violence."

Around us, hawkers jostle large water bottles, canisters of tea, sweets, and cigarettes. The instantaneous bush telegraph ensures, a silent crowd gathers, and every eye is fixed on Christine and me. Onlookers, melt away when we consistently fail to do anything interesting and are systematically replenished by their brothers and sisters.

"Australia. Ireland," Suez repeats amidst fluent Bangla explanations. "SCI. Volunteers."

"Ireland. Australia. SCI. Volunteers," echoes Bonny to another group.

We are joined by Pavel and Rehana, our hosts, and by Bachchu and Moni, and other volunteers as we wander across the scrub green park and along another hectic main road in the direction of a tall screen of flashing neon billboards advertising *Sharp*, *Grameen Bank,* and the *Dhaka Courier*, their colours muted by the fusty, thick, yellow smog. Behind the trees, the sun begins to set. A perfect orange disc, it sinks slowly, gracefully and in time with the reverential lowering of the Bangladeshi flag.

"Mosquito playtime," I sigh. I slap on repellent, attach citronella-infused arm and ankle bands, swallow an antihistamine along with half a dozen of Christine's homeopathic pills, and pull on knee-length socks. Finally, I am giving the locals the entertainment they are seeking. At least if I have to use the *Ana-Pen*, I will not go into anaphylactic shock in vain.

"No question why you married a pharmacist," Christine teases.

At the doors of an ugly functional block, ("Modern shopping centre for your interest," says Suez) we ride the humming escalator past an electrical franchise, through clothes and hardware departments and to a narrow, self-service café. Formica topped tables are adorned with plastic ketchup bottles and small pots of powdered milk. The coffee we order is served instant, weak, and lukewarm.

"Where are all the customers?" asks Christine.

"They shop in the bazaar. Here is maximum expensive," says Bonny. "You drink enough? We go."

It's now dark, the evening traffic is dizzying: cars, buses, rickshaws, scooters, all bumper-to-bumper and dancing a complicated, yet superbly choreographed, dance as they glide swiftly between one another. Only the rusting, dented bumpers and smashed headlamps demonstrate the frequency of accidents.

"Little crashes." Suez dismisses this occupational hazard of Dhaka streets.

At a major intersection, traffic swerves to avoid two men, their sandals neatly placed at the foot of the ladder erected in a desultory attempt to mend erratic traffic lights. Frequently they pause to consider their handiwork, but the colours still change at random.

"No matter," Suez continues. "These lights are decorations. In Dhaka, people stop and go as they wish. I find you a rickshaw, and then we all say goodbye and go to our homes. Pavel and Rehana will lead you. See, they are already in rickshaw in front. Okay? Bye bye."

"Okay," Christine and I chorus, "Bye bye."

A small girl with long, tangled hair and dressed only in a torn strip of cloth grabs at our hard-won rickshaw. She hangs on and is propelled roughly forward, her feet scraping the ground. Bruised and dirty fingers scrabble at our legs as she begs for *taka*, and then, content with a few coins, she jumps down and deftly sidesteps the wheels of a bus.

Wearily, we follow our hosts up the five floors back to the apartment where Mamun greets us eagerly. "Why you have been so long?" he complains, "I am waiting here with much advices for you."

"No more advice today," intervenes Pavel. "Now we have dinner and some cultural exchanges. Practice for Work Camp," he says. "Christine, you talk first of Australia."

Christine obliges whilst she picks at a small, black fish, nipping away the flesh to yield delicate, perfectly-formed skeletons. Green vegetables, rice, and dhal again are plentiful.

"Eat much," Mamun urges. "In my bazaar, is very cheap food."

Once we have finished and washed our hands, I prepare to be grilled about Ireland, but it seems I am off the hook:

"Now sleep," orders Rehana.

Only after Christine and I meekly disappear, not yet used to the Bangladeshi tradition to eat immediately before sleeping, do we realise that she was probably talking to Farabia and Alvi.

"We'd better shove up my net as a precaution against mozzies," Christine suggests, eyeing up my escalating bites. She rummages deeply in her suitcase and produces material resembling a tattered wedding veil gone saggy with age. We struggle to attach it over the bed. Mamun's help is invaluable. Clad only in his tight linen trousers, he leans on the doorframe—uttering instructions.

"Put it higher. Tie the knot tighter. This is not good mosquito net. You buy in Australia? How much? In Bangladesh, only 250 *taka*. I get it for minimum. Tuck in corners. Tighter."

The two of us crawl under this tepee meant for one, and have to slither out again to tuck in the corners. "See, my advice so good," says Mamun. And then again to fetch my torch, to locate Christine's book, to fill a bottle of water, to switch off the light...

"Can you hear buzzing?" I ask Christine suspiciously, as I return from a final foray into the dark.

"Right in my ear," she says. "The buggers must have got in through a rip in the material."

More cross than a bag of weasels, I bathe in insect repellent. And go apoplectic when I find another specimen waiting cockily on my pillow. For her own safety, Christine renders me gloriously semi-conscious with triple doses of fever reducing herbs.

"It's as if I've had a local anaesthetic washed down with a couple of litres of gin." I snuggle down happily, at one with all of God's little creatures, including my lovely little mosquito pets. "I'm floating from place to place."

"Here give me some of that." Christine crams the remainder of the remedy in her mouth in a most unladylike way.

"It must be your metabolism. I'm not getting anything." Christine frets two hours later. "Well, bugger that anyway."

3

Day 8 - Passage to Rajoir

"Right," says Christine. "Let's take stock. Today we travel, not sure where or to do what, so let's plan for every eventuality."

We pack. We unpack. We pack again. We worry that we have packed too much, not enough, forgotten something vital. We congratulate ourselves on limiting it to one bag each.

By seven o'clock, we have a final wrestle with our respective bedding and separate our money into piles. Twenty-five US dollars, the currency we were both advised to bring, yields *a lot* of *taka* notes. The bulk of my fortune is contained in a money belt wound several times around my waist, pinned and tucked into my knickers, and then hidden under a long shirt. It feels heavy and reassuring despite the eye-catching bulge at my stomach.

"You've licked the problem of spontaneous buying anyway," Christine notes. "Getting that money out in public would constitute an act of gross indecency."

Seasoned-traveller Christine has run up nifty squares of zipped cotton; pouches that can be filled with notes and secured inside her pockets, to her waistband, attached to her bra...

"A new take on *Pin the Tail on the Donkey*, really," she says. All that's required with her system is saintly patience and an elephant's memory as to where she actually put that emergency two hundred *taka*.

Mamun wanders in to get dressed, an activity he prefers to carry out in our company. He considers our antics with approval.

"Good. You make sense. On buses, sometimes are thieves. Perhaps hijackers. They rob rich foreigners first. Always in the newspaper. Christine, nice shirt. How much? In Dhaka, I get it for sixty *taka*."

The bathroom is virtually impenetrable due to the mounds of laundry being separated into untidy piles. The maid points out her child to us. He is laying curled up, thumb in mouth, on the largest heap of dirty towels.

"If you want to use toilet, you step over him," Farabia translates. "If you shower, please do not wet him or he screams and it is bad noise."

Alvi is the watchdog. When Bachchu and Moni are spied alighting from a baby taxi, he shouts for them to wait and Mamun helpfully moves out of the way as Christine and I haul our bags to the front door.

"Have care," he warns us kindly. "These are heavy bags. Really for a man to carry." He unfolds his arms to wave us off.

We bump and drag our bags down, take a brief, red-faced rest at the foot of the stairs, and then negotiate them into the street. With Christine pulling one end and me pushing the other, we manage to force my rucksack through the narrow doorway and dump it in the street. Bachchu, seeing Christine emerge, starts to shout a greeting. It dies on his lips as he views the coffin-like bag and me on its tail.

"Hi, there," I say, and we wave. "Back in a minute."

Christine and I lug her bag outside and abandon it next to mine right at the feet of Bachchu and Moni who are watching in disbelief. At last, Bachchu says.

"Both bags?"

"Yes." I smile. "Just one each."

He nods slowly. "Just one each," he echoes.

"Are they too big?" asks Christine. "We only brought essentials."

"They are...bigger than my bag, and Bachchu's." Moni is diplomatic. He is carrying a dwarf-sized holdall. Bachchu has a briefcase that matches his leather jacket.

"Is that all your luggage?" I ask. We look on in awe.

"But of course," Christine realises, and then laughs in relief. "You're going home. You must have everything there."

Honour dubiously restored, we wait whilst Moni hails another baby taxi.

"God. We were all supposed to fit into *one* of those blokes," mutters Christine. We start to giggle and are still smirking when we come to a halt at the bus station.

Gobtali Bus Station is an artist's impression of wretched urban decay. It is bleak, dirty, and smelly with discarded garbage and diesel fumes. Oil slicks and bits of broken bus accost the feet of expectant travellers and street-sellers alike. Once-shocking colours, now overlaid with a rusty coat, cover the scratched and battered buses waiting in ragged lines. We are directed to a pink and cream charabanc, its windows wide open with tatty, beige curtains streaming out of the windows.

Anne Hamilton

"A public bus," confirms Christine, as if we had expected a smart minibus, all air-conditioning and cup holders. She turns to me and whispers, "Hell. We should be wearing long skirts, not trousers. They'll be no privacy if we need to pee."

On cue, I need to go to the lavatory. Images of a bursting bladder or—God forbid—diarrhoea scuttles around my imagination.

"Learning to do it standing up is the key," Christine continues. "Pee that is. Or worse. If you're wearing a loose, long skirt, you just find a spot, let go, and nobody is any the wiser. Of course, splashing and wiping are the buggers..."

"Remind me how long the journey takes?" I squeak over these words of wisdom and the hysterical cramps in my stomach. "Suez and Bonny said four hours, is that right?"

Moni shrugs. "I think more like five hours. Six, seven. It depends on the time of the boat. There is only a small river crossing, but Bangladesh has few bridges and the boats are small."

I wish I hadn't asked.

The bus assistant urges us on board. Our seats are halfway up, but the aisle is crowded with travellers and well-wishers, a man selling oranges from a basket on his head, another carrying a bundle of plastic windmills, and our bags, which everyone, including the resident blind beggar, has to step over. As we depart, the woman in the next seat forms them into a makeshift bed and gently settles her small daughters on them.

After three hours of the city slowly merging into suburbs, it then evolves into small, kerbside shantytowns where workers shovel mounds of soil from the backs of trucks in the backbreaking task to make bricks. Eventually, the air clears into vistas of damp paddy fields; others fields are thick with yellow mustard seed. Here, brimming with boats, is the Padma River crossing. A continuation of the Ganges entering Bangladesh from the northwest, this will deposit us in Madaripur about a hundred and eighty kilometres due south of Dhaka.

Boat passengers, like armies of scurrying ants jumping from muddy quay to wooden deck, all push past a hundred others with the same intention to disembark. On the front deck of our vessel, a man bears a tray selling single cigarettes and plastic combs, another man shines shoes, and a third sells *gram*, a cheap snack made from mixed nuts and spices. Every seat, every space is filled to overflowing. People are hanging over the rails, and yet more passengers and luggage come. The ancient boat groans under the weight, and I wonder how it can possibly stay afloat. That it has crossed the river daily for decades makes for both consolation and apprehension. Of course it will make it this time...Will it? Will it? As Moni pointed out, there is a lot of water in Bangladesh but very few bridges. Instead, the country is reliant on boats and ferries to cross all but a handful of rivers. Since so many of the vessels are dilapidated cast-offs from India, there are hundreds of boating accidents annually, albeit most at night: scores of people lose their lives.

The landscape is increasingly tropical on the other side of the river. Verdant fields full of crops and lush palm trees glow beneath the midday sun. On the sandy riverbank, with its backdrop of swaying palms, nothing is static. More scenes of industry: bricks, a quarry, and boat building chum with domesticity, children bathing, women laundering, animals submerged. In a flash, we are disembarking, pushing our way to a second bus...and finally...

"In thirty minutes, we arrive in Takerhad," Bachchu says and leans back, rousing us from a travel-induced torpor. "A big town near Rajoir and close to our Work Camp."

But first impressions are blurred by the speed with which we, and our bags, are decanted from the bus and left, dazed and disoriented, in the middle of what appears to be the local motorway. Narrowly, I avoid being mowed down by something that looks like a rickshaw towing a cart, whilst Christine tussles with a herd of over-friendly market-bound goats.

"Would you like to take lunch now?" Moni asks us.

Christine and I look at each other; hot, dishevelled and mindful of the maxim not to eat from stalls in the street.

"We would rather get to the camp," we say in unison.

Moni is patient. "We think it is time to eat now. Come."

We stand corrected and follow them through the town, Bachchu pointing out landmarks as we go. "Our smart bridge—before this, a ferry is needed. Here is telephone office. We have no cell phone yet, but maybe in two years." Outside a dilapidated, deserted cinema, a few torn posters advertise films long gone and the rusty remains of a Coca-Cola machine. "It did not ever work," Bachchu confides. "My friend found it broken in Dhaka and put it here to make his movie house look like Hollywood."

Inside a small restaurant, Bachchu is hailed like a long-lost brother. Four empty tables sit behind a counter on which is laid a selection of sweetmeats and snacks. More sweets are lined up in a glass cabinet and bags of crisps and bananas hang from the canopy. A large black griddle is perched just outside, and cooked *paratha* (a type of fried flat bread) are piled up beside it.

Anne Hamilton

"Good hotel. My friend is manager," Bachchu tells us.

Hotel, restaurant—the semantics are illuminating. If I were to write home a description of this place, it would be something along the lines of, "a market stall with seats."

When we slip behind a strip of curtain to rinse our hands from a tin water jug, we nearly fall into the huge cauldrons of ready-prepared rice and meat. Lined up on the floor, each is conveniently open to both the elements and the rampant insect life. Seeing it, Bachchu, probably primed by Suez and Bonny, calls for freshly cooked food.

"Paratha, and fried egg with little bit onion and chilli," he explains as four, deep yellow omelettes arrive, served alongside hot bread on small plates lined with pages torn from *An Introduction to English Grammar* (1957 edition).

Here in the country, the rickshaws are rickshaw-vans; flat pieces of wood with four big wheels attached to the back of a bicycle. We bounce through Takerhad, one long street bulging in the centre and petering out to a thin strip at the point where we turn right. Over a small bridge, we reach a tiny settlement comprising a few stalls on either side of the road.

"Khalia village," Bachchu says. "To the left is our Work Camp in the Shanti Kendra Peace Institute."

In the late afternoon on this holy Muslim Friday, Shanti Kendra lives up to its name. Small yet distinct avenues connect a large compound of grass, flowerbeds, and vegetable patches. Little tin buildings are painted chameleon greenish-blues, and midway through the trees is a large, still pond. To the far right, like a benign, all-seeing Buddha, squats a large stone building two floors high with faded green shutters. It shelters a courtyard in the centre of which stands a sturdy water pump.

"Your home for three weeks," Bachchu says.

We cross the stone courtyard, warm and sheltered in the sunshine, and climb steep steps past colourful laundry drying on the ground. A muddle of bright-eyed little girls, eight- or nine-years-old crouch in a circle playing a dice game. An elderly caretaker in striped sarong ("it is a *lunghi*," Moni corrects me) unlocks tall double doors to a corridor empty save for a chipped and stained sink. With windows on the left and doors on the right, we are ushered into the middle room across which Bachchu strides to throw open two lots of shutters.

Cool and dim, courtesy of the white-painted stone walls, the room has two comfortable, four-poster beds to which are attached mosquito nets. Bachchu demonstrates the overhead light, delighting in the novelty of flickering electricity even if it is via a bare, yellowing bulb, crackling and sizzling with blue sparks. I make a mental note to fish out my rubber gardening gloves.

Further down the corridor is a large, secluded stone veranda with a broad view through the trees and across Shanti Kendra. In granite pots, shrubs and flowers add colour and fragrance to the warm air. The caretaker beckons us to the far end to view the lavatory, a dank, dark, spider-infested cubicle housing a stained, green, porcelain, long-drop toilet. We follow him into an immense cave of a bathroom with a diminutive sink and non-functioning shower cubicle.

"No good," the caretaker confirms, making a face at it. "Broke. Much broke. But here, water." He points to a knee-high cold tap fixed into the wall and does an enthusiastic and creditable mime of a coal miner having a brisk scrub down in the scullery, before producing a plastic bucket, small jug, a bar of soap, disinfectant, and a dusty and faded pink toilet roll. The latter is handed reverently to Christine.

Content we have all we need, Bachchu and Moni leave. "You take rest. We return 6 p.m.," Bachchu tells us.

Christine and I do an impromptu tango the length of the balcony, delighted with the beautiful if basic surroundings.

"It reminds me of a convent," I say. "Ascetic." We leave the sunlight and enter the dim, cloister-like corridor leading back to our room. "I see veiled nuns pacing, reading prayer books and chanting the rosary."

"Hmm. See them all you like, but if they start talking to you, I don't want to know."

"Do you want to swill or scrub?" I turn to more prosaic matters as we both squeeze into the toilet cubicle with a gallon of disinfectant. Close inspection has shown that the stains in the lavatory bowl are not hairline cracks but the residue of years of—

"Shit," says Christine. "I've sluiced away half the bottle."

"All the better," I say averting my eyes as I scour the pan.

"Toss you to christen it. I'm dying for a pee." Christine tests the facilities and pronounces herself content. "Squeaky clean and pristine fresh," she calls. "I won't say it's a pleasure to go, but oh, the simple joys of living primitively."

In the bathroom, I turn the tap in vain. The water is off and from now on we will remember to fill buckets for just this eventuality.

"We could practise using the water pump instead." I drag Christine downstairs. "You must have seen those in India? Show me how to use it."

"It's a question of brute force. Just grab the long handle." She suits action to her words. "And pump it up and down."

Anne Hamilton

She does this vigorously, the pump contraption grinding and squeaking in protest until she is rewarded with a sudden and violent vomiting of water all over her neat leather shoes. I jump backwards quickly, slip on the greasy residue of years, and try to prevent myself from falling by grabbing the back of Christine's shirt. She loses her balance and we roll around on the ground in a broad semblance of over-dressed lady wrestlers. Scrambling up, we brush ourselves down and meet the silently amazed faces of a dozen or so of our new neighbours.

Whilst the courtyard is open on one side, the other side faces a row of peeling blue and green wooden doors that look exactly like abandoned beach huts in an unfashionable seaside resort. That all these have a ringside view of the water pump has possibly not, until today, been much of a selling point. Now, the doors are all open, and every able-bodied adult and child, as well as an assortment of elderly relatives, infants, ducks and goats, have come out to seek the root of the disturbance.

"*Salaam walekum.*" Christine and I smile innocently, blushing cheeks and awry skirts notwithstanding.

We brazen out our social gaffe so easily that these people probably assume rolling on the ground is an ordinary evening ritual in certain strata of Western society. Beating a hasty retreat, we stretch out on our beds and listen to vague sounds of life: birdsong, rhythmic brush strokes as the yard is swept, the intermittent, confident call of the muezzin, and watch the setting of the sun behind baby-blue shutters.

The settlement is a different place at night. In the absolute darkness, I have no shadow, the breeze is barely a whisper against my cheek, and the sky is an expanse of taut black silk sprinkled with silver hundreds and thousands. With eyes unaccustomed to vision without street lamps, we stumble behind Moni and Bachchu with torches affecting only a pinprick of light upon the sandy paths. After the frenetic clamour of Dhaka, it is a glimpse of the Garden of Eden. Even my personal serpent—an ever-dutiful battalion of mosquitoes—has thinned out.

"We meet in the Peace Library," explains Bachchu, indicating the corrugated iron building. We slip off our shoes and pull back a thin curtain to enter a square room roughly carpeted and bare except for glass book cabinets and a blue and white banner announcing the *SCI Winter Work Camp 2002 (Rajoir Unit)*. Tiny flies buzz hungrily around the lone light bulb in the centre of the ceiling. The rumble of incomprehensible conversation from the assembled volunteers falters as we are ushered inside.

Bachchu introduces his brother, Munnu, who is also the Work Camp Leader, and their other brother, Mannu. Not only are their names near identical, but these two might be twins right down to their crooked teeth, except Mannu habitually wears a much more serious expression whereas Munnu is constantly smiling. I guess Munnu to be in his late twenties, and Mannu a few years older. Like Bachchu, they are wearing impossibly whiter-than-white loose shirts. Self-consciously, I pull my jacket tighter in an effort to mask my clean, but terminally creased T-shirt and long skirt.

"Is it a condition of SCI-Bangladesh that all the boys are so gorgeous?" Christine mutters in my ear. "Would it be ethical to grab me a souvenir toy-boy?"

There are perhaps fifteen others present, mostly young men, one or two elders, and three Bangladeshi girls, but the only other name I grasp is that of Tapon because he's wearing a bright yellow raincoat and carrying an old-fashioned camcorder on his shoulder. The meeting is a conducted in a curious mix of Bengali and English. Mortifyingly, even the local volunteers with only a smattering of English can out-perform my rudimentary Bangla.

Slowly and painstakingly, each volunteer is bathed in a pool of light, and Tapon's video camera is trained upon us as we synopsise our lives to date and stumble through our motivations for being here. It takes longer than the Eurovision Song Contest given the propensity of the electricity to fail every third or fourth sentence, and we must light candles and hold them aloft as if at an all-night vigil.

My moment of fame is straightforward. "I like to travel and to write," I tell them. "I've visited a lot of countries on holiday: Europe, Canada and America, the Middle East. A long time ago I volunteered on a kibbutz in Israel. But this is my first time in Asia. I just want to learn about Bangladesh, meet people, and be useful as a volunteer."

"...As well as working with children, animals and striving for world peace," mocks Christine in my left ear.

She soon gets her comeuppance.

"Now, Christine. Christian. So you are Christian?" Munnu asks.

"K-R-I-S-T-E-E-N," Christine hastily revises her spelling. "Actually I'm not a Christian."

"But you are called Christian?" Munnu translates, and there is a general perplexed frown.

"It's just a name," Christine flounders.

44

"If you are not a Christian, Christine, what is your religion?" Bachchu asks very politely.

"No religion."

"No religion." This is repeated around the circle in wonder. "Christine has no religion."

"And your husband?" he asks.

Christine all but groans. "I have no husband."

"Your husband is dead?"

"Not dead, no. Divorced." She leans towards me and mutters out of the side of her mouth, "For God's sake, help me out here. Tell them you're a Mormon transvestite or something."

"I'm a Christian," I interrupt and cross my fingers. No need to add that it's what my father-in-law calls *a la carte* Catholicism: look at the menu and pick off the bits you want. "So is my husband."

"Your children?"

"I don't have any children…"

"No children?"

"I wouldn't be here if I had…" And I, too, deflate in the mass gaze of benevolent pity.

We are saved by the supper gong.

Visible by the light of a hanging kerosene lantern is the remains of a small fire built neatly on the grass and shaded by a windbreak of two waist-high bamboo screens. One cast-iron cooking pot is sitting, smoking in the embers, and a bigger one is balanced upon two crossed sticks of wood. Tilted sideways, there is a steady drip of a hot, cloudy liquid into the hole beneath it—boiled rice being drained. Staggering under the weight of the cauldrons, two slender figures lift them, remove the lids, stir vigorously, and serve a generous bowl of food. Rice, meat curry, hard-boiled eggs, and salad are rapidly swallowed, and a runny, greenish dhal mops up the last of the rice. Every last morsel disappears, the liquid lapped up from the bottom of the bowls, the dishes licked clean.

"Let's escape to bed," Christine suggests as we pick our way back from the water pump and add our washed plates to the pile in the kitchen area. "There's only so much cultural exchanging I can do in one day."

Bachchu hears her. "First we plan our Daily Schedule," he says looking directly at Christine. "At what time do you think we take breakfast?"

Eyes swivel towards her. The group watches Christine expectantly.

"I think your domestic wisdom is being sought," I murmur. "You are the most senior women present."

"You mean I'm old, right?" she shoots back.

"Probably the oldest person here."

"With any luck then, I'm far too gaga to work."

Bachchu looks enquiring.

"Just discussing the schedule." Christine says. She takes a deep breath. "What about breakfast at 7 a.m., work from eight till one, half an hour for lunch, and more work in the afternoon, and then a house meeting at six. Dinner at seven and cultural discussions afterwards?"

There are uncertain nods during the translation of this practical business plan.

"Too many thank you's for your ideas, Christine," Munnu manages.

"Thank you. Most helpful ideas," echoes Bachchu looking shell-shocked. After a lengthy discussion in anxious Bengali, he speaks again, "So, we eat breakfast at eight o'clock or eight thirty, and we work between nine a. m. and one p. m. Except on Fridays when we do only two hours. Time is to bath before our lunch at two p. m., and afterwards we rest. The may be afternoon programmes to places of interest followed by a meeting at 7 p.m and dinner."

"It's pleasant to be asked anyway," Christine comments on her slightly tweaked plan. "Doesn't seem like we'll be overworked does it? Golly, their faces would've fallen less if *I'd* suggested bacon sandwiches to start the day."

"But have you noticed," I say, "that still nobody has told us what work we'll be doing?"

4

Week 2 - A Hard Day's Work

"So, Anne. Why do you visit my country?" Munnu asks as he escorts Christine and me to begin our still-unidentified work.

"I want to have a story to tell," I say simply and am gratified when he nods slowly, understanding.

"Of course. But why is your story about you and SCI volunteers in Bangladesh?"

I wonder how best to answer. With a mishmash of qualifications in social work, optometry, and general epidemiology, I have spent many years hankering over the idea of working overseas but cannot offer the time commitment or the expertise required by international aid societies such as *Voluntary Service Overseas* or *GOAL*, the Irish equivalent. Reading a newspaper article about the short-term volunteer opportunities available through VSI, I realised the solution. After a couple of information and training weekends in Dublin, I agreed that I could be flexible, adaptable, and a vehicle for cultural exchange, and finally identified my niche in the rural community development projects of Bangladesh.

"Okay," Munnu says. "And last night you say you like to travel *and* write. What writings?" he asks. "You write books? Or magazines, maybe?"

"Much more modest than that. I like to keep a diary when I'm travelling, that's all."

"You write a book-diary of SCI and Bangladesh. This is maximum good," approves Munnu. "We like to read it."

He is distracted by a shout from Aktar, another volunteer who arrived last night. In old fashioned parlance, Aktar would be described as a wide-boy; already it's clear he always has some kind of scam going. "You tell more later, yes? I have much interest," Munnu calls over his shoulder as he trots over to Aktar. "Bachchu looks after you now."

"I wish you'd told me sooner," grimaces Christine. "I'll have to keep a bloody check on what I'm doing and saying. Make me famous, not notorious, right?"

"Definitely," I say. "If you can define the difference."

Khalia School is adjacent to the Peace Centre, and this is where we head. As we stroll along the pathways first right, and then left, Bachchu runs a commentary.

"Here is main building of Shanti Kendra. There are kitchens and a room for television. Offices for administration. Please, turn here towards the pond. You can see the house of Asha. My family home is further along the path. Soon you are invited to tea..."

Our heads twist this way and that taking in this ordinary settlement so extraordinary to fresh eyes. It is a rural idyll from picture postcards and rare television documentaries—given that newsworthiness of poorer nations is generally judged by the scale of tragedy and famine—and one which, for now, I allow myself to believe in; enough to learn about the imperfections, struggles, *reality,* as the project progresses.

The narrow path snakes around the irregular pond, with its water still and gleaming in the sun, the green, stagnant edges could be naively mistaken for colourful aquatic life. Beyond is a low-slung, peeling, yellow building. A veranda runs the length of it with central steps leading into a main entrance.

"Our high school. Education centre for maybe a thousand pupils ages ten to sixteen," Bachchu continues his explanation.

"Not one thousand. I think one hundred." Munnu comes up behind us and claps his brother on the shoulder. "Aktar sends greetings. He will join later," he adds, "He has business in town."

We peek through the glassless windows and see a simple structure comprising a row of identical classrooms with individual desks and chairs set out in neat lines.

"I went to school here," Munnu tells us. "Also my brothers and sisters and our friends." He indicates to the other local volunteers standing around in small groups. "My father is principal teacher, now retired."

A playing field stretches out in front of the school, a cracked and arid carpet sprouting stiff and prickly grass at variance with the lush palm trees framing it and the tarred road opposite. During the rainy season, Munnu says, this field is deluged by floodwaters leaving patches of subsidence that make playing games erratic.

"So we wait now for our tools," he finishes, leading us to the school steps and motioning us to sit.

Tools?

"Digging," mumbles Christine. She speaks up. "Suez said we would be digging."

A silence ensues whilst the brothers look at one another, clearly hoping the other will speak first.

"Well?" demands Christine. "Is Suez right?"

Bachchu and Munnu both nod slowly.

"What kind of digging?" I pray for a little light weeding.

"We make flat the Khalia school playing field," Munnu states with endearing honesty.

"*What?*" I exclaim.

"We...are going to level the field?" asks Christine slowly, examining the lines and dips that form a parody of a mountainous rural map.

"Yes. We make it smooth enough for the Bangladesh cricket team," beams Bachchu. "It takes maybe five days."

Vague thoughts of shiny JCBs, turf rolling machines, and fluorescent-striped donkey jackets dart through my mind.

"Bloody hell," says Christine. "We'll be rolling rocks like *The Flintstones*."

The field is a veritable thoroughfare providing ready custom for the tiny wooden shop and café just behind it. Individuals and small groups of people use it as a short cut to the main road. Others bring their livestock, thin, beige cows and a muddle of goats, for tethering to the outlying trees and shrubs where lazily they chew their cud. The smallest, inky black goats have tufts of white at their feet and on the points of their ears. They rest their heads on their hooves as they curl up like puppies, and when they get hot, they stretch out cat-like in the sun.

Aktar is the first volunteer to appear. He carries two metal baskets that look like the mini bathtubs that were pulled out in front of the fire on bygone Saturday nights. Thrown across his shoulders in traditional milkmaid style is an assortment of spades. He is clanking and banging like an experimental one-man band.

Next comes the chugging put-put of a tractor towing a large trailer full of men and dry, grey soil. During an orgy of back-slapping, cigarette sharing, and that curiously male preserve of kicking vehicle tyres, Christine and I stand on the sidelines like pompom-less cheerleaders. Eventually, the trailer is tipped, a few spoonfuls of its load is dumped before trundling a few hundred yards to deposit another heap until the trailer is empty, and the playground looks like a rest home for incontinent elephants.

"Christine? Anne? Work time!" Munnu shouts.

Two people use the shovels to fill the baskets with earth; two more carry each load to a badly-pitted area of the field and tip the earth into the hole. The remaining volunteers smooth out the soil. We enjoy the frequent calls of "Take rest. Five minutes rest," and bodies relaxed by radiating sunbeams. We snack on cardamom-studded biscuits and more glasses of tea delivered from the nearby shop.

"Today, are many students at Khalia school," Munnu explains to us. "They and the teachers wish to meet with you. You can take many breaks to talk to them."

When school break time occurs, the doors are flung open, and like wasps to strawberry jam, the pupils swarm about us. The teachers admonish the children for such curiosity even whilst they lead the buzz. Mr Hussein is the young teacher of English, keen to practise his quite considerable language skills. Brushing aside concern for his dazzling white shirt and gleaming grey slip-on shoes, he swipes a mock leather cowboy hat from a surprised student, crams it low on his head and strides out like someone denied playing in the dirt during childhood. He bows as gracefully as a man clutching a bucket of mud.

"Madam, and Madam, conversing with you would offer me great mental delight," he pronounces. "Alas, is my fate to be a student of the written word." His jolly behaviour is totally at odds with the accompanying Jane Austen speech. "It is with consternation yet great joy that I commune with you, fair ladies."

So we lug sweaty wicker baskets back and forth over the playing field amidst the gentle harmony of nineteenth century garden party chatter. When the extended recess is over, he takes his leave as courtly as he began.

"Dear friends, would it be your pleasure if I depart for the schoolroom?" Mr Hussein waits for Christine and me to acquiesce, all but touches the brim of his hat, and then fairly skips back to work.

Exactly at one o'clock, work ceases. Aktar reloads himself like a sturdy packhorse and staggers homewards. In the manner of the Seven Dwarfs, single file and with implements dangling, we turn to view our handiwork.

"Is good, yes?" Bachchu's complacent gaze follows our dismayed glances.

The field looks like a Turner Prize exhibit.

"That made use of your social, optical, and epi-whatsit skills, all right." Christine grins at me.

But Bachchu is pleased. "We take lunch. Then we make a programme to visit Khalia village," he promises.

"So, no more work today?" I ask.

Anne Hamilton

"Finish," Bachchu confirms. "We continue tomorrow. And tomorrow and tomorrow. This is okay?"

"Very, very okay."

It is mid afternoon by the time we all meet up again. Khalia village is full of life. At the grocery store, shelves and counters are cluttered with food, hardware, bags of broken biscuits, bunches of fruit, sachets of washing powder, and shiny bars of Lux soap with a beautiful blonde staring seductively from the wrapper. Next door in his restaurant, a man, dexterous as a TV chef, sits cross-legged under a protruding canopy, cast iron griddle and a leaning tower of egg trays before him. He serves up omelettes, wrapped sausage roll style, in a twist of newspaper.

"And here." Bachchu points. "The men come for shaving."

This cabin is open to the road. A cracked looking-glass is taped to the wall in front of a man whose hair and beard is a distinctive gingery red. This is vanity, Munnu explains, the sign of a man who refuses to go grey or white with age and gets his hair dyed accordingly. Seated on a cockeyed leather chair, the elderly man gazes into the mirror whilst his chin is soaped from a kidney-shaped bowl. The barber stands back, one eye closed to fine-tune his work, whilst joining the conversation of customers squashed into the shop and sitting at the roadside.

"Every day the men visit here," Bachchu tells us. "They come for tea and talk. Maybe once per week only, they shave."

Beyond the village, soft pastures of waist-high mustard seed are a delicate swaying yellow. Alternating with stubby grasslands, both pastures are bisected by dry, cracked canals that will become gentle streams, and then flooded dykes as the year draws on.

We cross sandy clearings of tiny settlements, two or three wooden or tin houses roofed with a light brown thatch. Bright rugs and patchwork blankets are airing from the open windows. The man-made courtyards are swept free of stray leaves and hay by young girls who see us and down their witches' brooms. Young children creep forward, faces appear in doorways, and figures sleeping on raised porches lift their heads to call a greeting. Soon Munnu rivals the Pied Piper leading a motley parade of curious supporters.

"Here you see pottery making," informs Bachchu. "Hindu tradition, done by the hand."

We pass a scrap yard of discarded brown pots, all shapes and sizes, and all leaking or leaning heavily to one side. In a richer society, they would form an inventive backdrop to the latest must-have garden water feature. Crouched on the ground is an elderly, frail woman wearing the traditional white garb of the Hindu widow. Wisps of grey hair straggle across her lined cheeks as she deftly moulds the clay at her feet. She looks up, alarmed at our invasion of her light and her privacy. Seeing Tapon's video camera, she obscures her face with her bird's claw hand and motions for a younger woman to take her place.

This large and jolly replacement is not shy. She plays to the camera like a *Homes & Garden* expert. Gripping the soft grey circles of clay, she rolls them between long fingers and smooths the edges to create bowl after bowl, holding each out expertly for a video close-up. She invites us to see her husband at work astride the large pottery wheel. We—followed by the whole village—traipse after her only to meet the diminutive man himself plodding home, mopping at skin tinged with grey flecks. No matter, his wife instructs him, indicating to the camera and the necessity of filming for posterity that he must begin work again. Good-naturedly, or for fear his dinner will be fed to the hens, he does as bidden. The potter straddles a wheel the size of a human stride. With a large wooden pole at his side, he propels the wheel around, faster and faster until his pot magically takes on the lines of a large water pitcher.

In the background, a young woman is preparing the family meal. Beckoning us to come closer, a child is sent to bring chairs for Christine and me, and we end up with a mighty selection of pictures of Tapon videoing us taking photographs.

"This must be how Queen Lizzie feels on Commonwealth tours but without the anti-monarchy hecklers," Christine decides. "My boredom threshold for watching vegetables being chopped kicked in after the first million chillies."

She wanders off to look at a Hindu shrine. The tableau tells a bright and extravagant story; the figures are almost childlike in their crude forms and garish colours.

"Does your country have religious statues also?" Moni translates for an enthusiastic villager.

"Ye-es," I hesitate, stumbling through a description of the sedate roadside shrines to the Virgin Mary, knowing that the concrete basilica of Knock would certainly fail to impress.

"Now the joopy hospital," Bachchu says.

"Great," says Christine. "Er...what's a joopy hospital?"

"G-U-P," Bachchu spells it out. "Joopy. Another NGO—a non-government organisation—yes? Nearby Shanti Kendra. GUP works for rural issues: medicine, farming, arsenic problems...Oh, dear."

His attention is diverted to Tapon who, attempting to zip up his yellow anorak, appears to be buckling under the load of his camera equipment.

"Arsenic?" I ask Christine, something stirring in the recesses of my mind.

"It's a huge problem in the water. Lethal because there are no symptoms for years."

The GUP settlement is a single-storey building in a U shape around a grassy quad. There are thick bars on the windows, Bangla lettering above the padlocked doors, and a deserted, forgotten air lingering in the peeling paintwork and overgrown grounds. In the warm glow of the evening sun, it is like an old fever hospital left to ruin in the wake of modern medicine.

"Nobody is here now," Bachchu explains. "It was Health Centre and Children's Hospital. Very respected. It is closed maybe one year. Now people travel to Rajoir."

"Why did it close?" I ask.

Bachchu shrugs. "There is no doctor. Medical people do not want to work in rural areas with poor people's illnesses and few facilities. They like big cities with modern clinics where maximum money is for making."

As for nursing staff, he says, even the main hospitals in Bangladesh tend to rely largely on the "ward boys"—young men-of-all-work—leaving the brunt of all nursing and personal care to relatives and friends. Even more worrying, newspapers carry frequent reports of the scarcity of high strength analgesics like morphine. Post-operative patients survive, at best, on the lesser strength pethidine, or at worst on aspirin.

An ebullient family of picnickers lift the mood. Their tiffin boxes empty now; they are playing what appears to be Pass-the-Parcel with music provided by an old man with a harmonica. His notes die away as he catches sight of us. He motions his relatives to widen the circle.

"They want to know if you, Christine and Anne, are girls or boys," Munnu announces, laughing. "They say you look like girls, but you wear boys' clothes."

We look down at our baggy shirts and trousers, sun hats, and glasses and realise that in this world of colourful saris and bling jewellery, how asexual and hermaphroditic we appear.

Back in Dhaka we will go shopping.

"The foreigners are please to sit," the young father insists, as the party games continue. "For games then cake."

"Definitely no cake," Christine whispers as the package does its rounds to shrieks of excitement, not only from the children. "I once got typhoid from eating infected cake. It was in Indonesia and—oh..."

The music stops before Christine can toss the parcel to the giggling little girls on her left. She opens it to find a tiny lace-edged handkerchief, a gift the family insists she keep.

"Our honour," the young father explains respectfully. "You please us. In our country, old ladies like you are nearly dead, not outside taking the picnic."

"I'm only sixty," Christine wails. "I'm in my prime!"

"Would you like to drink coconut milk?" Moni rescues her tactfully. "Very healthy and good for the stomach. You see them, high up in the trees?"

"Always Aktar brings the coconut. In school we call him monkey-boy." Munnu grins. He throws a handful of grass, catching Aktar on the back of the head, and raises his voice. "Hey, monkey-boy. You bring coconuts."

Aktar jumps up with good grace, and with a series of nimble tucks, turns his *lunghi* into a pair of baggy shorts. He calls for a knife, which he clamps between his teeth and shins up the perpendicular trunk of the nearest tree. Soon, only the callused soles of his bare feet are visible, curled tightly around the bark. For a few minutes, it is raining coconuts before Aktar swings himself sideways, gives a Tarzan-like roar and, jumping crab-like, is suddenly hugging the bark of a neighbouring tree, thumping his chest and grinning down at us. The volunteers attack the yellowish-green shells with machete-like knives, gouging holes in the top, and the liquid inside is cool and sticky, like unsweetened fruit juice. Aktar, shimmying to the ground like a fireman down a pole, takes a bow. He devours two coconuts in quick succession and emits a supremely satisfied belch.

"*Dab* and *dim*. You know *dab* and *dim*? All you need." He grins at us. "Other food not needed."

"Coconut and eggs," nods Christine. "Good for me and for Anne. But what would you do without rice?"

Aktar rubs his tummy still laughing. "Be hungry. Be maximum hungry."

The picnic family, their share of the coconuts sucked dry, call for a farewell photograph. On a roll, Aktar is keen to form an acrobatic pyramid, him exultant on top. Christine, trying to prove herself not imminently grave-bound, also looks tempted. They are unanimously cried down.

"Gymnastics is a maximum bad idea," Bachchu says. "What will happen to our Work Camp if our volunteers break bones and take concussion?"

54

5

Week 3 - Ladies' Day

One week later, full of joy that the levelling of the playing field is over, and I will never ever have to do such a thing again, I open the shutters to an overcast sky. The courtyard is damp, and the air is cool with a fine mist upon the wind. It is almost raining in Khalia. I shiver as I brush my teeth at the draughty corridor sink and douse my face with cold water. I sympathise with the Bangladeshis who have already been wearing sweaters, scarves, and woolly hats.

Asha, flanked by Chapa and Mary, pay us an early morning visit. I remember these three girls from the first evening's orientation and have seen them around Shanti Kendra since, but until today they have only responded to our smiles and waves from a shy distance. Nevertheless, something has inspired their new-found confidence, and the three come in and wander around the room.

Chapa and Asha appear to be in their late teens, beautiful, olive-skinned girls with long, long hair neatly pulled away from their faces. Dressed in colourful *salwar kameezes*, the cheap woollen cardigans pulled around their shoulders are somewhat incongruous. Chapa has an aristocratic, almost regal profile in the contours of her face and neck. She is from a Hindu family, the sister of Tapon, our official video recorder. Asha's friendly gaze is open, enquiring and interested. Beside them is Mary who looks like a child. She is small and thin, a Lowry model with matchstick arms and legs poking out from her flowery cotton dress and trousers. Her short hair curls in towards her neck and accentuates the size of her huge brown eyes.

"You do not share bed," Chapa notes loudly, making me jump and bite my tongue. "Why you not share bed?"

"Er..." Christine is flummoxed. "In the West we just don't. Anyway, *she* wriggles."

"And *she* snores," I rejoin.

We are met with total incomprehension.

"Christine is the cook today," I say, changing the subject. "She's just going to make breakfast. How do you say 'breakfast' in Bangla? Breakfast? *Bangla kee bole?*"

"What?" asks Christine, looking at me.

"*Kee bole* means 'what word'...I think."

The girls laugh in delight. "Speak Bangla. Good. Good. Breakfast is *prahtorash*," says Asha

"You say," orders Chapa.

"*Prahtorash*," we repeat.

"*Prahtorash*." Christine fishes for her notebook and prints it phonetically.

For a few minutes the girls talk amongst themselves, and then Asha is put forward as spokesperson. She clears her throat.

"We teach Bangla," she says slowly and deliberately, thinking out every word. "You teach English."

The deal done, we all smile, broadly pleased with ourselves. Exhausted and relieved by the effort, Chapa, Asha, and Mary go back to conversing in Bengali while Christine and I revert to English.

"Typical," muses Christine. "Here we are in the perfect arena to see through female oppression, stereotypical fanaticism, and all the fundamentalism of a male dominated and predominantly Muslim country, and our means of communication amounts to bugger all."

"Why didn't I try harder to learn Bengali?" I bemoan my laziness. Again.

Asha coughs importantly. Out of the blue, she announces, "Christine to sing. Anne also. You both sing." The three sit on the floor and look at us expectantly.

"Sing? Now?" I ask.

"Before breakfast?" adds Christine.

"Yes. Sing. Now," Asha instructs. "We sing also."

They sit stubbornly, arms folded. It's a stand-off.

"I can't sing," Christine admits. "I'll warble like an old trout. Come on—think of something simple or we'll never get rid of them."

So we perform an animated, if not strictly precise, rendition of "Auld Lang Syne," with a "Waltzing Matilda" encore. The girls reciprocate with a surprisingly raucous medley of Bengali pop songs. The party thrives until hunger hits, and Christine flies off to breakfast duty. The girls turn to leave too.

"Happy putting on your clothes," Chapa bids me as the trio wander off.

Christine's partner in cooking for the day is Moni.

"Result!" she says. "He is a thing of beauty isn't he? Mean, moody and magnificent too, as they say."

"But he isn't mean and moody in any way," I point out. In my mind, the jury is still out on magnificent. "He's unfailingly quiet and polite."

"Exactly."

"But you just said—"

"Girl, have you no romance in that soul of yours?" Christine looks at me and shakes her head. "It's not what he actually does, it's what he hints he might do if he ever broke out of that calm exterior. Get it?"

I don't. Give me the cheerful and hot-tempered Munnu any day, or Bachchu with his innocent eagerness to show off his jacket (which he hasn't yet taken off as far as I can tell) and his motorbike.

"Your loss," says Christine cheerfully. "Heigh ho, off to work we go."

The rest of us, having finished off the school playing field two days ahead of schedule, turn to the gardens of Shanti Kendra. As I leave her, Christine is learning that there is chicken for lunch. Moni's non-verbal gestures indicate that said feathered friend is currently running happily around the farmyard and will remain so until the cook-of-the-day personally puts it to death and serves its little legs in a fragrant curry sauce.

Today's task is to smooth out the pathway between the wooden mosque and nursery school buildings (identical save for the elephantine mosquito net covering the veranda of the latter, where the smallest children take their midday siesta) and diminish the potholes, thus providing a pleasant trek for bicycles and rickshaws. Effortlessly, Mannu and Aktar are lifting hand ploughs high above their heads and bringing them rhythmically down, slicing neat lines through the dry riverbed as if cutting sponge cake. Collapsing red-faced and growing light-headed, I can barely raise one stroke, and queasy images of that luncheon chicken resurface. Thankfully, work is halted when the governor of Rajoir's District Council, his posse, the elected members and various hangers-on, arrive for inspection of the local SCI unit and visiting foreigners.

Christine escapes from the kitchen with a greenish tinge to her skin. "Moni wanted me to put my hand up the chickens arse and pull its guts out," she says. I dread to think what kind of picture the two of us present: dishevelled, sweating, and even paler than usual compared with the cool elegance of Chapa and Asha. Still, the Big-Man-On-Campus greets us courteously, mentions how honoured he is that "two big Western women" are visiting his country and yet how sad that we must do such manual work because so many indigenous "little people of sloth" refuse.

"Anne. What is sloth?" Munnu, who is beside me, whispers.

"Lazy," I tell him, less concerned to spare his feelings than to concentrate on the sudden wave of nausea washing over me.

Munnu looks duly insulted and refrains from socking the official on the jaw only by energetically stamping out our newly renovated path and muttering evil-sounding threats. Oblivious, the councillor completes his flowery speech by suggesting that he and "his fellow mighty dignitaries" would like to offer their "expert assistance" with future projects.

I swear that Munnu, in his best Hollywood impersonation, grumbles "over my dead body, loser."

"Give him the spade and tell him to start now." I try to lighten the atmosphere and am amazed when Munnu takes me literally. Seizing said implement from Aktar, Munnu marches forward and thrusts the spade under the nose of the startled VIP.

The man sidesteps quickly, lest his immaculate attire be sullied, but his words of protest die when he realises he is starring in Tapon's video. He manages a couple of ineffectual lunges before recalling urgent business in Rajoir.

"Anne," Munnu says. "You save me from fighting that man and bringing shame."

In a sudden fit of relieved patriotism, he leads the volunteers in the Bangladeshi National Anthem, and they bawl fervently like die-hard fans at an international football match. I see where Chapa, Asha, and Mary get it from, and fear that the puny efforts of Christine and I—she a well-known music teacher, and me a relatively experienced soprano—will not pass muster here.

"We like to make fine noise," Bachchu explains, smiling.

"Come with me to the kitchen of slaughter," Christine offers gloomily. "Whatever I'm doing, it's not cooking. Praise be that Moni isn't squeamish."

We enter the kitchen to find Moni scraping the messy remains of a plucked chicken from the kitchen floor. He peels sticky feathers from the soles of his sandals, and then immerses his hands into a bowl of pink water floating with unidentifiable bits of bird. I cause consternation when I announce my intention of skipping lunch. Bachchu is all but ready to call for the undertaker. But Moni thinks holistically.

"Maybe is not a physical problem?" he suggests. "Do you miss your country?"

I reassure him I am not pining with homesickness and realise with a jolt that I have barely thought of home in the last three days. I'm just slightly unwell with a great predilection to hypochondria. I go to my room to lie down.

Later on, Christine asks, "Puked yet? Any diarrhoea?"

"No, but I feel sick," I whine.

"Hmm. Take these for stomach cramps." She hands me a little pot of homeopathic remedy. "If it's the water, or something you ate, why don't I have it too?" she muses. "Could it be period pains?"

I look at her in horror. In my consideration of dysentery, gastric ulcers, stomach tumours, and arsenic poisoning, I overlook the mundane.

"No," I say.

"Are you sure?" Christine looks down at me like a school nurse questioning a fifth former who's trying to get out of playing hockey. "All this sun and travelling can play hell with the body, you know."

"Maybe," I agree. "But I don't think so. Anyway, I left all that kind of stuff in Dhaka. I wasn't expecting to need any of it til we got back." I lower my voice. "I'd have to drip my way around Rajoir."

"We'll ask Chapa and Asha what the local women do," Christine suggests. "Not sure how we'll get them to understand, but it's that or ask Bachchu. I know he said to ask if there was *anything* you needed but..."

"That's probably going much too far." We empathise over the image of poor Bachchu's gentle but pained face if initiated into a discussion on menstruation.

Christine fumbles through the Bengali phrasebook. "Well, I can find enema, erection, orgasm and penile warts, but nothing resembling the word for 'tampon.' I bet this book was written by a man."

"Rags and newspaper," I say. "I bet that's what the local girls do."

On cue, Asha bangs on the door for an afternoon chat.

"Mary and Chapa at home. They care for the babies," Asha apologises, uncomfortable alone. "Anne is sick? Or okay I visit?"

I smile bravely, but weakly, and motion for her to sit down.

"Asha, we need help." I seize the moment. "We need to buy..." I hesitate, seeking a comprehensible euphemism in case it is out of order to mention certain things even in exclusively female company.

"Ladies' things," Christine offers primly. "Private ladies' things."

Asha looks confused. "For lady?" she repeats. "Ah, you want to buy dress? At bazaar, yes?"

"Not a dress. Um, underneath." In a minute I'll be going pink and making coy references to *down below*.

"Underneath clothes? Vest?"

"No."

"Panties? Sock?" Asha tries valiantly.

We change tack. "Pain."

Asha nods eagerly. "Yes. Pain. Poor Anne. To buy medicine?" she asks.

"Not medicine." Christine looks at me. "Time to go for broke here and hang causing offence." She looks at Asha. "Period pain," she says. "Tampax. Sanitary towels."

None of this strikes a chord. "Towel?" Asha asks, glancing doubtfully at our bath towels draped becomingly over the shutters.

Christine is on a roll. "Stomach. Babies. Bleeding," she continues, clutching her abdomen and wriggling.

Asha takes a moment to compute this, and then jumps up, fear distorting her face. "No. Bleeding? Very bad. *Tamar dahktar.* I get doctor. Now."

Christine and I eventually get her calmed down, and we look amongst each other, a triumvirate of bewilderment. Finally, the metaphorical light bulb flashes simultaneously above our heads. Christine and I are inspired.

"Monthly bleeding," we chorus.

Bit by bit, Asha breaks into a smile. "Monthly bleeding. Monthly bleeding. Now, I understand." Then she frowns again. "Much pain. Very sick," she says. "Monthly bleeding hurts." She gets into her stride. "My monthly bleeding very bad. I go to bed. Head hurts. Vomits. Chapa also. And Mary," she confides. "So bad for ladies, monthly bleeding."

As an example of cultural exchange probably not on Suez and Bonny's original list, it is a definite icebreaker. She grasps the original question.

"Village women are making cloths," she tells us. "For monthly bleeding. In Dhaka City buy Modesse and Softex. We try this. We go to market. All girls to go."

As she gets up to leave, clearly keen to arrange this sortie, a thought strikes her. "You not speak this problem to boys?" she asks.

We reassure her of our reticence.

"Is better not," she confirms. "Boys—monthly bleeding do not like to know."

Motherly, she feels my brow and tells me to rest, and then pats Christine's arm. "I have pleasure you speak me this problem. Now are good friends. Soon times," she promises, "Chapa and Mary share much monthly bleedings with you. Now I must go to my home."

As it happens, that night I have a short, sharp, shock of diarrhoea, which yields immediate if exhausted release and confirms the source of my vague symptoms.

"Better not tell Asha that you've got the shits rather than *monthly bleeding*," Christine says the next morning. "She'll be devastated. We'd better join the great sanitary towel search as planned." She prods her stomach. "You know, I'm feeling a bit off myself. Nothing I can put my finger on exactly but..."

"Exactly," I commiserate. "That's just how I was. Stay near the loo."

"God," she goes on. "Hope the shits are a one-off. But remember, if either of us has to *go* on the way to town, just stop the rickshaw, find a ditch, and the other stands in front as a shield. Right?"

No sooner said, we are despatched with Chapa, Asha, and Mary on one rickshaw-van. Munnu, who allegedly has business in Takerhad, is chaperone.

"He not shops with us," Asha assures me, presumably to allay any embarrassment. She turns her rapt attention to Christine. "You are sick now. Maybe monthly bleeding also?"

Chapa frowns. "Not monthly bleeding. Not for sixty years old ladies." She leans forward. "Now I share my monthly bleeding with you. Okay?"

"Mary also?" Asha asks eagerly.

Poor Mary buries her scarlet face and anguished eyes deep in the folds of her *dupatta*. Chapa looks at her kindly. "Maybe she does not share. Mary is younger girl with less monthly bleedings. Is shy."

The four of us—a relieved Mary vanishing with Munnu—crowd into a small grocer-cum-chemist stall off the main market place and wait until the other customers leave. I cannot see anything remotely resembling what are at home labelled "feminine hygiene products," just a lot of soap and toothpaste and a shelf full of Old Spice shaving sticks. Asha makes her request to the shopkeeper in a mix of Bangla and English, but he just looks puzzled.

"Modesse?" Christine says hopefully.

"Softex?" I add helpfully.

"Ah, biscuits you want," he says.

I don't know whether types of biscuit with these brand names actually exist or whether the stallholder is chancing his arm as he reaches for a packet of chocolate chip cookies and another of custard creams. He pushes them across the counter.

"*Na*. No," begins Asha, but is saved by Chapa's careful scanning of the shelves. She points out a faded and dusty box way up on a back shelf, that burial place for items bought in a moment of wholesale madness and never to be sold. Except, clearly, to weird foreigners. The man climbs a stepladder, borrowed from the ironmonger next door, fetches down the box, and a second tucked behind it, whilst surreptitiously trying to dust them down with his sleeve to check that he has a respectable price mark-up.

"'Senora. Protection for the modern girl-about-town,'" Asha reads out laboriously. She and Chapa examine the containers in wonder. The faded boxes show pictures of mini-skirted models with thigh boots and bob-cuts posing in summer cornfields and looking demurely through Mary Quant eyelashes. To the uninitiated, it would be anyone's guess as to what the boxes contain. I bet piles of *taka* that the shopkeeper has no idea.

We settle on the smaller box, hand over the money, and wait, whilst under Asha's eagle eye, the package is wrapped and placed in a carrier bag. She illustrates—by putting her finger to her lips—that we should keep the purchase hidden as we leave the shop.

"You look as guilty as a priest hiding a Mills & Boon inside his Bible," Christine says as I tug at my *dupatta* to conceal as much of the bag as possible

Asha hurries us back to our room. She and Chapa are clearly dying to sample, as it were, the goods. I take the brick-sized parcel from the bag. "I could actually have a box of hair straighteners, or driving gloves, or..."

"Biscuits," supplies Christine. "Let's have a look."

I unwrap the packet, open the box, and with difficulty ease out the long, bulky contents. We all view the thick white napkins in silence.

"Bloody hell," says Christine finally. "I'd go with the rags and newspaper."

6

Week 4 - The Learning Zone

"Today we finish our work in schools," Bachchu shouts into the wind as his rickshaw-van overtakes a convoy of drivers running an impromptu Grand Prix. "We paint walls."

Christine and I exchange self-congratulatory smiles. For once, we are properly dressed on both counts. We had each packed a long skirt purely "for best" but decide they are actually needed to avoid further gender uncertainty, and we are—these being our dressier outfits—wearing them inside out for stain damage limitation.

We have had a busy week in various schools throughout Rajoir district. We have spoken English with the children in the first ever BRAC school[1], taken tea with a conference of local teachers, erected flagpoles for Sports Days, and cleared the grounds of a home/school for disabled youngsters. We've sat in on Maths lessons, Christine has taken a music class, and I have had a bash at telling Celtic fairy tales. Each session has ended with tea, more tea, and a song.

In today's school in Takerhad, rusty tin gates and a disintegrating brick wall protect a gaggle of small boys playing a makeshift game of cricket. Three broken bricks constitute the wicket, but they have a real bat, shiny and grass stained. Without delay, Moni, Munnu, Aktar, and the others join in the game. The little boys puff up with pride, the teachers smile benevolently, and the girls loftily ignore the entire proceedings and persist in walking through the middle of the match en route to their classrooms.

---

[1]The Bangladesh Rural Advancement Committee (BRAC) is one of the world's largest non-government organisations. It began in the seventies as a relief organisation, and then expanded into development work and is best known for its non-formal primary education programmes, especially targeting girls in rural areas–those most likely never to attend school or quickly to drop out. BRAC works for the children of the illiterate and destitute rural communities, the landless, and ensures that class times are flexible and lessons directed towards skills useful in family and village life: Bangla, English, Social Studies including health and nutrition and Arithmetic.

The girls' hostel is a basic, six-bed dormitory for all those whose homes are too far away for daily travel. The crumbling plaster walls are decorated with pictures of the latest Hindi movie stars torn from magazines and tacked up with pins. The door is open to a veranda protected from the courtyard by a fine metal grille—and this is what we will paint.

"First we clean away the rusting. Then we paint it shining red," Munnu explains. "We like it to be green to match the grass, but the students choose a happy colour."

"Back to the more practical end of cultural exchange," Christine comments.

Squares of stiff sandpaper are shared out and spread out along the veranda. We each pick our spot and begin the painstaking task of rubbing away years of rust and dirt. The orange dust falls like mellow rain, settles on our shoulders, in our hair, and mixes with sweat to stain hands and faces.

Ready to paint, we waste spend precious minutes watching a heated discussion between Munnu, Aktar, and someone who I presume is the school's general dogsbody.

"There is only *this*—and no brushes." Bachchu holds up a tin of paint the size of a can of baked beans. "Work waits until the boy makes free time to buy supplies at market."

"Could Christine and I go instead?" I ask.

But I may as well have suggested parading Lady Godiva-style through the town and paying for the paint in sexual favours.

"No, no. This is not your job," Bachchu explains.

What feels like a week later, the caretaker proudly returns with three brushes tucked neatly into the waistband of his *lunghi*. They are the kind of paintbrushes that a watercolour artist might use to sketch in fine lines. Chapa immediately co-opts one, using the handle to curl her eyelashes.

"What are we doing?" asks Christine. "Touching up the Eiffel Tower with nail varnish?"

Munnu throws up his hands in disgust and marches off in the general direction of the Principal's office.

"Well." Christine sighs. "What do we do now?"

"I Spy with my Little Eye?" I suggest.

We explain the rudiments of the observation game, and before long, all the volunteers are clamouring for a turn. It is a surprisingly effective way of teaching elementary English. Stuck on Aktar's "something beginning with Z" (it turns out to be President Zia as glimpsed in portrait through the Library window), Aktar is disqualified on a vote of five to four. The slim majority argues that the great man should be "something-beginning-with-P." Munnu has to shout before we notice his two threadbare rollers, an enamel tray, and a veritable barrel of red paint.

"Hallelujah, an archaeological fantasy," says Christine poking at the ancient yet serviceable equipment. "We've found the stuff Noah used to paint the Ark."

Exempt from the painting due to lack of equipment, Christine, Chapa, Asha, and I drag spare chairs from the nearest classroom and sit out in the sun with tea and *shingara* ("Like *samosa* but filled with potato and cooked until they puff up big," describes Munnu). Some of the girls are excused lessons to meet us but, "They want only looking at boys," Chapa says with disdain.

Clusters of them approach. Chapa and Asha act as our publicists and arbitrarily vet potential fans.

"You, girl, be my pen-pal friend," says one tall student. Her hair is braided into a sophisticated knot, her eyes confident. She steps forward, flanked admiringly by two of her less brave and far less pretty consorts, and holds out a worn copybook. "Write *nam*. Now." She turns to Chapa and obviously issues the same peremptory instructions in Bangla. "Tell girl," she finishes, nodding at me.

Chapa, taken aback at being addressed so by a younger, attractive stranger, answers haughtily. The two glare at one another. In less civilised environs, they would dissolve into a catfight, pulling each other's hair at the roots.

"Is best not," Chapa says to me after a final face-off. "If this student writes your name, all want. And." She sits up straighter and all but sniffs. "She is not nice friend for you. Not good girl."

"Positively common, I'm sure," Christine mocks.

I sneak a weak, apologetic smile at the girl who looks back condescendingly, gives a gracious flutter of her fingers, and retreats a safe distance to vent frustration on her luckless friends.

A long hour and a half later, a dozen similar life stories shared, and endless, identical, personal enquiries later, I wish Chapa were telling them all to clear off. Virtual prisoners of a tubby, round-faced girl who sits at our feet unravelling a short life of tragedy and woe, every time we almost get rid of her, her puffy eyes fill with tears, and she sniffles into her *dupatta* bemoaning her friendless state. She could write scripts for *EastEnders*. Chapa is charmed; the weepy girl acts as a totem to keep the real competition away.

There is no refuge in the staff room where we are lured for more "*refreshing-ments*." Two male teachers, with matching eighties perms and embryonic military moustaches, their trouser legs turned up around their knees, want to rehearse their dual aptitude for fast paced English conversation. Nearly prostrated by their frenzied dash toward us, Christine shakes her head before reclining on a surprisingly plush leather-look sofa. She runs a languid hand over her eyes.

"If there's any more tea going, wake me," she barks in my direction, and then alters her tone to address the panting teachers.

"I'm bushed, knackered, *very tired*," she spells out. "A lady of my position needs to rest. You boys *will* excuse me." The headmistress tone works. They give her a deferential wide berth and practically fall salivating on me.

"What is your good name, her good name, your job, her job, your good country, her good country, your age, her age, your marital status and hers?"

"How you liking Bangladesh, how she liking it? How you liking our English language, how she likes? How you getting us visa to your good country, how is she?"

After several rounds of this quick-fire elimination quiz, I have no idea what I'm saying any more. I simultaneously understand the roots of shell shock and why innocent bystanders give false confessions to zealous policemen. As they dash off to lead a whole-school PE class, I can feel Christine shaking with silent laughter.

"The sooner those boys get a good shag the better," is her verdict. "Did you ever see such bottled up sexual frustration?"

Since being so steeped in the education system, the Bangladeshi volunteers are concerned that they are not teaching Christine and me enough about the country. Before dinner, Munnu calls a special House Meeting, rounding up as many volunteers as he can find. As well as his brothers Mannu and Bachchu, Tapon, Aktar, Moni and the three girls join us in the library. We sit in a circle on the floor passing around a huge bag of *mori*, a rice snack that looks and tastes exactly like dry Rice Krispies. "First we talk of politics and religion," Munnu says. "Then we review Work Camp Programme."

"Better to start with subjects that causes less argument," agrees Christine.

"Christine. Anne. You understand the differences between Muslim and Hindu religion?" Munnu asks.

"Absolutely." Christine nods.

"I think so. Sort of. Well, in general," I say.

Munnu grasps this as an unqualified "yes" and hurries on.

Anne Hamilton

"That's religion done. Politics?" Christine grins.

Conversation revolves around the current spate of national *hartals*, (the Gujarati word for "strike") which are a constant feature of Bangladesh's chaotic political system. Moni describes it as succinctly as he can. "The Opposition Party calls for a strike a few days in advance, rallies the people to rise up and to form a mass outdoor protest about some policy or element of the Government." He pauses to crunch a handful of rice, and then continues. "Government is corrupt. Politicians are corrupt. It is not possible for many people to get a good job or a visa to travel or have an education unless they make good friends. There is a word in English—"

"Nepotism?" Christine interrupts.

"Yes. Nepotism. SCI tries to make difference but is very difficult."

"In Bangladesh there is a reputation that we are all poor with no food, and that we die in the monsoon floods. This is a bit true. But so many more people are less destitute but much socially disadvantaged." Munnu's face is both earnest with attempting to explain his country and faintly proud of his advanced English. He and Moni lead the others into an extemporized round of "We Shall Overcome" sung in English and Bengali. It is their theme tune, their call to arms, and not a day goes by without a rendition.

"What can we do?" Christine asks after they finish. We are at a loss. I am suddenly face-to-face with the fact that I cannot change the world, and that I am not trying hard enough, anyway. My Bangladeshi friends are, but the odds are stacked against them.

"You are here," says Munnu. "You tell your countries that Bangladesh is its own country, is not part of India. You say that we are not all bad people who visit your countries and do not leave when the visa is finished. You tell that Muslim and fundamentalist terrorist is not the same. You see that Muslim and Hindu live together here in Shanti Kendra, Centre for Peace. This is so all over our country. Only minimum people have problems. Since Liberation War of 1971, we fight together for People's Republic of Bangladesh. We wish to fight ourselves no more."

"Do you have a further question, any person?" checks Bachchu, who has sat quietly until now. "About Bangladesh or Christine and Anne's countries?"

There is a pause. Then:

"I like to say something." Munnu grins. "Christine asks how foreigners can give us help, yes?"

"Yes?" she replies.

"You can marry some of us and take us to Australia and Ireland. This makes us very happy."

"Try again, Casanova," Christine drawls through her smile.

Emboldened by the raucous laughter, Munnu pushes his luck. "Do beautiful girls wear mini-skirts in your countries?" he asks.

I choke as I remember Christine's prediction at our original orientation session that the volunteers are far more interested in entertainment, clothes and relationships than hard-end politics and religion. I can only nod vigorously. The boys are clearly holding their collective breath for more until Bachchu remembers his position of seniority and hurriedly suggests some good, clean entertainment. He produces a tattered game of Uno.

"Methinks we haven't heard the last of the mini-skirts," Christine says later as we lay side by side on the sun-warmed stone veranda just outside our bedroom. Dusk is coming quickly and the scent of the white flowers that straggle up the balcony, "It's called 'Night Queen,'" says Christine, "because—guess what?—they only smell at night." Their sweetish, vanilla scent mingles with the cigarettes Christine has cadged from a surprised Munnu.

"Funny the differences in what's socially acceptable here," she goes on. "Showing your midriff in a sari is okay, but bare shoulders and legs aren't. And the gobbing and snorting and spitting, not to mention belching that goes on in public is totally unself-conscious. God knows how the tight-arsed Brits ever managed in India."

"They didn't," I say. "They kept themselves to themselves and ostracised anyone who went native. Can I have a smoke?"

Taken unawares, Christine automatically passes me the cigarette— and just as quickly snatches it back. "What? Are you crazy? No, you bloody well can't. It's a disgusting habit, and you'll get addicted and die of lung cancer, and sue me." She draws deeply on the nicotine at the thought.

"How can I sue you if I'm dead?" I sulk. "It's just an experiment. It seems to keep the mosquitoes away."

"Bit drastic," comments Christine, cheerfully immune. Her blood must be the polar opposite to mine. "Maybe we could market it as a positive secondary effect, though. You know. Counteract all the death threats on cigarette packets with: *May prevent malaria*. Anyway, you're obsessed. There are only two mozzies here, and they hang around the light bulb in the loo."

"You can imagine my triumphant return home," I say, only half joking. "'What did you actually do in Bangladesh?' people will ask. 'What do you remember most?' What will I say? 'Cower under a mosquito net and worrying about bodily functions mainly.' So much for the intrepid traveller."

"So? At least you're here while you worry, not on your arse at home, making up excuses." Christine begins a sincere if confused philosophy: "Most people would—" She stops suddenly. "What the hell is that?"

Ghostly undertones are emanating from the cracks in the veranda. "Christeeeen...Annieee..."

"I think it's Munnu." I clamber up, lean over the balcony, and squint into the night. "Munnu? Munnu? Where are you, Munnu?"

"Move over, Juliet." Christine squeezes in beside me. "Maybe it's me Romeo after all."

"Anne. I come to ask if you like to make *kharbor* with me tonight?" Munnu's disembodied voice floats up.

"Why, sir, she hardly knows you," calls Christine. "And why her? What's wrong with my *kharbor* skills?"

As well he might, Munnu sounds mystified. "Sorry, Christine? I ask Anne because your first time was with Moni, but it was not pleasant for you. Tonight, I make it easy for Anne."

"Promises, promises..." Christine rolls her eyes.

I gag Christine with her cigarette, and tell him that I'd be delighted to make *kharbor* with him. "You do mean *cook* with you, right?" I clarify.

"Of course. *Kharbor* means food, meal for eating. What else do you think? Come down, let us go. Aktar joins us. Christine, you can play with the boys in their bedroom. Okay?"

"What an offer." Christine grins. "I'll be sure to keep the door wide open and one leg on the floor."

"Christine? I don't understand."

"She's making a bad joke that isn't worth translating," I tell the innocent Munnu. "Come on."

The kitchen is a makeshift affair straddling indoors and out. In the concrete room next door to where the boys sleep, the floor is piled with huge cooking pots, sacks of rice and cartons of oil. Vegetables bought from the market that morning are jumbled amongst them along with a red plastic bowl filled with raw chicken bits. There is a waist-high shelf for crockery, but most Bangladeshi preparation is done crouched on the ground using the *boti*, the huge village knife that resembles a small sword poking out of a block of wood. During the day, the actual cooking is done on an open fire outside, but in the darkness, Munnu coerces Aktar into helping him pump the indoor kerosene stove until they have orange flames leaping up the sides of the cast-iron cooking pot. They lean forward into the fire with self-congratulatory cigarettes balanced on their bottom lips. I wait for us to be launched into fuel-propelled orbit.

"Anne. Do you like our *kharbor*?" Munnu asks for the millionth time. "I can make eggs for you."

The food here is certainly repetitive, and to eat is simply to refuel. But it is also spicy, plentiful, and probably nutritious enough. Christine and I eat bread and vegetables with gusto, taste the meat, and enjoy the scarcer oranges and bananas. But we can't possibly consume sufficient quantities of rice to please our minimum-three-bowls-a-day hosts. As for the fish, it's less the fish itself than the water it comes from. "Shit coloured and shit filled," is Christine's eloquent description. Such foreign quirkiness means that she and I consume *a lot* of eggs: fried eggs served hot or cold, hard-boiled eggs served hot or cold, fried and hard-boiled eggs served hot or cold, fried and/or hard-boiled eggs with chilli and onions, without chilli and onions... "Your diary must contain nothing but lists of things we eat," Christine frequently observes—correctly. We could be in a Blyton boarding school.

"*Go to work on an egg*," singsongs Munnu. "Anne. Do you know this saying*? Go to work on an egg?*"

"I haven't heard that since I was ten," I remember in wonder.

"We have English books in primary school," Munnu explains. "Sometimes they have the big pictures, paper commercials ("adverts" I correct) for foods and refrigerators and cars. We like these maximum because no television comes yet. My brothers and me, we think to *go to work on an egg* is funny, like the book means the man travels to work on a scooter or a rickshaw." He frowns with the effort of explanation. "Is a joke. You understand?"

It is extraordinary to think that whilst I was being fed (literally), this media jingle in a parallel universe caused a classroom full of Bangladeshis—my peer group—to visualise grown-ups in the West flying to their offices on a giant, fluffy omelette. He reminds Aktar, and soon we are all ten again and chanting it with gusto: *go to work on an egg; go to work on an egg.*

Munnu waves me a safe distance back from the murderous knife/ garden tool/ torture implement combo—the *boti*—that he has dragged into the middle of the floor.

"Anne. I chop vegetables," he says masterfully. "It takes maximum years to learn use of this knife. I worry you injure yourself. Watch carefully."

Anne Hamilton

The knife remains static and the vegetables, fish, meat, whatever, are brought to the blade and viciously peeled or sliced. I watch carefully as Munnu proceeds to chop off his fingernails.

"Very lucky I wear sandals today, or my toes may face danger also." Munnu picks the clippings from the diced onion. He chucks everything—cauliflower, aubergine, onions, potatoes, chillies, tomatoes and cabbage—into a large pot.

"Shouldn't we fry the onions first? Then add the potatoes?" I wonder how the cabbage will stand up to half an hour of brisk boiling.

Munnu looks faintly perturbed. Clearly, my role is to watch, not to comment on technique or to do anything practical. For a second opinion, he calls Aktar, who has vanished next door, much more interested in the card game being played by Christine and the rest of the volunteers. Aktar laughs, seizes the cooking pot and hefts it into the meeting room next door where the others can no longer hear themselves over the mass rumbling of stomachs. Gleefully, he demonstrates the combined ineptitude of the Camp Leader and the foreigner. They all look and point, their merriment taking the edge off hunger. Munnu and I stand at the door looking hopeless.

"They all say we should cook each ingredient separately," Munnu admits to me in an undertone and waits for me to say *I told you so* to undermine his position in front of his mates even further. I smile serenely, say nothing, and, from his look of relief, I do believe he falls in love with me forever. We return to the kitchen and begin to pick out the different vegetables, give it up as a bad job, and stir fry them all haphazardly.

"If they are hungry, they eat," says Munnu, virtuous as a Victorian mamma. "There are maximum hungry people in the world who will be grateful to take our food."

I snort with laughter.

"Anne? Why is this funny? My mother always says this when we do not eat her dinners."

"Because *my* mother always said that if we didn't eat, she would send it to the starving children in Bangladesh. Where would *you* have sent it?"

"Africa." Munnu grins.

He is in fine form this evening. One-on-one, his English is clear and confident, and I realise how, Christine aside, I have been pining for general chitchat and silly jokes. Munnu is the first Bangladeshi with whom I am beginning to feel a strong connection and having the space and language to uncover a shared sense of humour has a lot to do with it. But as the curry bubbles away, he changes tack and starts telling me

71

all about his family, himself, his life. In fact, he is outlining his prospects. At first I think nothing of it, assuming he is redeeming himself in the light of the cooking debacle. But I begin to suspect his motives when he tells me of his love life and the girls who have not understood him.

"Bangladesh is not so different to your country," he assures me. "Boys and girls have places to be alone. There are many ways for this, Anne. You could be a shining Bengali wife."

He looks so innocent, and is so discreet in his suggestions, that I am not sure I am being propositioned. Not wanting to spoil a blossoming friendship, I am, ironically, able to miss the point (if indeed any point is being made), by not quite understanding his English.

Nothing more is said.

Later, Christine is in no doubt. "Why shouldn't he try his luck?" she says. "You're his age, blonde, and beautiful—don't roll your eyes at me," she admonishes as I pull faces at her. "Okay," she amends. "I'm exaggerating, but here, you really are exotic. Hell, *I'm* exotic—even if it is because I'm *nearly dead*. Wouldn't bagging you be a feather in his cap? Or," she adds, "he might genuinely like you. He's a very nice boy."

"But he knows I'm not Muslim. And I'm married."

"Not in any real sense from what they can tell. What do you expect when you can't cook, you haven't dropped any kids, and you've left your husband behind to go travelling? I'd put you down as a crap wife but great girlfriend material. And," she smirks. "You're a Class A flirt!"

"I so am not." I revert to teen syntax in protest.

"Bloody are. I've watched you at work. You've got that knack of looking cute and helpless down to a T. And men, being the naïve idiots they are, can't wait to grab your tools and fill your holes...as it were."

"This from a woman who can leapfrog the length of the veranda, hold the lotus position on the back of a rickshaw-van all the way to Takerhad, and still has all her own teeth."

"Stop exaggerating." She grins. "You know I've half a back molar missing."

"And yet," I resume, "she has the gall to pretend she was too old a lady to help me restrain two crazed teachers."

She doesn't hesitate. "It's called post-feminist grey power, and therefore it's allowed. Whereas you're just a flirt. Albeit an unobtainable, just-passing-through-and–therefore-highly-desirable one."

"When you say it like that, I suppose I'm a very hot property indeed," I agree. "You forgot to mention my comparative wealth and ability to entertain with an Irish jig."

"Hooray! The girl is developing that Bangladeshi self-confidence after all."

7
The Holiday Wardrobe

Whilst Christine tackles our laundry, I lie on the sun-drenched veranda supervising and trying to remember what I would otherwise be doing at home—like being on holiday, sick, or in an institution. Individual days have lost their meaning. The three weeks in Khalia has been equally a lifetime and has gone in the click of a finger, leaving me with my first incomparable experience of life in rural Bangladesh, one with which I will bore everyone in the West to death forever.

"I teach piano every morning 'til noon during term time," Christine is saying. "Then I try to practice for a couple of hours and do exam prep or admin. God, I need to get out more. Does Bangladesh count?" She crouches doubtfully over the leaking bucket, trying to coax a few more drips of water from the cold tap, and then gets drenched by a random splurge. "*If they could see me now...*" she croons.

"Wednesday is my *Jekyll and Hyde* day," I tell her. "Right now I'd be in a meeting deciding which of the children on my waiting list can't wait any longer to get their own social worker. Then I'd hand over, drive home, and spend the afternoon seeing patients and dispensing glasses."

"Less chance to get bored that way. Must be bloody hard to switch from one to the other, though."

"If you haven't learned to switch off quickly after ten years working in Child Protection, you're probably in the wrong job—or dead. And, at least you know where you are with glasses—either you can either see out of them or you can't."

"Not an obvious combination is it? Must be just Irish universities that offer a BSc in Social and Optical Sciences."

"Idiot. The optician stuff goes with the pharmacy. It's the family business. I sort of fell into it."

But Christine is no longer listening. In fact she is shrieking, rudely, crudely, and boldly, with an upturned bucket in one hand, and a pile of sopping underwear in the other.

Anne Hamilton

"What is it?" I rush in to the lavatory. "Have you burned yourself on a (for once) hot pipe? Slipped on a bar of soap and gashed your head? Had a close encounter with something leggy, slimy and venomous?"

"There go our socks and knickers! I've just poured them away!"

Dejectedly, she watches the surprising gush and swirl of dirty water as it travels along the gutter and vanishes down the drain. With an impressive tackle rarely seen off the rugby field, I do manage to salvage Christine's favourite long johns as they snake around the U-bend.

We hang over the balcony, squinting to determine where the effluent emerges but can see nothing.

"The system must be underground for once," I say. "And look. The drain isn't even blocked. Any other day a hairpin would cause it to back up."

"I don't know what's worse," groans Christine, her head in her sodden hands. "Losing half of the few clothes we have, or not even seeing them in the filthy water. Our 'whites' turned it black."

Downstairs, she and I meander illicitly through the garbage tip in the unlikely event that the outlet might just spew out somewhere convenient, but all I end up with is a scratched thigh, caught on rusty barbed wire placed to keep out trespassers.

"Oh, bother," I wail. "Now I have to worry about tetanus. As well as malaria, dysentery, typhoid, breaking a leg, and poison by osmosis from excessive insect repellent." Just because it's a miniscule graze, and I've had every possible vaccination, means nothing to any self-respecting, card-carrying hypochondriac.

"Maybe you'll get off lucky with a double amputation. Fool," Christine jeers. "Let me have a look. Actually, no don't—pull your skirt down. We're distracting all the holy mosque goers. Not to mention Munnu, who's rounding that corner and waving in our direction."

Munnu, who gamely pretends not to notice my dress up round my ears and Christine's rather intimate probing of my thigh, struggles to keep his eyes averted and launches into our programme for the day. It is a holiday, designated for sightseeing. We are advised on our wardrobe accordingly.

"Christine. Anne. For this programme, we all wear best clothes. In Bangla, means *fitfaht*. Smart."

"This has to be the greatest dilemma to date," Christine says. "If the reactions of Chapa, Asha, and Mary are anything to go by, we're buggered."

She's spot on. We have constructed a makeshift washing line that stretches the length of the corridor outside our bedroom, and after being rinsed in a bucket of cold and nearly soapy water, our clothes all hang there to drip dry. Almost daily the three girls creep up to finger the garments, smother their titters, and whisper amongst themselves incredulously.

"We have to be creative," I say. "What we need is bright, loose, long, and a couple of scarves."

"Skirt or trousers?"

"Both," I say, a sudden brainwave. "Trousers under the skirts will be a vague approximation of a *salwar kameez*." Very vague actually, but it is the best we can do.

We are surprisingly pleased with our efforts. Christine wears a long, multi-coloured designer over shirt ("From the best second-hand store in Sydney."), a blue skirt, and her purple trousers. I knew my flowery Laura Ashley summer dress would come in useful some day, and worn over loose, silk-like pants, and accessorised with one of Christine's many scarves, I do look reasonably dressed up. We even fish out Christine's make-up, which she expertly applies, and I daub on clown-like.

Definitely *fitfaht*, we agree with each other, repeating the word and savouring it, as we make our way downstairs to the library where the other volunteers are slowly congregating.

Chapa, Asha, and Mary, themselves dressed in their best outfits, smooth their hands over our clothes, stroke Christine's scarves, and offer their seal of approval.

"*Shundur, Anne*. Christine also *shundur*. Beautiful."

"Are we *fitfaht*?" Christine asks the boys as they arrive en masse.

"Very *fitfaht*. Christine. Anne. You are especially shining today," says Munnu.

"And you too. All of you are very *fitfaht*," I compliment them in turn. Moni, Aktar, and Bachchu are wearing neat Western clothes. Munnu and Mannu have donned Punjabi suits of embroidered white cotton. We spend quite some time forming a mutual admiration society in which *fitfaht* almost replaces *monthly bleeding* for our phrase of the week.

Waved off by what might be the whole of Shanti Kendra, we all walk a couple of hot kilometres through fields and small villages to the main road, where we loiter on the hard shoulder. Smoking, grey, industrial chimneys, and the lingering factory smell of wet tar is behind us. We watch men, faces lined and backs bent, pulling relentless convoys of trolleys loaded with bricks, unloading and restacking them.

Anne Hamilton

Munnu flags down a passing bus, and the conductor hauls us aboard an already overflowing vehicle. Even the section by the driver reserved for women is crammed with mothers and small children. We rocket along the road, bouncing and shuddering, horns blaring and headlights blazing.

"Very fast, hey?" Moni sways back and forth as the bus swerves to hit a rickshaw or two. "Always maximum speed. Many accidents happen."

Munnu is more specific, roaring above the engine whine. "Two days ago near Dhaka, a bus veers off the road and falls into the river. One hundred thirty-three people are killed. More injured."

I pray that my entry to the afterlife is not so imminent. It's already as hot as the anteroom to Hell. My amateur make-up is liquefying and dripping down my cheeks in streaky rivulets.

We screech to a halt on the outskirts of a pretty town called Jolipur. Jelly-legged, I totter after the others, soon lost in a maze of isolated, yet thriving, housing compounds.

"These are Hindu villages," Munnu explains. "Here we see much craftwork. Is a tradition for the Hindu community. Do not be shy to look."

We squeeze into a miniature, dim workshop where two large women, amongst a jumble of cardboard boxes, are squatting over a pair of grinding machines and making jewellery from a white shell material. One of the women gently removes the earrings Christine is wearing and replaces them with her own creation. Her colleague sweeps my hair up into a knot and secures it with a large hair slide.

"How much?" I ask, and am mortified to learn there is no charge.

"These are gifts from the community," Moni translates. "These ladies never see foreigners wear their jewellery. They are honoured you find pleasure in it."

"They cannot work outside because the light hurts their eyes," explains Munnu, "but this work means their families can eat one meal most days."

Christine and I look at one another. It's one thing to hear this on a news report back home, commiserate, and stick some change into an Oxfam or Save the Children collecting tin, it's another to be faced by the hard evidence of such poverty. Clearly thinking along the same lines, we both suddenly "remember" lots of cousins and nieces and friends who would love some of these accessories, and Moni barters for a good deal. The women are delighted yet maintain their dignity, and Christine and I are chastened, aware our few *taka* won't change the world, but not sure what else to do.

We cross a swinging bamboo bridge that has a single pole serving as an intermittent handrail. Tapon runs ahead with his video, and I have a nervous breakdown. Whilst there is barely a puddle of green, sticky water beneath us, the riverbed, sandy and arid, looks to be miles and miles below. The other volunteers, including Christine, skip across—Aktar does somersaults—and as I come in last, all are cheering me on as if I were the asthmatic fat kid in an egg-and-spoon race. Towards me, two small children run the gangplank, and an elderly man reaches up to his head to steady a bunch of cauliflowers in a blatant "Look! No hands!" gesture. One young boy wheels over his bicycle, a huge leg of beef on the seat. I fix my eyes on the two bamboo huts ahead of us and pray—any god will do.

By the time I crawl over, everyone else is rooting from under a white tarpaulin for raffia baskets and trays stacked in precarious piles. Baskets large enough to hold a newborn baby, smaller versions for storing vegetables, fat trays are for carrying tea glasses, curved ones for picking over the rice. There are unidentifiable containers of all shapes and sizes, boxes with and without lids, ornaments in the shape of lop-sided giraffes.

"They look as if they've had the raffia equivalent of a stroke." I squint.

"They are *Ganesh*, the Hindu elephant god," Bachchu plaintively corrects me.

"Seems kind of rude not to buy a few dozen to go with the jewellery," Christine comments.

Two middle-aged women seated on small stools expertly weave the raffia, braiding it, tying it, and forcefully bending it until the object takes shape. They peer myopically at their work, holding it close, shyly acknowledging our presence.

"They invite you to make something," Munnu says, indicating that we should kneel down for a brief demonstration.

As someone who cannot even plait hair and wouldn't graduate beyond threading needles in sewing class, I don't expect much of myself. I shrug off the gasps of wonder at my inability to braid three strips of raffia and—the *coup de grace*—actually to snap them in the process. The weavers gaze on in awe.

"They say they have never seen this before. They did not think it possible." Munnu grins.

Christine produces a most creditable effort. What she makes isn't anything as such, but it is a neat, tight length. If knitted by a six-year-old, it would certainly be the beginnings of a teddy bears scarf.

Eventually, Munnu says, "Now is the best point of our day. Very interesting visit to Catholic Mission."

Christine does well to mask her dismay. The usual reaction of an ex-convent girl turned atheist with a hankering towards Eastern philosophy would be to run away screaming. "Strewth," she mutters to me. "Flamin' mongrels took the best years of my life."

Actually, she doesn't say that. I've just been hoping that she would so I could quote her in the best Australian soap opera tradition. "Of course we talk like that," she says when I quiz her on the finer dialogue of *Neighbours*.

"Really?" I'm incredulous.

"Yeah," she replies. "About as often as the Irish say 'Begorrah!' and, 'top of the morning to yez!'"

In fact, the mission disappoints both my romantic notion of a Jimmy Stewart priest saying Mass at a simple, shaded, bamboo altar, and Christine's nightmare harem of sweet-faced, gimlet-eyed Sisters of No-Mercy. Munnu was using the term "*catholic*" to mean Christian. It is actually a large Kellog-Mokerjee sponsored Seventh Day Adventist school with an orphanage added on.

The beautifully cultivated flower and vegetable gardens are dissected by carefully-maintained walkways. The newest and largest of the two-storey buildings is the orphanage where boys reside on the ground floor and girls on the floor above. A large Bangladeshi woman stands proprietarily on the front steps, comes forward to greet us, and invites Christine, Chapa, Asha, Mary, and myself inside.

"No men," she says. "It is women who care for these children."

This formidable lady with the impeccable English is the warden, responsible for the welfare of the girls and all the younger children. She stands us in a line and interrogates us.

"My name is Mrs P. J. Thomas," she says. "I am here for twenty-two years. My husband is now dead, but he was from Cheshire, England. He was sent here to teach."

With understated pride, she shows us around her empire. Indeed, the facilities, though Spartan, are scrupulously clean and fresh smelling with bright, whitewashed walls. Fifty-six little boys live in one huge, open-plan room full of neat rows of bunk beds with a wall of lockers.

"For personal possessions," she says. "Most are empty."

Jumbo-sized French windows open out onto an enclosed green, a billowing line of little dresses and shorts are pegged to a washing line high above the ground.

"It has to be so high," says Mrs Thomas. "Otherwise the children would get tangled in the clothes and pull them down as they do their chores."

She points to a team of six-year-olds who have the task of sweeping the ground. One or two of them dutifully trail the brooms behind them; the others are attempting to chase their friends and swat them over their heads. On seeing strangers, they nudge one another and creep forward, a watchful eye on the Warden.

"I will let you practise your English for five minutes," she says to them, turning her wrist to see her watch.

Then, as if in the classroom, they recite in unison: "Hello. How are you? Very well, thank you. One, two, three, four, five. Goodbye."

"At five-years-old," Mrs Thomas says, "all the children begin school and work. Each has a job to do. They feel useful. They earn their keep, and it saves us enough money to feed and educate them. The older children learn trades in our workshops: cooking, sewing, farm work, and labouring. Sometimes one is offered a scholarship to college." As Mrs Thomas speaks, she takes us back inside, up a flight of stairs, and into the girls' room.

"There are twice as many girls as boys," she tells us, "and a mix of Christians and Hindus. Many of the children are not strictly orphans. They have a mother or father or grandparents, but the extended family cannot afford them, and they are sent here. Girls are less economically viable so they are sacrificed first."

"Do their families visit them?" I ask.

"Of course, if we know who they are. Some children are just abandoned—the parents know we will not turn an infant away. The others can visit their homes at holiday time, and their families may come here on open days. Visitors tell me my orphanage compares very favourably with that of Mother Teresa's in Calcutta." Mrs Thomas allows herself a momentary swelling of most un-Christian self-satisfaction. "But then," she recollects herself, "we, of course can avoid the worst excesses of a poor urban area, the crime, drugs, prostitution."

"She's great PR for the place," whispers Christine as we retrace our steps, Mrs Thomas still ahead of us. "Do you think it's all as *Pollyanna* as it looks?"

"I bet the children have to work much harder than she makes out. But they look happy and well-fed and, well, like children, not mini-adult drudges. So much for all religions living in perfect harmony, though. Didn't she say that there are no Muslim children here? I wonder what that's about?" I open my mouth to ask the question but am beaten to it by a voice calling from outside. Mrs Thomas hurries down the last couple of stairs.

Back outside, she hugs an extremely attractive young woman who, whilst clearly Bengali and wearing an elegant, emerald green and sky blue sari, looks strangely as if she would be more at home in low-slung skinny jeans and a tight T-shirt.

"Come and meet Ameysha," Mrs Thomas says fondly. "I looked after her for eight years before she was adopted by a good doctor and his wife. She, too, is visiting from overseas. Yesterday was her nineteenth birthday."

"Hi," says the girl, looking as if she would rather not have her life story made public. "Call me Amy. Where're you guys from? I'm from Canada. Not that you'd know it by looking." She plucks self-consciously at her sari, obviously struggling with a sudden clash of cultures.

"Is this your first visit back?" I ask.

"Yeah. Kind of strange. I keep remembering bits of life when I was a kid here. Mrs PJ was the best mom ever. I always write her." She gives the delighted warden another hug.

We have to drag the spellbound Chapa and Asha away. Even Chapa's haughty manner has slipped in the face of this novel character of her own age and background, yet living a life as far away from Bangladesh as is possible. The boys, too, are taking surreptitious backward glances as we say goodbye to Mrs Thomas and file out past the security guard.

"We've certainly been upstaged," remarks Christine. "I bet she definitely wears a miniskirt back home."

"Now, I have sad news," Munnu tells us as we wave our final farewells and stroll towards the next town. "The next visit of our programme is the milk processing plant, but sadly we hear it is closed. It does not reopen for many hours."

"Oh what a shame," I say, trying to hide the insincerity. "That would have been very interesting."

"What a total bugger," agrees Christine, pulling a face as if it has been her life's wish to tour the Co-op Dairy HQ, and this was the next best thing.

Munnu gives us a speculative look. "We can wait," he offers. "We sit here for maximum time. It is your choice." He turns away to light a cigarette.

"That's our bluff well and truly called," Christine mutters. "What do we do now?"

It's the cloud of mosquitoes around me that saves the day. So much closer to the river, they are swarming, and I barricade myself within a fortress of creams and sprays, socks, and shawls.

"Sorry all, but I think it would be a health hazard for Anne to wait," Christine says. "Persistent little buggers, aren't they?" she remarks, unaffected. "The chances of a mozzie getting to you should be on par with a sperm reaching a ripe egg."

8
Mammy Dearest

Traditionally, Munnu explains on the last day of the Rajoir Work Camp, all projects end with a celebration dinner and a campfire. In the meantime, though...

"Would you like to telephone your countries?" He grins, as we all but squeal in delight.

I never thought I was particularly materialistic, and I certainly have not cared about the lack of technology, or labour saving devices, ("or toilet paper," Christine reminds me). But a month in Bangladesh has shown that Christine's desert island luxury would be a hair-dryer and mine, much as I hate to admit it, would be a mobile phone. Never again will I take for granted being able to phone a friend, make an appointment, call home from work for no reason other than to say, "Howya, what's happening? I'm bored."

The telegraph office, off a side street in Takerhad, is a cramped room above a tailor's shop. Crowds attempt to follow us up the crooked staircase and jostle in front of a dirty counter piled with obsolete radio equipment and vintage Bakelite telephones. When asked to book calls to Australia and Ireland, the operator purses his lips and shakes his head like a plumber who has been asked if he can fix the washing machine sometime before the Christmas after next.

"There are three telephone lines only," Munnu translates reluctantly, the entire office suddenly silent and listening, "and one is broken. Cows eat it. This man has a—backlist? Sorry, *backlog*, for many days. I am very sorry to disappoint."

"Can't he squeeze us in? We'll be quick," Christine asks.

"Two minutes each? Or email?" I add, hoping to sweeten the deal.

"I am sorry." Munnu looks distraught. "Maybe in Dhaka?"

We are a drooping triangle of despair saved only by a commotion at the back of the room. Two strangers, matching Harris Tweed caps perched above their more traditional garb, push themselves forwards and thrust business cards at us.

"We couldn't help over hearing, love," the middle-aged one says, his North of England accent and easy informality both unmistakable.

"That's right," the other adds. "A right shame is that."

"So what you want, see, is a fax."

"Aye. They get sent through at night when it's quieter. We do it many a time. Better than nowt, in't it?"

I feel like I've walked onto the set of *Only Fools and Horses*. They are a Yorkshire version of Del Boy and his brother Rodney. In the West, they would own a successful chain of "Indian" (most curry houses in the UK are generically called Indian, even if they are really Pakistani or Bangladeshi) restaurants called the Taj Mahal, or The Bengal Tiger, or some such. In fact, Imran and Sajid (their real names) soon tell us that food is exactly their line of business—even when back home in Bangladesh visiting their aged and widowed mother.

"We've got restaurants in Bradford, four of them, and a couple of take-aways," Imran, the older brother, says.

"And a rota with our six brothers so that neither our mam nor the businesses are ever without family close by," adds Sajid.

Talking over each other in two languages, Imran and Sajid's welcome diversion gains immediate favour with Munnu.

"These are good men," he approves, calling for fax paper and pens. "We take tea here. I buy sweets to make you feel less unhappy."

Whilst Christine and I scribble a few banalities, pass the fax paper and a pile of *taka* to the operator (pointlessly because the messages never arrive), Imran and Sajid rearrange some cardboard boxes and a waste paper bin for us all to sit down.

"I spent four years at university in Bradford," I say, glad to find a common link.

Nobody has ever been so thrilled to hear me say this. The usual response is: "Oh, dear. Couldn't you get in anywhere else?" Soon I am deep in a bizarre conversation, which results in them sending a messenger to ransack their room and locate a dog-eared map of West Yorkshire and a dozen sample restaurant menus.

"See, here: Bradford." Imran stabs the map. "There's your college, and in town, the Wool Exchange, the Alhambra Theatre—last thing we saw before coming home was *Guys and Dolls*, our sister chose that— and right here on Richmond Road is our busiest take-away. Indian International, its name. Best mushroom *chaat* in UK, but you trying teaching English folk. Onion *bhaji* is all they want, that and chicken tikka masala."

"The newest restaurant is in Manningham—know Manningham do you?" Sajid breaks in. "Rough area, full of drunken students who'll eat owt. Thursday night all-you-can-eat goes down a treat."

I promise to visit the next time I am in the North of England, and Sajid presses on me a bundle of the menus.

"I do live in Ireland, though," I tell them.

"Belfast or Dublin?" Sajid doesn't skip a beat. "Our cousin, he's thinking about opening in Belfast. We said we'd put feelers out. Don't suppose you've any business contacts in Belfast, love?"

Having only ever passed through Belfast to board the P&O ferry, I have to shake my head. Equally, having no cousin, uncle, or brother in Sydney and accepting that a music teacher probably has little incentive to open a take-away, Sajid and Imran stop grilling Christine, and by tacit agreement, change tack.

"How about you ladies do us a right favour and...?" Sajid starts.

"Come and meet our mam?" Imran finishes.

"She'd be right chuffed," Sajid says. They look at each other and agree. "She doesn't get out much, see."

"Can we?" I ask. We look to Munnu for guidance.

He gives the customary twitch of the head in assent. "Why not? I must buy food for campfire and will join with you after one hour."

"Great stuff." Imran rubs his hands delightedly. "Come on then. It's right near."

"I'll go ahead and tell mam." Sajid suggests. "She'll appreciate a minute to spruce herself up."

We hurry down the stairs, scattering well-wishers and stray goats in equal measure, jog a couple of paces, and ascend an identical staircase. Here, a row of doors propped open demonstrate the frugality of the apartments with inhabitants and their lives spill out into the corridor: rugs, shoes, cooking pots, and children clutter the narrow space.

One thick, brown door towards the far end sits shut. In fact, it looks as if it has not been opened for years. Faded rags and yellowing newspaper are stuffed around the dusty frame and jammed along the floor.

"I thought it was only us Westerners obsessed with draughts," Christine mumbles.

"She's spent half her life in Bradford. Old habits and all that..." Imran explains.

Both brothers, all smiles, usher us inside. Ignoring the bound-up front door, we enter through the flat next-door, squeezing into a larder in the scrubbed scullery and pushing aside a sheet of polythene tacked over a sheet of dark blue velveteen. For a minute I think I'm walking into an American-sized industrial fridge.

"Mam worries about...safety," Imran explains. "She won't use the front door. You get used to it. Lucky, these are good neighbours."

"Aye." Sajid nods. "Mam is a bit...particular."

Such is the ensuing gloom in the lobby of Mrs Begum's flat, I expect floor-level lighting to illuminate and guide us to the exits in the event of emergency.

"Slip these on would you?" Imran avoids looking at us as he hands us each a pair of those plastic, elastic, overshoes usually only worn by swimming pool cleaners and coroners. We oblige. Even Christine is stunned into silence.

Sajid opens another polythene-protected door and motions Christine and me inside. It is like entering a sumptuously padded cell. A small, white room furnished with a white day bed, cheap white chairs (the kind seen at pavement cafes), and a matching white table. There are no windows, but a soft white material is draped over all the walls. The portable television looks as if someone tipped a pot of white paint over the casing. I imagine it's the kind of waiting room that St Peter keeps recent arrivals while checking out their credentials.

Mrs Begum, ensconced on the day bed, her white-saried bulk cushioned by infinite white pillows, looks like a vast, timeless Buddha. Her grey hair is cropped short, she is devoid of make-up and jewellery, and her bare feet are also encased in plastic covers. Only her darting, beady eyes belie her placidity.

"Come in, come in, ladies. Don't dither, and sit where I can see you. Hurry now." She bangs a white cane on the white-tiled floor. Without removing her gaze from Christine and me, she barks at her sons: "Dismiss, you boys. Go and do something useful. Go, go. Skeddaddle." They do, but not before she manages to poke both of them in the ribs with the white stick.

The woman has the astonishingly perfect, plummy tones of a 1950s BBC presenter coupled with the foghorn volume perfected by centuries of the British upper classes calling home the hounds. Her sheer presence is overwhelming. Perched on the edge of the garden chair, I feel as if I'm about to be expelled from finishing school. Mrs Begum looks at us through half-closed eyelids. The only sound is her wheezing breath squeezing its route out of gurgling lungs.

"Ladies," she booms finally, and I nearly fall off the garden chair. "I don't serve refreshments. Snacks here are unsanitary. You, young lady, do you agree?" Her eyes bore into me, and I hasten not to offend the massed citizens of Bangladesh and agree with her. Not quickly enough, obviously. She sighs and rolls her eyes. "I see not. Gels today have different standards. And in itself, indecisiveness is not an admirable trait, is it?"

"Well...no?" I stutter.

"Are you a student?" she continues. "You give the appearance of a Home Economics student. Do you know your stain removers from your bleaches?"

"I'm not..." I whisper.

"Speak up, girl. Can you bake an apple charlotte and sew the hem of a pinafore?"

"I'm not a student," I croak, "of Home Economics or anything else. I'm a, well, just now I'm a social worker."

"'*Just now,*' the girl says." Mrs Begum mimics. "Are you or are you not? Smacks of flibbertigibbet. I can't abide flightiness." She leans forward, rolls of fat wobbling like a lukewarm jelly. "What do you wish to portray by the term 'social worker?' Are you a bona fide statutory employee who has sufficient *nous* to remove offspring from their feckless parents, or a wishy-washy do-gooder who panders to the inept? Think about it, girl. This country alone is full of volunteer 'social workers' who are, in truth, layabouts."

"I don't think—" Sufficiently outraged, I find my voice but lose it again under her bell-ringing tones.

"You." Mrs Begum waggles a finger at Christine. "You should have more to say for yourself. You're no spring chicken, but I'll grant beggars can't be choosers. I take it your child-bearing years are done with?"

I can feel Christine's thank-God-for–the-padded-cell-now-bring-on-the-strait-jacket train of thought, but all she says silkily, her own received pronunciation turning up a few notches, is: "How refreshingly to the point you are, Mrs Begum. Why do you ask?"

The old lady *tut-tuts* impatiently. It brings on a wheeze that would embarrass a steam train at full throttle. "Is it not obvious, dear girl? A kind, but stupid, man like Imran is no man at all. God forbid he should bring children in his likeness into the world. Imran requires a wife sufficiently aged..."

"Wife?" Christine all but shrieks. "*Wife?*"

"I think there may be a misunderstanding..." I begin.

But the elderly woman is on a roll and rides roughshod over interruption. "Sajid naturally will spawn sons, although three or four shall be sufficient. I assume you—" she stares at me, and my ovaries shrivel—"can reproduce? As to religion, I shall turn a blind eye. A heretic is surely better than no wife at this late stage, and in the godless depths of West Yorkshire, who, precisely, will care?"

Luckily, the image of godforsaken Bradford causes her to pause, grope for, and suck on an asthma inhaler. Whilst she's going purple and trying not to die, we take the opportunity to regroup.

"We're not here to marry Imran and Sajid. We met them an hour ago in the telephone shop. That's going some even by arranged marriage standards," Christine objects.

"Is that why they brought us here? They told *us* you would like to meet us. Maybe we should leave now," I add, polite as possible.

Mrs Begum flaps at us. "Sit." She wheezes. "Sit down. If you wish to avoid matrimony with my sons, so be it. I fear you are hardly unique in that. Yet, a mother must do her best for even the runts of the litter." She gasps this last, and I jump up again in alarm.

"Let me get you some water."

"No! No, I said, girl. Sit down. Sit."

"Leave her," Christine whispers. "Let the old bat choke. She's a nutcase. We should gather our skirts and leg it."

The conversation dies down a bit.

Slowly, Mrs Begum's breathing evens out, and she collapses into her wall of white. Either our unease or her ill-health moderates her tone, if not the content. "No person may open a door when I am in the middle of an attack, do you understand? As for offering me water, you might just serve poison." She lowers her voice further, and glances around the room as if suspecting a hidden microphone in the wall-hangings. "Do you understand, I say?"

"Well—no." We say it in unison, shaking our heads.

Mrs Begum sighs. Clearly, she cannot believe that a moment ago she was offering daughters-in-law status to such a pair of simpletons. "The arsenic. It's the arsenic of course."

"The arsenic?" I look doubtfully at Christine. It is a subject she knows far more about than I do.

"Yes, yes. My dear girls. You must know of the arsenic?" Mrs Begum's vowels remain perfect, but suddenly she is an ordinary old lady, fearful, and slightly confused. "You *are* one of us? You *do* know of it?"

"Sure do," Christine says and explains, mostly for my benefit. "It occurs naturally in the water and is being drunk from the table wells and pumps. One of those silent-but-deadly diseases that cause long-term health damage. It's an enormous problem in Bangladesh."

"Yes, yes. But are you *one of us*?" Mrs Begum is impatient. "You are, aren't you? I can see it in your eyes." She takes another hefty dose of Ventolin and continues in a stentorian whisper. "Arsenic in the water is only the official story, you know. Oh dear, yes. It's the air-arsenic that's the killer. We breathe it all the time," she confides. "It's chemical warfare to reduce the population, you know. The FBI has infected us all."

"I don't think that's possible..." Christine sounds sceptical.

"Don't you be fooled, my dear. It creeps in through the gaps in the walls and the doors, and you breathe its deadly germs. It clings to the bottom of your feet and works its way through your skin, you know. Two things alone stop it. You," She barks at me suddenly, cane erect once more, headmistress voice back. "Name one of them?"

"Plastic?" I venture, given the polythene over the doors and encasing our feet.

"Good. And the other?"

Unable to hazard a quick enough guess, she tells us. "Newspaper," she whispers. "Only a few of us know this. Newspaper blocks the arsenic germ. You must stuff all your empty bottles with newspaper and the print soaks up the germs and kills them. Each time you do that one, two, three thousand arsenic invaders are thwarted. White, the colour white, is good too." She plucks at her sari and taps the sofa. "White blinds them so they bump into each other and die from the impact."

"The arsenic bugs...die?" I ask.

"Yes, silly girl. What else could I mean?"

"I don't think that's possible." Unwisely, Christine tries again. "It's the water that needs treating."

"Are you doubting me?" Mrs Begum's eyes narrow. "Ladies, do you doubt me?" The eyes turn to slits. "In fact, I am beginning to doubt you. In fact, I have reason to believe you are not ones of us at all."

"No—"

"Yes—"

"Ah ha! Dissention in the ranks! As I thought. Infiltrators," she accuses. "First you girls present yourselves as brides, albeit of the most feeble demeanour, and then you pretend to be ones of us. Where are you hiding them? Where are you hiding the marauding arsenic germs, you hussies?"

Sadly, she is never to find out because Imran and Sajid take that opportune moment to barge in, get whacked with the white cane, and likened to "bumbling, curry-cooking fusspots." Whilst they are completely unperturbed, Christine and I wave an unfocused adieu and fight our way through the marauding arsenic germs to exit—stage left.

Munnu is waiting in the hall. We fall on him as if he is Santa Claus, Johnny Depp, and the Dalai Lama rolled into one.

"Do you enjoy your visit?" he asks, nervously untangling himself.

"Enjoy it? Oh, nearly as much as my last cervical smear test, thanks," Christine replies. "She's a complete and utter luna—"

I manage to nudge Christine as a beaming Sajid and Imran appear behind her.

"—Lovely person," she amends. "Unconventional, maybe. But some interesting opinions."

"She explained all about the arsenic problem," I add. "Fascinating."

"This is good," approves Munnu. "I had a plan to take you to GUP arsenic programme today, but maybe you have enough?"

"Oh, we've definitely had enough," Christine agrees.

"Thank you for the visit," I tell Imran and Sajid." It was nice to meet you. And of course, your mother." We smile politely to Imran and Sajid, sympathy outweighing the need for truth.

"Eh, you've no idea how we appreciate you coming," Imran says earnestly. "It'll give mam something to talk about for weeks. Make our lives a bit easier until we can get back to Bradford."

"Aye, it's hard enough to keep the old dear happy, but we try what we can," adds Sajid. "I hope she was...alright with you? She can be a bit forthright at times, can mam."

"She didn't want you to wed us or owt silly like that then?"

The brothers stare at us anxiously, willing us to reassure them.

"It was fine," Christine says at last. "Your mam kept calling me a 'young girl.' I can always forgive a bit of eccentricity when someone knocks thirty years off me."

And when Munnu invites the brothers to this evenings' end-of-camp party, neither of us begrudges them the rare night out.

In preparation for the open-air last supper, we build the campfire to end all campfires. Branches, leaves and kindling rapidly amassed, fail to ignite to Aktar's dramatic standards, so he compensates by haphazardly adding lashings of kerosene. When he has a conflagration worthy of Satan's playground, he urges a game of leapfrog.

Chapa disapproves. "Little children," she says. "Boys very silly."

"He won't be fathering six fine sons if he doesn't stop pretty soon. Ooh." Christine winces as the flames tickle his crotch.

There is a lot of prancing and dancing and clapping, and soon we are immortalised on film doing an impromptu conga around the blaze. Munnu chairs a committee of himself, Aktar, and Moni who play a delightful game in which they pick on one of us and decide what sort of a "turn" we will do. It's worse than an Irish wedding party.

"I feel as if they're going to ask me to show my knickers," I complain to Christine as the boys grin evilly in my direction.

Obviously, there is no such request, but when I am asked to do an Irish jig or sing a traditional song, I do seriously consider distracting them with the less embarrassing knicker option. Then I recall my greyish, sagging, and inexplicably torn underwear and warble my way through a ballad in my own colloquial Gaelic—otherwise known as gibberish. I expect Imran and Sajid see through me, but that just makes us quits. Following the musical theme, Christine sportingly attempts to lead us all in a canon version of "Frère Jacques." Forever more, the residents of Shanti Kendra will be singing "flared-red-jacket, flared-red-jacket..."

Midnight comes and goes and the food is cooked and eaten; meat and pudding marking it out as a special occasion.

"Anne must eat more than three potato pieces," Munnu insists, launching a sack of King Edwards and half a dead cow onto my plate. He then hefts up a catering-sized serving of what resembles apricot Instant Whip but is actually curd, delicious and only slightly sweetened so that the Bangladeshi faces screw up with the bitterness of it and, to a man, they yell urgently for the sugar bowl.

Later, when the evening, scented by the nocturnal Night Queen and illuminated only by firelight, grows chilly, Christine and I are ushered into the boys' touchingly tidied bedroom for a nightcap. Glasses of cola are slurped and Bachchu carefully announces that it is time for any final "exchanges of cultural information." If he is expecting a serious discussion, he is sadly mistaken. Aktar asks to be taught a selection of not-quite swear words in English.

"Wiffle," I say. "Wiffle is a very good word when you are cross with someone."

"Pondlebom," Christine adds, not to be out done. "Very rude indeed."

He spends the remainder of the evening mouthing our invented gems to himself, occasionally cutting across the conversation to check his pronunciation.

After Christine and I have written our words of wisdom in the newly established Camp Logbook, the evening draws to a natural close with a vocal group hug that is half a dozen choruses of "We Shall Overcome."

And it really is goodbye, because in the morning, only Chapa, Asha, and Mary are around to receive small gifts from our stores of pencils, postcards, and perfume samples. The sincerity of their tears is deeply affecting.

"Your visit is very good," Asha assures us. "Always we remember, Anne, when I think of monthly bleeding, I am thinking of you."

Selfishly, it has hardly occurred to me that our visit is as significant for them as it is for Christine and me. It is so easy to get wrapped up in my own "whys" and "wherefores" that I forget the huge strides these girls have made. Mixing with foreigners and with young men on more equal terms than ever before, their horizons are changing. Whilst they may have only crossed a compound to join the Work Camp, mentally and culturally it is the same half a world that Christine and I have travelled.

As we turn at the corner and wave one last time, it is not the silent, deserted, and idyllic Shanti Kendra of origin; now it is alive with friends and memories.

We relax in a Takerhad restaurant owned by an uncle of Bachchu, sipping tea and challenging sentiment and premature nostalgia. Munnu, also coming to Dhaka and the lookout for the tardy bus, is the one who drags forward our copious luggage and hurls himself across three front seats when it eventually trundles into view.

"Hurry," he calls. "No reserved seats. You must take your place."

Semi dozing and occasionally pondering events of the last few days, we travel the unravelling road ahead without incident. That is until Christine suddenly jerks, gives a yelp, and digs me in the ribs. Her face is contorted with disgust.

"There is something wet and warm and ever so slightly solid running over my foot," she whimpers. "What is it? What the hell is it?"

I yank up my feet in unconscious sympathy, and nervously look down.

"Yuck," I say when I see the lumpy grey mass.

"What? What is it?" Christine groans. "Oh, God. Someone has puked on my shoes haven't they?"

By now, Moni, barefoot, is affected. He takes stock of the situation and politely informs the elderly gentleman in the row behind us that the newspaper and string lid of his porridge bowl has come undone. The milky oats are now making their slow and fragrant escape all over the floor and forming puddles in the ladies' shoes. Seeing his rations rapidly spilling away, the old fellow gives a cry to outdo Christine's and is galvanised into action. On his hands and knees in the aisle, he frantically tries to scoop up the porridge and put it back in the pot. A true gentleman, he then wipes Christine's shoes on his *lunghi*, spits on them, rubs them to a shine, and returns them in as courteous a manner as would befit Prince Charming with his glass slipper.

Nearly five hours later, Dhaka hits in a steaming cloud of fumes, smog, and pollution. With three weeks' experience of the country, my perspective has easily shifted and the noise, the people, the stray animals, and makeshift homes are recognisable entities. I climb down from the bus with a blasé swagger—and trip on a pile of stones. I land in an undignified heap and spill the contents of my bag into the gutter. I am mortified as Bachchu, Munnu, and Moni come running.

"Don't get in a flap," Christine jeers. "At least you haven't got porridge between your toes and saliva on your sandals."

9

Week 5 - From the Ridiculous to the Sublime

I think we have crossed what is commonly known as the "cultural divide." Geographically, it may be only from one side of Dhaka to the other but...Wait.

I am getting way ahead of myself.

We spend one further night with Pavel and Rehana, who welcome us back like old and valued friends. Alvi reverts to treating us like his own, live comedy duo, mimicking our every word and refusing to take his eyes from our faces. Farabia hankers for stories of the country girls, Chapa and Asha; and Mamun is at the peak of his strutting skills, posing half-naked at the end of our bed like a frustrated male model and asking, "How much?"

"This soap—how much? Pah! In Dhaka, Tk 2... The blue shoes—what is the cost? Tosh! I get for Tk 20 only...Your hair cutting? Bish! You pay much. In my country—"

In the morning, the family departs for a short trip to Pavel's distant home village to commemorate the anniversary of his father's death. Christine and I, nonchalantly, hail two surprised rickshaw-drivers, or *wallahs*, and haggle nonverbally over the fare. We arrive at the SCI office on Sir Sayed Street well before any of the staff.

Shahardot gives us free rein to use the phone, the computer, the kitchen, anything, as long as he may watch our antics over a surreptitious cigarette.

"At least you can catch up on your diary." Christine sits down at the table, puts her head on folded arms and promptly falls asleep. But when she wakes an hour or so later, I look up from a page on which I have scribbled only the date and share concerns about my poor grasp of local news and politics.

"Don't stress," Christine advises. "You're not writing a treatise on the Bangladeshi nation—and if you were, nobody would give a toss. Neither of us has a clue what's going on. It's enough to get our heads around *living* here."

Even though it's a cop out, she has a point. Life is so different and new that we are totally taken up with the practical environment. "It would be the thickest layer of icing on a three-tier cake to understand it all as well."

"Make it all up. Everybody in the West knows that '*all these Indians*' are the same," Christine teases. "I know, I know. That's exactly why you want to set the record straight."

"Let's face it," I mourn. "I'm a product of Western materialistic culture. My security, and therefore my happiness, is reliant on possessions, things, objects."

"So? Our friend Mamun hasn't got any nearer to Western culture than MTV, and he's obsessed with *things*."

Blasé world travellers will sniff at my naivety and recall how "character-building" it was stranded in the Kalahari and surviving on ear wax for a week, or how "liberating" it was to pee against gravity on a recent excursion to the moon. Bangladesh? They were here when it was East Pakistan but—yawn!—left three days early. Perhaps so, but this is my first big adventure, and I reserve the right to be spellbound.

With still no sign of Bonny or Suez, Christine telephones a Bangladeshi acquaintance with whom she has promised to make contact. She puts her hand over the telephone receiver to look at me.

"Hasina wants to know what you're going to do?" she asks.

With the conclusion of the Rajoir project, Christine has all but completed her official contract with SCI, whereas I have the option of attending two more Work Camps. However, the free time between them, potentially a week or two, is my own and I have no real plans.

"She's inviting you to stay." Christine grins. "She's very insistent. Go on—say yes! She'll fetch us this afternoon." While Christine discusses the final details, Suez and Bonny arrive, surprised to see us thus installed.

"Yes. You have returned from Rajoir," remembers Suez.

"Yes, and today you should take rest," Bonny admonishes.

"But we're here for the formal Camp Evaluation," I say. "Pavel said you'd arranged it for today."

"Today. Is this so?" If Suez had a beard he would be thoughtfully stroking it. He tips his head sideways in that indigenous gesture of okay that we have learned to recognise. "Let us begin."

"Here are the official evaluation forms." Bonny hands a thick document to each of us.

We go through them like a team of Hollywood lawyers checking the small print of a superstar's pre-nup. Suez listens to our thoughts about the SCI programme, the role of Bangladeshi women in the work projects, the chaotic and paternalistic political and social system, and the arsenic situation.

"You feel that our country has many difficulties and that you are not assisting where most it is needed? That your skills are overlooked?" He sums up our joint concerns.

"Ye-es." I hesitate. Put like that, it sounds as if I am Lady Bountiful come to oversee a four-course dinner for the needy and am put out by being asked to wipe down the plastic tablecloths instead.

"Maybe you come with a false expectation?" Suez repeats what both the SCI and GUP volunteers in Rajoir have already said. "Your place in our organisation is not for field work, or famine relief. It is not the Red Cross or MSF. Short-term volunteers experience cultural exchange. Maybe you call it 'public relations,' yes? You share, you learn. The people here, they share, they learn. Your small tasks build big foundations."

"People realise we're all the same underneath, and the world grows smaller and safer?" I sound like a Sunday School sermon. "I wish it were that easy."

"It *is* that easy," Suez insists.

"Well, I feel liberated," says Christine. "Unconditional permission to enjoy this jaunt."

"Okay," says Suez. "Good. And you, Anne? We think you do not enjoy. Often you look worried."

"But Munnu says that sometimes your face lights up with a big smile, and you shine," adds Bonny. "We want to see more of this."

I spend the rest of the day impersonating the Fastnet Lighthouse on a foggy day.

"All else is okay?" Suez asks. "Have you plenty of food?"

"We really enjoy it," I admit, "but we just can't eat everything we're given. People are hurt and think we don't like it, or that we are sick."

Both men roar with laughter. "This is Bangladeshi culture. Always, people want you to eat. Always they say, 'little bit more, just little bit more.' This happens in every family. It is an—insolvent?—problem."

"Insoluble," corrects Christine creating a diversion.

"The same as oil in water? Insoluble?" Suez checks.

"But *insolvent,* too, is a true word?" adds Bonny.

"Then what is the exact meaning of *insufferable*?" Suez wonders.

We bluff our way through an impromptu English lesson.

"Anne, why do you not put off your clothes?" Suez asks me earnestly, and I choke into my bottle of water. "You *put* them on," he elaborates. "But you *take* them off. Why do you not *put* them off?"

A good question. Much to their mutual disappointment, Christine and I are stumped. Tentatively, I mention the next potential Work Camp. "I would like to go to Srimangal." The nature of the work there has never been specified, but after the variety of Rajoir, I'm probably past caring. All I know is that Srimangal is one of the main towns in the Sylhet division of Bangladesh, the area most renowned for its tea gardens. It sounds like a beautiful place to visit.

"Ah, maybe that Camp is postponed..." Bonny says. He has the grace to look a little embarrassed.

I feel a sense of déjà vu.

"We think you prefer Jessore," persuades Suez. He explains that this is a medical initiative. "An excellent project. Social and public health programmes in very poor villages. I think there are many doctors and dentists involved."

"Also, eye specialists," intervenes Bonny. "All your fields of interest, I think. This would be good for you."

"And the glasses and drugs you send from Ireland are gone already to Jessore," Suez says, playing his trump card.

"Somehow I get the impression you'll be heading for Jessore in the near future," Christine whispers, grinning.

Somehow, I have the feeling she is right.

"Of course, it is necessary you remain in Dhaka for your wedding," continues Suez.

I stare at him.

"Congratulations!" Christine grins. "So there was hanky panky over the cooking pot after all?"

"Not Anne's own wedding. She has a husband," Bonny reminds us. "Her friend from Ireland, Borhan," he says. "Mr Borhan calls this office to say he is in Bangladesh and gets married on Tuesday. You are invited. I keep his telephone for you."

"Who's Borhan?" asks Christine, confused.

"He's a friend of mine from home." I explain slowly, somewhat in the twilight zone myself. "He has an Indian restaurant there. But I didn't expect him to be here. And as for getting married..."

The arrival of Christine's friend Hasina halts the deliberating. From the residential suburb of Gulshan, Hasina is a beautiful woman who must look decades younger than she really is. Her dark hair is immaculately waved and styled, her make-up as discreet as her gold jewellery and as simple as the dark green and black pattern of her *salwar kameez*; it has clearly been tailored for her. Her very entrance illuminates the drab office.

After a quick discussion with Suez and Bonny as to her credentials—although Hasina appears to be doing most of the quizzing—the men escort us downstairs.

"Anne. You must keep contact. Call this office tomorrow," orders Suez.

Shahardot longingly strokes the paintwork of the upmarket, navy blue Honda as he stows our shamefully shabby bags into the boot. Hasina's driver runs around opening and closing doors until the three of us are settled into the back seat. The air-conditioning is activated, and we drive off behind tinted windows.

Christine is a friend of Hasina's youngest daughter who now lives with her own family back in Sydney, so the two women are meeting face-to-face for the first time. However, Hasina immediately confirms that she is inviting us both to stay with her indefinitely—as long as Christine and I will not mind sharing a bed. "Um, isn't that where our story started?" says Christine.

"Please do not be polite and refuse." Hasina leans over and pats my hand. "Of course I can find a nice neighbourhood hotel to accommodate you, but why do this? It will be nice for my family to have you. When I lived overseas, I relied on kindnesses of people. I wish to repay this."

I gulp, and thank her, wondering at my unbelievable good fortune.

"I think both of you need rest after the strain of the villages. You look tired and thin." Since her English is impeccable, it is natural-born politeness that prevents her using the more accurate words like grubby and scruffy.

"My husband is CEO of National City Bank," Hasina explains. "This is his car and driver. We go now to Motijheel—the commercial district, yes?—and collect him. Thursday is his half day."

The car noses its way through the huge stone arches that herald the financial area of Dhaka. As expected, it is crowded and thick with rickshaws, baby taxis, and cars fighting for scarce parking places. Sober-suited men hurry in and out of the myriad money institutions. Parking attendants and traffic police are attempting to move on both the vehicles and the hawkers and beggars alert to rich pickings.

At the pillared entrance of one of the more impressive buildings, uniformed doormen stand either side of a carpeted lobby. Our feet sink into plush carpets, our eyes feast on exquisite sculpture work, and we are smoothly and silently elevated to the top floor. As we emerge into a hushed and expensively panelled reception area, I feel like a bag lady being shown around Buckingham Palace. I know Christine feels the same when she surreptitiously tries to clean her scuffed shoes on the backs of her legs.

"I was like one of those 1950s housewives who greet unexpected callers in an overall and hair curlers," she confirmed later.

Courteous to the nth degree, none of the staff appear to notice this as they deferentially greet Hasina and usher us into Mr Hoque's simple yet skilfully decorated and vast corner office. We perch on a brocade sofa within shouting distance of his desk, and an elegant receptionist serves us milky coffee from the best china. It's lukewarm and weak, but has only a dash of sugar, which is such a novelty after being in the villages, that both Christine and I sip it slowly with the respect usually saved for best champagne.

Mr Hoque seems the archetypal businessman, immaculately dressed, with large dark glasses. With a crushing handshake, this high-flying executive who hobnobs with the global good and great greets us like the prodigals returned.

"We will take lunch," he says. "Mrs Hoque says you come from the villages. Ha! I bet you eat nothing but rice. Rice for breakfast, rice for lunch, rice for dinner." He roars with laughter. "And dhal. Always dhal. Do you *still* like rice and dhal?"

"We do," we both insist. "We like the spices, the curry, the breads. But..." I look at Christine. "There was *a lot* of rice in Rajoir."

"See!" Mr Hoque smiles. "I understand such things. In my village in Jessore: rice, rice, rice. For lunch, Mrs Hoque and I bring you to a different restaurant. Less good for the figure–(he pats his ample stomach)—and the cholesterol, but tasty."

We retrace our steps to the waiting car.

"She is coming too." Hasina nods to the receptionist who has pulled a wool coat around her shoulders. As Mr Hoque takes the passenger seat next to the driver and we four women compress ourselves into the back, Hasina explains:

"She—" (the receptionist, upon whose knee I am half sitting) "—is Mitali, my daughter."

Mitali is charming, perhaps my age but much more self-assured, and as welcoming as her parents. "My son and daughter are waiting so long to meet you," she tells Christine. "Bobby," (her sister in Sydney) "—talks of you often."

"Mrs Hoque and I lived in the UK, London, for five years," her husband tells me. "We never visited Ireland. Such a shame."

"But Paris, Rome, Vienna..." Hasina lists the majority of the European capitals.

"And." Mr Hoque smacks his head with his hand, groaning theatrically. "She brings home furniture from every place. Pictures, glass, lamps. Two containers bring it all to this country. Two! We live in a museum."

Offer me a million pounds to predict where exactly we will have lunch (Members Only dining room? Ambassador's residence? The National Assembly canteen?), and I wouldn't even get the booby prize. We pull up on a busy main street and march into the plate glass and Formica-topped table premises of a *Helvetia* fast food outlet—Burger King or McDonalds by any other name. Hasina looks disappointed as we queue at the counter, and Christine and I choose egg burgers ("Don't trust the meat," whispers Christine in my ear), fries, and about a gallon of Sprite.

"You must eat more. The chicken is so good. Our favourite. Try just a little bit?" Hasina coaxes, but gives in gracefully when we demur. I think she assumes we are decently choosing the cheapest items on the menu.

We take an orange plastic seat midway in a restaurant full of college students who are tucking into little paper bags of food like their comrades the world over. Every few seconds, a red light comes on over the counter and, "Now serving no. 55...56...57," flashes onto the screen.

"Here is our order." Mr Hoque is despatched to collect the trays. There is something very humanising in seeing an all-powerful executive, who can hire and fire at will, meekly balancing fried chicken and burgers on an insubstantial tray.

"Just like you have at home, heh?" Mr Hoque beams. "No rice. No dhal."

"Dad, they enjoy Bangladeshi food as well," mediates Mitali. "Like we do."

We assure them that, yes, we love the indigenous diet and yes, we are also enjoying our first taste of Bengali fast food.

There are subtle changes in the environment as we get nearer to the affluent suburb of Gulshan. Not only are there many more cars and fewer—if still apparently millions—of rickshaws, but some of the building structures are less jerry-built and the shops are not necessarily down at heel. Nonetheless, all remain intertwined with garbage banks, shanty dwellings, beggars thumping on car windows, and the inevitable potholes and road works. That the area seems quieter and more sophisticated is probably due to being inside a comfortably cool car with a reasonably intact suspension and an experienced driver. We pause at a local supermarket.

"Come in and look around," invites Hasina. "Many foreigners, diplomats, and expatriates live in this area, so you find all the food you like."

Christine and I dutifully coo over Kellogg's Corn Flakes and tinned peaches and little triangles of processed cheese tucked amongst the more typical Bangladeshi fare. Back in the car, we cross a busy roundabout and swerve dramatically to the right.

"You always recognise our street," notes Hasina. "Turn at First National Bank." She indicates a small corner building with the distinctive neon green logo, and we enter a residential street full of white and cream apartment blocks behind locked security gates. On the left is the Golden Bird Residence for Foreigners. On the right, the driver, whose name is Hanan, beeps at two uniformed attendants in a small cabin. They pull back the gates, salute, and we drive into a car park.

A small, dark girl, who wears baggy trousers under a tattered, pink, party dress, opens the apartment's oversized wooden and brass doors, the bell of which echoes an eerie rendition of "Clementine." Two other little girls wait in the background. Through a dim vestibule, we enter a combined living and kitchen area that sports no Asian influence whatsoever. From the huge, chest freezer to the floral-patterned china and matching Eternal Bow-patterned toaster and kettle, it is comfortable and homely, but further on the apartment widens into a large, open-plan room, which, as Mr Hoque rightly describes, would not be out of place in a museum or a stately home.

The furnishings seem luxurious: deep sofas, chaise longues, teak sideboards and occasional tables. The paintings, photographs, and wall hangings are eclectic in the extreme, complementing the lamps and mirrors, the rugs and ornaments. What sets this room apart is that each piece has a special memory, a history, a carefully chosen position in the room. Cheap and well-loved souvenirs sit in harmony with their more expensive counterparts.

"And how much it cost to ship here! Two containers. Two," Mr Hoque shouts, but he winks covertly. "So bad for my blood pressure. The headache of importing a crystal chandelier!"

The room has double French doors leading onto a small balcony overlooking the street. From here, we watch the security guard summoning a rickshaw and see staff smoking cigarettes on the neighbouring hotel's front porch. A little way along the road, a group of barefoot, lunghied men are huddled around a mobile tea cart.

Hasina drags us away to the guest room, points out the large double bed with a beautifully embroidered coverlet, elegant wooden furniture and another balcony. The bathroom even has a corner tub and a pedestal toilet.

"There are screens and shutters everywhere. You should not be bothered by mosquitoes." Hasina's concern is a discreet reference to the fetching red and angry blotches all over my body. She's probably crossing her fingers and trusting to luck that they are insect bites and not some kind of contagious, flesh-eating disorder.

"Come and take tea in the drawing room," she continues, interrupting herself to issue instructions to the little girls who now stagger under the weight of our luggage. I get the impression that to protest would be a social gaffe, so I say nothing. I assume they are maids, servants, house girls? I search for the politically correct term. Christine has no such qualms.

"Who are they?" she asks. "Do they work here?"

Hasina nods. "They help with food and cleaning. Moshina, Vouvulay—" She calls them back and introduces them, but they just look down at their bare feet and giggle. "There is also Parvin, the cook. She is an older cousin and looks after them."

The glorious surroundings are, of course, terrifying to a clumsy oaf like me who will trip, spill, stumble, and dribble whenever remotely nervous, a disability exacerbated in situations of extreme refinement. Christine is the perfect guest. She talks easily, shows an intelligent interest in her surroundings, and hands out gifts from Bobby, Hasina's daughter, and her family in Australia.

"Hush, the telephone rings." Hasina, head cocked to one side, appears to sense the call seconds in advance of its shrill jangle.

Conversation ceases whilst every Bangladeshi present delves for the source. Mr Hoque examines the minute cell phone nestled in his jacket pocket, Hasina and Mitali frantically rummage through their respective handbags, emerging with three mobiles between them. One of the maids picks up a landline receiver shaped like a tomato, and another appears from the kitchen to say there is a call on the fax telephone. As if on cue, the doorbell rings with "John Brown's Body," and Mitali's children, Oninder, a boy aged fourteen, and Fiona, who is seven, tumble in, heading for the refrigerator and the television respectively.

"We have an apartment on the first floor," explains Mitali. "My husband is there, but he is very sick and a boy comes to care for him during the day. My children say hello to him, and then visit here when they return from school."

Anne Hamilton

Hasina, having momentarily disappeared to her bedroom, wanders back into the drawing room, halts as if struck by a thought, turns and—

"Belly. Belly," she roars. "Belly!"

I jump a mile, biting my tongue which is poking out in the concentration required to balance cup, saucer, spoon, and side plate full of cake on a trembling knee. Even Christine gives an involuntary ladylike twitch. Nobody else even seems to notice.

"Belly. Belly," shrieks Hasina again. For a beautiful and gracious woman, she would not disgrace herself at a fishwives' convention. I expect to see her roll into a ball clutching her apparently agonised stomach. Instead, she introduces us to another member of the household, a good-looking girl who drifts towards us carrying a mug of tea. She is dressed in a long, grey skirt and red jumper, and wears discreet, rimless glasses.

"This is Bely, my daughter-in-law," beams Hasina. "She and my son, Mithu, live here also. He is at work now."

"Hello, *salaam walekum*." Bely speaks very loudly and carefully. "I know little English. Welcome."

Mr Hoque returns from the telephone having changed into casual clothes of baggy trousers and an oversized linen shirt. He is rubbing his hands together with the aura of one who has just pulled off a huge deal.

"Tonight Mrs Hoque and I go to a function at Uttara Club," he tells us as he paces up and down the tiled floor. "Members only. The Minister for Expatriates and Overseas Employment is to inaugurate the new Executive Chair. You both will join us."

"It is a nice club," persuades Hasina, obviously in case we are concerned about the class of people with which we will be mingling, or just might have something better to do. "There will be dinner and a show."

"It will be so nice for you to dress up and go out after all your work in the villages," Mitali says.

The sound of "Greensleeves" playing on the door chime heralds the arrival of Hasina's sister on her way home from work. Soon the family are all crowded onto the sofas and shouting happily at one another. Christine and I take the opportunity to slink away and agonise over our potential evening dress.

"Talk about a remake of *Cinderella*." Christine roots through her bag in disgust, discarding first this skirt, and then that shirt. "It'll have to be the Oxfam special over the least-stained pants."

"At least it's a designer shirt," I moan, determined to be worse off. "And you have smart shoes. Look at my tatty sandals."

The extraordinariness of the situation strikes us, and we giggle our way through bathing and dressing, marvelling at how far we have come in the last forty-eight hours. It is then strangely satisfying to find that despite the luxurious bathroom fittings, the water is little more than a lukewarm trickle and the lavatory flush is erratic.

"Thank God. We're back in Bangladesh," breathes Christine.

Hasina enters the living room, perfect in a gold and blue sari, which is intricately embroidered. It looks as if her hair, makeup and jewellery are straight from a top salon, yet I know it is the result of a bare twenty minutes alone in her bedroom.

"You look so beautiful." Christine and I both compliment her.

"Yes, she looks beautiful. Of course, she is always beautiful. But at what cost? Hours. Hours. We are always late because the ladies take so long to dress," Mr Hoque bemoans. It doesn't take long to learn that this is almost a mantra, and that nobody ever leaves the house until this cry has gone up.

"We are not late," soothes Hasina. "We are never late. We will arrive to an empty hall. We always do," she tells us.

Uttara Club is a large, white, neo-classical building in the next suburb. Set back from a residential street, its impressive façade is strung with columns of tiny golden lights that stretch around the grounds and light the way to a huge marquee. We walk the red carpet to the entrance, weather a glitch when the hostess cannot locate our names—mine and Christine's I'm sure—on her list, and are greeted by the Chairman himself who demotes the unfortunate woman to rice cleaner forthwith. We sit in a virtually empty tent immediately behind the VIP seats.

"We are very early." Hasina is smug. "The function begins an hour, maybe an hour and a half late. But the men like to talk first."

Indeed, as the place fills with people matching Hasina and Mr Hoque in the appearance stakes, it is a networking dream. Tactile businessmen are hugging one another, shouting down a cacophony of cell phones, making introductions, and swapping company cards. Their wives smile politely and look elegant. On stage, the speakers and amplifier are tested with a medley of ABBA hits.

The function begins with the inevitable, incomprehensible speeches and half the audience, Committee, and various Members of Parliament being invited forward for endless photographs and sustained applause. "Kiss-arse in any language," observes Christine. When the cameras are turned on the rest of us ("For the diary pages in the newspaper," Hasina tells us, "and for television"), Christine and I are in the limelight.

The entertainment kicks off with an obviously well-known and liked band, although I don't think I catch its name.

"Welcome—Big Bastards," the compère announces to cheers of approval.

"What?" Christine asks Hasina.

"Big Bastards," repeats Hasina. "The name of the group."

"Who?" I turn to Mr Hoque.

"Big Bastards," he confirms.

It is weeks later when I see a newspaper article about the *Beat Masters* that the penny finally drops. It's nearly midnight when Hasina nudges us and suggests that we eat. We follow her and Mr Hoque out of the marquee and into the main building where guests are milling around a large buffet. Once inside the door, men and women are segregated, the men turning to the left and queuing at a long table against one wall, the women doing likewise on the right. With a wave, Mr Hoque disappears into a huddle of his peers.

"Men and women eat separately at these functions, and at weddings and formal dinners," Hasina tells us. "It is not a rule, just tradition." She ladles large dollops of food onto our plates with the skill of an old-fashioned, school dinner lady. "Come. We sit here, and I bring glasses of cola."

We set the laden plates on our knees, drinks at our feet, and begin to eat. Hasina hands us forks; maybe half the company are using them, but the remainder are comfortable with their hands. Occasionally, a friend or acquaintance pauses beside Hasina, but largely we are left to ourselves whilst the serious business of food consumption continues.

"Everyone wants to look at you," Hasina informs us. "They are all so curious. But they are more used to seeing foreigners than village people, and they think it is not polite to stare." She pauses, considering. "Maybe villagers are just more honest in their curiosity. So now, we will get some little sweets."

Obediently we accept paper bowls of glistening sweet milk and sugar balls smothered in a sauce with the consistency of melted ice cream, and then catch up with the concert. Despite the noise, the glitz, and the dancing in the aisles, the only way I can keep my eyes open is to surreptitiously claw at a new batch of mosquito bites clustered around my right elbow. From her clenched muscles and ramrod back,

I guess that Christine feels the same. When we leave, around two o'clock, the party is still in full force and snacks are just being served.

"Sleep late tomorrow," orders Hasina.

"You must rest," agrees Mr Hoque. "Here in the city it is very humid, easy to get dehydrated and exhausted. Then you have palpitations. I rise at six a.m. for golf. Good exercise."

10
A Spending Spree

Far too early, my alarm clock starts to bleep. Blearily, all but knocking a priceless china lamp, two glasses, and a jug of water onto the tiled floor, I pat the bedside table in an attempt to silence it, and then realise it is somewhere in the depths of my bag. The noise gets more and more frenzied before I locate it, stamp on it, and find myself surrounded by a huge mess of my belongings. Neither of us can sleep again, and eventually a bang at the door brings one of the maids making eating motions. She tells us that her name is Moshina.

"I think she wants us out. She's going to clean the room." Christine indicates the small stool and an array of cloths the child has under her arm. "It's only eight o'clock. So much for a lie-in."

We go into the kitchen area where Hasina, looking relaxed in a faded, long house dress, is drinking a mug of something hot, brown, and strange-smelling.

"Parvin has made you your proper breakfast." She motions us to perch on the high stools at the counter. "And Moshina will wash your clothes." Hasina waves away our protestations. "There is a machine and the ironing is sent out. It is no trouble. But if you have anything delicate, do it yourself. She is often hopeless."

Luckily, we are not required to answer. Hasina and Parvin look proudly at the Rice Krispies with fresh, warmed milk, cold, poached eggs with sliced white toast, and mugs of tea. With somewhat startled murmurs of appreciation, we begin munching.

"I hope it does not make you feel homesick?" Hasina commiserates. "Anne, I expect you and your husband sit down to breakfast together each morning?"

Clearly she pictures us cordially sharing *The Irish Times* over plates of bacon and eggs before he blows an affectionate kiss my way and heads off to his spotless dispensary. Reality is my getting up late, resetting the alarm for him, and then dashing straight out of the door—generally without keys, petrol, or money. We generally have our first conversation of the day over RTE Evening News.

"Some mornings," I agree. Well, we did once for a whole week (on holiday, Jersey, 1993). "I'd quite like to phone home from here. How could I do that?"

No sooner said and Hasina, the fairy godmother, has me bundled into the car, at the Post Office ("We must be quick. It is open only one hour today."), and cramming myself into a glass phone box. Not liking to mention that it is barely 6 a.m. in Europe, hence no chance of any self-respecting Irishman heeding a call at this hour—he would either be out herding cattle or sleeping off last night's excesses—I leave a message with myself on the answer-machine and dial my mother in England, knowing that she can vacuum the house, walk the dog, and possibly wallpaper the hall, stairs, and landing all before a sunrise breakfast.

My mother—when we finally establish contact—share a lot of ghostly "Helloooeee? Yes, helloooeee?" on the line—seems pleased, if disorientated, to hear from me. No doubt I've inadvertently called on her annual (until eight o'clock) lie-in. She does appear somewhat disappointed to hear that I have not been abducted for the gratification of the white slave trade or contracted dysentery.

"Not even a hint of an upset tummy?"

"Not even a twinge," I reassure her smugly, "and no, I haven't been mugged once. In fact I'm in the lap of luxury." I twitter on as the telephone units go down like wounded soldiers.

"Well, I'm glad you're safe and well, of course," she says, her voice fading. "But it's not much of a story is it?"

She has a point. I mean, what can she say to the neighbours? "Oh, yes, my daughter's in Bangladesh you know. Well, she always was a bit strange. Doing? Oh, she's staying in a nice apartment in the city... No, she didn't actually say anything about grappling with Bengal tigers or rehydrating dying babies, but then it was a bad line. So, how goes *your* daughter's life-saving work with victims of random drive-by shootings in the favellas of Sao Paulo?"

Next time, I vow to pepper the narrative with anecdotes to make her hair (and the hair of all the neighbours, and probably the hair of the people in the next street) stand on end.

Since Mr Hoque, Mitali and Bely are all free for the rest of the day, Hasina suggests various forms of entertainment.

"Today we have the car so we could visit Savar, the National Monument, or we could go to Sonargaon, which is the medieval settlement. Also, there is a boat trip each Friday. We could go to the Liberation Museum—"

"Or we could go shopping," intervenes Mitali.

Bely claps her hands. "Shopping. I maximum like shopping," she says loudly and slowly.

"We're clothingly challenged," Christine adds. "We want sparkly dresses."

The shopping mall, a middle-of-the-road outlet, is neither a cheap and busy market nor a particularly expensive centre, and could be anywhere in the world where bedraggled tower blocks are a 1960s icon.

"I think *salwar kameez* is a good idea." Hasina looks at us critically. "You would not be able to wear *sari*. Too complicated."

So we bypass the first floor, which specialises in material for sari lengths. Hasina, Mitali, and Bely are professional shoppers. We fly around the stores like housewives on a supermarket trolley dash. The shops are near identical: open at the front with large counters, shelves stuffed with clothes, and hanging garments against the walls. Eyes gleaming, the assistants are keen for sales. They vastly underestimate the haggling skills of our three frustrated, Broadway wardrobe mistresses—and Mr Hoque amiably brings up the rear.

"All *salwar kameez* are one size only," Hasina assures us. "Fits everyone. Anne, you like this dark blue? See the fine embroidery? Christine, you prefer the long sleeves, yes?"

Christine says yes to mauve cotton, me to navy georgette. We imagine ourselves sashaying around in the folds of the material, and the deal is done. Well, not exactly. The bartering starts. Hasina is in her element. There is rapid dialogue between her and the shopkeeper, a pause for Hasina to look first incredulous, and then disdainful, and they begin again.

"He asks for Tk 1220 each," Mitali translates. "My mum says she will pay Tk 800 each only. She tells him it is not fair to charge so much because you are foreigners."

"Come," says Hasina grandly. She raises a silencing hand to her adversary. "We go to another place. He asks unreasonable prices."

The retailer resumes his plaintive diatribe as we troop unashamedly into the arms of the merchant next door. His young assistant is dispatched to entice us back. Whilst Hasina seems barely to notice the small boy, she is actually listening carefully for the magic number, and then she stops suddenly, causing us all to fall over like dominoes.

"I offer Tk 800 each. The boy is now saying they will take Tk 1200 for both. This is a very good price." Hasina, designated money-keeper, removes the money from a soft, red purse hidden inside her bra.

"Finished? Then we take lunch. *Frusca*." Mr Hoque, still patiently behind us, rubs his hands gleefully.

"*Frusca* is so good," Mitali says. "Our favourite."

In a small take-away café of rocky tables and orange plastic chairs, Hasina calls our order to the man behind the counter. "You taste little bit of *frusca*," Hasina says to Christine and me. "But, I get chicken soup for you also. You must not go hungry."

Quickly, they tuck into plates of deep-fried filo pastry balls stuffed with vegetables and hot tamarind juice, and then call for seconds.

"Bring one without chilli," commands Hasina. "For you to try." She nods at us. Christine opens her mouth to point out—again—that neither of us objects to chilli, decides it is useless, and makes exaggeratedly happy slurping noises over her soup which (the soup that is, not Christine's eating habit) is truly disgusting. Primrose in hue—my family home had a bathroom suite that exact colour when I was about six—the soup is the temperature and texture of matte emulsion complete with unpleasantly exploding powdery lumps. The frusca however, is excellent.

"We now go to buy *shals*," says Hasina rising with her last mouthful, politely failing to notice the congealed yellow fluid in front of her ungrateful guests.

Christine has both a self-confessed weakness for shawls and a detailed list of like-minded friends who would appreciate one or six as a homecoming gift. Hasina, dutiful mother-in-law that she is, takes the opportunity to teach Bely how to recognise a bargain and to hone her bartering skills accordingly. We each choose a low stool in front of the long counter—a few buzzers and we'll become contestants in a budget game show. A selection of materials, various colours, and patterns are passed along for our perusal. Christine quietly intimates those she prefers, and Hasina doggedly guides Bely in the art of fair trade. The shelves get emptier and the pile in front of us grows so huge that the only way to make contact with the shopkeeper is to climb up on the stool and wave a white handkerchief. Christine selects eight shawls before being physically restrained and dragged screaming from the shop, soothed only by the promise that she can come back another day.

Anne Hamilton

A subsequent hunt for postcards becomes a treasure hunt in disguise. Entrepreneurial vendors shake their heads and tempt us with alternatives: posters, diaries, calendars—from a range of years between 1996 to 1999—key rings, and a set of six, pink, mini ashtrays in the shape of love hearts. Bely almost succumbs here, but ultimately she cannot get the price sufficiently reduced. Finally, one bemused shopkeeper roots in the far reaches of a distant drawer and brings forth a meagre contribution of ancient postcards, brushing off the dust and uncurling their edges as he places them on the counter. We choose from *Floods in Dhaka 1988, Boats at Low Tide - Anywhere in the World,* and *Chittagong Airport by Night.*

Hasina nearly short-circuits on hearing the lowly asking price. "Bad. Very bad, indeed. I do not believe this man has such greed." She turns to tell him so, and he shrivels like a pricked balloon.

"I tell him that the cards almost crumble to dust when we touch them. They will disintegrate to powder with the little weight of a stamp," she exaggerates. "They will tear when you write."

Rallying well, the resourceful vendor takes this as a cue to tip a shoebox full of biros onto the counter. Most are mementoes of the Taj Mahal ("Not even the real one," complains Hasina. "These advertise a restaurant in Banani."), except for one with the name "Michael" inscribed.

"Where next?" Mr Hoque demands, as we sit in a traffic jam. Christine and I are using the opportunity to write our postcards, shamelessly boasting about grappling with cross-cultural relations and levelling school playing fields.

"We need to change some more money," Christine remembers.

Mitali, Bely, and Mr Hoque intimate that they cannot face much more excitement, so we drop them at home before taking a fifteen-minute drive to a small private bank about three minutes' walk away. Hasina would be at home in Los Angeles, the No-Pedestrian city. The manager sits in a compact-yet-smart office, attractively carpeted in pale orange shag pile. An old-fashioned and unwieldy computer is in pride of place on the shiny desk, its connection leads, plug, and adaptor still in a sealed plastic wrapper, the power button untouched by human hand. The staff is silent, their desks clear.

"Unfortunately this bank cannot change your money." Hasina frowns. "The person responsible for foreign currency is not at his desk."

We gaze at the inactive staff.

"What about the others?" enquires Christine. "Couldn't one of them deputise?"

"They cannot. It is not their job," says the manager, via Hasina.

"They're not qualified to do it?" I ask. "Not permitted under the financial rules and regulations, perhaps?"

"No, no." The bank manager is impatient. "Each of them knows how to exchange the cash and is licensed to do it, but they may not. Foreign currency is not their job," he repeats.

"Even though none of them is doing anything else?"

"That is irrelevant."

Once back in the street, Hasina holds out her hands and grasps Christine's left wrist and my right. She appears about to impart bad news of gargantuan proportions.

"It is regrettable," she tells us, "but we must..." The pressure of her fingers tightens, she takes a deep breath and says, "Go to a public bank for your money."

Hasina interprets our baffled silence for one of horror, and she shakes her head apologetically. "I wish you should avoid the experience, but there is no option. It is good I know the manager. I phone ahead and he sees us in his office."

A couple of doors down, the institution is tall and grim. Its entrance is manned by a gaggle of security guards arbitrarily refusing entry with the sneers of hardened nightclub bouncers.

"Or maybe they're just aiming to comply with statutory fire regulations as laid down by the Lord Mayor of Dhaka and strictly adhered to by the loyal citizens of this country," Christine mentions primly.

"If so, they're failing dismally."

One cross shout from Hasina, and they immediately melt into the background providing us with a tunnel into the bank's darkest interior.

"Keep your head down," Hasina instructs. "Walk forward. Do not make eye contact. Do not lose sight of me. Do not pass *Go*." She speaks as one might to a party on safari, lost and about to become dinner for a commune of starving cannibals.

"You are okay?" She looks from one to the other of us, we nod, and then: "Let us go, go, go," she exhorts, all five feet of her marching manfully into the fray.

In the seconds it takes to cross the crumbling, high-columned concourse, I gain a vague impression of millions of people crowded around makeshift desks. Some are shouting and waving pieces of paper in the air, others are holding their heads in bemusement and staring glassy-eyed as if they called in for a quick bit of business three years ago and are still waiting. Some areas are cordoned off with thick, black grilles, and glass boxes double as cupboard-sized offices making the workers within resemble goldfish at an experimental aquarium. The noise is so deafening as to be almost indefinable: voices, footsteps, shuffling of papers, the thump of rubber stamps, jangling of keys, banging of doors, and silent screams of despair. It is the mass sound of weary humanity heaving and groaning in an enclosed and frustrated space. Everyone looks poor and ragged.

"You okay?" hollers Christine.

"I think I've just seen Jesus overturning all the tables in the Temple," I yell back.

She grins. "See what you mean. Muslim or not, this lot would've been with him. Not," she screeches, "that a bit of desk bashing and chair throwing is likely to be noticed."

At the back of the building, Hasina launches us into a curtained room with as much force as if we are being flung from a burning deck into a lifeboat. She takes a moment to smooth her hair and adjust her dress before announcing herself to a surprisingly tall and dapper moustached man extravagantly entertaining two clients. His clerk stands like a footman behind him. The manager instructs the clerk to snatch the untasted cups of tea from his visitors' mouths. A messenger drags them from their chairs and hustles them to the door. The two men seem singularly unworried, smiling even as they fumble in their respective wallets and throw a selection of business cards in our general direction. Their chairs are dusted down, the tea is given to us instead, and the messenger is despatched to turn our dollars into *taka*.

"We do not pay commission," Hasina says with authority. "You have good value here."

"Could we have some small denomination notes?" asks Christine. "For rickshaws and things."

The request is relayed from the manager to the clerk to another a messenger, each of whom looks more surprised than his assistant. We realise our mistake when the money arrives. At fifty-seven *taka* to one US dollar, we expect to receive a big bundle of cash for the three or four notes we hand over. We have vastly underestimated the strength of our position. The first messenger returns, his steps slow and ponderous, his body bent double with the weight of the notes he is carrying. He can do nothing but lean over the desk and regurgitate the money onto it like an apologetic but desperate drunk vomiting lavishly onto his neighbour's shoes.

"This is all for us?" I whisper, wondering how we are going to carry it.

"No, no." Hasina shakes her head, and Christine and I exhale simultaneous sighs of relief. Short-lived sighs of relief.

"This is only a little bit of the exchange," she continues. "The other peon brings the remainder."

Indeed, a *clickety-whirr-whirr-squeak* over the stone tiles heralds the entrance of a sweating office boy pulling a small cart. It is stacked with brown mailbags.

"Ah. Here it is now." Hasina smiles.

The Great Train Robbers have nothing on us. Knee-deep in big, big bundles of notes laboriously recounted before our eyes and shared out equally, it becomes *Monopoly* money. With our bulging pockets, purses, money belts and—copying Hasina's example without the decorum of a soft wallet—bras stuffed with the overflow, we might as well wander the streets carrying bags marked SWAG.

"I've just exchanged $25," Christine says, "and become a millionaire. As for you," she eyes me up. "Money can certainly buy a cleavage. God, I love this country."

We emerge into the sticky evening, drive a little, walk a couple of steps and climb some stairs which are rejects from a multi-storey car park—concrete, smelly, and with odd-looking people loitering on them—and into a sweatshop arcade full of identical tiny tailors' shops. This is the New Market.

"I go to one place for the making of a sari and another for finishing. One that is an expert in fine embroidery," explains Hasina. "These are saris for special occasions. They are made of fine silks and lace."

The bell jangles overhead the door of her chosen store where the staff is peering through cramped rails of hanging garments to watch a portable television high up in the corner. Christine and I are given low stools to perch on and handed cups of tea. The ready-made clothes hang on squeaking hangers above our heads.

"It's like being trapped under an enormous washing line," I complain, flicking at a Punjabi suit that persistently tickles my neck. I would not be surprised to see a packet of crayons and a colouring book being brought out to amuse us, but I suppose we have got each other to play with, and Christine at least looks old enough to behave herself whilst Hasina and the tailor shake out bales of material and discuss designs, check on work already underway, and argue over accessories.

The second place is even smaller, simply a counter opening onto the arcade and meltingly hot despite three whirring and grinding ceiling fans. I feel limper than a wilted lettuce and probably look just as fresh in the midst of impervious shop assistants who coolly smooth the material lengths to display exquisite beading, perfect mother of pearl buttons, and intricate stitching. I keep my hands well behind by back, afraid of leaving greasy palm prints smack in the centre of the crushed, peach-coloured silk.

What must it be like here in summer?

We return to a blissfully air-conditioned car, drive to a blissfully air-conditioned supermarket to buy Australian muesli and homemade curd, and then sit in a blissfully air-conditioned waiting-room for Hanan and the car to be miraculously summoned from the depths of a parking lot via a security guard's loud hailer.

"Now to the pharmacy," Hasina says and leads us to hypochondria heaven, a medicine shop with a few tubes of toothpaste thrown in. Boxes, jars, and bottles of every pharmacological substance ever invented are neatly packed on shelves and in glass cabinets. The service is akin to a busy McDonalds drive-thru, and buying a cocktail of drugs—as long as you have a vague name and approximate strength—is easier than choosing which flavour milkshake.

"Would you like any ointments with that?" the pharmacist asks as I buy two Mogadon tablets. Not that I need them. Working from my emergency first-aid kit, I could act as wholesaler to this man. I get them, like a dog snapping at flies, just because I can.

Christine wants a cheap new toothbrush to see her through her last few days in the country, but Hasina, sniffing out another bargain, insists on helping her become the proud owner of a complicated electric version complete with spare batteries and cumbersome carrying case.

"See?" Hasina soothes a disgruntled Christine. "For only a little more than the ordinary toothbrush, you get something to keep and take home."

"I have one at home," Christine mutters, but impotent in the face of infuriating kindness.

"And now you have a spare one also. So useful."

"It is a bargain." I try to convince her.

"So is five pounds of fish heads for a few rupees, but I don't want those either," Christine retorts, catching a glimpse of said delicacies staring glassily up from a bucket balanced by the kerbside.

"Shopping done, and we are all happy." Hasina beams, oblivious. "Let us go home for tea."

11
Bengali Wedding Belles

Remembering Suez's message, I try to phone my friend Borhan. When the person answers and speaks no English, Hasina takes over. She has a long conversation, apparently swapping life stories with the woman on the other end.

"He is not home," she reports finally. "I have left a message for him. But he is in Dhaka, and he is getting married. Actually, the wedding celebrations have already begun."

"Should we buy a gift?" I wonder aloud.

"A gold ring for the bride is traditional," Hasina says. "Gold has value all the time. I know a good jewellery store. We go there later. Now I must go shopping for vegetables. It is in the Cantonment—the military area, yes?—so I cannot take you with me, as foreigners are not allowed. Perhaps you can watch television?"

"We'll be fine," first Christine, then I assure her, but she remains unconvinced.

"Bely! Bely," she calls and her daughter-in-law, wearing a long, red dressing gown and furry slippers, appears from the bedroom. Bely spends a long time alone in her room, her huge TV full on whilst she paints her nails and touches up her immaculate make-up.

"I look after you," Bely says carefully. "You watch movie of my marriage."

"You will then understand what happens at Borhan's wedding," Hasina approves.

We sink into Bely's large, floral, and be-cushioned bed where she prepares us for the Big Picture with a library of photographs that suggest her family and the Hoques are acquainted with all but three of Dhaka's fourteen million inhabitants. The wedding video itself has an additional cast, a colourful, pictorial, docu-soap with a romantic soundtrack that eventually becomes hypnotic in its circularity.

"The families mix about as much as attendees at a 1950s formal school dance." I wonder if this is deliberate.

Christine is ahead of me. "No, look. If you watch carefully, the film cuts between two ceremonies: one for Bely and her relatives, the other for Mithu and his. See? It's a different room."

Bely would keep up a running commentary if only her English or our Bengali was up to it. She almost stamps in frustration at our inability to grasp the significance of the rituals on screen. It is very, very long.

"Lovely wedding. *Shundur*," we chorus.

"No. No," shouts Bely.

"*Not* a lovely wedding?" I am confused.

"Not *wedding*. Wedding is next film. This is *Gae Halud*. Bride and husband *Gae Halud*..." Words fail her as Christine and I impersonate simpletons. "More?" Bely asks.

"Another day," Christine begs her.

"Was good. Very good, my marriage days." Bely sounds wistful.

I wonder if life afterwards can ever match this three-week spectacle of which she's only shown us a brief interlude.

"How is your marriages?" Bely hopefully demands of us both. But even without the language issue, Christine's long-since divorce and my own quiet wedding in a church on a Paris side street are set up to disappoint.

Bely is startled out of her pensive humour by the ringing of her mobile phone and, in the uncanny synchronicity unique to this house, the main telephone as well. One call is for me, Suez from the SCI office. The work project in Jessore is confirmed, and the luckless Munnu will be my nursemaid and companion. The other call is from Hasina, downstairs and summoning us to the car. Bely decides to accompany us.

"Did you enjoy Bely and Mithu's marriage movie?" Hasina asks as we sit in traffic.

"Great," says Christine. "But what's a *gah ay holuth*?" She stumbles over the pronunciation.

"*Gae Halud*? It is the turmeric ceremony. It is ancient Bengali tradition, I think more cultural than religious. This is the start of the celebrations," explains Hasina. "There is one ceremony each for bride and groom. Turmeric is put on their faces to help make them pretty for the wedding. First, the groom's family—without him—go to the bride's house with gifts for her to wear. She is beautiful with sari and many flowers, and the groom's mother ties *rakhi* around her wrist..."

"*Rakhi*?"

"It is like a bracelet, gold with long fringes. It is symbol of betrothal and must not be removed until the wedding. The guests put turmeric on the bride's face and on their own, and then they feed her sweets."

"And the same thing then happens for the groom?" I check.

"Yes. This was as you saw with Bely and Mithu. But for Mitali and her husband, the *Gae Halud* was made into one ceremony for both."

By now we are nosing down a narrow cul-de-sac off the main market area toward a cluttered two-storey row of gold, silver, and jewellery shops, but Hasina orders Hanan to pull over whilst she finishes her explanations. "I wish you to be prepared for Borhan's evening," she stresses again.

She explains that the *Akht* ceremony comes next, to register— legally and in the eyes of God and society—the union of the couple. The contract is specified, and with witnesses present, the groom proposes marriage, and the bride accepts, and then they sign the registry and are formally blessed. Having made their vows, the *Mala Badol* is hosted by the bride's family wherein an exchange of flower garlands and of food symbolises the union.

"It is a little more complicated, but I think you hear enough," finishes Hasina. "Come. We shop for the gift."

Choosing a simple gold ring for a girl I have never met and of whose tastes I know nothing is easy: pick something I like and hope for the best. However, so as not to disappoint Hasina, graduate of the Leisurely School of Shopping, I try on, and Christine tries on, every ring in every tray in the shop. When we are unanimous in our decision, the gold is weighed, and the price is fixed on today's value.

Then Hasina leans on the counter and ruthlessly barters her way to a Tk 1500 discount for the making up and setting.

There is a constant stream of customers, all women, all in small groups, and I watch Bely anxiously check out their clothes and their looks, relaxing when none of them reach her own well-deserved high standards. One enormous black-clad woman evaluates a heavy gold necklace set, matching bangles, and earrings, an ensemble Tutankhamen might have passed over as *de trop*. Bely cannot keep still.

"Very not *shundur* lady," she whispers loudly to me. "What is English word?"

I want to say ugly, but charitably amend my thoughts to "plain."

Bely nods approvingly. "Good for plain lady wear burkha. Hide her."

I worry she is about to go over and compliment the woman on her clever taste.

Anne Hamilton

"Anne?" Hasina, interrupted in her deal by her cell phone, turns to me. "Finally, this is the family of Borhan. His cousin Ashiq comes at seven-thirty to take you to the wedding. He says you, Anne, will know him when you see him. He is manager of a restaurant near your home." Her brow creases. "Let us go home. You must have time to get ready."

Given the combination of Bangladeshi and Irish time involved, I calculate it will be about 9.40 p.m. by the time our escort arrives. Meanwhile, we pass the intervening hours learning what marriage might mean in the villages. Hasina has been employing girls from the northern Rangpur region for years, as do her sisters and sisters-in-law.

"I think Parvin here is the oldest. Maybe she is now twenty. But most times even the girls themselves do not know their true age. They do not keep birthdays and they become adults very young. Sometimes the children return because their family has arranged for them a marriage."

"And is that legal?" I ask.

"Yes. But it is getting more unusual except in the poorest of places."

"The villages are very backward," dismisses Mr Hoque. "You see that Parvin?" He nods in her direction. "Her brother has two wives. Two! And they live not just in the same house, but in the same room of the family house. Imagine that. Crazy, crazy."

"And is that legal?" I repeat.

He shrugs. "In Muslim law a man may take four wives. In theory, his first wife has to agree to the second and on and on. Usually the woman just does as she is told. She is not educated. She has no power. Me." He puffs out his chest and roars with laughter, looking towards Hasina. "I have only one wife. Enough. Sometimes too much."

Later on in the evening, "Amazing Grace" rings out from the door bell.

"You're twenty-five minutes out." Christine consults her watch as Ashiq and a driver arrive in a large, white minibus, the roof strewn with garlands of bright flowers. Ashiq is tall and slender, young, and as perfect looking as any of the stars of the Hindi television serials. His traditional Punjabi suit is pristine white with the slightest hint of silver embroidery.

"Anne. It is wonderful to see you again. You are most welcome. And of course, your friend...?"

"Christine," I supply.

"Of course, Christine. Welcome to Bangladesh." His English is perfect.

"You didn't say he was absolutely gorgeous," Christine accuses me as we climb into the minibus.

"I didn't know. I've never seen him before in my life," I confess. Ashiq is tall and slender with milky-brown skin and unusual hazel-coloured eyes. In his pristine white Punjabi suit, he looks like one of the Bollywood moviestars peering down from the hoardings on the side of the main roads.

"God, maybe this is all a ruse, and Mrs Begum is kidnapping us back to Takerhad to marry her boys. Bags I don't tell Hasina." She shuts up hurriedly as Ashiq jumps in the bus and it speeds off.

"Borhan was married three days ago," he tells us. "Tonight is the *bou bhat* (literally "bride's rice"), the reception party from the groom's family. It symbolises the beginning of their new life together, so it's the first time that Borhan and his new wife step out socially as a married couple." He pauses. "You understand about Bengali marriage ceremonies?"

We describe our intensive lesson courtesy of Hasina and Bely and explain that we get the general gist.

"Both families are very religious, so you will see all the women wear the burkha, and there will be many prayers. Also, the men and women keep separate."

I offer up a silent prayer of my own, giving thanks for our traditional, modest outfits, and quickly follow it with a petition that nobody will notice my black, plastic shower sandals.

"There is a code to follow," Ashiq continues. "First you greet the groom and are introduced to his father, and then you will meet the bride and be taken to eat with the women. Don't worry. I have permission to help you with anything you don't understand. You are both honoured guests."

"We're honoured to be here," I say. "Looking forward to seeing Borhan and—what is the bride's name?"

"Shakila. Her name is Shakila."

"When did they meet?" Christine asks.

"Formally, a couple of weeks ago when Borhan arrived home from Ireland. But our families have been friends for a very long time," Ashiq explains.

We pull up in front of a brightly lit community centre decorated with a huge flowered awning of blushing roses and golden sprays intertwined. Ashiq leads us along a strip of red carpet whilst the flash of a camera and the blazing lights of a professional videographer blind us. Whilst I squint and stumble, Christine is as gracious and elegant as an actress receiving her eighth Oscar. I follow her like an inept lady-in-waiting. Beyond several rows of folding wooden chairs, there is a raised, canopied platform festooned with swathes of heavy material. Cross-legged, impassive in all his gold-and-white glory, and strewn with pink rose petals, sits Borhan on the dais. Like any self-respecting bridegroom, he looks proud, nervous, shy, bemused, and a bit silly at being the centre of attention, particularly, I imagine, after several days of this.

"Please. Sit." Ashiq motions us towards the platform. I perch on the edge. Should I talk? Sit here silently? I look to Ashiq for guidance.

"Both of you sit up beside him. I will take your photograph together." Ashiq hijacks my camera and waits for us to clamber up without disturbing the beautiful cream coverings.

"Shoes off!" Christine issues a timely, gangster-like warning from the side of her mouth.

Kneeling on either side of Borhan, smiling this way and that, we take part in the photo opportunity of the century. I have a brief and urgent whispered conversation with him. "Congratulations...be very happy."

"Thank you."

"Didn't know you were getting married..."

"My family arrange this. Thank you for coming...so pleased."

Borhan's evident delight in our presence, the linking of his traditional home and family with his new life in Ireland, finally allows me to relax.

Ashiq beckons us onward. "Come now and meet my uncle, Borhan's father." We are introduced to him, and then to the bride's father, and are received cordially with grave nods by both elders. I am ashamed of my personal stereotypes that have reared their ugly heads. I automatically expect these serious, religious men to be at best suspicious, at worst hostile, of two Westerners play-acting in *salwar kameez*, and yet I am greeted with quiet courtesy and thanked in their modicum of English for taking time to share this occasion.

The bride sits in a small anteroom. She, too, is upon a platform, her female relations and other guests gathered around her. Shakila is small and thin, appearing very young and doll-like. As still as a regal waxwork, she is almost dwarfed by the rich, red and gold silk sari enfolding her. Her hands, intricately hennaed, are clasped in her lap, her eyes are modestly turned downwards, her countenance as traditionally expressionless as is her groom's. Shakila's face, when she does turn slightly to acknowledge our greeting, is beautifully made up; she looks exquisite. Climbing up to sit beside her, I resemble a lumbering elephant; one false step on the hem of an over-long tunic, and I will flatten her.

Fatima, Borhan's sister, a plump and comfortable young woman wearing large glasses, is our protector. Her face is one huge smile.

"Welcome," she says over and over. "Welcome to *bou bhat*. Salaam walekum."

Covered head to toe, as Ashiq promised, in a plain black burkha and white lace dupatta, she could easily be mistaken for an old-fashioned nun. Some of the other women have coloured or patterned outfits, but in all cases, only their avid eyes are visible. We make what conversation we can, admire the bride, the small children, the decorations, and by popular demand, model our own *salwar kameeze*s. Eventually, Fatima leads us to a deserted dining area. "Please to sit," she says, pointing to the head of the table, where two velvet-padded chairs stand out amongst the plain wooden ones.

"Where is everyone else?" asks Christine.

"You are special guests. You eat first."

Christine and I look at each other. Using mime and sign language, we convince Fatima we would like the other women to join us. After all, the bride is the important one here. Surely she isn't expected to wait for us?

Glasses of *borhani* await us. Gingerly we sip the green, spiced, peppery yoghurt drink that resembles corn flour-thickened cabbage juice. Definitely an acquired taste, it would make a fortune if served for breakfast at a health farm. Fatima clears a space between the caterers' standard curry and rice dishes.

"Shami kebab. Prawn bhoona." She beams at us. "Made by mine own hand for honoured guests." She serves us lavishly and stands over us as we eat. "Now to excuse me. Shakila comes to eat."

The bride is the last person to be seated. She slides silently into the chair on my right, letting Fatima cluck around her and pile her plate high. I offer Shakila the kebab and prawns, and with great reluctance ("It is for you honoured guests"), Fatima accepts on her behalf. Shakila eats heartily, reassuringly, for such a remote and frail-looking girl. Her intricately hennaed hand and gold ringed fingers move quickly to and from her mouth.

Shakila's father arrives at the door, gesticulating at his watch, and the bride is pulled from the table mid-swallow, her hands given a perfunctory dab, and she is manhandled back to her ornate platform. Christine and I are directed by Ashiq to follow her and sit directly in front of the platform. Each time we attempt to change position so that family and friends can see more than the rear of our heads, Fatima moves us back with a broad but determined smile. Ashiq provides a discreet running commentary: "Now the groom will be brought to his bride, and tonight they go home together."

Borhan is led into the room by two young flower girls strewing petals in their wake and trailed by an assortment of family members. Willing hands help him climb onto the platform and take his place beside the demure Shakila. The couple do not look at each other. It may well be a joyous occasion, the marriage an achievement for all involved, but for the young couple, it must also be nerve-racking. Despite a long association between the families, the number of times that Borhan and Shakila have met can be counted on one hand. Borhan returns to Ireland in a few weeks time; Shakila will follow him only when her visa is granted, a formality which will probably take more than a year.

Garlands of flowers, bright, full blooms in red and white, are pulled from a carrier bag, placed around Borhan's neck and pressed into his hands. Turning awkwardly, he holds them out towards Shakila, reaching forward to hang it over her head. Shakila is shaking visibly. They look very nervous, and the audience goes quiet. There is a short version of the symbolic ceremony wherein the happy couple are fed morsels of sweetmeats by members of each family, and then the two fathers come forward to sit on the edge of the dais. Borhan's father leads the families in prayers, and then Shakila's father makes a short and emotional speech and is in tears by the end of it.

The ceremony is over in a flash. Borhan climbs down from the platform with the aid of his mother and father, touchingly showing his navy blue and white cotton socks that are so out of place underneath the regal tunic and trousers. He is immediately swallowed up by the crowd of male friends and relations.

Meanwhile, Shakila undergoes the cumbersome task of being fastened into the plain black burkha necessary for the journey home. Her sisters and the many willing female hands dress her without disturbing her hair, her gown, her jewellery, and then, indistinguishable from all the other women, she follows Borhan out to a decorated white Toyota. The couple and their respective fathers squeeze into the rear of the car, two or three others get in beside the driver, and they are waved off excitedly in the traditional wedding manner.

Immediately, Ashiq beckons us to the waiting minibus already crammed with other guests en route home and with odd bits of furniture and utensils left over from the reception. We set off through the quiet back streets. Last stop, Gulshan.

"Have you enjoyed your evening?" asks Ashiq, pressing a box of cakes into our hands. "A gift for your friends."

"Very much," I assure him, and Ashiq, showing his Western affinity, kisses us soundly on each cheek, and then enters the minibus that roars off down the street.

"See you in Ireland!" he yells out of the van window.

12

Farewell Christine

We are in the midst of an international Muslim gathering in Dhaka. The annual *Biswa Ijtema* is a large-scale religious pilgrimage, second only to the Hajj to Mecca. It is the third and final day of ceremonies in which three million men have converged on land on the outskirts of the city to pray for peace and the guidance of Allah.

"Have some nuts," says Hasina, reaching into a brown paper bag and handing over brimming fistfuls. "It might be a long trip."

We are en route back to Gulshan from the SCI office, where Christine has said her tearful goodbyes to Bonny and Suez, and I have learned that my next project is under negotiation. "Call tomorrow or the next day," says Suez.

Actually, the traffic is unusually light, and I begin to wonder if *Biswa Ijtema* is an urban myth to keep people off the streets whilst Dhaka City Council revamps the road system. Or if I've completely misunderstood the muddled stories I've heard and three million men have *left* the place. Then, in response to clanging bells and lights that would probably be flashing if the bulbs were replaced, we slam on the brakes at a major railroad crossing.

"Quickly, Christine, Anne." Hasina twists and points. "The main train that travels west. You see many, many of the Hajji's travelling."

The clatter of a train advances steadily. We wince at the screams of those who don't clear their makeshift villages from the tracks in time, and around the bend trundles a thin, snaking train held together by rust and the faith of the passengers.

The compartments are full to bursting. The thinnest and youngest men are hanging out of the windows or standing on the running boards, held on only by the tight grasp of willing hands from within. The roof of the train is invisible, submerged under ragged lines of white clad and cross-legged figures sitting as easily as if on a football pitch. The current cold front sweeping the country today (read: a typical Irish summer's day) of fourteen degrees Celsius makes news

125

headlines but is no deterrent. There is a thunderous murmuring from the ranks as they continue their prayers. Hopefully they will disembark before they have to kneel and bow to Mecca or there will be carnage.

"Hell," says Christine. "Are all the pilgrims on the same train?"

I lean so far out of the window that I nearly topple, and she yanks me backwards. "I need you on a bloody pair of reins," she scolds. "You'll kill yourself trying to get World Press Photo of the Year."

In the apartment, Hasina advises Christine to pack her bag. "Then," she says, surprising us both, "my masseuse will arrive, and you can both have nice relaxing massage."

"Your passion for shawls certainly comes shining," I tell Christine as I fold up woollen item number eleven. In the guise of gifts, she has managed to beg, borrow, or buy twenty new *shals*.

"I'm betting on Sydney customs impounding the lot," she admits. "And as for *this*..."

This is a giant molasses cake, a homemade favourite of Hasina's daughter in Australia and reluctantly couriered by Christine, assured that there is no difficulty whatsoever in transporting a dessert large enough to contain several pounds of Class A drugs. "Some happy sniffer dog is going to wolf that down." Christine warns Hasina who just laughs at such pessimism.

As promised, Hasina's masseuse arrives. Reka is a huge peasant woman, dark, almost black skinned. At thirty-odd, she looks twenty years older, and her purplish skin tone, the sheen of sweat on her brow, and her laboured breathing suggests she is chronically unwell.

"Her blood pressure is huge. Huge!" says Mr Hoque, himself just back from the Hajj. "She could drop dead anytime. Right now even. Mrs Hoque takes her to our own doctor, but then she does not take the medicine. A time bomb! Is lucky we have the equipment to check her."

He turns to the stolid Reka and shouts all of this at her whilst Hasina rummages for an old-fashioned sphygmomanometer, struggles to fit it around Reka's upper arm, and expertly pumps the bulb until she gets a high but not astronomic reading.

"My own blood pressure rises," grumbles Mr Hoque, not reassured. "The worry of all these women. I feel the pounding in my head. What do I do?"

"Take tea," Hasina says. "Parvin has made sweets. The pumpkin and the coconut, the pita..."

"More food," moans Mr Hoque. "First the hypertension, now the cholesterol. My life will be cut short. Short!"

For once Christine agrees. "I'm feeling a bit off," she confides—and dashes for the bathroom. "Diarrhoea," she wails. "On a bloody eighteen-hour journey to Australia. Get me drugs! Now."

And she invokes the East-meets-West argument re treatment.

"Christine?" Hasina, able to detect malady at a hundred paces, intercepts her on, luckily, the return leg of a bedroom-bathroom dash. "Are you sick?"

Christine plays it down. "Tummy," she says. "I'll be fine if I starve myself and drink plenty of fluids. I've a heap of re-hydration sachets."

Hasina frowns. "So sad on your last day. But you cannot stop taking food. You get so weak. Today especially, you eat good meals, even little bit will help," she instructs. "Each time, you take Flagyl. You know Flagyl? Very good medicine for the stomach."

But Christine is adamant, and even Hasina's determination cannot coerce her to tuck into the Bengali equivalent of a colossal fry-up.

"Okay." Hasina eventually, reluctantly, gives in. "But you must take rice water. Parvin mixes it immediately."

It is a noxious food supplement, a concoction procured from the American Hospital, a putrid, slimy liquid, the texture and consistency of frogspawn.

"Is best swallowed straight down when still warm." Hasina holds out an expectant glass.

"God. It's enough to make the other end start spewing" is Christine's ungrateful verdict.

The soupy mixture is produced hourly. Christine tries in vain to find somewhere else to dispose of it, but Hasina stands over her and watches every last mouthful go grimacing down.

Reka sits patiently. She has literally been waiting for hours.

"Anne, you take first massage whilst I make Christine more rice mixture," Hasina instructs.

Someone in anticipation has placed a small mattress covered in a bright eiderdown on the guest bedroom floor. As she noisily cracks her knuckles, Reka indicates that I should undress down to my knickers and lie face down on the mat. With a bottle of olive oil and great physical skill, she leaves no part of me unpummelled.

It is abundantly clear that my poor specimen of a body will be Reka's talking point for weeks, if not years, to come. Alternately horrified and amused by my pale skin and thin limbs, she pokes and prods and squeezes various bits of me, and then her own ample, fleshy curves. Over the colour of my skin she sighs in envy, "*shundur*," despite her naturally, gloriously-deep tan. She taps my flat chest and concave stomach, shakes her head, and pinches her own firmly rounded torso.

"You eat rice," she orders. "Too much rice. Stay in my country, eat rice. Grow big and strong." She flexes a Popeye—post spinach—like muscle.

"You husband big? Strong?" She mimes a giant, offering me a line to reel in credibility.

"Well, not really. *Na*. No."

"Children?"

"None."

She squeezes my arm sympathetically. "Too thin. Eat rice. Get plenty baby."

Not literally, I hope, given the three-times-a-day platefuls I am currently consuming.

It is a short drive from Gulshan to the airport and the traffic is somewhat less dense, if still crazed. Commercial trucks predominate. These are allowed into the city only after 8 p.m., so they wait in the suburban roads forming an unintentional convoy.

Departures is a floor above the arrivals hall, and it is a novel experience being back here four weeks after I stepped into the absolute unknown. We pull up to unload, a process for which armed security allows about three seconds. Hanan, our driver, has Christine's bags out of the boot and onto a trolley before I emerge from the car. Christine chooses this inopportune moment to decide she has lost, or left behind, the keys to her luggage. She searches maniacally through her handbag. Nothing. I search frantically through her handbag. Definitely nothing. Mr Hoque starts advising, and Hasina and Hanan take it in turns to fend off the whistle-blowing policemen. Both appear indifferent to the very big guns in the grim possession of these impatient people.

One policeman daringly taps the bonnet with his truncheon causing an irate—and I feel misguided—outcry from Hasina. By now, I would usually be taking this time to worry about being shot, but my hands are full with Christine who is recklessly undressing to get at all her hidden pockets. Half the police swivel their eyes to view this spectacle; the others holler to get the car moved. Fortunately, Christine utters a hysterical cry and holds up the missing key with all the reverence of the Blessed Sacrament.

"Pinned to my skirt all along," she smiles.

So far, so good—no shooting.

Anne Hamilton

"All talk. No action." Mr Hoque dismisses the scowling policemen in a louder voice than I would have chosen. "Power crazy, these men. Bah."

There is a growing rumble in the ranks, when who should appear but the genial *gendarme* who expressed his undying adoration to me upon my arrival to Dhaka. He pushes through the circle, his face aglow with happy recognition.

"You. You. I love you." He grins, turns to Mr Hoque and folds him in an unexpected hug. "I love you," he repeats, pointing at me. His presence is a blessing, restoring affability with the traffic cops and cutting short our tearful and predictably inane farewells. Only one fee-paying person may accompany each passport-holding traveller into the airport terminal—not even the laughing policeman is love stricken enough to bend those rules—so Hasina goes inside to organise Christine.

"Email me," Christine says to me. "Every week. Send me pictures. Send those postcards to Chapa, Asha, and Mary, won't you? Oh and be sure to send me a copy of that infernal diary of yours. After all, I am the star. I'll read it in my dotage when I'm in the poor house and living on beans."

Driving back, I am in a happy little dream world thinking about Christine, so glad that we met, musing on fate throwing people together, and wondering exactly how I will manage without her.

Then, completely without warning, the car swerves onto the kerb and screeches to a halt at the top of a long, official looking and security-fenced driveway. Like actors in some cop show, Mr Hoque and Hanan open their respective front doors, get out, slam them, walk round the back of the car, and open the boot. Meanwhile, Hasina is frantically fumbling inside her bra for her purse.

"What is it?" I squeak, heart pounding. "What's happening?" Two scenarios spring to mind: either we are being robbed, kidnapped, or hijacked, and, not knowing the niceties of such a situation, I have missed the signal, or the men are disposing of something illegal and possibly grotesque like a big can of trash or a dead body.

"Look! Quick, look!" I point out to Hasina.

She clocks the three soldiers, weapons poised, walking purposefully up the drive towards the car and she climbs out. She thrusts a bundle of notes at Hanan—for a mad moment I think this might be for him to bribe the military for some reason, but Hasina explains later that it was his wages—who, bin liner in hand, makes a run for it across the busy road. Hasina continues around the car and buckles up in the front seat.

129

"Hurry! Hurry," she shouts at Mr Hoque, who jumps in, rubbing his hands and bellowing—with laughter. He puts the car in gear and roars off.

"Nearly shot twice in one hour, hey Anne?" He chortles.

"I tell you it is a mistake to drop off Hanan in front of American Embassy to dispose of the trash. It does not matter if he lives right across the road. We look suspicious." Hasina scolds. "My blood pressure rises. Probably Anne's too."

I turn to giggle with Christine, stop short, and remember that from now on it's just me and my imagination. Not necessarily a comfortable twinning.

13
Week 7 - Jessore Beckons

Another day, another bus ride.

Hasina waves me off, and I renew my acquaintance with a glum-looking Munnu at a muddy rendezvous—an overnight rain shower has left the ground sodden and smelly—at the Eagle ticket booth at the bus station. Rows of these offices run the length of the parking lot, each identifiable only by Bangla script above the doorway. Munnu hefts my bag inside and motions for me to sit on a vacant piece of bench already occupied by two large ladies wearing black burkhas, identical gold-rimmed, dark sunglasses, and Nike running shoes; a scowling young man who holds his shiny, black briefcase as a shield—almost certainly a lowly assistant bank manager reluctantly relocating to Benapole; and a skeletal, very elderly, bearded man.

Three officials are squeezed so tightly behind a desk that they appear to be one enormous body with three heads and a variety of arms flailing out of holes in their knitted tank tops. One bit of the entity verifies our names on a barely-legible passenger list, another copies the details to our tickets and assigns us seats, and the third answers the phone and keeps an eye on the window for passing Eagle buses.

I remain in my small corner, dealing with a constant stream of hawkers selling newspapers, fruit, early morning tea, crisps, nuts, boiled sweets ("I have chocolate for you, sister"), biscuits, *gram*, gum, and magazines, whilst Munnu is outside inhaling lethal doses of nicotine. A sudden whistle induces that glorious stampede usually reserved for Ryanair flights. The fat burkha'd women are remarkably agile—Nike might want to consider a sponsorship deal—reaching the narrow door simultaneously and so are momentarily jammed there, which allows the emaciated old fellow to crawl nimbly through their legs, thus reaching the bus a whisker ahead of the failed bank manager who is trampling women and children without prejudice. My instinct is to be up there with them, but I think better of it in case they are actually answering a pre-boarding communal call of nature or prayer.

There is only a handful of people on the bus: Munnu and I, my friends from the Eagle booth, a middle-aged women elegantly dressed in a cream satin sari with gold accessories—not a speck of dirt in sight—and a young man in a multi-coloured poncho at whom Mr Bank Manager looks distastefully whilst edging closer to the chic sari lady. She, in turn, ignores him, calmly produces a nail file, and begins a manicure.

"Why so few people?" I ask Munnu as the doors close, and we begin the tedium of departing the bus station.

"A/C buses cost more than the non a/c, so in winter few people travel a/c."

He sneezes and I learn the reason for his morose humour. Air-conditioned buses are cold and passengers are banned from smoking on them. After the hot and sweaty trip to and from Rajoir, I am responsible for today's air-conditioned choice and boy, do we get our money's worth over the next six hours. The system blasts out cold air to rival a refrigeration plant. Even the complimentary bottled water already placed in each seat pocket is icy. A dull, overcast morning, heavy with pregnant clouds, renders the air conditioning obsolete and makes me responsible for Munnu's incipient pneumonia. I wonder if my cure-all first-aid kit comes complete with those tinfoil thingies for warding off hypothermia. I picture the two of us wrapped up like oven-ready turkeys.

I am diverted by a sudden commotion at the front of the bus. Exhibiting a surprising amount of vitality, the shrivelled old man is trying to get the sari lady to join him in remonstrating with Mr Bank Manager. She listens carefully and seemingly waves her arms in agreement, or maybe she is simply drying her newly applied nail polish (deep green with silver shreds).

"What is it? What's happening?" I struggle to get a better view. The great thing about travelling in Bangladesh is that every vehicle quickly forms a firm, if transient, community and nobody is left out. By the end of this journey, I will know who has a brother in England, will receive three offers of a mattress for the night if ever I am stranded in Chandpur, learn where to buy the best sacrificial animal for Eid, and be asked (confidentially) if I can help brother/uncle/cousin/friend/self to get a visa into the UK, possibly by marrying said relative. I will share the salient points of my life history in return.

Anne Hamilton

Munnu and the two ladies in black have now joined in the debate; each is shouting from his or her own seat. The bus assistant is respectfully attempting to referee.

"What?" I ask again. "Is it a mutiny? Has somebody forgotten something and wants to turn back? Are they fighting over the radio station?"

Munnu turns back to me. "The old man and the ladies ask that the a/c is turned off because it is a cold day. But the young man says he has paid for the a/c and it must stay on. So the bus boy can do nothing."

I wish the worst on Mr Bank Manager, who, assured that his rights are not compromised, settles complacently behind his newspaper and ignores his fellow passengers. Nevertheless, this incident breaks the ice and, on request, I provide a full and frank expose of my life thus far to a captivated (captive, anyway) audience. As a reward, the beautiful sari lady offers to paint my nails, but we agree that her selection of colours—midnight purple and fire orange in addition to the deep jade—unfortunately clash with my baggy and oversized cerise shirt. Instead, she offers to henna my hands, but the air is so cold, the brown mixture is stuck resolutely in its tube.

Just as I expect us to launch into a convivial singsong, the trundling bus jerks to a halt behind a queue of already stationary vehicles. As one, the men alight.

"Is this the ferry crossing?" I turn to ask Munnu, but he, too, is already half way down the aisle, cigarette in hand.

With a lavish gesture, I pull back the curtains expecting the Lawrence River and a couple of Sealink ferries. Instead, I cast my eyes at a green hedgerow barely five feet away and bordering a vista of scrubland, along which a uniform row of men are standing—facing me—to urinate.

Unfortunately the hedge is only mid-thigh height on the average male. I gulp, let the curtains fall, take a drink of water and concentrate on the hawkers already climbing onto the bus. Each looks cheated to see that there are more of them than of us.

"We wait here for the boat," says Munnu, soon back on the bus and looking much happier after his nicotine fix. "It is only a small boat and there are five, six buses ahead of us. Also cars and trucks. Maybe we wait two hours. Anne. Would you like chips?"

A boy with a big, plastic bag of assorted snacks hovers in front of us on the scent of a sale. I would love some crisps. I yearn for additives, colourings, and artificial flavourings. I would offer to marry (for the sake of a visa) anyone with a packet of Chicken Corn Chips, or Spicy

133

Tomato Stix complete with enclosed sachet of sauce. However, since none of my companions so far ever snack on anything bought (as opposed to that offered in people's homes) except fruit, I assume that this kind of junk is expensive and therefore to be refused.

"No, thanks."

"Oh." Munnu's look of child-like disappointment galvanises me.

"Okay, get some," I say. "I've changed my mind."

Munnu is surprised at my vehemence, probably reckons it my first definitive statement since I entered the country. And so begins a beautiful friendship based on furtive enjoyment of childish treats. I make a mental note to email Christine whether she would swap the worthy banana for a bag of Tangy Mango Fries, the delight Munnu and I are currently chomping through.

Every few minutes the driver releases the handbrake and we roll forward another couple of inches. Eventually, we crawl through a busy market town, the sandy ground turned to mud, the ramshackle buildings waterlogged and shiny with rain. The mass devastation of the monsoon becomes understandable if one night of rain causes this much damp and mud. Near the water is a large dairy farm where herds of skinny, coffee-coloured cattle mingle on sodden earth. Even with sacking coats tied loosely around their waists, they shudder miserably, eyes blank. People walking barefoot, their ankles caked with dried grime hold torn plastic sheeting over their heads. Otherwise the weather makes little difference. People still crowd around tea stalls, strain to view a fuzzy cricket match on a precariously balanced black and white television, and cook rice squatting on an outdoor raffia mat.

The driver grinds the gears of the bus. The engine emits a high-pitched whine and makes tortuous and uneven progress up a metal ramp and onto a boat named something odd like the *Anna Karenina*. I had expected a roll-on roll-off ferry, old and rusty, a cast off from some richer nation, but large and reasonably equipped. Reality is a square-ish deck barely able to accommodate the length of the bus, wide enough to take maybe three such vehicles and a couple of cars or a small truck. Incidental rickshaws, carts, fruit and tea vendors squeeze in, the passengers leaning over the rails, flapping, as at a pesky wasp, in the direction of the odd beggar who has unobtrusively boarded.

Outside it is warm and wet. The swell of the water reflects the dullness overhead. The only colours in the landscape are the iridescent pools of oil, slippery on the metal deck. Leaning on the wet, flaky rails, there is no evidence of the tropical lushness or life that has been

Anne Hamilton

Bangladesh to date. Although the boat gives the impression of one of those two-stroke pools where you swim on the spot, barely half an hour later, the dock is in sight and we are waiting to bump onto land.

Back on the bus is a party atmosphere. The radio is turned up so we can all enjoy hits from the most recent Hindi movies, and the elegant sari lady is chatting volubly with the burkha ladies, their heads tightly together. The skeletal man is stretched over three seats, noisily sleeping, and Mr Bank Manager is itching to kick him—after he has kicked and broken the radio. Every now and again I see him reach stealthily into a bag, take out a piece of cake, and slip it into his mouth, chewing carefully so as not to attract attention and—God forbid—have to share.

"See the little boy?" asks Munnu, pointing out the window. "I think he is quicker if he drops his pet."

Three small, naked children squat on a flat cottage roof, jeering at their friend climbing painstakingly from a kitchen chair to a foothold half way up the corrugated iron wall and trying to stretch a skinny leg onto the roof. Certainly the tiny black and white goat he has dangling from under one arm is not helping his progress, and neither does our bus at which he and his friends turn to wave enthusiastically.

"I think Jessore is the next town," Munnu tells me, peeling an orange and breaking it up for us to share, handing a piece to each of the other passengers, even the bank manager who accepts it without shame.

Jessore is generally described as a "typical Bangladeshi country town," distinguished by being the oldest of the country's modern cities. It is also the largest town before reaching Benapole and the border into India. Nowadays, Jessore is only a small part of the Khulna region and far smaller than the urban city of Khulna itself, but geography has ensured its significance both during the British Raj when it was an outreach post of the district headquarters in Kolkata, and in the more recent Liberation War.

Now, a combination of modern plate glass, large, shabby stone buildings, and ramshackle tin huts, the town is a confused jumble of old and new, of English and Bangla. The bus station lies on the periphery of the congested central area. One minute we are travelling the straight and empty main road, the next we are in a dense municipal sprawl.

A circle of rickshaws gathers instantly at the bus door, drivers clamouring for fares and grabbing bags as they are passed down the steps. Mr Bank Manager is first off, followed by the two burkha ladies who, with the ease born of long practice, wedge their curves onto one of the sloping seats and are driven away on the jangle of a bell. The elegant sari lady presses a bottle of her prized nail polish into my hand and urges me to visit her second cousin's shop which is just along the main street and is famous for its *nakshi kanthas,* the indigenous, multi-layered, and embroidered bed quilts.

My bag is hoisted between modes of transport, becomes our foot rest for the next part of the journey, and the last I see of our little community is the bus assistant gently trying to rouse the old man, now tousled and disorientated.

Away from its core, the town is quieter. There are fewer cars and more rickshaws on the wide, poorly maintained roads where the dust of winter is watered down to a beige mud. Shops and houses, cafés and hotels, are crammed along the sidewalks. They thin out slightly, and then as we turn left and cross a disused railway line, they build up again in the suburbs. Despite its size, Jessore feels like a small town, friendly, with cleaner air and a less frenetic lifestyle than Dhaka. It is cooler, too, less humid, and this alone reduces an incipient claustrophobia.

Munnu and the driver, engaged in prolonged, hand-waving discussion, are evidently considering our directions. The rickshaw crawls along as they call out to curious passers-by, who offer geographical advice, turn to their neighbours for second opinions— one man disappearing into a bank and emerging a few minutes later with the manager and a hand-written note. The trade-off for this information involves lots of words like "Dhaka," "Rajoir," "SCI," "volunteer," and "Ireland." I switch off from this peculiar, yet universal, ritual of male bonding: "Where are you off to? Mohinney— *where? What?* At this time of day? Take you a good couple of hours that will, mate. Thinking of taking the Benapole road were you? Hear that, Channu? They were only going down the Benapole road to Mohinneycarty. Yup, can you believe it? No mate, now, what you want to do is turn round and...who's your lady friend by the way?"

Ignoring the food and hardware stores, a pharmacy, telephone office, and restaurants, I wile away the time choosing my ideal base for our week-long project. My hopes rise in front of a large, neat health centre, a school with a carefully maintained, flowering courtyard, and a smart YWCA building. They plummet as we ride past.

Finally, in a coincidence that could only occur in Bangladesh or the West of Ireland, a young man on a bicycle draws up and yells a wobbly greeting. He just happens to be the Assistant Secretary of SCI Jessore Unit and has just finished a college exam. He and a group of fellow volunteers are also en route to the medical project.

Anne Hamilton

We chase the bicycle up the street, pausing frequently and suddenly as the boy stops to chat with an assortment of his friends and others who want to know who I am. I seriously consider composing a one-page personal profile, getting it translated into Bangla, and arranging its advance distribution to all neighbourhoods on our itinerary. Think of the time saved.

Behind the counter of a small, roadside drug-store, three men sit watching a portable black and white television balanced on the knees of a fourth person opposite them whose job it is to hold the attached wire aerial at the correct angle. The shop is crammed with drugs, dusty, battered boxes and bottles shoved at apparent random into glass-fronted cabinets and onto deep shelves.

Lite, the pharmacist, is tall, thin, and wears a carefully-ironed white shirt, and neat black trousers. His company are college boys about to join "our" project. Whilst Lite and I swap spookily similar stories about life in small-town pharmacies thousands of miles apart, he ensures that in a small hotel down the street the cook is roused from his slumbers and coerced into making a very late lunch. Our lunch is soon delivered, and a plate of paratha and fried eggs is placed in front of me. Munnu favours rice and meat, but we have barely begun when Lite excuses himself briefly, returns, looks apologetically at me, and speaks rapidly to Munnu.

"Anne. Come," says Munnu, swallowing with difficulty. "The bus leaves. It is more early than Lite expected." He pauses to gulp down two tall glasses of water and toss a banknote to the vendor, and we hurry to the small square where Lite is holding up the bus for us. This time it is a local passenger bus with as many people on the roof as inside. Lite finishes his conversation with the driver and we rattle off. Seconds later, we are revisiting our lunchtime hotel, flagged down by the excited owner. The bus driver looks between him, Munnu, and me. I note—with a sinking feeling—Munnu nodding gravely as the man shouts down the aisle.

"The owner of the hotel says we do not finish our food," Munnu tells me. "Maybe he wants to return our money."

With difficulty, Munnu stands up and calls to the driver since the aisle is too crowded for him to go forward. The driver relishes his role as intermediary. Neither he nor the other interested passengers appear worried about the delay of their journey.

"I tell him the money does not matter." Munnu turns back to me. "But he insists we must be served properly."

Through the window I watch the vendor disappear into his restaurant and emerge almost immediately followed by a small boy.

Both of them have their arms full. As the objects are passed from person-to-person down the bus, I realise it is not Munnu's change that is stopping at us, but the remainder of our lunches. Munnu's lunch is still sitting uncovered and half eaten on an enamel plate while mine pokes out of a screw of newspaper, the paratha folded carefully around the remains of the fried egg to make a sandwich. My teeth marks from the last bite are still visible. We call embarrassed "thank you's" down the bus, force the window further back and lean out, seeking the hotel vendor. He grins and waves, and the little boy runs alongside the bus as it begins to draw away. I feel in my pocket for change, knowing that the child will retrieve it however impossibly it falls.

Well beyond the twenty-kilometre ride to the town of Jhakargacha, sits Mohinneycarty, the next Work Camp venue. The sun, a blushing circle in a bland sky and partially obscured by the sturdy palm trees whose shadows frame the lanes, is dipping almost imperceptibly to merge with the horizon. There is no artificial light, save the momentary shine of oncoming headlights, no sodium street lamps or electricity cables. In the one-street, apparently-deserted village, the sparse shop front that marks the bus stop looks abandoned. Sticking limpet-like to Munnu, I crawl off the bus whilst my bag is heaved out of the open back window where it hits the ground with a thud. My fellow volunteers take the same route off the bus.

The silent, inky night closes warmly around us, and my eyes begin to adjust. A cluster of small shops and stalls stand on either side of the road, but in the gloom it is impossible to discern their business. We re-group, move off down an alley, and head towards a flickering light of a candle in the window of a low, flat-roofed building. Munnu forms the advance party.

"*Salaam*, Miss. What do you think about my surgery?" A voice from the shadows steps forward to join us and makes me jump. The figure— the doctor?—turns to me and raises his bushy eyebrows. He appears to be only a few years older than I am, tall and broad with a bushy head of hair and is faultlessly dressed in a blue blazer and grey trousers. Before I can answer, Munnu reappears at the door with a short, slightly-built man whose huge grin is camouflaged by an impressive moustache and large, tinted glasses.

"Anne. Here is Ali, our Camp Leader."

Ali pumps my arm up and down eagerly. "*Salaam walekum.* Welcome. Very welcome." He continues in rapid Bengali, and then waits as Munnu translates for me.

"Ali says he is very pleased to have you as volunteer. He apologises because his English is not good. He introduces Dr Musa."

Anne Hamilton

I smile at the man standing beside me. Dr Musa narrows his eyes. "Miss Anne and I have met," he says. He pauses as Munnu says something to him and Dr Musa corrects himself. "My apologies, Mrs Anne." He beckons to me. "Come. We take tea and we talk."

We retrace our steps across the grass and emerge into a village instantaneously reborn. It is as if the spotlights on a theatre stage have been switched on (enough to depict a very dim evening anyway), and the actors have taken their places. At the teashop, jars and boxes and tins and packets line the shelves. Fruit hangs from the roof. Carefully situated for maximum visibility is a large, unwieldy, and very old television. Somewhere in the depths of its snowstorm are intermittent commentary and a distant cricket match. We juggle glasses of tea and sweet biscuits.

Dr Musa reaches for a banana, dusts it down, inspects it microscopically, and hands it to me. He tells me he lives in Jhakargacha with his four children and a wife who is a schoolteacher. Dr Musa and a colleague, Dr Bashir, have their main clinic there, but as members of SCI, both volunteer to treat villagers who would not be able to afford neither doctor nor medication. This week, a local eye specialist, and a dentist will begin to do likewise.

"Come." Dr Musa tosses his own banana skin into a corner and stands up. "You see more of the surgery."

"Is this a new health centre?" I rack my brains for intelligent conversation as we move towards it.

"Yes, a new health complex, built recently, maybe five years ago. It is for the people of all nearby villages, not just Mohinneycarty. Here the nurse and doctor also come to see babies and give vaccinations."

Inside the clinic, three boys have formed a pyramid and are playing with wires and fuses and light bulbs. The one on top is fixing a lamp high upon the wall. He gives the order to flick a switch. There is a buzz, a flash, darkness, brightness.

We have light.

I examine all the little niceties of furniture and creature comforts. Inside the door are two high, stretcher beds padded with blue plastic mattresses. Beyond them, a shelf doubles as the kitchen, complete with cooking pots and crockery. There are squat toilet compartments either side of an internal water pump, and two largish rooms either side those. One appears to be an office, and the other is open to reveal the average teenager's den. Roughly lined with a temporary cloth covering, the floor is piled with bedding and pillows, bags leaking clothes and shawls, random saucers of cigarette butts, and dented bottles of water. Towels provide a blackout over the two shuttered windows. Desperate burglars with diplomas in Ransacking and Looting could not better it.

"So here is where you live for the next days," Dr Musa confirms. "*Inshallah*, you will sleep soundly."

Ali calls a house meeting, sitting in a circle in the hastily-tidied sleeping room. I try, uselessly, to imprint faces and names—Dostogir, the second-in-command, Rakim, a first-year medical student, Shantu, voted minute taker—and to concentrate on the muddled translations of pedantic Bangladeshi discussion.

"We have days for dental camp, for eyes camps, and for medicine camp." Munnu offers a simultaneous translation as Ali or whoever, is speaking. I feel like a UN delegate with an interpreting ear piece, except that Munnu frequently interrupts himself to join in the Bangla conversation. Here, the camp machinery—metaphorically speaking— is less well oiled than in Rajoir. Daily tasks are vaguely defined, reporting is ad hoc, and the cooks have little responsibility thanks to the "caretaker" next door. Munnu clearly has the urge to firm up the organisation, so the information I get is wonderfully erratic.

"The opticians hang a chart outside to which patients point or clap...We provide a bucket for spitting out the dentist's bad teeth or the floor becomes slippery...Dr Bashir enjoys a packet of sweet biscuits for examination...The rose garden is now in bloom, and we visit early one morning...Twenty posters to hang at dawn...We bath in the pond at midday..."

"Where do I bathe?" I ask, and with a pang, miss Christine.

The lads look at one another. Presumably they expect the liberated Western woman to join the daily male conga down to the river, towel around my neck, *lunghi* at my waist, part shares in the communal bar of soap, to partake chummily in the violent splashing, mock drownings, and spontaneous *a capella* chorus that is camp ablutions.

"Yes. You are a girl," Ali states.

It is a brainteaser. There is the village water pump in the square, but that is probably more suited to washing dishes and clothes; a crowd might gather if I took out my shampoo. Or, they could lock me alone in the building with the windows covered to use the water tap. The source is cold and intermittent, the pump very stiff but...

"That's fine. Really." I interrupt what is in danger of becoming a mammoth debate. "I will do that when you go to the river."

Another thought strikes Ali. "We all sleep here." He waves broadly around the room. "But all are boys." He pauses. "You are a girl," he reminds me again. I think he is trying to convince himself, like orphans in nineteenth century England (the uneconomic girls obligingly dying off), SCI volunteers are by Jessore Unit definition, male.

I leave them to come up with a solution they find satisfactory. My objection to sleeping with them en masse is not moral but practical. The physical discomfort of squashing onto an already overcrowded floor surrounded by discarded underwear, cigarette butts, snoring, farting, heaving, throat-clearing mob, is a recipe for sleepless nights and subsequent grumpy, very grumpy, days.

The group eventually concludes that quantity is the issue. Would it be okay, they suggest, if I shared the surgery room with, perhaps, two of them—a big space between us naturally. I *could* have the room to myself but with the four new volunteers from Jessore, and Munnu, this bedroom would become very uncomfortable. I agree and the subsequent dialogue as to who should share with me carries us through a simple, but substantial, dinner of rice and dhal.

After the table is cleared and the examination room turned into a bedroom by covering the floor with a large, hairy blanket, the real business of the night sets in. Fortified with a supply of cigarettes, biscuits, and a jug of water, the volunteers settle to playing cards. With the bare light bulb glowing a harsh, orange light over their heads, the hazy fug of smoke and raucous laughter, wrapped in their shawls, they look like the last bastion of a remote bandit outpost. I opt for bed, blowing up my inflatable mattress and spreading my sleeping bag carefully in one corner of the room. Munnu explains that Ali and Rakim drew the short straws and will share with me. He, Munnu, is not abandoning me, but, he intimates delicately, it would not be etiquette for him to sleep beside me. Since we already travelled alone together, our relationship might be misinterpreted, my good character dented.

"Mine also," he adds, looking as if he'd give his left arm (the right would be *too* awkward) for a racy reputation.

"Me, I protect Anne." Rakim interrupts his card game to state his position and glares at Munnu who bristles back.

I fear pistols at dawn.

There is nowhere to attach the mosquito net I borrowed from Hasina, so, with fingers crossed around a bottle of insect repellent, I crawl into bed. Since the light has to be on in the entire building or off completely, it is like trying to sleep in the Big Brother house.

14
Eyes Wide Open

I awaken to the tiniest hint of dawn beyond the shutters. Two huddled forms sleep against the far wall of the room, a crater the size of the Grand Canyon between us. I untwist myself from the sleeping sheet, throw on some clothes, and creep outside to locate my flip-flops. The door to the other room is ajar, revealing more of my slumbering companions piled on top of each other like friendly puppies. In the corridor, two others are precariously laid out on the stretchers.

Aiming to fill a bucket and quietly wash, the splash of water on my face rivals the crashing waterfalls of Niagara. Closing and bolting the lavatory door generates clatters, bangs, and thuds akin to lock-up in a high security gaol. Since nobody stirs, I continue my one-woman percussion band out through the front door and into the hazy promise of a sunny day. I stand on the steps luxuriating in absolute solitude and soaking up my new surroundings, adjusting last night's vague impressions.

The health centre is brightly whitewashed with green metal doors and shutters. On one side is a part-wooden, part-tin dwelling secluded by a crude fence, behind which I spy a lick of flame and wisp of smoke curling upwards from an outdoor stove. To the front is a large, square clearing with rough grass and sand underfoot, a couple of straw sheds, and a centrepiece of an angular, red, water pump dripping rhythmically into its covered drain. Beyond lies the village, the shop yards visible through a scattering of trees, a glimpse of the tarred road through the alley beside the tea stall. Slowly, I turn a full circle. The complex is built against a backdrop of open fields, uneven, sparse, and randomly populated with clustered trees and shrubs. The river, its bed dry and gaping despite yesterday's rain, runs parallel with a wide and well-established dirt track. It is not an arresting landscape. The beauty is in the mellow, pink first-light stealing over the land illuminating the ordinary and lightening the spirit. It is in the silence, the minimal but true notes of birdsong. It is a fluid place, its personality evolving between day and night.

A tousled head with eyes half-closed peers out between the doors, gives a protracted, phlegmy, hacking cough, snorts deeply from chest to nose, and spits lavishly, forming a perfect arc and *splat!* onto my romantic illusions. He, whoever he is, starts a trend. There are rumblings from within, and in various states of undress and complaining about the cold, these fine examples of Bangladeshi manhood stagger to life. Full of team spirit, I seize my toothbrush, share out paste to all comers, and join in the communal cleaning of teeth.

Theoretically, today's Eye Camp is due to begin at nine o'clock. Ten, eleven o'clock, half past, come and go. Patients begin to assemble. Small and large family parties settle down on the grass, groups of men congregate to smoke and talk under the trees, and a cluster of women hang back, carefully observant. No one is particularly perturbed to note that the doctor and his team have failed to arrive, and there is a general air of jollity never yet recorded by the NHS. All of them, however, do need to know, as a matter of urgency, exactly who I am and why I am here. It feels like an international press conference with a million reporters and one translator. There is fervent nodding and smiling.

"This is social occasion. A day away from their own villages," Munnu tells me. "In Rajoir, it is the same. They pack a picnic, and the family travels in a bus or rickshaw van. They meet relatives and friends. Today is very good as you give free entertainment also."

Ali arrives and unearths the package of glasses and drugs from Ireland via Dhaka and hands it to me to open. The volunteers crowd round as excited as if Santa Claus has muddled up his dates and religions.

"We have pleasure that the gift arrives," Munnu explains. "Maximum times, the mail is corrupted, and the box is put open and robbed." He eyes the tightly bound wrapping approvingly. "The taping here is so much that any robber gets bored and chooses easier box."

Half an hour and ten torn nails later, I see his point. My husband (responsible for sorting and sending) might well have had a previous incarnation as Head of Mummification in ancient Egypt there is so much masking tape. Everything then, is intact and in perfect condition. And with the bonus of all that bubble-wrap, the volunteers swoop down with shouts of joy, and only then do they turn to modelling the various pairs of glasses and crowing with merriment. Rapidly I hand the donated drugs to Lite for safe-keeping. The consequences of Dostogir, Rakim and the others popping a few diuretics, or vision-distorting eye drops might be hilarious in a *Carry On* film sort of way, but would throw the day seriously out of kilter.

Lite himself is pleased with the stash. I only wish it were more than a few practically out-of-date leftovers. He checks them over and writes names and quantities into his record book before locking the tablets away. Scattering the last bulky packet over the desk, he picks through them, frowns, and then grins.

"Anne, I think these must go in a special place. More suitable for Work Camp volunteers than patients, yes? I prescribe two per person, twice a day."

He is referring to a selection of Cadbury's best, Fruit Pastilles, and Wine Gums. I can't remember a nicer surprise, and it makes me want to go home.

Still no sign of the ophthalmic professionals, but into the fray comes the health centre manager and a doctor from one of the local hospitals intent on a spur-of-the-moment vaccination programme. The bush telegraph kicks in and a steady stream of women produce eligible babies. The morning is punctuated by the universal, offended wail of an infant being unceremoniously jabbed with a large needle.

By midday, we need crowd control. Somewhat over-zealously, all women with small children are directed to the immunisation clinic. Puzzled by the mothers' greater reluctance than usual to hand over their offspring, the doctor questions them closely, puts down his needle and calls for a show of hands. At least half are escorted from the health centre.

"They are told that there is a strange white lady here, and they come to see her," the exasperated doctor says. He turns to me. "They come only to see you, ma'am, and I nearly inject them."

Ali takes stock. He invites Rakim to collect the potential vaccinees, and Dostogir to shepherd those waiting for an eye examination. Ali himself takes control of the remainder who circle around me, content as artists in a still life class.

The rest of the volunteers disappear to bathe.

I am told to take a break and so sit on one of the benches basking in the sun—whilst all around me snuggle into their shawls and shiver under their hats—and pretend to write my diary, knowing that any time I look up, someone will catch my eye, smile, and engage in vigorous sign language. Regularly, I sense movement behind me. A shadow falls over the white page and, looking round, my head collides with the person peering over my shoulder. The women chatter amongst themselves, willing me to lose my constipated smile and understand them. One or two of the braver ones lean over to stroke my face and my arms, fascinated by my paleness and bare skin. They gently take down my hair and smooth it over my shoulders. They pull me down to join them and plait my hair, pass me bits of jewellery to model, express amazement that there are no holes in my ears or my nose.

Every few minutes someone approaches me, pointing at his or her eyes or at those of an accompanying wife or child or friend, obviously giving me the low-down on the difficulty. One terrified child is plonked on my knee whilst his mother all but inverts his upper eyelids and pokes at the inflamed skin underneath. She motions that I should write a prescription.

"*Ami dahktar na*," I say repeatedly, pointing to myself and shaking my head. "*Ami dahktar na*." I hope that this is the pidgin equivalent of "I am not the doctor."

This woman looks as if she doesn't care. She simply wants relief for the streaming eyes of the child who appears—and I am not an expert—to have a nasty case of papillary conjunctivitis. A complaint exacerbated by his mother continually jabbing her finger in his eye, which she does about every ten seconds to show how bad is the condition.

Another elderly patient is led by his twin brother. Close up, both of his eyes have the milky and unfocused opacity of advanced cataract. This time I don't attempt to explain and just sit them both down in the middle of another bench and assume they get the message to wait. They do as bidden. In fact, had I produced a penknife and removed the cataracts there and then, I think they would have sat quietly throughout, nodded their thanks, and been on their way.

Luckily, the return of the bathers coming single file, towels thrown over their shoulders and singing loudly, coincides with the abrupt arrival of the real ophthalmologist and his team bumping violently over the grass in a small, dusty Toyota. Like advancing armies, both parties meet in no-man's land. A small, wiry man bursts out of the back of the car, wrenches open the other doors, starts yelling instructions, and then makes his way to the health centre at a run, waving back the crowds to make room for his entourage of five colleagues and two cardboard boxes. There is little time for introductions or for explanations in English; I just deduce what I can, do as I am told, and keep out of the way.

"Dr Sawar is main man," Ali tells me briefly. "Very old man. Hurting feet. See him?"

The doctor has a full grey beard, traditional dress, and wears thick, black-rimmed spectacles. An old-fashioned hearing aid dangles from his right ear, and he adjusts it every few minutes like a television reporter with a dodgy microphone.

"Also young man doctor and two assistant people," Ali continues. "The busy man. I do not know him in English. Maybe eye tester?"

The manic man is probably a dispensing optician. He has Harry Potter glasses, the ubiquitous nylon slacks—a horrible yet strangely common habit of lower-grade professionals here (cheap, I imagine)— and is in his element. He struts around with a "don't disturb me, I'm on very important business" frown, barks orders about tea, furniture, drugs, and then settles down to roar at the patients' universal stupidity. Thankfully, the crowds appreciate this as humour and guffaw in unison.

The system is orderly if primitive. Details are recorded in a small copybook; the patient is handed a scrap of paper on which is written his or her name and a corresponding number. Each patient then waits to see Mr Manic-and-Important who has supervised the attachment of a cardboard Snellen Chart showing *Landolt's Rings* (the so-called "illiterate E's) onto the outside of the shutters. It is rigged up with string and dangles lopsidedly at precisely the right distance from the benched patient. The optician puts a frame on the patient's face and yells instructions at them with his nose an inch away from theirs. One of the assistants stands at the chart holding it square and pointing at each figure in turn. If the patient cannot see where the gap in each circle is or makes a mistake, the assistant walks towards him, holding up fingers to count, to ascertain whether the patient's vision is very poor, or if he does not understand the system.

If Mr Important gets too impatient, he snarls, gets up with a force which knocks over his chair, shoves aside the assistant, who is about three times his size in height and weight, and does the pointing himself, leaning into the patient's face and intimidating him or her to improve results. His technique varies for nobody: male, female, young or old. Yet, whatever the content of his staccato speech, he frequently manages to raise a laugh from the crowd and a nervous smile from the contestant. Indeed, as the day wears on, I realise that it is all a persona. Not the officious creep he pretends to be, the eye tester is reconciling his awe of Dr Sawar and playing to appreciative and responsive spectators in the manner of a stand-up comic. The results of the eye test are then scribbled onto the piece of paper and the patient is waved inside the health centre to await one of the two doctors.

Anne Hamilton

The ophthalmologist's main method of examination is to shine an industrial-sized torch into each eye, perhaps ask a question or two, and then write out either a prescription or a letter of referral to the local clinic. After being ushered back outside, the patient then hovers beside Mr Important until he decides to notice and interrupt the eye testing, grabs the paper and, at high speed, explains the instructions thereon.

Those needing glasses receive the nearest possible approximation to their prescription from the meagre selection of donated cast-offs. Each pair has their lens strength taped to the side of the frame, making it a simple matter of matching that with the doctor's written direction. The spectacle frame is then adjusted to fit by hand: bending, tweaking and cutting the sides. There can be no concession to style or colour, and indeed nobody cares: the happiest little boy of the day goes off with a pair of orange Deirdre Barlow's.

In total, ninety-odd people are seen in this manner, always at the centre of a crowd of delighted onlookers jostling for space and shouting words of encouragement or commiseration. When the noise gets too loud for even Mr Important to hear his own voice, or the view of the Snellen Chart is obscured by the enthusiastic hordes, there is a pause whilst he clips people around the ear and manhandles them away, but the multitude is not to be deterred. Those who have had their consultation are reluctant to leave. Each wants their turn at jeering and laughing at fellow patients. Other people have no intention of being tested. They are simply here for the fun.

The exception is the older women. Escorted by husbands or sons, they are unused to being beyond their own home compounds and are shy and understandably reluctant to be on such public display. They whisper their responses, sometimes to their husband/son who relays it to Mr Important, and then they scuttle into and out of the doctor's makeshift surgery, heads down.

As the stream of patients becomes a trickle and finally dries up, Ali calls me over. "You are international SCI volunteer. You offer snacks to Dr Sawar the main man and the less men."

The group refuse tea or water, but do accept the raspberry creams that I right-handedly remember to hand out individually rather than less politely offering the packet. Spewing enthusiastic crumbs, Mr Important offers me a bite, and then takes the opportunity to shout at me long and loud. Since he is grinning, I take this as a friendly overture. When he realises I understand nothing, he shouts louder, and then instructs Munnu, who is taken aback by such peremptory orders from someone not his brother, to translate.

"He thanks you very much for your help. He wants you to know that he works for Dr Sawar in Jhakargacha and would be proud for you to visit the clinic. It is the best clinic in Jessore area, and Dr Sawar is the most respected doctor."

Even before Munnu has finished, the man is racing off to open the car door for his beloved employer, barely beating the elderly doctor triumphantly to it. Ali looks equally agitated.

"Anne, you thank the Dr Sawar for service. Hurry, hurry."

We race across the grass to where the car is ready to depart. Ali knocks on the window and holds up his other hand like a traffic cop. The stragglers and other volunteers waft over.

"Anne gives thanks for what we receive," Ali prompts me.

A vision of me shouting an incomprehensible grace-before-meals at the startled doctor means I am holding back giggles as I peer through the closed and murky car window, yelling—see, even I'm at it now as it's the only way to be heard—official SCI thanks for the team involvement. Attempts from inside to wind down the window fail when the knob comes off in the driver's hand, causing Dr Sawar to struggle back out of the car, listen politely to my stuttered ad-libbed speech, accept the thanks graciously, and offer his own in turn to us. The driver revs the engine, spinning the wheels, and shoots off, narrowly avoiding a head on collision with Dr Musa who is put-putting his scooter through the narrow alley towards us.

En masse, we seek out the inevitable tea at a new place in the centre of a row of shops. The heat of the day has gone along with the last of the light. I rearrange my *dupatta* across my shoulders and tuck my feet into the usefully wide trouser legs of my outfit.

"Mrs Anne, you are cold?" Dr Musa asks, sitting down beside me.

"No, just afraid of mosquitoes."

"There are few mosquitoes here," he says dismissively. "It is winter."

"They still find *me*," I whine, and graphically describe the itching, swollen eruptions that will decimate my skin if even the oldest, laziest, half-dead specimen gets the merest whiff of my blood. Dr Musa looks sceptical until Munnu comes to my defence.

"She is right. In Khalia..." His face suggests he is recounting a macabre tragedy rather than anecdotes about my mosquito-induced tantrums during the Rajoir project.

This fascinating subject is brought to a close by the arrival of three new SCI members: two sisters in their twenties called Rokeya and Shuna, and Islam, a middle- aged man, who I think is their father, maybe an uncle, or perhaps just someone who likes the company of girls whose combined ages total his own. Islam immediately accosts me with one of those questions, the answer to which is bound to inspire self-loathing and the need for hours in a psychiatrists chair for someone. Probably me.

"These two girls are sisters. Which is oldest? Tell us, which you think is oldest?"

The two sit placidly opposite me, smiling a little. Doubtlessly, this is not a new situation for them. They are beautiful, big-boned girls, nearly identical, with long, silky black hair tucked into their *dupattas*.

"Well? Which is oldest?" Islam persists.

"I don't know. They both look wonderful."

"Guess. Guess. Which do you think is older?"

"I don't know," I insist. "You tell me."

"It is I," Rokeya relents. "I am four years older."

"You can be friends," Islam tells me kindly. "You cannot be so much younger than them."

It is not so much on the tip of my tongue as past my teeth and hopping up and down on my lips to insist he guess *my* age, he being plainly unaware that, himself and Dr Musa aside, I am easily the eldest person here—something I never thought I would want to admit. Still, as I am also the stupidest (in this context that is. I don't believe I am a stupid person per se: neurotic and a bit hopeless maybe...On second thought, let's not go there), I decide not to pursue it.

"Maybe you can guess Anne's age?"

I look up sharply at Munnu who is leaning back against the counter, legs crossed, lazily inhaling a cigarette. There is nothing to underwrite my suspicions that this is more than an innocent component of desultory small talk; not even the faintest wink to show that we share the same sense of humour and are united against a common foe. Islam isn't listening anyway. He is calling loudly for raw tea and making room to sit at the feet of his daughters.

I don't know whether Shuna and Rokeya are reinforcements brought in to placate me, the token female volunteer. If so, I applaud the concept. Unfortunately, by the end of the evening I am heartily sick of these talented and accomplished fat girls. Islam is chairman of their appreciation society and announces their many and varied skills like a top Hollywood agent. The trio join us back at the health centre where we congregate in a cross-legged circle for a pre-House Meeting. Islam tells us stories of previous SCI camps he has attended.

"Last year I was in Bangalore. The camp leader became sick so I took over. I built a school for handicapped children. It had fourteen floors and a swimming pool in the roof. Then the other all volunteers got sick too, and I alone had to roll a cricket pitch. I extracted stones from the earth with my teeth, and then I successfully played the entire Pakistani team in a test match. In my free time, I eradicated smallpox and prepared a manifesto for world peace."

Or something like that. Maybe there is a little exaggeration in the translation. Modestly, he switches the limelight elsewhere.

"Rokeya is a beautiful singer. Maybe she sings for us now?"

We murmur assent, and Rokeya closes her eyes and taps out a rhythm on her knees as a prelude to wailing her way through a traditional folk song. I cannot comment on her skill, since wailing is what one is supposed to do in Bengali, and she certainly has great lung capacity. Let me state now that my enthusiastic clapping is not just because the musical interlude is over. I cannot wait any longer to see what Shuna will do to entertain: back flips, a belly dance, solving mathematical equations by abacus? Islam promptly obliges.

"Shuna is a great reciter of poetry. Her own poetry."

And oh, happy day! She just happens to have several, typed, A4 sheets of completed works, and several hundred pages of jotted notes to read out for our mental delight. Indeed, the rise and fall of her mellow voice is mesmerising although it's anybody's guess as to content (I didn't ask for fear of Islam giving me a line by line interpretation to be followed by an oral and written test tomorrow morning).

Is my irritation justified? Of course not. Is it founded on pure jealousy? Definitely. I am so insecure, that if I were a building, I would be the Fallen-Over-and-Smashed Tower of Pisa. *I* want to be able to do something special for all these people so they recognise that I am not the speechless, talent-less, unable-to-cook-clean- write-sing person that they see before them.

Pride and belief in oneself is a general characteristic of the Bangladeshi volunteers. There is no namby-pamby mock modesty ("Oh, I couldn't possibly," "Gosh no, I'm so hopeless"); rather chests are thrust out and "Me, I am a good singer/games player/whatever" is commonplace. No doubt it comes with the ability to graciously accept a compliment.

The limits of my tolerance are defined during the subsequent House Meeting. During the allocation of tomorrow's tasks, it is unanimously agreed that Shuna should take over as cook. She instinctively knows the format and immediately reels off an appetising and balanced menu. Rokeya's contribution is to restructure the working day to build in a morning visit to local flower gardens. Islam, nominated Time Keeper, smiles at them fondly.

Anne Hamilton

"See?" he says to me. "They know everything very well, and this is only their first work project. This is already your second project." He doesn't actually add "and you are useless," but he might as well.

"Right," I say. "Just send them to a country with an alien language, unfamiliar culture, and totally foreign way of life and see how well they cope. Even better," I am warming to my theme, "stick *her* in my kitchen and demand she rustle up a three-course gourmet feast for a group of Japanese diabetic vegetarians on the Dr Atkins diet. If she succeeds, then she really is a better man than me, my friend, and I concede defeat and will eat her humble pie."

Of course, I don't say this out loud. I would probably gain far greater respect if I did, but thinking it makes me feel better. Actually, it makes me realise what a self obsessed and ungrateful ninny I'm being, and I'm extra nice to Rokeya and Shuna for fear they will read my mind and their feelings be hurt. Not to mention that underneath, I have the sneaking feeling that they are really very nice girls.

Dinner is best passed over, literally and figuratively. The food has been waiting for a while, probably since lunchtime (it probably *is* lunch—last week's lunch) and has settled at that lukewarm temperature ideal for breeding bugs. The partially covered pots are sitting on the floor in the corridor, the plates and food-encrusted spoons balanced on top of a sack of dried rice, and a community of flies are hovering protectively. I pick at the throat-burningly spicy *dhal* and try not to think about lurid activity in my intestines.

Some of the volunteer students now return to Jessore to sit their college exams, which means that we three females are able to sleep alone. It is neither better nor worse than sharing with the boys, except the sisters talk endlessly, and later, their snoring is much worse. It turns into a veritable slumber party. I learn all about the doomed marriage and subsequent divorce of Rokeya. Or maybe it's Shuna. And they paint my hand with henna.

"See what an excellent design artist she is?" I hear through the closed door.

Guess who?

15

Like Pulling Teeth

The comings and goings during the night rival those of a thriving brothel. It seems that mine is not the only stomach assaulted by yesterday's food, and there is quickly established an involuntary rota for journeys to and from the lavatory.

When Rokeya, Shuna, and myself are awoken by a thunderous pounding on the door, I alone jump up to greet Armageddon; the others probably assume that it is a desperate someone mistaking our room for the bathroom, and they shove their heads under their pillows. This endears them to me. At least they are not the healthy, wholesome types who rise before dawn to meditate, jog, and brew prune and bran tea. The commotion is actually a nauseatingly hearty Islam, fulfilling his time-keeping duties. Since nobody had explained to me that we would be rising in the middle of the night to view the promised rose gardens, I just suppose that he has recalled some outstanding achievement of his daughters which he forgot to gloat about last evening.

Breakfast, the putrid remains of last night's feast, is refused to a man. It's the first time I have ever seen a true Bengali decline food. Ali instead plunders the village for dry biscuits, creating ample opportunity to take part in the favoured Bangladeshi pastime of comparing diarrhoeal symptoms.

"Me, I am disturbed by loose motions last night," announces Dostogir between handfuls of puffed rice.

"I also," agrees Rakim, peeling an orange. "I have to drop many stools. But now my stomach is empty, and I feel good."

"We call diarrhoea p. p.," they tell me helpfully. "If you go to the doctor and say you have p. p, he will know exactly the problem. P.p. is short for..."

Despite much animated discussion, they find they cannot remember the meaning of the abbreviation.

"Anne, do you have p. p?" enquires Munnu in a spirit of comradeship. They all turn interestedly to me.

"Yes, during the night I had p.p. But now I am fine," I reassure them.

"Rokeya, do you have p.p.?" Ali enquires.

This novel breakfast-table conversation takes some time.

"Shuna has the worst p.p., the very worst. She suffers p.p. like no other," Islam pipes up.

Someone should alert him to the fact that being the best (or worst) at everything, particularly at having diarrhoea, is not exactly an asset for one's CV.

Finally, when everyone's bowels have been satisfactorily opened and examined, as it were, we depart for the flower gardens. It is a cold morning. The rising sun, already a washed-out tangerine haze, is obscured by damp mist. I burrow deeply into my scratchy peasant shawl, and we commandeer a convoy of rickshaw vans, their wood carefully insulated against the moist morning with thin raffia matting. We pause in two villages to spread the word about the forthcoming Dental Camp. Ali or Munnu or Dostogir climb onto the vans and announce the attractions. We might be missionaries conducting an open-air evangelist revival.

We ride and ride through the deserted countryside. First, the tarred roads, and then branching onto the narrower, uneven lanes where, framed by waving, yellow mustard seed crops, cotton and wet paddy fields lie back to back. An occasional farmer, deep in the grass, straightens to squint at our singing wagon train, watching with shaded eyes as we disappear into the distance only to return again as the leading van back pedals from a dead end or impenetrable track. It is a bouncing, butt-numbing, gut-jerking, *dupatta*-tangling two-hour journey of aerobic exercise, bending, and twisting to look this way and that.

"Anne, look at the jack fruit tree."

"Anne, watch the sun rising."

"Anne. Please to get down. We must walk this path."

"Anne, see over there quickly—you see the dead cow?"

"Anne, listen to the happy chirping of the birds. As they eat the dead cow."

"Anne,"—finally—"here is flower gardens."

A lesson soon learned in Bangladesh is the relativity of wonder. Sightseeing will hardly yield the Taj Mahal or the Coliseum. The natural world is beautiful but rarely splendid in the manner of, say, the Great Barrier Reef. The fascination of the country, the colour and vibrancy, the imagination and enthusiasm, is in the personality of the people as they wander through the daily grind against a backdrop of untouched landscape.

Arriving at the flower gardens, I surreptitiously rub my bottom and make my way down a random footpath bordering large, flat grasslands. A longish field is sown with row upon row of almost-red almost-roses. Small and spindly bushes hold their heads up weakly, and sprout modest little flowers that might have been eagerly pruned by Edward Scissorhands. Kneeling in the soil, a handful of men share a frayed piece of string—for measurement—and carefully plant the roots of new seedlings.

"See how carefully they work?" Munnu asks me, impressed. "I do not have this patience."

"*Salaam walekum,*" Ali calls, handing over his cigarette and going ahead to meet them. The gardeners look up through the glazed eyes of the terminally bored, chuck down their cuttings, and practically trample them in the scramble for a distraction. Seven minutes later, we've seen all there is to see.

"This visit is very short; very inferior," Munnu comments. "In Rajoir, we had many more visits. Anne. You enjoy the free time in Rajoir?"

"Very much."

"But you did not see the milk processing factory," he regrets. "One day maybe I can take you there," he assures me, and then changes the subject, reaching under his shawl. "Anne. I have a flower for you."

I hear an intake of breath from behind me.

"I also give her the flower." Rakim glares at Munnu, and pulls a veritable bouquet from beneath his baggy jacket. "Mine is big," he boasts.

"Nice," acknowledges Munnu, ever the gentleman. "Mine is smaller." He is not crestfallen for long. "But perfect," he adds.

They start a trend. Ali alone asks the foreman if he may pick a stem, and the others embark on a floral smash and grab, rapidly assembling for me a bouquet of red and pink roses. The scent of the barely open buds is glorious, sweet, and perfumed, powerful enough to compensate for the blood I am dripping from the deadly thorns. Pushing my nose into the petals at least hides my gloating smile. Nobody else has been given roses. Surprised, I glance around for this apparent failure on Islam's part, but no, there he is, still talking to one of the gardeners.

Do I really see *taka* change hands?

No doubt there are now two new varieties of rosebush called *Shuna* and *Rokeya*.

I have no chance to ask as Islam gathers his protégés up and says they are unexpectedly expected in Jessore forthwith, and we must manage as best we can without them. Their rickshaw pulls away, propelled by my insincere wave.

Preparing the health centre for the dental camp involves, for a place with such deficiency of fixtures and fittings, a surprising lot of reorganisation and movement of furniture. A desk up-ended in the corridor and one of the hospital stretchers have to be hustled into "my" room to make an examination suite for the dentist. Since the doorframe is smaller than both objects and at a queer angle off the corridor, it is a logistical nightmare that would make the ancient Egyptians, having easily thrown up the Pyramids, scratch their heads.

Still, I need not worry my silly little head about such things. My job is to sit in the sunshine and audition for a seventies rerun of *Blue Peter*.

"You mend little packets for the dispense of the tablets," Ali says. "The paper is very old. Is dampened. Those pieces here"—the seams and flaps on the envelopes—"get unstuck." Ali enterprisingly demonstrates the use of sticky grains of cooked rice as glue.

Whilst I'm thus employed, Lite explains to me the major causes of tooth decay and gum disease. Apart from the inevitable lack of awareness and access to dental services, the chewing of *paan*, a mild intoxicant made from betel nut, lime, and spices wrapped in an edible leaf, eventually turn the gums red as if internally bleeding, and then rots and blackens the teeth. Another startling side effect is the Jack-the-Ripper trail of red spit blobs along the pavements and gutters. Sold at food and tea stalls all over the country, the widely consumed *paan,* like gum, is not swallowed.

A little while later, the volunteer dentist from Jessore is ushered into the room of the desk and stretcher, and two of his colleagues sit themselves at a table in the corridor. Patients are quickly registered and sent into the inner sanctum of the dentist where it seems that the heroic efforts with the stretcher were quite superfluous. The man is adept at standing behind his victim, cradling the head to give a false sense of security, and then, quick as a flash, grabbing the scalp with one hand and the jaw with the other. Afterwards, he either sends the relieved patient out to collect medicine, or the poor unfortunate goes to the outer table and to the mercy of the two assistants.

"What are they going to do?" I ask.

Lite looks up. "Who? Pobble and Dink?" he says indistinctly, his mouth full of banana. "They take out the teeth. Anne, please count the sachets of saline."

Pobble and *Dink?* I must have misheard. Can two grumpy men at a table in a corridor, with names that would turn the Teletubbies green, really be extractionists extraordinaire? Their meagre equipment comprises a sheaf of tissues, yellowing cotton wool, a tube of Savlon, two hypodermic needles, and a torch that projects only a feeble beam. But as the men go on to demonstrate, the size of the tool is immaterial; it's what they do with it that counts, and they can certainly hit the spot. Adjacent to the table is the least-rickety kitchen chair, and at their feet is a green plastic wastepaper basket.

Discreetly—unlike the hyperactive rubbernecks, well-wishers, and sightseers jostling at the open windows and crowding the doorway—I watch as the first nervous patient sits down. Pobble and Dink spring to life in an animated and orchestrated double act. Pobble gets to hold the torch, Dink makes do with the patient's head, and they both peer deeply inside the open mouth. Then Dink grabs the syringe and injects the gum. I don't see what they're using, but the soundtrack would suggest that it is not Novocaine. He gives a few random jabs until, with a cry of delight he yanks out a sad, little tooth and holds the trophy high.

What they lack in technique they make up in dedication. No matter what heart-rending groans or wails are manifested by the patient, Pobble and Dink beaver away until the job is complete. My teeth ache in sympathy, particularly when Lite mentions that the syringes do not contain analgesia or anaesthetic but simply adrenaline to reduce bleeding.

By mid-afternoon, 176 patients have passed through the chamber of horrors, from seven-year-old Nasreen (who makes her anxious father wait outside whilst she sits motionless, her clenched fists buried in the fur of the mangy stray mutt she calls her pet) to the infamous bicycle man.

"Anne. Here is Bicycle-wallah. Very old man." Ali calls me outside, where the laggards are enthusiastically greeting a local institution, though whether they mean the elderly man or his amazing mode of transport is debatable.

Bicycle-wallah greets me like a long-lost niece, points out every last part of a machine he has painstakingly built himself from write-offs and other bits of abandoned mangled bike, and reverently invites me to cycle around the green.

"Very maximum honour," whistles Ali. "He says, he holds, and you get leg over. Okay?"

"Okay," I agree dubiously, swiftly entreating my constant companion, St Jude, He of the Hopeless Cases (I often wonder what he did to get stuck with that job) to be a celestial stabiliser.

The gravity of the occasion is brought home to me by the sudden silence of the crowd. I might as well be attempting the world land-speed record, or going solo with Concorde's prototype descendent. The old man intimates that he will run behind me for balance—I bless his prescience—and we perform a victorious, if wobbly, lap of honour. The onlookers let out a collective sigh of relief and excuse an action replay, thankfully. The cord in my *salwar* is loosening alarmingly and the dentist has issued a summons: If Bicycle-wallah wants to see the dentist, he must come now.

He roars with laughter, the crowd roars with laughter, and even Pobble and Dink raise a grimace from behind their torch. I get the punch line only when he comes close and gives a wide and apparently toothless grin. But no, I see he is waggling one lone and blackened molar as he marches toward the smiling dentist.

"He tells the dentist to—out," Ali says, making his meaning clear with wrenching movements and agonising gurgles.

It appears that the dentist agrees as Bicycle-wallah emerges and plonks himself on the kitchen chair in the extraction zone. As Dink pounces on the torch and Pobble, muttering crossly, goes to position the head, the voluble old man holds up a protesting hand. He talks like a movie jammed on fast forward, looks wildly around him, spies me packing up the drugs, points vehemently and, crossing his arms and clamping his jaw stubbornly shut, prevails on somebody to translate. Nobody can do so because they are hovering on the edge of mass hysteria. Eventually, the calm and collected Lite pulls himself together.

"Anne, this man likes you maximum. He wants that you take out his tooth. He says that if you do not, then it stays in."

Feverishly, I try to explain that I cannot extract his tooth. I have neither the know-how nor the apparatus, and judging by the manner in which the affronted Pobble and Dink are protectively clutching their pliers and torch, they would be reluctant to share anyway. Ultimately, reluctantly, Bicycle-wallah gives a sorrowful flick of the head to signify "okay," and, with a sadistic glint, the extractors go in for the kill. Or try to.

With only one tooth in the entire mouth, I had assumed it easier to grab and snatch. Apparently not. That one plucky tooth holds on by a whisker. The old man hangs in there for as long as his patience will allow—about ten seconds—and then gives a disgruntled snort, pushes Dink aside and waves Pobble's pliers away. Opening wide, he puts his own hand into his mouth, twists and wiggles, and with a grunt, he triumphantly holds the tooth aloft. He spits lavishly in the direction of the waste bin, wipes his mouth with the back of his hand and acknowledges the raucous applause. He beckons me over, chatters happily, and palm upward, he holds out the grey and wizened tooth. I am at a loss.

"*Bhuchi na,*" I say. "I don't understand." I wait for Lite to rescue me. Ha, some hope.

"He wants that you accept the tooth as a token of esteem. A gift," Lite says.

Yuk. Yuk. Yuk

16
Operation Cupid

The final day with the Jessore Unit of SCI is spent in the town of Jhakargacha. Dr Musa forces me to a sweet shop.

"Mrs Anne, the doctor prescribes sweets. You eat."

Trays of sticky, sugary sweetmeats lined up in the window are shielded from the strength of the sun by a piece of curling yellow Perspex. Little round balls of different pastel colours resting in beds of liquid, syrupy goo, coconut covered cakes the size of bricks, and lurid green triangles of indeterminate ingredients.

"Well? Which do you choose?"

The other volunteers are salivating, their noses all but pressed against the glass. They look at me hopefully.

"You pick." I tell Dr Musa, who looks gratified and saunters into the shop. He is pushed to the front of the queue and ladles two fat, golden sweets swimming in liquid sugar into a polythene bag. The colour of anaemic goldfish, they wobble as a pair of warm testicles might. I carry them gingerly, fearful of spills. Later I get rid of them via Rakim who bundles them coolly into his trouser pocket, zips it, and sits on them with no adverse effects.

Before we settle down to a general surgery session, Dr Musa invites me on an extensive tour of his clinic. "Here is Sigma Medical Centre. I and Dr Bashir share it. The largest clinic outside of Jessore City."

The building is one amongst many along a busy street. Two steps lead through a gloomy, slate-grey entrance where the small dispensary is located amidst a number of totally unrelated businesses: shoe repairs, electrics, hardware. A once-white curtain emblazoned with a big red cross screens a waiting area and general consultation booth. Up a dark and winding stone flight of stairs is the "hospital," a small, two-bed, stone cell for sick in-patients. Without ceremony or invitation, Dr Musa throws open the door. Inside is a young woman wrapped in a woollen shawl and huddled at the end of her narrow bed.

Her face is flushed, and she is dabbing a sore, red nose with a scrap of material. She struggles to get up but is waved back.

"Don't go in," Dr Musa tells me. "She might be infectious. Influenza."

Behind this bare room is another, home to antiquated x-ray and ultrasound machines. Chipped and battered, adorned with large silver buttons and black knobs on cream ceramic surrounds, they are large and unwieldy. I am reminded of entering a how-we-used-to-live museum and looking at a 1940s designer's impression of prototype medical equipment. Both appliances are in more or less working order and are cranked up as the need arises. The x-ray machine jerks and grinds and rattles, glowing ominously and emitting a constant hum.

There are two small offices for the doctors. Dr Musa's office has a slender balcony looking over the street, a place he uses for filing and storage, the files and notes weighted down by pieces broken from a clay water pitcher and protected from the rain by a thin sheet of plastic.

"Now, Mrs Anne." Dr Musa beckons me to continue the tour. "I show you my speciality. In French, my wife says it is a *piece de resistance*." He pauses for dramatic effect outside a square concrete room screened from the corridor only by a flimsy and ill-fitting door. "The operating theatre," he announces.

In the centre of the room, raised on an oval pedestal, is the operating table, a tattered couch covered in black plastic. Above this, swinging from a long metal chain, is a bright, white light, and to the right is a table and shelves littered with intriguing bits of medical equipment.

I search for words, try to imagine even minor surgery taking place here, wonder about sterility, the lighting, and marvel over the lack of gleaming surfaces and fancy gadgets.

"You find this a strange place, Mrs Anne," says Dr Musa. "It is to you like something from the Charles Dickens. I hear European doctors say this."

"It is fascinating," I say. I long to poke around, sniff the stoppered bottles of anaesthetic, and take out the polished tools of incision. "Absolutely fascinating. I would love to watch you work here," I tell him, smothering the inner voice that tells me that I am no better than the wealthy Victorians gawping around Bedlam. "What surgery do you do?"

Dr Musa shrugs. "Whatever is needed. Yesterday I remove an appendix, last week a ruptured spleen. I mend broken legs and arms here. For big operations, on maybe the heart or liver, the patient must go to Dhaka, sometimes to Bangalore. My clinic is simple."

With time to spare before patients arrive, Dr Musa reaches onto the top of a skinny wardrobe and pulls down a crinkled carrier bag.

"Now, Mrs Anne, I test you," he announces happily. He peers into the bag like Santa Claus into his sack and pulls out a strip of tablets, tossing them onto the desk in front of me. "What is this medicine?" He sits back, his arms folded.

We run through his limited supply of antihistamines, antibiotics, and antacids. That I manage to sound like a competent pharmacologist pleases him greatly.

"Good. You become my intern," he tells me. "SCI leaves you here to assist in my operating theatre. We start with general surgery now. Okay?" The look on my face compels him to roar with laughter. "I am teasing you, Mrs Anne."

I sit back in relief. For a second there, I had visions of performing a quick appendectomy before bedtime.

We are all—Ali, Dostogir, Shantu, Rakim, Munnu, Dr Musa, Lite and me—sitting around, on, or under the desk when a few patients drift in. A woman, age indeterminate in her frail, skinny body and lined face, hangs back by the door, shy of so many expectant stares. Impatiently, Dr Musa demands her reason for consultation. She bows her head and mutters incoherently, her fingers scrabbling at the well-washed flowered cotton of her sari. Dr Musa motions to the volunteers to leave the room. He calls me back.

"You stay. She has a woman's problem and wants only you to hear it."

The woman creeps forward and murmurs deferentially, now hugging herself with both arms. She is focusing solely on me, I presume to reduce her embarrassment and nodding encouragingly. I only wish I could understand her.

"An infection of the urinary passage," Dr Musa quickly diagnoses. He turns to me. "She has no money to go to market for medicine. You give her some antibiotics and some iron preparation." He nods towards the crumpled bag of drugs from which I select a card of penicillin, rummage around for half-a-dozen iron tablets, and hold both out to the now-smiling woman.

"The remedies work better because they come from you," notes Lite, who has left the other volunteers to poke his head around the curtain and ensure I am not poisoning anyone.

The next patient is a young man who saunters in, re-knotting a *lunghi* that sits low on his hips. He is relaxed, relates his problem volubly, and with great gesticulation in the groin area. The man looks expectantly at me, and is about to remove his clothes when Dr Musa intervenes.

"This man is suffering from sexual dysfunction," Dr Musa tells me. "Impotency. His wife has borne four children, but he hopes to give her more boys. He thinks you might have new treatment from Europe."

The man leans forward and interrupts.

"He says he has much money. He can pay you."

Now is the ideal moment to produce a stash of *Viagra* and establish a lucrative black market economy. Unfortunately my bags contain less prosaic remedies. Dr Musa offers some kind of explanation, advice, even consolation, although the patient does not appear in any way perturbed by his affliction. He flicks his head sideways in the "okay" gesture and departs, still talking.

"He says that if you change your mind, you go to his shop after surgery."

I say firmly that it is not a case of changing my mind. The last thing I want is a respected reputation as a drug dealer. Imagine the local police getting a search warrant out on my bag. I'd never be able to repack it. Or explain Christine's homeopathic medicaments.

A variety of minor ailments—coughs and sore throats, aches and pains—are examined, prescribed for, advice and medicaments offered. The prescribing is largely led by drug availability, limited to little more than an antacid, an antibiotic, an antihistamine, the coveted *metronidazole*, (the Flagyl that Bangladeshis seek at the first sign of an unexpected bowel movement), Vitamin B, and iron tablets.

"Some people are not sick," Lite, counting tablets, confides. "They come because this surgery costs no money. To them we give three B-Complex tablets. Others that have fear of the doctor come to ask me for help."

There appears to be displeasure with the Vitamin B. Several people examine their treatment and immediately return it, pointing instead at the penicillin.

"Why do they all want an antibiotic?" I'm puzzled—and impressed that so many realise they are being fobbed off.

Lite laughs. "They do not know it is antibiotic," he says. "They want penicillin because it is a blue tablet. Coloured pills are maximum prize. They work better than white ones."

Periodically, he calls out that we are running low on one substance and scripts are rewritten accordingly. A few patients are advised to go to market for eye drops or cortisone creams, but I suspect that their bits of paper never get further than being taken home and used as insulation somewhere. It all makes me very grateful to be from a place where we moan about the state of medical care but still take certain standards for granted.

Munnu and I say a formal goodbye to Dr Musa who packs us, along with Ali and Rakim, into a friend-of-a-friend's estate car, whilst our luggage is heaved into the boot on top of a load of bricks and four large baskets of cauliflowers. En route, we drop off Ali and a curiously excited Rakim who hardly pauses to wave farewell.

The sun is shining, totally transforming the place from the wet, drab town we met on arrival. There are law courts, a university, a cluster of girls' schools, and more for boys. The driver takes us past a huge, colonial Post Office building and an enormous garage selling Japanese motorcycles. Next door, like crooked teeth that have pushed their way into an already crowded mouth, are cramped little shops, their entire stock comprising a couple of fourth- or fifth-hand Singer fridges in shades of beige and sludge green.

With spot-on planning, Munnu grabs two seats on the next (non-air-conditioned) bus to Dhaka. Buses come and go constantly, linking the town with places across Bangladesh and into Kolkata via the Benapole border. Munnu and Ali wander off to look for provisions and come back with a prized bottle of Seven-Up and a dozen oranges and bananas.

As Ali shares a final, brotherly bear hug with Munnu, I tie up the wispy blue curtains and recline to take in the view. And miss a triumphant Rakim forcing open the door and slinging his backpack down the gangway. He sits firmly, and unexpectedly, beside me.

"I come to Dhaka City," he declares. "Anne, first I offer you flower. Now we make maximum serious talk. We have too many hours."

Too many is right. I grimace as the wind rushes in through the windows and the bus careers down the road blowing its horn. Munnu, relegated to the seat across the aisle, says nothing but looks perturbed. I tell myself not to be so arrogant. There is no reason why Rakim should choose me for his undying love. He could well want to confess a secret. Maybe he wants to talk about...well, being gay or having an affair with his brother's wife. Or something. But without preamble, he hands me a banana and pipes up.

"Anne. I am much in love with you. Do you love me also? Do you now marry me?"

While not unexpected, the delivery is.

"No," I say, and then realise how unkind this must sound. I try and temper it with an explanation, point out the slight impediment of my existing husband and my intention of keeping him. I protest to Rakim that he hardly knows me, can barely have a conversation with me, and probably would not enjoy my company a week hence.

"Ask Munnu what it's like to travel with me," I say. "It's like being with a three-year-old on her holidays. I can't talk the language or count the money. I get sick all the time and can't be left alone. I need special water and have to be taken to the toilet." Not literally. I mean I have to be helped to find the physical location of the lavatory. I watch Rakim carefully compute some of what I am saying, and see him realise there is no window of hope.

"For you, I would do those many things." He bites a morose chunk from his banana. "Do you love Munnu-*bhai*?" he adds suspiciously.

"No," I say. "He's my friend. You're my friend. That's all."

He shrugs. "I keep silence and love you from afar."

From his stoicism, I gain the impression that I am not the first to rebuff Rakim's amorous intentions. Nursing his heartbreak, he changes seats and consoles himself with the company of two girls and their brother travelling to Motijheel.

Munnu slips in beside me, looks superior, and falls asleep.

I sigh. The only arms I want to fall into right now are Hasina's, followed closely by the welcoming embrace of a proper, permanent, boy-free bedroom.

17

Week 8 - Culture Clash

Two days later, when I am indeed settled back with the Hoque family, Munnu wakes me—figuratively speaking. He is on the telephone and arranges to show me the sights of Dhaka. We agree to meet at the SCI office, and I prepare to make my first unaccompanied journey across town. So concerned is she, I expect Hasina to check that I'm wearing clean knickers and have a nice new handkerchief.

When I am ready, Hasina instructs me that Parvin will accompany me downstairs and ask the security guard to hail a baby taxi and fix the fare. Fine, until Mitali reads that the scooters aren't running today because of a strike. I am in the bath by this time, so Hasina, on her way out to the Cantonment, relays all this through the door and tells me I must use the much-slower rickshaw instead. No problem, I say. Twenty minutes later, I am climbing out of the bath when she telephones.

"Anne? Don't go. Do not even think about leaving the house. Do not pass Go. Do not collect £200."

Apparently, many of the roads between Gulshan and Mohammad-pur are closed. I do not grasp why, but Hasina definitely knows best. It is not only the lack of language which makes me wary of venturing out alone, or that as a lone, white female, I stick out like a potato in a rice factory, or even that Hasina would kill me; rather everyone has been so kind and welcoming to me, it is easy to forget that crime and violence are as rife here as in any big city and probably exacerbated, given the density of the population.

Yesterday, shortly after we left Motijheel, *The Daily Star* headlines claimed a businessman and his aide were robbed as they emerged from one of the leading banks. Three men shot the victims before taking a substantial amount of money. This was witnessed by a large crowd, which angrily banded together, chased the robbers, set fire to them, and watched them burn to death. And this is not an isolated incident. The same newspaper reports that countrywide there have been twenty-eight lynchings since the beginning of the year. Acid throwing is another issue, a so-called "punishment" for young and vulnerable village women whose behaviour for some reason labels them morally defective or disobedient.

I phone the office. The ever-patient Munnu tells me to wait. He is on his way. I pass the time listing all the Bengali words I know, or think that I know. This takes under five minutes and will not get me far unless I need a banana, a green coconut, or a doll. The last comes from Fiona (aged seven, remember) whose English is fluent enough to teach me a few words one day and test me on them the next.

"Teach me how to count to ten in Bengal," I suggest.

Fiona looks at me kindly and shakes her head. "No, auntie, you cannot do it," she says. "We talk the English numbers until you are older."

So, I loll around on the sofa watching Hindi television, fascinated by the drama and over-acting that appears to be far more central to success than the plot: a variation on boy meets girl, arranges to marry her, falls in love with her sister who has a terminal illness, they run away together, she dies, he comes back to the girl, and they live unhappily ever after.

Mid-morning, Munnu arrives and gently explains that I have got the wrong story entirely about the striking scooters and the closed roads, so God alone knows about what else I am living under misapprehension. Apparently, baby taxis have two-stroke engines—already the science bit is beyond me—that emit problematic fumes and seriously add to urban pollution. On foot of legislation allowing four-stroke engines only, the government has ruled non-converted two strokers off the roads for a trial period. The separate, but connected, difficulty for incompetents like me is that to minimise congestion, rickshaws are banned from certain routes—such as the direct roads from Gulshan to Mohammadpur.

We revert to buses, and then a rickshaw, to cruise the University district, sailing down the road, swerving in and out of traffic and heading for Curzon Hall.

"Anne," Munnu yells above the sound of the wind. "Everyone looks at us." He sounds delighted, sits up a little straighter, and quenches his cigarette. "Do you not notice?" he asks.

Strange to say, sometimes now I don't. Increasingly I forget I look different, noticeable, and just assume—incorrectly—that the greater familiarity I have with Bangladesh, the more imperceptible I become to its residents. But Munnu is correct. Pedestrians stop and stare, tinted car windows are rolled down, and scooters veer. A rickshaw driver in our path stares hard, turns back to urge his passengers to take a long look, and in so doing, fails to see that his colleague ahead has slowed down likewise. He drives straight into the back of the second rickshaw.

There is nothing new in this per se: ramming into the vehicle in front is an approved stopping measure alternative to using the brakes, but usually it is gently done, a nudge rather than a jolting collision. In this case, the front rickshaw is bumped with such abrupt force that it causes the driver to topple sideways and fall from his bicycle and almost under the wheels of a third rickshaw, which swerves into the path of an oncoming car. Horns blare and our rickshaw-driver follows the golden rule of accident etiquette: get away from the scene as fast as possible. Craning my neck and feeling guilty, I estimate that no lasting harm is done, except maybe to the ego of the original driver. Munnu has no such qualms. He is laughing out loud and pointing.

"Anne. You cause a road traffic accident. RTA. Like in American movie. How do you say—a pile up?" He sits back, sighing contentedly.

The highly decorated rickshaws have developed a distinctive art counter-culture. Pictures of wealthy cities, of idyllic rural scenes, of animals, of images from movies, all tell complete stories in brightly coloured drawings and abstracts, and are further decorated with bells and tassels. The artwork represents both the working man's dreams and the commercial nature of the business. Rickshaw builders—mistris—compete to win contracts from the fleet owners, the maliks. Many of the estimated 600,000 rickshaw wallahs in Dhaka—the Council insist the number is far less—are rural migrants who rent their vehicle and work shifts; thus they are very selective about where they will go and when. Trying to travel in the opposite direction to the particular depot a driver uses at two o'clock in the day when they are about to finish work is nigh on impossible.

It is in rickshaw-land that the class divide screams. The extreme exercise faced by the drivers takes care of a carbohydrate-laden diet. They have none of the rice-induced bulk of the sedentary businessmen who perch like squat Buddha's on the narrow seats behind them, or of the heavy women who are literally hauled up and down relentless slopes. Apparently, great mirth is achieved when the few tourists who visit Bangladesh decide to attempt to cycle themselves. A few feet is usually the limit, and that is without a client.

In my opinion, there is only one thing more difficult than driving a rickshaw and that is mastering the technique of being the passenger, that is to say gripping ones knees tightly together and grabbing onto anything available to stop falling off.

Curzon Hall, named predictably for Lord Curzon, former Viceroy of India and British Foreign Secretary, is the nucleus of the Science Faculty of Dhaka University. It dates from 1921, and this particular building is the accepted masterpiece of the campus. It is a red-brick building, elegant with a projecting bay in the centre and wide, horseshoe arches below the roof. Despite its city-centre position, it is set in a green, tree-lined park, and with the sun behind it, it looks like an ancient haven of tranquillity. We circumnavigate the building, past the less spectacular halls of residence and the low slung, rustic yellow of Madhu's Canteen. The remainder of the University buildings are modern, functional and faceless structures and spread over a large campus bordering parkland. Students, seemingly as many girls as boys, congregate on the steps and in hallways, carry books, buy snacks.

"When does the academic year begin?" I ask Munnu.

"It is complicated," he says. "There is no yearly date set. First the exams are taken. This may be in April or May or June—whenever they have been written. Maybe it takes two months for them to be corrected and more time for the results to be published in the national newspaper. Then, if the student has passed, he applies to the university. When all have sat admission exams, the term may begin."

"May?"

"Start dates often are much disrupted by politically-active students who hold rallies and conventions and so prevent the registration."

He goes on to say that start dates can be delayed for days or weeks, perhaps indefinitely. Chittagong University was closed for months following the shooting of a student on campus.

"It becomes clear to you why the country has chaos?" asks Munnu.

Although primary education was declared compulsory in 1991, inadequate government commitment makes for a colossal shortage of teachers and accommodation. Frequently, extreme poverty means that many children withdraw to work or to care for younger siblings, and even with the BRAC programmes, illiteracy runs at a rate of forty-four percent and is greater for women. Secondary and tertiary education—tuition and textbooks—has to be paid for, making those in higher education a minority. For most families, the costs are prohibitive, the scholarships are few even for the very brightest students, and the means of entrance to schools, colleges, and teaching posts are invariably under scrutiny for favouritism and nepotism. The lucky students head off to India or further afield. All newspapers carry advertisements for affiliated colleges in Australia, Malaysia, and the USA.

Anne Hamilton

We detour to the University's Annual Book Fair just off the main thoroughfare. Here, the university grounds with their neat stalls and odd marquee manage to emanate an ambience of village church festival. There is even a covered podium upon which an obscure local poet is reciting his work to a sprinkling of nodding students.

"The books are Bengali, but I think there are beautiful girls selling them." Munnu reveals his ulterior motive.

We make a whistle-stop tour of the outdoor sale, the girls apparently not up to Munnu's standards, and my examination of the books necessarily cursory. Frustratingly, in the manner that reading a newspaper over someone else's shoulder always renders tantalising copy, many of the books are eye-catching.

"Not very interesting," Munnu says flicking through two I pick out. "That one is called *Bluff Your Way in Botany of the Qu'ran*, and this is *Beginners Guide to Corruption*."

Or something like that.

"Not *Harry Potter and the Magic Thingy*?"

"Anne. Who is this Harry Potter?"

Next on Munnu's list is the National Museum, and for a Tk 2 fee, we enter a cavernous, echoing building. The reception area is bare but for stairs.

In the basement is an exhibition of interesting, if incomprehensible, modern art and installations by Bangladeshi artists. On the upper floors the rooms are poorly kept: dirty glass cases, bare light bulbs and dangling wires, cracked and blistered paint from seeping damp. Still, the displays themselves are varied and comprehensive, ranging from handicrafts to fine folk art and presentations of tribal life. An entire section is dedicated to artist Zainul Abedin's artwork depicting the Great Bengal Famine of 1943 with paintings of arid landscapes where emaciated figures are stalked by fat birds of prey. One floor commemorates the beloved National Hero, President Zia Rahman, who, in 1980, was machine-gunned by a group of soldiers, and another floor memorialises the 1971 Liberation War which includes the first ever, and handmade, Bangladeshi flag.

We scoot around. Me, because I find that my tolerance for static museum exhibits only goes so far no matter how interesting they are, and Munnu, who is clearly dying for one of his interminable cigarettes. In the street, we take tea brewed in a condensed milk tin and sloshed into newly rinsed glasses and watch business at the flower market opposite. The vendors in their shiny, bright saris are as colourful as the blooms. In front of them, rickshaw drivers await fares, and once we have again bartered the price—fair skin and blonde hair dramatically inflates it—we make the limping, bruise-inducing journey into the winding depths of Old Dhaka and Lalbagh Fort.

Theoretically, the speediest way to the monument is through Old Dhaka. In reality, nothing moves quickly through this frenzied and intense microcosm of the wider society. Originating long before any condescension to town planning, it is a jumbled maze of narrow streets and winding alleys overhung with crumbling buildings and crammed with small subsistence stalls and shop fronts—shoe cleaning, rebottling, fabrics, rice picking, snacks—alongside thriving engineering and masonry businesses.

The old city heaves with humanity. People are everywhere shoving, scurrying, shouting, coughing, and spitting out the taste of petrol fumes, manipulating huge loads through the crowds, dodging the trapped rickshaws and baby taxis, and fighting for their inch of dense walkway and breathable air. Herds of cattle lumber past, towering linen carts trundle by, and nearer the river is a veritable industry of ironworks and recycling plants where, courtesy of the rolling of barrels, the banging and grinding of tin and tarnished metals strikes a painful cacophony. Above all, it is hot, sticky, and smelly with the intermingling of sweating bodies, dead chickens, rotting food, engine oil, and grease. Beggars, their limbs missing, cuts and grazes bleeding, thrust emaciated frames forward, hold up tiny, wide-eyed children, and demand money for food. Men squat in the gutter to pee, their *lunghis* providing a modicum of decency.

Behind the façade of grime and bustle, I strain for a glimpse into the life and work of the shopkeepers. In rows of small stores all selling fabrics, house men sitting cross-legged in groups of two and three who call out civilised greetings to potential purchasers and to passers-by. Around them, in the cramped and tiny quarters, rolled material is displayed and stored neatly. Colours and shades are grouped together with an unerring eye for detail, a spectrum of fire-engine red to the palest blush pink, vibrant lush green fading to a delicate apple tint.

Immediately, we step into grounds of Lalbagh Fort that is enclosed by a heavy stone wall and the noise abates. The formal gardens are all but deserted. Down a long path, three honey-coloured monuments date, according to the guidebook, from 1684. These are all that remain, indeed all that was ever built, of this unfinished fort. Prince Mohammed Azam initially ordered its construction in 1677, and then it was taken over by Shaista Khan but never completed following the so-called omen of the death of Khan's daughter. Her mausoleum still stands here. On the Western side, is the Quilla mosque, and on the East is the governor's residence housing the Diwan, the Hall of

Anne Hamilton

Audience, which is attached through a large archway to the hamman baths.

Both of these are now museums, but their doors are securely padlocked when we rattle them and peer inside. Instead we wander around the grounds, enjoying the peace, which is suddenly, and very rudely, shattered by a shout. An elderly man in a candy-striped *lunghi* and dazzling white shirt strides towards us shaking his fist and muttering rapidly. What unwritten rule have I broken? My arms and legs are covered; I am not picking the flowers or throwing stones into the sludgy green pond. I stand by whilst Munnu and the old man talk.

"This man is—janitor? Yes, janitor, of Lalbagh Fort," Munnu says finally. "He is taking rest when the guards tell him a foreigner is here."

The caretaker hears him speaking, stops walking, turns. "Janitor, *ha.*" He points to himself. "You foreigner. Visit my country. I open museum. Special for foreigner." The effort of speaking English labours his breath, and he frowns in concentration. "You visit my country," he repeats. "Maximum thanks to you."

"Thank *you,*" I say.

The small museum comprises the inevitable weapons of war: swords, knives, guns, as well as an exquisite display of calligraphy and of Mogul miniature paintings. Inside the square hamman, the caretaker indicates, are the domed and tiled central chamber and a smaller room for bathing, body massages, and keeping hot and cold water.

"How much money should I offer him?" I ask Munnu, when the brief tour is over. He turns to the old man and asks him what he expects, and the two of them haggle enthusiastically.

By this time it is rush hour and not possible to rush anywhere. We queue for a government bus whilst fending off the beggars who are at their busiest. Munnu says it is now the trade of youngsters; the unaccompanied and barely clothed children who roam the streets is a growing issue.

There is a short article in the daily news commenting on the organised begging rings that plague the city. In the poorest villages, small children—names, birthdays, and origins unknown to the authorities, probably to the children themselves—are recruited for so-called employment by unscrupulous middle men out to make a fast buck, and then sold between professional adult (usually women) beggars. Touted on a day-to-day basis, they go to the highest bidder, their role changing accordingly: son or daughter, brother or sister. Some of these "rescued" children describe being stripped, bruised, or made to cry—it all adds to the pathos—before being pushed forward into slow-moving traffic jams. Little care is taken with their safety, for who will bother if they are killed beneath the wheels of a scooter?

I gaze from the bus window and muse on the state of the city. I see banks of urban detritus—papers, rotting food, tin cans, and bottles—black with scavenging, cawing crows and hungry humankind. If vermin armies rule the gutters, they do so indiscernibly. All residents can distinguish between "good" and slum areas, rich and poor, but still, lean-to stalls are erected next to huge, featureless, concrete shopping malls, and wooden and cardboard shacks shelter beside new apartment blocks. Despite the billboards and flashing neon lights, the twinkling, golden lights and glitter decorating upmarket shops and restaurants, nothing appears new or clean or particularly cared for. The dust, smog, and pollution do their part in dulling any newness. Once again, it is the people, their movements, their interest, which lifts it—most of it—beyond the bleak.

On my return, only the house girls are home, tuned in to their daily Hindi movie. With no common language, we enjoy a full and lively conversation. It must appear like a drunken and hilarious game of charades. They insist on switching television channels

"Auntie, auntie," they call. "English TV."

We watch an episode of *Ally McBeal* until Bely appears. She is disappointed in me wearing my old clothes. "I give you *salwar kameez* as gift," she shouts. "I give you maximum. Wear all days. Look *shundur*."

Nails abandoned half-painted, she takes my hand and drags me into her bedroom. "You sit," she orders. She yanks open the elegant wardrobe doors, scans racks of brightly coloured, well-made, and expensive outfits. She pulls out a random selection: primrose yellow cotton, embroidered peach silk, red and black chequered taffeta. "These so good. You try."

The shades and textures are too good to resist, as is Bely's desperate attempt to rid herself of the daily ennui of the new daughter-in-law. She seems to accept that she sees Mithu scarcely more than I do. He appears perfectly nice but works long hours, eats late, disappears straight to bed and spends weekends meeting his friends. Occasionally he ferries Bely, excitedly clad in her finery, to her mother's home across the city. Today we play dressing up with Bely tirelessly tweaking and gathering and pinning material, eventually resigned that I am not, unlike in the best fairy stories, transforming into the new-look Cinderella. Standing back, she observes me swathed in the delicate peach, tottering on her high-heeled, strappy, gold sandals, my hair crudely tied up.

"Look nice," she says critically. She insists I take a good look in the mirror and we admire the difference, somehow striking even without the tanned skin and dark hair. Bely parades me through the apartment, seeking praise from Hasina in the same way that Fiona does after drawing a picture, and, being kind, Hasina joins in the game.

"Now, Anne, you are true Bengali wife," she says. "Your husband will not recognise you. Turn this way, and this."

She and Bely talk rapidly over my head. Bely claps her hands delightedly and rushes out of the room. I hear excitement in her rapid, high-pitched speech, and the careful repetition of "Bengali wife" as she talks to the house girls.

"She tells that now you must learn to cook Bengali. Come." Hasina smiles. "We make *samosa*."

Parvin is coerced from the afternoon movie to demonstrate the making of *samosas*. In fact, Moshina and Vouvulay, jabbering in fascination at my get-up and tentatively stroking the folds, decide this is greater entertainment than TV, and all three squeeze into the scullery. Shoved bodily against the sink, with me beside her, Parvin placidly prepares thin sheets of pastry whilst Hasina and Bely, peering over my shoulder, shout conflicting instructions and criticise her technique.

Parvin does not use weights or measures. Instinctively, she mixes flour and water, melts ghee in the cupped palms of her hands and stretches the finely-formed dough into near-transparent lengths. Moshina, so small she uses an upturned pail to stand on, reaches into the larder for a tureen of fried mixed vegetables, passes it to Hasina who pokes in a testing finger and sucks it meditatively, and then offers the pot to me. Parvin drops little vegetable piles onto the pastry, cuts it, and folds them into neat triangles. She stands back, wipes her hands on her cardigan and folds her arms.

"Try." Hasina encourages me. "Is so easy. Try."

"But Bely's beautiful clothes..." I protest. It will be like trying to make scones in a wedding dress, trying to keep it pristine for the ceremony whilst egged on by several intoxicated bridesmaids.

"Bah. It washes clean." Hasina dismisses my concern.

I metaphorically roll up my sleeves and copy Parvin's casual kneading. By the time I have flour reaching my elbows, grease spots on my chin, and a stringy, holey piece of pastry, Mitali, one of Hasina's sisters, and Reka the masseuse have joined us.

Mr Hoque's head even appears around the door. "Women. Chatter, chatter. So much eating. I go to rest."

"Now, put in the vegetables—like this." Hasina leans over and deftly hides the doughy holes under the pea and potato mixture. Laboriously, I make rough, triangular folds and, pink with exertion, hold up six *samosas* for inspection.

"We eat them hot. One each," Hasina enthuses.

Parvin takes over again and deftly fries the snacks in hot oil. She hands the cooked platter to me. Uneven and misshapen, the pastry is by no means thin and crisp as it should be.

"You serve," Hasina instructs me. "The Bengali wife serving her guests."

"Who is Bengali wife?" Mr Hoque appears at the merest sniff of food, rubs his hands, eyes alert. Bely, claiming responsibility for my transformation, gestures at my outfit, the hot food, speaks rapidly. Mr Hoque roars with laughter. "A blonde Bengali wife. Very good. Very funny. I must taste her first meal."

He bites the offered *samosa*, chews, and nods his approval. "Okay."

"Okay," everyone choruses, munching. "Okay."

"Today we see Ahsan Munzil," Munnu announces, the following day. He is determined not to stint in his role as tour guide but is thwarted in his attempts to get a fair price for the rickshaw ride. It leads him to drastic measures.

"Anne. I leave you here." *Here* is well back on the pavement of a wide street and partially obscured by green foliage. "And get rickshaw. When we pass, you jump on. Do not leave this spot, or I worry."

I loiter, completely inconspicuously, in the bushes, watch Munnu run across the road, hail an unsuspecting rickshaw, immediately agree a price, and climb up. He points vaguely in my direction; the rickshaw turns, I leap out, and a victorious Munnu hauls me aboard. The driver yells a bit, but admiring Munnu's audacity, he is grinning by the time I recover from an inelegant sprawl over the seat.

"They like to charge double for the pleasure of your rich, white ass," grins Munnu daringly. "I tease. Please do not be offended."

"It's okay. I like to watch their neat brown asses as they cycle." Munnu looks as if he cannot believe his ears, and I remember too late that he is not Christine.

Along the Buriganga River in the smelly, teeming heart of Old Dhaka, we halt in the midst of a convoy of trucks depositing their loads at the docks and make our way on foot.

Anne Hamilton

"You can walk slower," yells Munnu above the inhuman din and clatter filling our ears, his words demonstrating my failure to adapt to Bangladeshi ways.

The river itself is a panorama. Anchored beside the quay or floating gently out is an array of boats small and large: a cargo carrier, speedboats, tugs, paddle boats, motor launches, tourist cruisers, feluccas with sails like huge, cotton sheets, and overloaded rowboats. And—as with the land traffic—all are travelling in contrasting directions. Lone crewmen are painting or repairing their crafts, preparing one-pot meals in an open galley or stripping down to bathe. Others squat, resting and watching.

On the far bank are tin and cane slum dwellings. Lean-to sheds open to the elements whose occupants live their whole lives on public view, their hanging laundry contrasting with the grey sludge of the churning water and the lines of coloured plastic bags laid out for drying and recycling.

"See the *bara*," Munnu points out, shading his eyes against the glare of the sun. I see an ancient and worn out houseboat, a peeling pink rose on the near side is its only decoration. It is wedged with people, all eating.

"It is floating restaurant. I think you say 'canteen.' Yes? Very poor people go for food. Is never empty or closed."

Past the Sadhargat boat terminal, the pinkish façade of Ahsan Munzil, the Pink Palace, looms. The house, dating back to the 1870's, is reputed to exhibit a fair summary of life for the ruling classes during the Raj. It sits in benign, timeless contrast to the bustle of the Old City and the Buriganga, protected by large formal gardens in full flower. Crumbling slightly despite rare, ongoing renovation, the house is probably the country's remaining tribute to the foregone glories of the nineteenth century.

"Here was once a factory," Munnu tells me. "Then Ahsan Munzil was built by the Nawab Abdul Ghani. Very wealthy landowner."

After being seriously damaged by a tornado around 1890, it fell into disrepair until being restored nearly a hundred years later. Now open to the public, it is protected by armed security guards.

The interior is ours exclusively. It is cool and dark, faintly musty, and the contents declare understated middle class (Western) good taste, lacking the glamour and warmth of any Eastern influence or philosophy. It is furnished, I read from a plaque on the wall, to match the era of its original construction. The huge, curved wooden staircase crossing two floors, domed at its apex, is very impressive but too unstable for ascending. The furnished rooms have been recreated from the detailed black and white photographs of 1902 still mounted on the walls of the drawing room, dining room, and a bedroom, as well as the portable latrines that were once manned twenty-four hours a day by dedicated servants. There is something almost ghostly in its reserve and the echoing emptiness; it is less like a museum than a house in which the family has stepped out for a moment and time has stood still.

We exit through great French windows onto a first-floor terrace and descend to the gardens via a grand stone stairway. Behind the gardens is a row of trees, and the river is in constant view, a perfect backdrop from this distance since the noise and smells are muted to leave only the dreams and romance of passing sea craft.

"Anne. Maybe we sit on the grass and take rest?" suggests Munnu. We try to loll carefree beside the roses, but we might as well be on the receiving line at a wedding, so many people come over to talk. By the time I have heard Munnu's repetition of "Ireland, SCI, volunteer" about eight times, even his enthusiasm is beginning to wane. We decamp to the SCI office.

Suez and Bonny have already left, probably scarpering out of the back bathroom window as I enter the front door. There is a succinct message for me:

> Anne.
> Sadly, Srimangal project is postponed. Maybe
> we make a different programme if you are able
> to travel alone to Sylhet district where you will
> be met...

Munnu looks concerned. "Anne. Do you know how to get to Gulshan from this office?"

"Not really," I admit. "Get in a baby taxi, if they're not on strike. Hold out a large denomination note. If that doesn't work then—"

He nods. "Yes. I think it is not good for you to travel alone. Maybe you can do it, but so many people want to be with you, it will not be nice. Girls do not travel alone in the country, and you are very shining."

I am torn in my response, touched by his perception and his disquiet on my behalf yet ashamed that I remain a liability. Munnu delivers me back to the apartment where Moshina leads me to the master bedroom to join Hasina and Mr Hoque, who are sitting on their bed, watching a Hindi medical soap. Hasina gathers me to her bosom like a fourth daughter.

Anne Hamilton

"You are so late. We were worrying. Mr Hoque nearly sends the car for you. What happened to you?"

"She worries for nothing. Always worries. I knew you would return safely." Mr Hoque dismisses her unease and winks at me.

I interrupt their television drama ("I do not watch such rubbish. I am keeping Mrs Hoque company only," claims the dutiful husband), to outline my latest dilemma. I want to visit Sylhet but am wary of lone travel.

It is enough to shuttle their respective blood pressures sky high.

"Ohmigod." Hasina's voice goes up two octaves. "It is not safe for any girl alone, especially not safe for you. I say no."

A machine-gun-style staccato conversation is fired over my head before Mr Hoque produces his cell phone, speaks to three different people, with Hasina avidly listening and contradicting him as necessary. As he snaps the phone closed, Hasina beams at me. "We make your programme to Srimangal. We all go by car for two nights to Lungla Tea Estate. We go at the weekend. All arranged by a colleague of Mr Hoque. It is little bit holiday for us also."

I stammer the obvious objections, and as these are thrown aside, I switch to thanking them profusely.

"Women are so emotional. Just a short tour. So easy to arrange. What is the big deal?" Mr Hoque dismisses my effusion, but looks pleased all the same. "It is good for her," he explains, jerking his head at Hasina. "Always we used to take one short trip each month, but since Mitali's husband is now so sick, Mrs Hoque thinks she cannot leave. This is good opportunity for her."

"You also," protests Hasina to him. "Always working. Too hard. You need a programme also."

"I like only the quiet life. If you are happy—you are happy, yes?— then we all travel. The end of the story."

18

More Tales of Dhaka

When I tell Suez and Bonny that I have alternative plans for Srimangal, their relief is palpable.

"Very best idea," Suez says.

"When do you leave for this programme?" asks Bonny. "We have one more task for you to do if there is time."

When I explain I still have two free days in Dhaka, I am handed another evaluation form for SCI intended to aid future volunteers that welcomes my opinions on the things one should and should not do whilst in Bangladesh. I am on number 436 of the *Not Do's* when I am interrupted by Bonny calling me to the office telephone.

"Anne. Munnu here. I wish us to visit the Trade Fair. When shall I come?"

"What? Munnu?" I hardly hear him because of the raised voices in the background.

"Anne. Please wait." Munnu continues, "I have problem." He bangs the receiver down and, judging by the subsequent noises, he engages in a shouting match, punches somebody on the nose, receives a kick, apologises, washes his hands, and returns to the phone. "Anne? Good. You wait..."

"What's happening? *Who* is that?" I ask, when, in ghostly cyberspace, I hear someone crooning my name: "Aaanne, Aaanne, Aaannie..."

"That," says Munnu distastefully, "is Rakim. Maybe you don't remember Rakim from Jessore Unit?"

"Ye-es. I remember Rakim," I say, trying to hide the smile in my voice. "But, um, what is he doing?"

"I think he cries in pain." Munnu is matter of fact and does not elaborate.

There is a reluctant pause.

"He asks to visit the Trade Fair with us. Do I tell him yes?"

"Fine," I say. "But Munnu, he does remember the conversation on the bus, doesn't he? He knows I'm not going to marry him..."

"I, Munnu, have just reminded him of this."

When we meet outside the SCI office about an hour later, there is an obvious state of truce in the rickshaw.

"We fight," announces Rakim. "But Munnu-bhai and me, we make friendship again."

"Good."

"You are knowing why we fight?" Rakim asks.

"She does not need to know," Munnu says quickly.

"Maybe she likes to know."

"No, she does not like."

"Already she knows I love her from afar," Rakim reminds us.

"Hello?" I interrupt, "I am here. And no. I don't want to know why you're fighting. I just want you to stop it." I ignore Munnu's proprietorial air, and pretend not to notice that Rakim's "loving me from afar" is to watch me with Labrador eyes and sigh deeply.

When Munnu stops the rickshaw to buy the Trade Show tickets, Rakim leans towards me urgently. "I know you are not loving me back, but can I see you?"

"Yes," I say, puzzled. "We can see each other sometimes."

"You mean this?"

"Yes. You're my friend."

"Then tomorrow I take you somewhere."

"What do you mean? Where?"

"The house of my cousin where I live. There we are alone."

"I don't think that's a good idea. I think—"

Rakim interrupts. "How do I see you if we are not alone?"

I am not being deliberately obtuse, but feel I have missed something and am now out of my depth. "But you're seeing me now," I say.

"No, no. I am wishing to *see* you. You say is okay." He lowers his voice even more. "I never *see* a girl before."

Ahh. He is talking "*see*" and not "see."

Mentally, I add to my list of things not to do in Bangladesh: *No. 942 - Do not agree to let anyone "see" you without understanding the meaning.* In Rakim's seventeen-year-old world, "seeing" means literally seeing all of me, that is, undressed, without clothes, naked, starkers. I think. It may mean just breasts. I feel it inadvisable to demand clarification.

Hurriedly, I explain the misunderstanding, do my best to limit the embarrassment—well, mine, anyway. Rakim has none. His mouth, and possibly the rest of him, too, simply droops with disappointment.

"I do not touch," he assures me. "I do not wish harm. Just to look and admire."

Gently I say that whilst I am aware of the absolute thrill it would be for him to feast his eyes on my pasty, mosquito-bitten skin, cellulite-encrusted thighs, and pancake-flat chest, I am afraid that I have to say absolutely no way, Buster.

"Contrary to popular belief," I lecture him, "Western girls are no more likely to strip off than the average Bengali girl." I floor him completely by asking what he would do if I asked him to remove his clothes and dangle his assets. He understands this well enough, rallies with the equivalent of "I'll show you mine if you show me yours," and makes one last effort to cast me in the role of Mrs Robinson.

"You teach me. You married woman sees naked man. I," he reiterates, "do not see naked girl. Especially one I maximum love."

"Yes, exactly." I ignore the avowal and seize on his other words. "I am married. How would you feel if you were my husband?"

"I be maximum unhappy," he admits. "I fight the man who sees you. But," he adds. "I do not let my wife leave for travel."

This point is not debated because Munnu returns brandishing tickets, and I slowly become aware of my surroundings once more. At 8 p.m., the wide avenue leading to the grounds of the Trade Fair is teeming with cars, rickshaws, baby taxis, and coaches chaotically leaving, arriving, and being abandoned in a spoof of parking. An enormous candyfloss concession, its generator zapping the National Grid, acts as an impromptu roundabout and serves pink wisps of sugar larger than the children already juggling plastic cricket bats and rag dolls, buying it.

The neon advertisements of the largest exhibitors—Sony, Panasonic—are visible through the smog. Inside the turnstiles, most of the stands are Bangladeshi, some from Pakistan or Iran, a few more from India. It is an outdoor Ideal Homes Exhibition, and displays range from state of the art electrical equipment and audio-visual goods to Kashmiri weaves, Persian carpets, wicker garden furniture, cosmetics, and perfume. It is bright, smart, well organised, and deceptively prosperous. This could be any city in any country, a far cry from the everyday Bangladesh outside these walls and another new perspective on this endlessly changing world.

"Can many people afford to buy these things?" I ask Munnu. I seriously doubt that many of the visitors have the financial wherewithal to purchase a 45"-wide, plasma, surround sound, digital television, or a one-off cherry wood bedroom suite complete with leather reclining sofa.

"Some of them have money. Rich people with fancy houses. The diplomatic staffs. Ordinary people come only to look. It is a nice programme for the evening, Anne. Shall we eat? We taste *chatpuri*. Is very good."

There is no shortage of refreshment stands serving burgers and sandwiches, soft drinks, doughnuts, even fish fingers and French fries. We share a table with a family devouring chicken nuggets smothered in tomato ketchup, drink excellent coffee, and wait for our *chatpuri* to arrive. When the heaped paper bowls are put in front of us, steaming and fragrant, Munnu looks crestfallen.

"I forget you do not eat salad." He pokes at the dish. "There is pepper and onion and chilli. Also tomato and cucumber. All raw."

"To hell with caution," I say, ignoring the hovering spectre of Christine wagging a warning figure. "I'm sure it will be okay." I am rewarded by Munnu's huge grin.

It is a spicy mish-mash of a dish. The aforementioned "salad" ingredients are mixed with hot, stir-fried vegetables and lentils, slivers of hard-boiled egg, and crushed poppadum with a blob of natural yoghurt on the top. It is very tasty and very, very hot. Eyes streaming, I remember something. "Where did Rakim go?"

Munnu smiles. "Oh, I meet two girl colleagues when I get the tickets. I tell him how beautiful girls they are and how interested they are to meet nice boys."

"Well, I'm glad his true love for me hasn't stood in his way. Again."

Two hours later, the evening warm and balmy, Dhaka is thriving. Its people are out in throngs, the markets are open for business, their trade now in foodstuffs like fruit, vegetables, nuts, and spices. Set on the edge of the sidewalks, those markets without electric lights are lit with candles or gas lamps. The very poorest vendors build small campfires and lay out their wares, often cigarettes, on the ground.

The rickshaw driver delivers us back to Gulshan via circuitous and unlit side roads with craterous potholes. We travel past a dark truck stop, owners and mechanics busy with bodywork, painting and changing and repairing of tyres. We pass over the central railway crossing where the red warning lights and clanging bells are still ignored by people walking the tracks, those with rickshaws parked up for the night, others with carts hawking *paan*, nuts, pulses, plastic combs, brillo pads, and soap. Along the perimeter of the tracks lies a transient shantytown. Every night semi-permanent dwellings and shops spring up. Children sleep outside, huddled beneath thick rugs whilst their parents cook and chat and smoke beside them.

"What happens when a train comes?" I ask Munnu, visualising a ten-ton Intercity Express thundering down the line, decimating this makeshift camp and causing carnage.

He assures me that a) there aren't many trains, b) they always go slowly and, c) people just get out of the way.

So that's me reassured then.

"Tomorrow Friday. I come at eleven a. m.," Munnu instructs as he leaves me in Gulshan. "We go sixteen kilometres to Mirpur to visit the zoo and botanical gardens."

The entrance to the zoo is a mess of buses and rickshaws and baby taxis. All are dropping off visitors and touting for further business amongst patrons of the unofficial tea, fruit, and sweet vendors.

The zoo itself is not nice. It stretches throughout large, sadly-unkempt grounds, full of even sadder, bored, and lethargic animals.

"The management is corrupt." Munnu shrugs. "Sometimes they do not feed the animals, and you maybe see the tiger lying down dead." Bad enough in itself, he is including the endangered Royal Bengal Tiger. Given their rarity due to over-zealous hunting, this is probably the only place, outside their natural habitat of the Sunderbans, in which anyone will see the animal...preferably alive.

The parkland is nothing but scrub and long grass. Many of the compounds are empty; in others the animals are alone or paired in functional concrete cages and are mostly sleeping—I hope. Even the infinite numbers of monkeys are immobile. Lions and tigers, the leopard, are all prostrate beside huge, bloody chunks of rotting meat and bones, and I try to banish the mental picture of a hungry cat turned cannibal. We stand still for a long time, eventually rewarded by momentary movement of the leopard. Like an arthritic octogenarian, it struggles to its feet, stretches unenthusiastically, and then licks its lips.

"There are supposed to be one hundred species of animal," Munnu says, watching a huge but scabby, as opposed to naturally wrinkled, grey elephant. "But I do not think so. So many empty cages."

We work hard to find something positive, and indeed many of the birds are impressive, their plumage thick and colourful. There is also a fine looking zebra in the middle of its personal field.

"Anne," Munnu observes as we sit on the grass for a rest, "more people are looking at you, and also at me, than at the animals."

Anne Hamilton

People are veering off the paths to observe my behaviour in this unnatural habitat. I expect an entrepreneurial youngster has erected a sign and is charging admission. One small child, his mother pushing him from a safe distance, throws me a banana, but I like to think this is indigenous hospitality rather than a desire to watch the animal feed.

The one-room museum is a paradigm of grotesque planning. It houses a stuffed, teeth-bared and tail-cocked replica of every animal—save the elephant—in the zoo. The centrepiece is a series of corked jars filled with preserved eggs, foetuses, and stunted bodies of snakes, monkeys, birds, and I don't know what else as I don't venture close enough to examine them. Like a chamber of horrors, fascinated children shout "yuck" and hide their eyes, daring one another to tap on the glasses and poke at the stuffed animals.

The redeeming feature is at the farthest perimeter of the zoo where a beautiful and natural lake fringed with palm trees is found. The birds and ducks—I'm sure some of them must be unusual or special, but in my uneducated eyes, they are identical to their Irish cousins—are plentiful, seeming happier in a natural and free habitat. In an adjacent watery pen reclines the real draw—two enormous...

"Are they hippo or rhino?" I ask Munnu.

"Maybe one. Maybe the other."

Okay, two rhino-hippo are lazing, gloriously content in the muddy water, completely still but for the occasional twitch of eyelids or tails warding off flies and bugs.

We dither outside the neighbouring botanical gardens, sceptically reading the billboards that promise, in Bangla and English, "a shady, tranquil and exotic heaven." As *bijou* means small and *deceptively spacious* means cramped, no doubt this is estate agent-speak for "dull, lifeless, and will make you wish you were dead." Tacitly, we agree to move on. After all, I have been here six weeks, and nobody as yet has grabbed me and cried, "Oh, but darling, you mustn't miss the botanical gardens. They are too, too divine!" If anyone has been there, and I short-sightedly missed gardens full of splendour, I stand corrected. It will be my loss.

We disappear into the depths of suburban Mirpur, not that I recognise it as being any way different from downtown Dhaka. We take lunch in an average restaurant, which, in addition to the regular canteen tables, has curtained booths or *Ladies Cabins*. These are filled with young families, parents gently chiding their offspring for spelling out their names in rice on the table and spilling Cola over their good clothes. I accept a tasty biryani but push away the side order of greyish scrag-end.

"It is a shame you do not eat sweets," Munnu commiserates as we rinse our curry-stained fingers. "There is a very good shop here."

"Why do you think that?" I am incredulous and think guiltily of all the sugar ingested at Hasina's expense.

"I never see you choose sweets," he says. "In Rajoir, you and Christine say you may get sick."

"I've changed my mind," I admit. "Did the *chatpuri* kill me? Now lead me to the sweet shop."

"Ice cream also?"

Tactfully, I try to explain it is the storage conditions that make me wary, the lack of refrigeration, and resultant armies of snacking flies.

"Anne. I choose clean shops only. It is my best wish to take care of you."

Munnu is as good as his word, ushering me into a small store which doubles as a café. There is standing room only. "What do you eat?" he asks.

I might be Charlie in the chocolate factory. My eyes are wide as saucers, bigger than my belly as I view the shelves of goodies.

"I know," he continues. "You say I must choose."

Leaning on an industrial-sized ice cream fridge, I am fed a bowl of curd and two melt-in-the-mouth halva cakes. I taste brown, oval sweets, light beige ones, square white ones, and orange balls. Since everything tastes overwhelmingly of milk, sugar, and maybe a hint of mixed spice, I suspect similar ingredients and a spot of food colouring, but who cares? I eat until the pressure of my money belt straining around my waist brings me back to reality.

"Anne. I like to show you places in Dhaka now. The homes of my family. Maybe we meet some young brothers of mine. Is okay?"

Munnu engages a rickshaw by the hour. He points out nondescript landmarks, substantial but worn-out apartment blocks, and shares a knowledgeable and often incomprehensible family history. About to comment sympathetically on the amount of children his mother has borne, I remember that the terms "friend" and "brother" are largely interchangeable, and for once I do not show my ignorance.

These "young brothers" to whom I will be introduced are all strangely absent, whereabouts unknown, from their usual hangouts, and even I become familiar with the streets we circle.

"Now they will not believe I have you," Munnu complains like a little boy forbidden to play with a new toy.

"What have you told them?" I ask suspiciously.

"That you are SCI volunteer and my good friend Anne," he says. "Not *girlfriend*," he emphasises, looking hurt. "I only speak good of you."

"I know." I feel bad. "You can have a cigarette if you like," I offer graciously to make amends. Too polite ever to light up without seeking my permission, he responds with alacrity and inhales deeply.

"Now, we go to the tailor where I must pick up two shirts and two trousers for me."

Just in time, as he narrowly misses burning a hole in brother Bachchu's borrowed-without-asking-first blue linen shirt.

Thwarted by a roadblock (a piece of string slung at decapitation height across the road and protected by a gang of medium-sized children), we have to circumnavigate the thoroughfare. We pay off the rickshaw driver and duck beneath the barrier into the depths of an all-male street party. I practically trip over the polythene-lined plywood coffin before I realise it is a funeral, and I am hurriedly retreating to the fringes before Munnu can utter a warning shout.

The pale, rectangular box is placed in the middle of a street in front of open garage doors—a mosque, community centre, funeral home?— and the white-clad mourners receive condolences from behind a respectful, though invisible, cordon. No visible outpouring of grief, no observable anguish; there is simply a leaden air of resignation.

With a brusque "Anne. Wait here," Munnu strides over, gives a cursory glance at the open coffin and sympathises with the attendant family.

"This is a young brother of mine," he tells me. "Dead. He is killed with a gun. His elder brother, also political activist, was shot many months ago. His family cannot believe it happens again."

What to say? "I'm sorry," I offer feebly. My mind is spilling over with questions. Why, exactly, have these brothers been murdered? By whom? Is it a gang thing? Does it happen often? Not able to gauge Munnu's feelings, I keep quiet. Like senseless death anywhere, it puts a pall over the day.

"We take tea," Munnu says.

Obviously the restorative properties of said hot beverage are not confined to small islands in the Western world.

"Is why we do not meet my friends," he explains as we find seats in a café—its convenience possibly outweighing its filthiness. "All go to the funeral."

"Should you go too?" I ask, willing to be shipped immediately back to Gulshan. "Do you want to?"

He shakes his head. "No. I give my sympathy. This is enough. I do not know these brothers well. We only share classes in university."

As Munnu shouts for tea, and glasses are quickly slopped down in front of us, he takes notice of our surroundings for the first time. Everywhere—floor, tables, work surfaces, chairs—are slimy with grease. Congealed dishes of pre-cooked fish, mutton, and chicken are lined up on the counter for daily topping up. Great pots of curd, uncovered, their crusted ladles protruding, fight for space with the sticky greying rice. Through a small green hatch, I spy a tiny, black hell hole which is the kitchen and store combined; upended sacks are leaking rice, lentils and beans.

"Anne," Munnu states ruefully. "I break my promise. I say I take you only to clean places. This is very dirty place. Can you forgive me?"

"The tea is fine," I say, gratefully scalding my lips. "Very hot water. No problem." My mind, probably his neither, is not on cleanliness. "I can't imagine a friend of mine being killed like that," I say.

"It is bad. Very bad. Life over in one second."

"For politics?"

"For beliefs," Munnu corrects me. "But this time, I think of his parents. Today they care minimum about beliefs."

We call it a day.

When I return, Hasina is pleased to see me. "Just in time. Anne, you and I make a visit to the beauty parlour. We each receive facial. Come."

My senses reel again.

The salon is only a couple of streets away, but we take a rickshaw anyway.

"Not nice to arrive all hot," justifies Hasina.

The entrance is narrow and up a flight of stairs lined with signs saying: *Private. Beauty Parlour. Strictly Ladies Only.* We enter what might be an empty, doctor's waiting room: no soft lighting or relaxing music, no lingering perfumes or massage oils, just a clinical white box with a grave receptionist in a grubby, white overall and a largely blank appointment book. An adjoining room has four cubicles on each wall with high beds just visible beyond the partially drawn curtains. It looks like a hospital day ward specialising in barium meals or in-grown toenails.

From the cubicle next to mine, Hasina holds up a white, waist-length shroud and tells me I should undress my top half and put on this garment. I struggle to do so, pulling it up under my armpits and tying the cord, although tight as I knot it, it falls down when I let go. Hasina peers around the curtain to see how I am doing.

"Hmm. I think it is made for more bosoms. But do not worry, it is fine when you lie down," she reassures me.

The facial is slow and gentle, the beautician's hands following an automatic routine, her neck and shoulder massage exerting ideal pressure. I recline in blissful silence, the language issue banishing the duty of small talk. Feeling cosseted, I am singularly unprepared for the ice-cold pads that suddenly smother my face and the freezing unguent plastered over them and weighting them down. With an instantaneous ice-cream headache deep in my eye sockets, I involuntarily breathe in hard and nearly choke on a mouthful of cold compress. Just as I am about to shout—pointlessly in English—"Surrender!"—the therapist placidly removes them. Tingling all over, I comfort myself in the knowledge that I must have added a whole new life cycle to my skin and delayed the onset of wrinkles by five years.

"Good, yes?" Hasina, fully dressed again, is glowing. I hope my skin looks half as fresh as hers.

We leave in a hurry, summoned of course by the telephone. Hasina, with Mr Hoque as reluctant chauffeur, has promised to take Parvin, Moshina, and Vouvulay to Wonderland, a children's fun park. They are beside themselves with excitement, dressed in their best, and Hasina has to return to calm them down.

"I am sorry there is no room in the car for you." Hasina frets.

Mr Hoque winks at me. "I wish there was no room for me," he whispers. "Wonderland is a very awful place."

"So grumpy," complains Hasina, overhearing. "He likes it very much," she confides. "He is glad to come."

"She talks rubbish." Snorts Mr Hoque. "Is full of crazy families. Mothers who do not try to keep their children in control. They smile at bad behaviour. Huh."

19

Week 9 - From Tea Gardens to Rubber Plantations

The Sylhet division of Bangladesh is famous for its terraced tea estates, small areas of tropical forest, and seasonal pineapple plantations and orange groves. It has the highest rainfall in the country and generally registers as the coolest division with the lowest humidity. Excellent conditions, Mr Hoque tells me, for tea production.

"Approximately one hundred and fifty tea estates," he continues from the front seat of the car, "generate annually—mostly for export—in excess of thirty million kilograms of tea. Thirty million, heh?"

Sylhet also boasts a couple of gas reserves requiring large numbers of employees, thus ensuring there are more migrants here than anywhere else in the country.

Hasina, Mr Hoque and I, driven by Hanan, head for Srimangal, the location of the postponed SCI Work Camp, to a town described as *the* tea centre of Bangladesh. We make good progress until we reach a small village with what appears to be a large traffic jam. In fact, I should have realised by now that this is the queue for the ferry necessary to cross three inches of water.

"I say we should go via Comilla," says Hasina gloomily.

"No worry, no worry," shouts Mr Hoque. "You worry, your blood pressure goes up. Wait here."

"I tell him Comilla," Hasina repeats to me. "But men, they think the women have no road sense. None. You see the result?"

The temperature, once the engine and therefore the air-conditioning are stationary, rockets even with the windows fully open. Leaning out and fanning herself and instructing me to do likewise, Hasina and I are targets of the street vendors' army who know they are on to a good thing. We refuse short, fat cucumbers, ready peeled and swimming in a barrel of water, but buy a carton of dried roasted nuts and a brace of bananas.

"It is so hot," says Hasina, pulling at the neck of her thick dress. "I expect the cold, so I wear winter clothes. Made from wool."

Anne Hamilton

"Ha! Melting Hasina! Melting Hasina!" Mr Hoque teases, returning to the car with bottles of ice-cold orangeade and singing loudly to the tune of "Waltzing Matilda." He says to me, "See this juice? Made by a huge company called *PRAN*. I sanction large finance for them. A very successful piece of business, if availability and sales are anything to go by."

A young boy comes up and bangs on the bonnet.

"Now, we join the front of the line." Mr Hoque turns to Hanan who, ignoring the clear displeasure of those around us, eases forward. Mr Hoque grins. "A benefit of the private car."

It is obvious that one can locate the Ferry Port director, offer him money, have a number of minions manhandle the vehicle through the crowd, and thus secure an earlier place on the next departing boat. It takes a thick skin to ignore the outcry from fellow travellers who cannot afford said bribe or whose mode of transport is too large to inch in and out of the queue, but Hasina sits sanguine and I copy her. Mr Hoque does not notice, too wrapped up is he in lecturing me on the health benefits of cucumber and vitamin C.

We rattle up the creaking gangplank, park for the twenty-minute crossing, and wait another hour for departure. We have a perfect view of the sturdy railway bridge built by the British during their rule of India, over which the frequent and fast trains to Sylhet travel. Eventually we bump off the other side and enter Sylhet Division.

Still flat as yet, there is none of the promised greenery and rolling hills of my guidebook. At least the roads are predictably unpredictable. More than once, we are bumping onwards, scaling almost-vertical bridges, when the road ends: no warning sign or explanation, just a dead stop with either a dirt track or an expanse of dried grass to cross. Sometimes roadworks are evident, such as reparation of a disintegrating bridge, but often it appears as if the workers wandered off for the afternoon and got a better offer.

"The money runs out," shrugs Mr Hoque. "It is not considered an important route when there are fast trains. Mrs Hoque, where are the bananas? Bananas are very good complete food, high in potassium."

"The train is very good," Hasina agrees. "But what then happens in Srimangal? No car, few buses. Stuck."

So we bump and grind and covet a 4x4 instead of a city-suitable Honda barely visible through the clouds of earthy dust spewing out behind us, always hoping there is no unscheduled rain to render mud or flood.

"In monsoon season the roads are impassable for many days," Hasina explains.

"For weeks," confirms Mr Hoque, pausing in a diatribe on the evils of fried food.

"Do not mind him," Hasina whispers. "Car trips bore him, so he talks of food."

"One time we had a programme in Srimangal and could not return. We took the train and Hanan collected the car later. Many weeks later." Mr Hoque reminds Hanan of the occasion, who in turn, looks as if he would rather drag the car through the mud with a rope between his teeth than be stranded again in Sylhet.

Then, without warning, the flatlands and waterlogged paddy fields merge into large and lush tea plantations. We negotiate a meandering bend, and the landscape alters before our eyes. It is, in contrast to anything else I have seen in Bangladesh, remarkably English in appearance except for the row of palm trees.

"It is a pity that the first garden you see is so poor." Mr Hoque looks dispiritedly out of the window. Indeed, the land is unkempt and water starved with no sprouting greenery.

"It is owned by a Bangladeshi family," Mr Hoque informs. "The Bangladeshis never keep the estates as well as the British companies. Too many politics. Here the family are feuding since the death of the father and nothing is done."

"Such a shame," says Hasina.

"Very bad for business," admonishes Mr Hoque.

The situation improves vastly as we see further estates run, as he describes, by British growers or thriving Bangladeshi businesses. Acres of plants are laid out in neat rows, closely packed, green and rich. The trees offer both shade from the heat of a potentially scorching sun and a partial umbrella throughout the monsoon deluge, and they, too, despite their annual scarcity of leaves, look healthy and well tended. The estates go up into cultivated hills, back as far as my eyes can squint, and the uneven green carpet surrounds us. Where one ends, another begins, and in between them, the villages are flourishing. Still on the main Dhaka-Sylhet road, we pass through Srimangal.

"Look around," says Mr Hoque. "Look carefully. Do you see the railway station? No. The SCI office? No. How could you arrive here alone, heh? You? You make the right decision."

"I might have managed," I reply, self-doubt in every word.

"No matter." Hasina is peacemaker. "We are all here now. All happy now. Yes?"

Anne Hamilton

Patiently waiting at a busy junction just beyond the town, we are met by ex-colleagues of Mr Hoque, two men given the job of directing us to the appropriate guesthouse.

"They expected us after five hours. We are so late," frets Mr Hoque. "It is already 4 p.m. 4 p.m.!"

I want to tell him not to worry, to think of his blood pressure.

"Do not worry," says Hasina. "Think of your blood pressure."

Following their jeep, we drive and drive and drive some more until the roads become bouncing tracks. A gang of *lunghi*-clad labourers, scratching their heads while standing around a collapsed bamboo bridge, enthusiastically indicate that we should veer around it. Luckily, the dry season makes this possible. We don't actually have to take a sheer drop into the riverbed and claw our way up the other side, or pause to count fractured bones and collect missing car parts, but that's the level of discomfort we face.

We swerve off onto private land and are waved, by a dazed and grizzled old man, through a homemade, string security barrier.

"Now we pass through the leper colony," Hasina tells me, struggling to heave herself back upright.

Intrigued, I see small houses, a shop, and a neatly-maintained school and community centre in front of which a large crowd of little boys are playing an impromptu game of cricket. I crane to gawp at real life lepers and can't see even a small one. It is only during a moment of night-time clarity that I realise Hasina said *labour* colony. All the workers live on the tea estates, their homes, food, education and health needs all met by their employer.

"Thirteen hundred workers live on this plantation. Both husband and wife work," says Mr Hoque. "Some produce tea, others work the rubber."

Still we drive. I begin to feel edgy, irritated, and sympathetic to the plight of the second Mrs de Winter on her homecoming to Manderley, the mocking rhododendrons replaced here by tall and thin rubber trees. They stand erect like soldiers on parade, eventually and abruptly yielding once more to the squat tea bushes huddled in terraced hilly rows and flanking a large sign.

"Duncan Brothers Tea Estate and Rubber Plantation," Hasina reads out loud. "We arrive at last. Have an orange."

The land stretches to infinity, silent and lush against the setting orange sun, the peace interrupted only by the crunch of tyres and the soft thud of falling fruit as Hasina discards the last of the skins into the dirt. The path bends to the right where wrought iron gates sweep round a circular drive. A perfect, green lawn and flower gardens surround two white-washed bungalows. A bearer in spotless white makes his regal way down the steps of the main house, opens the car doors and stands respectfully back. Mr Habib, the estate manager, follows in casual contrast. I have joined the cast of *A Passage to India*.

Until the 1970s, the English tea producers sought local labourers—often migrants whose families originated in India—but still exported their managers from Britain. Now, having learned that the Bangladeshis are perfectly capable of running the plantations, the management reins have been handed over.

"The Madam" has her bags carried through shuttered French windows to a large front room leading directly off the porch. High and white walled, a ceiling fan slowly circulates above a large mahogany bed. Simply furnished with embroidered cloths protecting a writing desk and dressing table, there is also a round table and two easy chairs. Three screened windows overlook the gardens, and there is an attached bathroom, cavernous and anciently tiled, with a claw-foot bath and square enamel wash basin. It is an uncanny miniature of Ahsan Munzil, the Pink Palace.

The entire bungalow is furnished similarly, as if a museum exhibit of a military hill station. Instead of a moustached Army man, the smiling Mr Habib officiates an escorted tour of bedrooms, offices, a large sitting room traditionally for the reception of more important visitors, and the dining room with curtains hiding the kitchens. Beside the main bungalow, a smaller rest house is fully self-contained with meals served from the rear kitchen of the main house, again so designed that the bearer is able to move between the two without disturbing the gentlefolk on the verandas. This rest house was originally designed to guarantee the privacy of supervisors and visitors from the English offices who might sail out for a month or more with family or entourage.

Traditionally, when a new manager comes to post, he has nothing to bring beyond his clothes. Furniture and furnishings are passed through the generations. Today, Mr Habib and his wife and five-year-old son (both living in Dhaka during the little boy's first school term) are looked after by a staff of seven: one cook and his two assistants, and four bearers alternating two shifts. The gardeners are extra.

Class distinctions remain very much in evidence and all—management and the highly-professional staff—would be offended if the rules were broken. Here, Mr Habib explains, the bearers pride themselves on total discretion and maximum efficiency. If they cannot pre-empt a guest's request, they have failed in their work. With my guilty instincts to help fetch and carry thwarted, it actually takes about twenty seconds for me to realise that I was born to be *Upstairs* rather than *Downstairs*. I mentally compose my next email to Christine.

On the veranda, varnished cane chairs and small tables are strategically placed for shade and view, and gas lamps are lit as the evening falls. As the crickets emerge, punctuating conversation and drowning the mosquitoes' whine, we sit back and admire the gardens; extravagantly watered, bright with flowers, and a swimming pool discreetly curtained by manicured hedges. Light-footed bearers serve ice-cold drinks, tea, and biscuits from a linen napkin on a silver tray. Later on, as it grows dark over the hills and the heat of the day disperses, a two-tier trolley is wheeled out smoothly and silently.

"How is this done?" Hasina wonders. "Anne, do you see trolleys like this in your country? We try one in London, but it is so noisy."

"We had one just like that in 1978," I say. "It was the rule for all aspiring middle class households."

"And did the wheels squeak and rattle?" Hasina is interested.

"Almost certainly."

She nods. "Here, the wheels would not dare squeak."

The trolley is filled with a selection of alcohol unlikely to disgrace the average Irish hostelry.

"The tea plantations may legally hold a licence for hard liquor," Mr Hoque announces gleefully, "for entertaining the many foreign visitors. Sometimes I take a drink if I wish not to offend the host."

"Sometimes you take many drinks," Hasina scolds.

"Sometimes," says Mr Hoque with dignity. "My host is easily offended."

So crestfallen is Mr Habib on my refusal of a very large gin that I hurriedly agree to a glass of white wine, which he interestingly and thankfully fills to the brim with ice and water.

At nine o'clock, another silent tray appears at my right elbow with a selection of sweets and cake complemented by *samosa* and rare slices of hard cheese. By ten o'clock we are sipping hot consommé from a china tea service and shattering crispy poppadoms over the floor tiles. By eleven o'clock, and despite the lateness of our arrival, we are called to the dining room.

"What, no gong?" I ask sadly.

"Only at lunch times," Mr Habib explains.

There we consume four full courses, and then we are despatched to bed. The bearers have already turned down the beds, closed the shutters, and laid out towels. Once they dim the veranda lights, the silence is absolute save for the cicadas and the occasional cry of a fox.

The Duncan Brothers' Estate comprises a total of fifty-five thousand acres, and Mr Habib offers to show us around the portion adjoining the bungalow. The dense, green fields are empty and silent at present, as plucking of the tea will not begin until the first of the rains come at the beginning of April. The few labourers we see are tending the tiniest plants still beneath bamboo shields or in hot houses. Others pass by on the road to market and children return from morning school. Mr Habib keeps up a running commentary.

"Tea plants can go on producing for one hundred years, but ideally they cease using them at sixty years," Mr Hoque translates.

We pause in front of a board stating that the field beside us was planted in 1978.

"This is medium age," Mr Habib continues his explanation. "Each area is labelled because at all times there are several different ages being worked. Now, in the dry season, any unused area is cleared for new plantings." Up in the hills, he points out more outhouses filled with minuscule plants being individually nurtured, and then replanted into larger pots, moved inside, and finally removed to the fields.

"Such a shame you are not here to see the tea being picked," Hasina commiserates. "They take two leaves and one bud from the top of each plant. Like this. See?" She reaches into some of the partially mature cuttings and starts tweaking at the tiny growths, much to the consternation of Mr Habib who, hopping from one foot to another, is too polite to tell her to stop.

"In fact," he tells me. "We must be commercial, make competition. So we pick three and a half leaves. The tea is not quite so pure, but still it is good."

Sure enough, the tea here is a far cry from that which I've come to expect. It is light and delicate with a pool of leaves at the bottom of the cup. Generally served black and unsugared, it is beyond the pale to slosh into it a load of milk. As I drink the inevitable cup after cup, I ashamedly hanker after the over-sweetened, condensed milk concoctions of the less enlightened villages.

Down at the low-slung factory buildings, workers are preparing for the new season. The machinery is being tested, parts replaced, the warehouse painted. All looks old and unwieldy. The cumbersome machines are rusted and flaking; ancient sits beside new.

"They do not use these things," says Mr Hoque, kicking at something that looks like a combine harvester circa 1948. "Monstrosities shipped from England in the 1950s. Now they are out of date and too expensive to run, but too bothersome to move and destroy. See? No work ethic any more..."

He is well into his stride by the time we finish the tour of the factory, luckily all in English or he may well be lynched by the tired and hard-working labourers who stand back to let us pass.

"Come, Anne," Hasina says. "Have your photograph taken at the entrance." We pose, including the cigarette-smoking Mr Habib, at the gaping mouth of a big barn and directly underneath a sign warning: *Photography Prohibited. No Smoking*.

"Such unlikely rebels." Mr Hoque gives a bark of laughter.

The Lungla rubber plantation, also run by Duncan Brothers, is adjacent to the tea garden. The trees are tall and lean like palms, the bark tied at measured intervals with inverted plastic containers. Daily, before dawn, the bark of each tree is scraped down and the cup placed upright into which the liquid rubber will drip. By noon, workers empty the containers and turn them upside down, thus extracting only the ideal amount of liquid rubber for manufacture.

This factory is much smaller, barely more than a pre-fab bungalow. All around it are squares of rubber stretched in various stages of drying out and solidifying across bamboo canes. The smell of latex permeates the air at every turn. I am quite hazy about how the liquid turns to transparent sheets and actually becomes the solid, black material forming shoe soles and tyres—a selection of both are lying around the grounds—but:

"Enough to know that it does," Hasina says easily.

After lunch—I can hardly bear to think of the one hundred and fifteen courses, beautifully prepared, efficiently served, reluctantly swallowed—and a well-earned rest, we set off to visit Karimpur, a sister tea plantation some forty minutes the other side of the main road, for (wait for it) afternoon tea. The bungalow and grounds are similar to those of our host, but larger and not quite as tasteful or as nicely kept. Rather than a relic of the Raj, this place would fit comfortably into a high-roller estate in Marbella, right down to the bar and barbecue area beside the kidney-shaped swimming pool. Even the bearers lack finesse, and their thought-reading skills are as yet undeveloped. To his obvious chagrin, the estate manager sometimes has to prompt them to action, and one of them even clattered a teaspoon against a china saucer. Mr Habib is far too much of a gentleman to snigger, but he sits up a little straighter, a little prouder. Keeping up with the Jones's is an international sport for sure.

It would be a relief if the servants had either forgotten afternoon tea entirely or at least tipped over the catering-sized platters and ruined the food. Since they do not, we eat. Then we go home for tea, snacks, and soup, which keep us going until dinner, the main performance of the evening. I realise the seriousness of the situation when Hasina speaks up.

"Mr Habib," she begs. "Tomorrow morning, just a very light breakfast. Maybe Cornflakes and toast. Nothing else. Please."

"Anne eats maximum one egg," he promises, shocked but agreeable.

"Anne's about to *lay* an egg," I mutter as I waddle the few yards to my room.

I wonder what the plantation workers will have eaten today?

In the morning, Mr Hoque demonstrates a restlessness that not even a high-powered half hour on his mobile phone can allay.

"How I long for my cup of coffee," he confides in a stage whisper. "Tea is not so interesting on the third day." But then he brightens. "Today, I call some colleagues and arrange we visit the Monipuri."

Historically working as weavers, the Monipuri tribal peoples are apparently of Oriental descent and indigenous to the Sylhet region since the eighteenth century. They are close relations of the population of the Indian state of Manipur.

"They wear traditional Monipuri costume," Hasina explains whilst Mr Hoque makes the kind of arrangements usually only necessary for State visits to unstable countries. "Is different to our *sari* and *lunghi*, a tunic and long loose skirt for women."

"Okay. Okay. So now we go." Mr Hoque rubs his hands together. "We visit traditional tribal village. Then we go into the hills and make a visit to friends of Mr Habib. I tell him so now."

What exactly the polite and quiet Monipuri community, which appears *en masse* to greet us, thinks of two wealthy Dhaka-ites, an enthusiastic foreigner, and a gang of dark-glasses-wearing bank officials who inexplicably turn up in a convoy of shiny black cars, I have no idea. Having formally watched the chief, a roly-poly bearded elder with a goat under his arm, invite us to make ourselves comfortable in the grounds of the village compound, the apparently incurious villagers melt away back to their work. We wander from house to house, each decorated with carved awnings and personalised religious offerings, simple and without colour, so different to the comparable Hindu relics. We pause briefly to watch geometrically-patterned clothes and blankets arising from hand looms, intricate and

Anne Hamilton

deceptively simple contraptions, dwarfing the yards of the makeshift tin cottages.

The visit lasts minutes, nothing to do with the hospitality or otherwise of the Monipuri people, but because of the constant head shaking and glancing at watches of the bank staff. Substitute the mobile phones for a couple of two-way radios, and it would be like being hurried through a presidential walkabout by meticulous *Men In Black* bodyguards. Mr Hoque is in his element. Half a dozen of them accompany us into the hills, the remainder returning to their banks in time for lunch.

As the remote roads narrow and small towns become memories, Mr Habib navigates faultlessly. He tells me that the location of this next tea estate is even more beautiful than his own home.

"I would like very much to be manager here," he says. "I am offered the job, but my wife says no. She finds it is too far from Srimangal. Also, she thinks the bungalows for the manager and his assistant are less good. Maybe so. We are very happy at Lungla."

We climb curving and uneven stone steps to reach the back of the main property and the manager's bungalow that is positioned on top of a hill accessible only by foot.

"Why do they not widen the roads?" puffs Hasina.

"You must do more exercise," Mr Hoque chides. "Take a walk each day. Shopping is not good exercise."

"If I do not shop, you do not eat."

"Ha! So how is it that your dress shopping feeds me?"

"Oh, quiet," says Hasina good-naturedly. "Enjoy the view."

The view encompasses a huge valley saturated with lush vegetation, distant, rugged, and sandy hills peeping through. With the sun beating down, a warm breeze and colour everywhere, one feels, literally and metaphorically, on top of the world. Certainly, the residences are less highly maintained than those of Mr Habib or his colleague in Karimpur, but this only serves to give them character and makes them real homes for the young families who live here. Toys litter the porch and a broody chicken has pride of place on one of the comfortable chairs. We sit around her. The gardens, running round the houses in full circle, are gorgeous. The plants and flowers are rich and plentiful, and the tiered lawns perfectly green and smooth.

"There is a competition between the estates managers to keep the best looking house and grounds," Nanda, our hostess says. "The wives are responsible for making sure the work is done."

"In Britain, we have seen—what is it called, Anne? Ah, I remember, a *Tidy Town* competition." Mr Hoque mystifies the assorted company.

"Here, it is a *Tidy Tea Garden* contest." He roars with laughter at his own wit.

As we follow Nanda in the direction of the second bungalow, she bends her head to Hasina and speaks quietly. Hasina turns to me.

"She is apologising that you will enter her house through the back kitchen. To go to the front door is a long walk around the gardens."

It is a revelation to compare back and front; the grubby, cramped quarters of the servants and the shabby but neat, comfortable, and very large sitting room belonging to the family. Via the smoky stone walls of the kitchen, a heap of garbage, Spartan utensils, vegetables, and pots heaped on the floor are being cleaned, along with his hands, by an elderly man using the corner of his well worn *lunghi*. The kitchen leads to an ante-room draped with laundry in the comfort of which another hen noisily concentrates on laying an egg. Content to sit quietly, I get swallowed up in the cacophony of staccato Bangla.

"Anne? Anne? You are dreaming." Hasina taps my knee. "We talk about you."

"No surprise, hey?" Mr Hoque winks. "Always some person talks about you." He clears his throat. "Anne, I am asked to make you a suggestion." He pauses. "Would you like to be the school teacher here?"

I presume this is a prelude to a joke and am already smiling when it dawns on me that they—tea estate folk, bank officials various, and Hasina—are serious. The entire company are nodding approvingly, waiting for me react favourably to such an honour. But...*school teacher*?

It does make a nice change from offers of marriage.

Perhaps Hasina has actually got me and Christine muddled up, and that is why the family has allowed me to stay so long with them?

Hasina shouts at Mr Hoque, "She does not understand. I tell you she would not understand. I must explain."

"What to explain?" Mr Hoque rallies. "She is not stupid. She knows exactly what a school teacher is. So, Anne?"

Hasina gives Nanda and me that universal eyes-to-heaven look that says "Men!" and ignores her husband. "There is small primary school near here," she tells me. "For children of the estate managers and assistants. Now, they are thirty children of ages five to ten. The children come each day to—"

"Yes. Yes. Okay," Mr Hoque interrupts the leisurely description. "I continue. There is no permanent teacher. The education department can find nobody willing to live in a remote place. So the wives of the estate managers, who have been to college, offer basic education."

Anne Hamilton

"Then we must send our children to Dhaka to secondary school," Nanda breaks in.

"So, the mothers and fathers would like a proper teacher. One who teaches through English medium. This is required for the children to progress. They feel you would be a good person."

"You have a house, your own bearers, a cook and gardener. A driver to take you to the school. You get holidays often. Adequate salary." Mr Hoque gets down to the practicalities.

"We look after you when you come to Dhaka. It would be so good. One year only to start." Hasina is at her most persuasive.

Nanda hands me a photograph of the school. Smudged and out of focus, it still manages to look like an advertisement for a new life in South East Asia, of a soft, pink building gleaming in the sun with scrubbed steps broadening onto a veranda upon which a dozen beaming school children are gathered in uniforms of grey and blue. Two luxurious flower baskets hang from the windows, and a small garden stretches out in front. I nearly ask when I can start. I imagine a peaceful, worthy life in the sun, imparting knowledge and wisdom to young minds...and then I think of the language barrier, the monsoons, the isolation, oh and the slight impediments of a life elsewhere, my husband, and not being a teacher. I try to explain all of this, balancing enthusiasm and gratitude—both genuine—with realism. Hasina is surprised at my adamant refusal.

"You have a good education, degrees. You work with children. Other qualifications are not essential."

"You can learn Bengali in Dhaka," shrugs Mr Hoque. "Three months."

"Christine. Why not ask Christine? She'd be good," I babble. "She's a proper teacher and she wants to work overseas."

I am off the hook. I offer to swap letters with the school children, send them photographs of Ireland and post the odd gift: leprechaun egg cups, shamrock fridge magnets and useful items like that. Hasina thinks she will email Christine and suggest the scheme to her.

"So then, Anne. It is time to leave Sylhet," Hasina commiserates. Her eyes glint. "This time we go home via Comilla. No, I insist. We go to Comilla."

Mr Hoque closes his mouth, his objection dying on his lips.

The border town of Comilla skirts a bypass linking Dhaka and Chittagong. Travelling this way back to the capital probably doubles the journey in terms of kilometres, but is by far a better road (that is, most of it exists) and negates the need for a ferry crossing.

"Also it is the home of the Bangladesh Rice Research Institute. A great shame to miss that," Hasina says enthusiastically.

Mr Hoque's back tenses in horror.

"But we have missed it," cries Hasina in dismay. "It is so dark, we see nothing."

"Oh, bother," I say politely.

Mr Hoque relaxes.

"There is also important military cantonment," she adds. "Off limits to foreigners." (Of course.) "And the remains of a Buddhist temple. Very old and very well preserved. We can visit this?" Hasina sounds like a good hostess who, even though her feet really hurt, is determined to do one more trip around Harvey Nicks rather than be accused of failing in her duty.

"Well, it would be interesting, but as it's getting late..." I hesitate.

Hasina seizes the excuse. "This is true. So maybe..."

"So maybe we stop in a café for Coca-Cola, yes?" Mr Hoque chips in before Hasina can suggest anything else.

In her relief, Hasina describes the temple at great length. "Now you know as much as if you had seen it."

If Mr Hoque was less of a gentleman and did not adore his wife so much, he would undoubtedly be shouting something along the lines of: "Woman, would you bloody well *shut up*? You're doing my head in!"

We pause to refuel and, what feels like twenty hours later, join the convoy of trucks waiting to enter Dhaka City. Finally, in the middle of the night, we arrive back in Gulshan.

"Did you enjoy your trip?" Mr Hoque asks as we wait for the lift up to the apartment.

"I loved it," I tell him. "Thank you so, so much for taking me."

"Yes," he nods. "Sylhet is like no other place. Beautiful. Peaceful. I can only stay two or three days. The silence worries me. My blood pressure goes up."

20
Week 10 - Valentine's Day Surprise

Once back in Dhaka, I spend a few days in cosy domesticity with Hasina. Between shopping trips and meeting her and Mitali's friends, I manage the occasional visit to the SCI office and think about what I might do next. About a week after our return from Srimangal, everything takes off again. The day in question begins frustratingly and ends, or rather doesn't end at all, but merges on a crazy note into the next.

Hasina is overseeing the house girls' packing. The three of them, plus two more who work for Mitali and four others placed with an assortment of Hasina's siblings, are all leaving tomorrow for their annual six weeks' visit home. Hasina is hiring a microbus plus driver, and she and two of her sisters are chaperoning the girls to Rangpur, some six or seven hours north of Dhaka.

Parvin, one eye on a selection of bubbling cooking pots, is sweating behind a huge pile of dough. Before she can join the others giggling, chasing each other, and shrieking over their packing, she has to fill the deep freeze with enough meals to last out her absence. As the oldest and the cook, it is Parvin who decides the duration of the holidays: three, four, five weeks—Hasina is accommodating—and from the mutinous look on the girl's face, it could be a long while.

I am still deciding whether to accompany them or whether to join a forthcoming *Parjatan* (Bangladesh Tourist Board) trip to the Sunderbans, when—

"Anne. Your telephone call. It is Munnu."

"Anne. I hope you are well," he says formally. "I like to invite you on a programme to Rangmati to my young brother, Rana. Is a very beautiful place. My favourite. Also, sea beach at Cox's Bazaar. We leave tonight. I like you to come very much."

What's the overused adage about three buses arriving at once? Moderation is not my strong point. I want everything, preferably as soon as I have thought of it. I want to go to the Sunderbans *and*

Rangmati *and* Rangpur. After all, I can justify my greed. Bangladesh is not the Isle of Man. I will not be able to hop over on a whim on a wet weekend and see the place again.

Hasina overhears my dilemma. "You invite Munnu here for lunch," she announces. "I tell the guards to send him up. I like to meet him. Maybe you go to Rangmati instead of Sunderbans and Rangpur." She alters tack. "Now, you wear nice dress to have your first guest here? Special occasion. I change also."

Such a social whirl. I rush to comb my hair and put on my best dress. Parvin helps me clasp Bely's second-best gold chain, choker style, around my neck, and I am ready, if a little over-dressed, for lunch.

Munnu is nervous, having not expected this royal audience. He also seems a little surprised by my glamorous (for me anyway) get up. He rises admirably to the occasion, easily bridging the social gap by being polite and charming to Hasina and friendly to the maids who all but drool over him. I stand demurely in the background, the embodiment of a blushing maiden whose gentleman caller is being vetted by her elders. Hasina is evidently satisfied that Munnu's intentions are honourable because she beckons Parvin to serve chicken and lots of rice, and then retires gracefully to her room. Munnu has no need to champion his cause. After this charade, I owe it to him to go to Rangmati, Chittagong, and Cox's Bazaar.

"I am very happy," Munnu says. "It gives maximum pleasure that you accompany me. My brother Rana likes to see you also."

"Two conditions," I say firmly, intent on there being none of the Rakim-type misunderstandings. He nods enthusiastically. "We go by train overnight—"

"Okay. There are sleeper trains. What else?"

"The second condition is that *there are no conditions,*" I say. The drama is lost on him.

"Anne? I do not understand. How can a condition be not...?"

"What I mean is," I glance around, lower my voice. "I am not going to take off my clothes. Nobody, not Rana, not you, will be...*seeing* me."

Munnu chokes on a chicken bone. After I have performed the Heimlich Manoeuvre and salvaged the guilty piece of meat from Hasina's favourite pot plant, he protests his good character.

"Of course I understand. Why do you think I might ask this? I enjoy your friendship. Is all. Who else makes you think this way? Is it Rakim? If so, I kill—"

"And Bachchu?" I interrupt. "He agrees to your travelling with me?"

"He gives permission. I tell him we are going to Rana's family." Munnu calms down, watches closely my reaction to this three-quarters-truth, but if his conscience is clear, so is mine.

"Good," I say. "Then I will tell Hasina."

She must have been hovering. She returns with haste and proceeds to grill Munnu about the travel arrangements. Satisfied, she then offers him a typed list of instructions concerning how often I need to be fed, what time I go to bed, and that I must be encouraged to wear warm clothes in windy areas.

"Sorry," I whisper, but loving Hasina for it all the same. "I know you were not expecting this."

"Is okay. She is protecting you, this is all. This is good." He pauses. "Anne. I tell you again. I do not expect you to put off your clothes. We do not mention it again."

As I open my mouth to agree, a thought seems to occur to him. "Unless," he goes on speculatively, "you change your mind. If ever you wish to put off your clothes, then you will tell me immediately. I go now to make the programme."

I am still grinning, mostly amused and only slightly apprehensive, as I turn back to Hasina.

"Very nice boy," she concludes as the door closes behind him. "I think he will take good care of you. In Bengali, he promises me this."

"Me also." I smile my best *Mona Lisa* smile.

Munnu returns late evening. We are wandering down the road to hail an auto rickshaw when he clears his throat.

"Many Happy Returns for Valentine's Day. I forget this earlier. I have bad news," he says in one breath. I panic.

"You have to go home instead? Rangmati is closed to tourists? SCI are cross that I have disrupted their programme and my visa is cancelled. What?"

"None of those things, but you might be unhappy. I go to the train station, and I wait for two hours, but there is no sleeping berth tonight."

"That's okay." I wouldn't have expected anything else.

"This is not the bad news. There are no first class seats and no *sulob*—the second class—either. Also nothing in third class."

This last is a relief anyway. Picture the London Underground between King Cross and Leicester Square on a Friday evening, add people hanging out of the doors and sitting on the roofs of the trains, and you have some idea of this type of travel. It is very cheap.

"I suppose there are buses?"

"Not air-conditioned buses," Munnu says. "The problem is Eid. So many people travel home at this time of year."

"And?"

"I have bought for us the last two seats on a non a/c bus direct to Rangmati. We depart 11.30 p.m. and arrive 8.30 a.m. tomorrow. Only Tk 200."

Nine hours—at a conservative estimate—on a bus. "Does it stop on the way at all?" I ask.

"I check this for you," Munnu says proudly. "I know you worry about toilets. Yes, it stops at four hours. The man said that most do. Definitely," he assures me.

Possibly. Maybe. Am I so transparent that my bladder concerns are common knowledge? And how liberated of us to be discussing such things in mixed company. Chapa and Asha would be horrified.

"Is it safe? What about hijackings? Crashes?" I think back over newspaper reports from the previous few days: frequent hold-ups on night buses, passengers robbed, drivers falling asleep and careering into trucks rushing to beat the curfew into Dhaka city.

"I think it is safe. I take good care of you."

I know he means this, and I open my mouth to thank him when he continues conversationally: "Many weeks ago I ride a city bus that was hijacked. Three robbers had knives. They threaten the driver and ask for money."

"And? What happened? Were you hurt?"

"No. One passenger was a friend of the robbers. So they get off our bus and go to hijack another."

I don't know whether to laugh, cry, or refuse to take another step. It doesn't really occur to me *not* to travel. Having been to so many different places, including the trip to Srimangal in a large, air-conditioned car, I understand that no cross-country journey is going to be physically comfortable or on time. But it will be endurable, and the end (so far) justifies the means. I suppose it might as well be done as cheaply as possible.

"Come on then." I am resigned. "But if I get robbed or murdered, *you* will have to explain to Hasina."

At the tiny, back-street bus depot, we sit in a heaving waiting-room that gradually empties as various buses in declining states of roadworthiness pull up at the door. Munnu vanishes into the market to buy bananas and oranges, and I sit quietly, eyes decorously down-turned, and entertain the looks of other passengers. Soon I am the only person left, and I have a sinking feeling...

Munnu comes rushing in, hurls a couple of paper bags and a bottle of Seven-Up in my general direction, yells at somebody behind a desk, they yell back, and the next thing I know I am being hustled into the back of a baby taxi to chase the bus we have just missed.

"We catch it in Motijheel. The next stop. The only stop," Munnu roars above the sound of the engine.

Our driver has waited a lifetime for this challenge. Theme park customers would pay folding money for this kind of ride! With a maniacal chuckle, he puts his foot to the floor, screeches around corners, bounces over craters in the road, takes a moment to wave cheerfully at irate traffic police—who are drawing attention to the startled family of five and their goats and cattle who have been all but mown down—and narrowly avoids (I think) a blind beggar. I have one hand clinging to my bag and scarf; the other digs into Munnu's arm. My feet are clamped onto the luggage piled in front of me, and I'm straining to find out what exactly is happening. "Maybe this is a sign that we shouldn't travel tonight," I bellow into Munnu's ear.

"It is the fault of the bus people." Munnu leans forward, unnecessarily urging the driver onward. The driver takes this as an invitation to actively seek out victims.

"Can we wait and go tomorrow? Please?" I beg.

"We have tickets. Your money is wasted then."

"Ah, yes." I sigh. That extortionate four dollars. "I'll sacrifice it, put it down to experience, miss breakfast." My throat is getting sore with shouting. "Let's find a hotel instead."

Munnu jerks his head to look at me. I can see him waver. Perhaps I would, in the chaos, let him share the hotel room and thus make him one up on Rakim...But no, honour overcomes desire. He says we will get this bus and arrive in Rangmati at 8.30 a.m., and that we will bloody well do.

Up ahead a bus draws into a dark side street. Our driver takes his hands from the wheel to give a jubilant clap and, steering with his knees, aims for the back of it. Then he groans: right company, wrong bus. The driver and passengers gladly point in the correct direction, only none of them can agree as to which way this is. The auto rickshaw turns full circle, lurches dangerously, rights itself, and continues tearing through the night. Honking madly for it to pull over, the rickshaw finally reaches the trundling Rangmati bus.

Leisurely, Munnu pays the baby taxi driver, argues over the fare, and has to go into a small shop for change. He and the bus assistant have a full and frank discussion regarding the allocation of blame, shake hands like best friends, and usher me aboard. At which point the paper bag containing the fruit finally gives way in my hands and oranges tumble artistically—and I'm sure, in slow motion—down the steps. The bus assistant clutches his head in horror, and despite my hysterical pleas, he evacuates the bus of all able-bodied men in a dramatic rescue attempt.

"Anne. You sit," Munnu commands.

I scuttle down the aisle avoiding all eye contact, and slink into a seat near the back. Eventually, Munnu slides in beside me and translates for the earnest bus assistant who hands me an illegal plastic bag (Plastic bags are supposedly banned in Bangladesh because of the pollutants. Instead, string or paper bags are usually provided). "He says he is sorry, but one orange lodges underneath the wheel of the bus. The driver almost certainly must squash it."

I accept the parcel with all the dignity I can muster, offer him two of the slightly-worse-for-wear fruits as a miserly reward, and tuck the remainder carefully under my seat. Beaming, the driver retreats to the front of the bus.

"Did he really say that?" I ask Munnu.

"Yes. He is afraid you are cross."

"*He* is afraid that *I* am cross? After I delayed the bus for a few oranges?"

"Oranges are expensive. Especially for unskilled workers." Munnu reminds me. "He does not like that you lose them."

I wish I could buy him a truckload of the things.

"Smile," says Munnu. "Accept you are rich white girl. Be happy we have made the bus. Anne." He looks around. "I fear this is not a very good bus."

This dinosaur might once have been a bright, shiny, passenger-worthy vehicle with windows that shut and seats with springs. At the end of its life, it looks fit to be buried in the scrap yard to become a nesting place for rodents and feral cats. Still, after a few half-hearted coughs, the engine croaks back into existence, and we rattle slowly down the road, and if the force and resonance of the hooter indicate viability, this bus is up for an excursion to the moon, let alone a nine-hour domestic journey.

The journey passes remarkably quickly. In the early hours we stop at a hotel for toilets and burgers. We pause twice more to collect early-edition newspapers and half a dozen crates of squawking hens. Shortly after dawn, we enter the borders of the Hill Tracts. I force my drooping eyelids open, wipe the dribble from Munnu's shirt—I appear to have inelegantly dozed on his shoulder—and read a few pages of my guidebook. I nudge him awake.

Anne Hamilton

"It says here that foreigners might need permission to enter," I announce cheerfully. "Maybe I'll be put on the next bus back to Dhaka."

"You get signed in at the checkpoint," Munnu replies, rubbing his arm and making a face. "There is no problem unless there has been a kidnapping or hijack recently. Anne? Are you sore from the bus? My shoulder pains me very much, like a sack of rice has crushed it."

Chittagong District is in the southeast of the country bordering India and Myanmar, and as the "Hill Tracts" name suggests, it is a hilly, mountainous area that merges into the coast, eventually becoming the seaside resort of Cox's Bazaar. Unresolved difficulties between the government—none in particular, just whichever party happens to be in power at any one time—and tribal rebels of the dense and remote Hill Tracts make areas like Rangmati and neighbouring Banderban politically volatile and potentially unsafe for visitors. Despite a peace settlement in the late nineties that included reduced travel restrictions, there remain periodic kidnappings of both Westerners and prominent, wealthy Bangladeshis. The rebels have a single criterion: fair game is anyone likely to make international news, thus highlighting the cause and demonstrating the (alleged) corruption of the political system. Attacks are random, treatment of hostages erratic.

Fundamentally, as Munnu points out, it is an example of how guerrilla warfare between (in this case, Bangladeshi) army and certain indigenous tribes (in this case, the Chakma) has officially ended, but the "cause" has been taken up by splinter groups who have apparently lost sight of what the original fight was for and are now just fighting.

It's impossible to imagine any of this as we approach Rangmati at dawn. The bus slows down at a bamboo checkpoint incongruous with its backdrop of striking mountains and ripple-free lake. The red and white barrier is raised, and the winding road ahead looks peaceful. There are two, maybe three men in view, strolling, smoking, and relaxed, their *lunghi's* topped with bright sweaters. My fellow passengers, aware that a bus containing a foreigner is akin to the latest Hindi movie in the entertainment stakes, are shaking each other into wakefulness and sitting up straight. A soldier, not youthful (In fact he would fit unobtrusively into Captain Mainwearing's Home Guard) but correctly dressed and wielding a large gun, boards the bus, and Munnu and I are called to the front.

"Bring your passport," Munnu tells me.

I fish out a bedraggled photocopy and stumble forward. Three minutes later, I am standing on the roadside, and Munnu is passing our belongings out of the open window. Please God, don't let me drop the oranges again. Everyone else leans out shouting comments of encouragement or commiseration.

The foreigner has been denied entry to Rangmati.

21
Week 11 - Worried, of Rangmati

I stand with Munnu, drooping and dejected, carrying our homes in two carrier bags, and watching the bus chug slowly through the checkpoint and disappear around the bend without us. Seconds later, the back end of the bus reappears; faces are pressed at the window, arms are waving, and the bus driver's assistant is leaning out of the door.

"The driver reverses so that the passengers take a final look at you," notes Munnu.

Then there is silence.

Escorted across the road by the Army officer, I am ushered into the bamboo sentry box and invited to sit down and "shelter from the cold." Well, it probably is chilly to those who do not know the joys of Ireland in February. Another man, even older than his colleague, with a bushy beard, woolly jumper, and gingham *lunghi*, chatters away to Munnu in rapid Bangla with occasional reference to me.

"Foreigners take permission from the Ministry. Takes five to seven days. Or entry refused and foreigner turns back," the Army officer intones without breath and in a monotone (E-flat, I fancy). But he smiles to indicate that it is nothing personal.

The only place to which I wish to be granted entry at this moment is the lavatory. I make urgent faces at Munnu who admirably grasps the situation and mutters discreetly to the soldier.

When I emerge, I am greeted by a third person dressed in striped *lunghi* and brown leather jacket. He and Munnu are enjoying a comradely cigarette outside the sentry box. It is evident, even to the foreigner, that they are hatching a deal. After this man—later when in uniform, transpires to be Mr Chief Army Officer (the older men are his assistants)—has pored over my photocopied passport and attached driving licence, puzzled over the vaccination certificate and copies of travellers' cheques. He folds his hands and speaks.

Munnu translates that he (striped *lunghi* and leather jacket soldier) *might* grant me permission to enter the Hill Tracts for the weekend, but it is not strictly his decision and will certainly depend on the organising of a microbus as the public bus is not secure, which will incur a fee, and will involve *much* administrative work and *very expensive* documentation.

"You mean, he's saying 'pay me enough, and I'll overlook the problem'?" I ask cynically but quietly. This soldier has a very large gun.

"Ye-es," says Munnu.

"What?" I prompt him.

The simple reason for the soldier's reluctance to let me enter Rangmati, he describes with obvious relish, and Munnu—I know him well enough by now—picks over and selectively interprets for me. Unfortunately, the soldier is unaware of this nicety and punctuates Munnu's narrative with ghoulish gurgles and throat-cutting antics.

"He says that yesterday there was a kidnapping. Ten Bengali men are taken from their microbus. Two are found unharmed. The others are mostly still missing."

"Mostly?"

"One is dead…" Observing the soldier's garrotting motions, there is no need to ask how death occurred. "…and one injured."

"Injured how?"

Munnu, pained at my insistence, finally yields. "His fingers and toes are no more attached to him," he admits delicately.

Chittagong suddenly looks very inviting, so inviting I think we should go straight there. I have an abrupt urge for a large, bustling city with a pleasant waterfront and access to a tropical beach. A place that is safely in the opposite direction and full of people who will want to stare at me, perhaps even stroke my hair and ask me to marry them. What they will not want are my body parts as souvenirs.

I open my mouth to demand immediate expatriation to civilisation, and stop. The tableau of rolling hills, winding roads, the dazzle of the sun turning the ripples in the water silver, that early morning slant of light promising a glorious day, is the most perfect image I have ever seen.

Naively, I refuse to believe that anything bad will happen to me here.

Stubbornly, I refuse to waste the opportunity to drink in more of this Nirvana.

Politically, I refuse to give in to terrorist threat.

And, fatalistically, I refuse to give up on my mantra: *regret the things you do, not the things you don't do.*

"When is the next bus back?" I counter.

"Ten-thirty. Tonight. Local bus. Change for Chittagong."

"And you are sure that Rangmati is beautiful? So beautiful that it would be a mortal sin to miss it?"

"I promise." Munnu nods. "It is worth inconvenience."

"Worth being the last place on earth I ever see? Worth looking at with a rebel's gun pointing at my head? Worth the world being denied my travel diary serialised on *Women's Hour*?...Don't answer any of that."

"So if the guard grants permission, we go into Rangmati?" Munnu confirms. "You are sure?"

I have fleeting visions of Hasina's fury should anything untoward happen, how the already-overwrought Bely might be tipped into a nervous breakdown if her stunning clothes are filched by a kidnappers moll, how my prized return-business-class-flight ticket will be wasted and the upgrade probably given to an unappreciative nun. I take a deep breath.

"Yes, I'm sure."

Apparently surprised that we are not fleeing screaming, the soldier concentrates on keeping his paperwork fully up to date just in case I am mutilated, murdered, or missing and my litigious relatives sue him for malpractice.

Munnu is told to make himself scarce whilst the soldier interrogates me. I follow him into his little booth trusting that Munnu would not have been so quick to scarper however great his need for a cigarette, or would have at least mentioned it if I am expected to offer sexual favours or some other payment in kind for my visitor's permit. Quite honestly though, that might be the easiest option. I do not know how else we are going to communicate. The soldier holds out his hand to shake mine.

"Me *nam* Shoehorn," he introduces himself formally. "You, Miss Ann-ie."

This is shaping up to be on par with meeting Shahardot at the airport. I wait patiently, but the quiz does not go as expected.

"Man. Munnu." He jerks his head backwards. "Is friend?"

"Yes. He is my friend. Another volunteer with SCI." I know I am wasting my breath but cannot help myself. "We met in Rajoir Work Camp."

"Is friend?" the soldier persists.

"Yes. So are his brothers and his sister. I met all of his family."

"Family? Hmm."

I wait for him to gather his thoughts.

"Man. Munnu. You choose him?"

"What?"

"Man. Munnu. You choose him?" Sgt Shoehorn insists.

"Yes. I choose him as friend," I say but the answer is not the one sought.

"You *choose* him?" He looks intently at me.

I give up. "*Ami bhuchi na,*" I say. "*Bhuchi na.* Don't understand."

The soldier sits back, screws up his eyes and breathes heavily. He emits an air of brutal constipation. Suddenly he is inspired.

"Man. Munnu. Husband. You *Mrs* Ann-ie?"

"No," I say. "Not husband. Friend. Me, husband in Ireland."

"Huh?"

Somewhere, on the edge of the twilight zone, I begin to see what he is getting at. But I still haven't a clue how to explain that I certainly have a living, breathing husband, but it just doesn't happen to be the man with whom I am travelling. Alone. In a Muslim country. Maybe, it occurs to me, I should not try to explain. Perhaps Munnu has already said that he and I *are* married and this is a test at which I am dismally failing. Taking a speedy glance around the hut to guarantee that the soldier is not within means of shooting me for insubordination (or immorality), I stand up and yell for Munnu to come back.

The soldier obviously feels he has done his tortuous duty. He joins in my shout, calls to a junior, lights a cigarette, and laughs.

"*Nashka.* Breakfast. You share," he instructs me jovially. "No talk more."

Whilst I am being forced to lower my head into a saucepan of hotchpotch so hot that both my mouth and my fingers are burning, Munnu and the soldier, now best-buddies, all-men-together, joshing like locker-room-lads, laugh over any misunderstandings. I feel I should apologise for not having grasped the rules of the game.

"He must make sure that you know me well," Munnu confirms. "That I am not kidnapper who already kidnaps you."

It's a novel point but fair enough. "What about the marriage bit?"

"Anne. If you are my wife, and then responsibility for you is to me."

"Is mine," I correct automatically.

"Yes. Is mine. So you sign that we are married. We pay Tk 500 fee. We go to Rangmati. Easy."

And, I think, finally cottoning on, if there is a problem, the military bears no liability because they have officially handed me over to the care and protection of my "husband."

Anne Hamilton

"To think I was under the impression that Sgt Shoehorn is concerned for my safety and my moral welfare."

So, adrift in a foreign country, I lie to a bona fide officer of the national Armed Forces, fraudulently sign an incomprehensible yet official (possibly) piece of paper that probably makes me Mrs Munnu ("Quick, how do you spell your proper name?" I mutter since most Bangladeshi's are called by a nickname) under Muslim law, and hand over a paltry bribe. I disclose the year of my birth and share Sgt Shoehorns joy that we are the same age. I swap autographs with him and agree that Ireland is England under another name. There is one slightly dodgy moment when my new best soldier friend lowers his voice and asks if it is possible for me to procure UK visas for unattached, loving Bangladeshi men, preferably by marrying them, himself for example. He really, really wants to go to England with a beautiful blonde Bengali wife. Sadly, I point out that I would love to help him, but as he now knows, (tapping the signed document) I am already married. Married twice in fact: once in a country he does not believe exists and secondly, as of about three minutes ago, to the smirking Munnu.

Our microbus arrives exactly as I am congratulating myself for having been on the outskirts of Rangmati for one hour without being shot by either terrorist or army personnel, though it is not before word of mouth has brought car, truck, and busloads—including the bus I was thrown off, *with* the same passengers aboard (who greet me proprietarily)—of locals down to the checkpoint to get a first-hand look at a live foreigner as opposed to all the ones who have all been abducted and subsequently bumped off.

One glance at the somnambulistic driver of the bubble-shaped microbus and his faithful assistant does not reassure me of their combined capacity to protect me from even half-hearted tribal rebels who are weary of the cause and considering voluntary retirement. What it does suggest is that one or the other, probably both, are related to Sgt Shoehorn and are on a nice little earner.

As a parting shot, the soldier lets slip that our trip will entail stopping at a second checkpoint over which he has no jurisdiction, sorry. There may be a further financial charge, sorry.

"Thank you, and have a nice day," he enunciates clearly.

Mentally, I begin to calculate how many Tk 500 administration fees I can afford before we become *Down and Out in Rangmati*.

We ride up a deserted mountain road. Framed with leafy, luxuriant trees, these occasionally part to expose a sickeningly steep ravine, the valley thick with forest and nigh-on impenetrable, given the low-slung bamboo bridges which swing across the canopy. High in the hills above us, still dense and green, I think I see a wisp of curling smoke, a glint of sunbeams on water, the illusion of movement, but when I turn my head, it is gone. On sporadic ridges sit clusters of wooden cabins, tin houses, and corrugated sheds. It is a fantasy land, a flawless hiding place, a perfect locale for vicious and precise snipers. I sit well back from the window and pull my *dupatta* peasant-like over my head and across my mouth.

We would have roared straight through the next security point were it not for the armed guard stepping bravely into the road from his nondescript bus shelter furnished with one bench and a poster exhorting visitors to Visit The Splendids That Is Rangmati Area.

"Oh, how I'm trying." I sigh.

No banter here, no deals, no chatter, no sense of comradeship. This soldier is solemn and unsmiling. Munnu takes stock.

"Anne. Stay quiet. Say nothing. Look like you understand nothing."

"Tricky. But I'll try."

The man listens sceptically to Munnu's story, makes about five unexplained phone calls each lasting ten seconds, insists that Munnu call another number and explain himself, and all the while his eyes bore achingly to a point in the middle of my forehead. If this man is shown a photograph of me in twenty years time after I have had a sex change and he is registered blind, I have no doubts whatsoever that he will recognise me without delay.

Just as I am about to make a false confession to the guard's choice of crime, suffer a bout of Tourette's Syndrome and scream with tension, we are dismissed. Munnu shoves me back into the pope-mobile.

"You can stay only today and must leave by sunset. You must be with me every second of the day. I must give them the name and address of my young brother, Rana. He tells me a list of places forbidden for you. You must not take photographs. You must do nothing that makes people look at you."

"How can I cease to be?" I snap with nerves. "What a shame I didn't know earlier. I could have packed my invisibility cloak. Oh, and I hope the lavatories are big around here."

"Anne? I do not understand."

"To fit both of us inside if you're coming everywhere with me."

Munnu begins to laugh. Unwillingly, but ashamed of my outburst, I join in.

"You are very funny-type girl. Very exceptional but very funny also," he says happily.

Anne Hamilton

"You're not the worst either," I respond. It is a peculiarly Irish compliment, but I amend it with the more traditional, "You're a decent enough bloke yourself," and inadvertently dig a bigger hole for myself. A lot of convoluted explanation later, Munnu is pleased with his new take on colloquial Anglo-Irish language.

"I am not the worst. I am a decent enough bloke," he repeats. "Anne. I am pleased to learn. When you hear bad English grammar and wrong words, please correct me."

"Okay," I agree dubiously. Vocabulary is one thing, but his grammatical mistakes could jump up and slap me in the face, and I probably wouldn't recognise them.

It is barely ten o'clock in the morning. I force myself to relax and enjoy the extraordinary terrain. All around me is yet another facet of the Bangladesh landscape. Verdant and hilly as Sylhet, this place is also tropical in the extreme. Rangmati is the backdrop to Kaptai Lake, a shimmering dew pond picturesque right down to the obligatory sailboats in the distance. Designed in the 1960s as a hill-station town, it is clean and well maintained. The population statistics is well below the national average which means that the inevitable slums are confined to certain areas rather than spreading over the entire district.

Like the Monipuri settled in Srimangal, Rangmati is the home of the Chakma peoples, notorious, Munnu tells me gleefully, for their tradition of brewing a stronger-than-methylated spirits-brand of almost-pure alcohol.

"I do not remember the name," he admits, but assures me his friend Rana will have a healthy consignment under the floorboards.

"It sounds like puchin," I say. "That's a really potent Irish home-brew."

Munnu dismisses this. "This drink is puchin with attitude. It kicks ass," he boasts, relishing this carefully memorised choice phrase.

"Tell me what there is to see here." I change the subject, even though the current surroundings alone are sufficient for any visitor.

"This is perfect place to take a holiday," Munnu says, switching into tour guide mode. "You can take a boat tour on Lake Kaptai and see tribal villages. There is a special Tribal Institute museum. Rainforest and banana plantation. Also many Buddhist Temples."

"And," I ask. "How many of them am I allowed to see? Two places? One of them?"

There is an embarrassed silence before Munnu breaks the news. "None of them," he admits, and then adds conspiratorially, "But my young brother Rana helps us. We sneak out and take minimum risk."

"I don't know whether that makes me feel better or worse."

If ever I needed proof that fear breeds paranoia, I find it in Rangmati. Suddenly, all the stares, the half-smiles, the half-formed questions, the small crowds forming around me, are no longer benign. I keep my head down, treat passers-by with inward suspicion, and despise my defensive instinct for self-preservation. It does not spoil the day, but it takes the ease out of it. Yet somewhere deep down, a tiny, tiny part of me does respond to the thrill because, with my talent for fictionalised living, all of this is going to make a great story one day. Oh, as long as I can avoid getting kidnapped, of course.

After copping us for a full tank of petrol and an extortionate donation for their "best protection," the microbus driver and his sidekick drop us at a baby taxi rank situated in the golden curve of a natural harbour. Unusually, there are no scooters waiting for fares.

"They are always busy," Munnu explains. "Look around. Because there are no rickshaws. Rangmati is very much too hilly. Anne. You wait. I find baby taxi for us on the street."

I brace myself like the proverbial sitting duck. If any rebel faction has followed us from the border aiming to take a pot shot, they will never have a better opportunity than now. Where I stand alone on the pavement, "shining" as Munnu would say, they could use me for target practice. There is not—and read this carefully because it is the only time I will ever say it—a single other person in sight.

"Why did you take so long?" I growl, as Munnu helps me into the hired baby taxi fifteen minutes later.

"You were afraid? But you are safe." He gazes around and echoes my thoughts. "There is nobody else here."

"Exactly. I was waiting to be shot."

He manages not to laugh out loud. "You do not get shot." He is supremely confident, explains tribal rebel etiquette to me. "First they kidnap you only. They cannot make headline news and bargains if you are already dead. Only later, if they are upset, they shoot you."

This provides a certain amount of cold comfort.

"We now go to Rana's house. You feel very safe there. His family like foreigners." Munnu uses his most soothing voice. "Anne. Can I smoke?"

I nod mechanically as something else occurs to me. "Is Rana expecting us? Does his family know we are coming?"

Munnu takes a long drag on his cigarette and shrugs. "Maybe. Last time we meet in Dhaka I tell him I visit soon. He says to come any time and bring my friends."

"That's all right then," I say, hoping to settle into a well-earned and satisfying coma.

22
Underhand Underground

Word that we are in town has preceded us, and Rana's sister Shilpy is sitting patiently at a dusty kerb-side in the quiet side street that we seem to find at random. Shilpy and Munnu are not acquainted, but it is not hard for her to recognise us.

"How did she know we were here? Is she a spy? Is somebody following us? Where are they?" My voice is shrill. I look jumpily over my shoulder, the one that is not frozen with tension.

"Anne. Be calm. A young brother of Rana knows the soldier we meet at second checkpoint. He passes on messages. Very simple. Okay?"

I know I am being ridiculous. I pull myself together and smile at the friendly Shilpy. She is in her mid twenties, has a pretty, cheerful face, and wears a sunny yellow but much-mended *salwar kameez*. From her gestures, I know she is apologising for greeting us in her work clothes. Munnu waves her contrition aside and points to his own supposedly-crumpled garb, which is a gentlemanly thing to do because his striped, white shirt and grey trousers look fine. I am the one who appears to have slept in her clothes, which, of course, I have.

"*Shaba shokale,*" I try out my Bangla. "Good Morning." I make a huge effort to use the words. Shilpy speaks no English. Neither do her mother, cousin, and sister-in-law who share the family home.

"What about Rana?" I ask Munnu.

"He has the same English as you have Bengali," he replies.

In addition to the usual nod and smile, Shilpy puts out her hand, briefly touches my upper arm. "*Obhinondon,*" she says.

I wonder why she is congratulating me. Possibly for getting this far in one piece, all digits and appendages intact, but I presume *obhinondon* is one of those non-specific, general words of greeting.

We follow Shilpy up a flight of steep stone steps that lead to a wide lane flanked by curiously subterranean houses. The path is dusty, the stones are a sandy, reddish colour, and there is an enveloping sense of peace. This, with the warmth on my back and the very faint breeze in my hair, is almost enough to calm my jangling nerves. Almost. There is the high, plaintive sound of an unseen young girl crooning Bengali folk songs, the muted clatter and whoosh of water as someone else collects a pitcher of water from their pump. From one small, open window screened with thin, flowered curtains, I catch the crackle of a transistor radio and nothing else but the patter of three pairs of sandals.

Other than telling us that Rana is not home, (he went out yesterday and they still await his return), Shilpy is content to keep silence, seemingly incurious about us and unfazed by our arrival. Afterwards, Munnu will disclose that she had just received news of the recovery of two more bodies of the abducted businessmen. Her low profile, as I wandered on oblivious, was to avoid drawing attention to us. "I think we can trust our neighbours," she had said. "But it is best to take care."

"It is very beautiful. *Shundur*," I say shyly to Shilpy who stands at my shoulder.

Her face lights up. "*Shundur, ha.*" She goes on and Munnu translates for me. "She say, she lives here all her life and still every day, she thanks God for making this her home."

Shilpy introduces us to her cousin, Shimu, a small, slight girl, and her sister-in-law, Naly, who might be much older than both of them. Her face is lined despite the huge smile, and she is very heavy, carrying her bulk awkwardly. Both look at me with something akin to awe and carefully take in my pinkish-brown *salwar kameez* and the incongruous fair hair above it. Their eyes dance with interest between Munnu and me. Both offer me welcome and again, congratulations. Before I can respond, Naly leans over to Shilpy, whispers in her ear, and Shilpy nods and does likewise with Munnu.

"Anne," he says. "Naly wishes you to know that she is fat only because of medication. She has had cancer of the breast. Before, she was much less fat. Like you."

"Steroid," Naly elaborates. She thumps her chest. "Cancer. Sick."

"Tell her I'm sorry. That I hope she is feeling better now," I say ineffectually.

Naly is as pleased with my inadequate words as if I have offered a cure for her insidious disease. "*Pabi*," she says delightedly. "*Pabi.*"

"Why is she calling me *pabi*?"—*pabi* is the title used to address an older brother's/friend's wife—"And why are they giving me so many congratulations?"

Munnu looks mystified too. "I also wonder this. I think they just try to make you welcome as friend of friend of their brother."

Shilpy hustles us into a narrow room, the far wall taken up with a covered bed, the privacy curtain pulled back for daytime use. She motions me to sit down, talks at length with Munnu.

"She tells us to lie down and take rest whilst she prepares food for our lunch."

"Both of us...here?" I look at the bed.

"I think they have no other place."

We lean side by side against the wall, legs stretched out in front of us, half dozing, saying little. Minutes later, Shilpy returns with a small card table that she sets in front of us. Shimu follows her with a laden tray of sweet and savoury snacks. They sit and watch us eat crisped rice, sticky maize twiglets turned pink and blue with food colouring, sloppy rice pudding, oranges and bananas. When this is cleared, we are served a large platter of fried eggs and paratha keeping warm under a teacloth adorned with a rucked picture of the Empire State building.

"You are eating more." Munnu looks approvingly at my empty plate, and spoils it by reaching over to pass me another paratha. "This is good. I am afraid you get too, too thin. Remember my sister, Muktar? She worries about you eating three pieces potato only." He launches into a long description of my odd eating habits, clearly both amusing and horrifying Shilpy and Shimu. I see their resolve to feed me up before nightfall.

We troop into the main room where Shilpy and Rana's mother is sitting, half-lying on a large daybed. As Shilpy pulls me forward and says my name, the old woman's face remains expressionless. It is only her faint squeeze of my hand that suggests she is content for me to invade her home. Shilpy leaves us alone with her, and to Munnu, she is slightly more forthcoming. In fact, whatever she says to him, he becomes tongue-tied, opening and closing his mouth like a hungry guppy. For a second, he puffs up with—pride? Joy?—and then he lowers his head in modesty, or embarrassment. I don't know.

"What did she say?" I ask when we are back in the original room. Shilpy, having shown me the lavatory and the washroom, suggests I should sleep, and she retires for her own siesta. I presume Munnu, rooting through his bag for his toothbrush, has been directed— probably to the porch—for his own rest.

"Anne," Munnu begins, a farrago of emotions crossing his face. "Do not be angry. There is mistake. At first I do not understand. Now is late to make it right."

"What is it?"

"Rana's mother. She thanks me for bringing my new bride to her home."

"What!"

"Anne. Ssh! You wake all. You know I have to tell the soldier we are married. We have signed paper. Yes?"

I nod.

"So when message comes to Shilpy that we arrive, she thinks we are husband and wife."

"Which is why they have been congratulating me and calling me *pabi*." And why this room has been designated "ours," and we are resting together. Of course. It is so obvious except I've been too wrapped up in the fear of being assassinated to have noticed.

"Did you arrange all this on purpose?" I ask the now-grinning Munnu.

"No. I promise I did not."

"But you're enjoying it," I accuse him.

"Maybe little bit. I do not like to have untruths with Rana's family, but I like to be married to a shining Bengali wife."

"What shall we do?" It is one of those absurd sit-com moments when half an hour of banal television depends upon an unlikely misunderstanding causing the characters to tie themselves up in knots before coming clean in a hilarious dénouement.

"When Rana comes, I explain all to him," he promises. "Is not a problem."

"And our...*rest*?" I indicate the single bed.

"Is it a problem if we both stay here?" Munnu asks. "We sleep."

"I don't mind," I say. "But I don't want Rana's family to think I'm the whore of Babylon."

"Anne?"

I put it in his terms. "I don't want them to think I'm a fast, white, Western girl."

We compromise by curling up at separate ends, only our feet meeting in the middle and the curtain and windows wide open. The next thing I know, I am struggling to sit up as the door is thrown open and a slender, extremely good-looking young man bounces in and grabs Munnu in a wrestle hold. This, I take it, is the elusive Rana. They talk at high speed with much gesticulation before Rana turns to me and says laboriously: "Hello. Welcome home. Pleased to meet." He then returns to haranguing Munnu, who hangs his head bashfully.

"What is he saying?"

"He wants to know why he was not invited to our wedding party."

"Tell him the truth," I order.

"In a little while," says Munnu, merrily milking the situation for all it is worth, complacent in the knowledge that all I can do is glare impotently at him. Rana eats up our leftovers, and then he and Munnu decide they will go out and try to "solve my problem."

"We find Rana's friend who is the friend of the soldier and see if we receive permission to stay longer," Munnu explains.

"Before or after you try and score some dope and some alcohol?" I enquire. Despite the fact I have no evidence that Munnu is partial to the odd spliff, from his expression, I gather I have hit the nail on the head.

"The girls take care of you," is all he says.

They do. As soon as Rana and Munnu are safely out of the way—we hear Rana's motor bike shatter the peaceful afternoon—they invite me into their bed-cum-living room and show me their treasures. Naly has the bottom drawer of a large dresser filled with her wedding trousseau: hand embroidered tablecloths and napkins, a lace-edged nightgown, and four pairs of cotton bed socks. She shakes each piece out, shows the fine detail, the neat stitching, and the Bangla signature that I gather is her own. I think she tells me that her husband is in the army and at present is serving away from home, but equally it could be that he is a lion tamer in the Bangladeshi National Circus.

I admire their jewellery box of pretty trinkets (coloured stones and plastic bangles) and try to refuse, without giving offence, the gifts they press on me. Instead, Shimu hennas my feet, paints a neat and intricate design from toes to ankles whilst Naly braids my hair and fixes it high on my head with gold and silver combs.

Shilpy has changed from her working clothes into an afternoon dress of midnight blue decorated with tiny silver rhinestones. Whilst by no means as expensive or ornate as any of Bely's clothes, it is simple and elegant and I attempt to tell her so. Pleased, she shows me her other, obviously best, clothes: a red velvet *salwar kameez* and pale green brocade sari. Naly, pulling at her folds of bulging flesh, looks mournfully at the slim outfits, and explains again that her weight is not self-inflicted. Trying to reciprocate their hospitality, I open my bag and show them the dresses I have, courtesy of Bely. They are passed from one to the other and commented on at length, but there is apparently something fundamental missing. Naly rummages deep in the canvas holdall, comes up empty handed, and has an earnest conversation with the other two.

"Sari?" says Shilpy to me. "*Sari na?*"

Anne Hamilton

Inexpertly miming, I admit that I do not know how to wear it, and that coming to terms with the two-piece *salwar kameez* has been effort enough.

"You like?" Shilpy persists.

"I like. *Ha.*"

Naly is already on her knees in front of the dresser drawer. She chooses a thick length of material just like a super king-size bedsheet but a good bit larger. It is crimson satin and unusually plain save for some fine, gold embroidery around the edges. Shimu helps me out of my clothes, the green baggy trousers and flowery Laura Ashley dress which, at least, have the distinction of being clean and ironed, and I stand in my knickers in the middle of the sitting room.

Shimu pulls the tiny sari shirt over my head, a deliberately tight and short-sleeved little number designed to show off the midriff. Unfortunately, but not unexpectedly, I do not fill it to its best advantage. Naly identifies the problem by running her hands down the counters of her own figure being sure to exaggerate the curve of her bosom. Pityingly, she makes a concave shape when it comes to demonstrating my assets. Shilpy, with a neat nip and tuck, compensates by making sure I display an extra lump of flesh around my middle.

Shimu holds the floor-length skirt in position just above my right hip whilst Naly and Shilpy wind it round and round my body. And round and round some more. Then a bit more, until about fold thirteen when I feel trapped in swaddling clothes and the edge of the material is pulled over my shoulder, crosses my back and chest, and is unobtrusively pinned. The dress is too long for comfort, when Naly motions for me to walk forward, I all but trip over it and fall headlong into the dresser, but this is easily rectified with a pair of gold stiletto heels.

Disappointed with my unadorned ears, nose, and belly button (for a moment I am worried by the speculative glint in Naly's eye and expect her to produce some indigenous hole-making implement), the final touch is to stick a tiny gold dot between my eyebrows. Only then am I led, with as much care as if I *am* a new bride—guilt hits me afresh—to the full-length if somewhat warped mirror.

Naly, Shilpy, and Shimu have the good manners to be pleased with their handiwork, even though it is clear that I lack the grace, elegance, and sheer know-how of wearing the beautiful sari. I am not transformed, but rather I resemble a little girl in a Nativity play, awkwardly dressed up to play the Virgin Mary. Still, my new friends insist that I sit patiently and wait for Rana and Munnu to return.

Shimu longingly folds my discarded dress, and I motion for her to try it on. She does so with alacrity, and she and Shilpy take turns wearing it for the afternoon. Eventually sated, Shilpy reaches for a large mahogany box that I eventually recognise to be an accordion. "Can you play?" I mime a squeezing motion.

It takes little persuasion for her to tune up and entertain us. The music is mellow, verging on melancholy, but she plays well, and when she lifts her voice and sings the songs, it is almost hypnotic. The rise and fall of the cadences are perfectly pitched. Shilpy's repertoire is limited even with the aid of a music book, but it is enough to hear her repeat the same tunes over and again. It is some time before she comes back to earth, and we notice that Munnu and Rana have returned and are sitting quietly on the back door step, listening closely.

Hauled upright, I pose without managing the demure yet supercilious demeanour of the well-dressed Bangladeshi bride. The boys smile gallantly, feign interest, and Munnu pleases my dressers by asking if they could make him look so good.

"Bengali wife." Rana is unknowingly unoriginal.

"My beautiful blonde Bengali wife," charms Munnu, not to be outdone. I smile prettily and resist the urge to stick the heel of my shoe between his toes. Instead, I ask about his endeavours to lengthen my stay here.

"Is okay. We stay tonight." Munnu evades my question.

"Who said so? Have I proper permission?" I ask.

"We do not find the soldier. We find nobody at the checkpoints. So is okay to stay tonight," Munnu repeats.

"Are you sure?" I am unconvinced by such vague arrangements. It appears that I am going to be spending the night running from the terrorists because I am white and allegedly rich, from the military because I have disobeyed strict orders, and from a new and enthusiastic "husband" for obvious reasons. Some of my anxiety must penetrate, because Munnu and Rana have another rapid conversation.

"If you are very unhappy, we take a bus in one hour," Munnu admits. "It is your choice. But I think and Rana thinks it is okay you stay here."

Rana speaks and Munnu translates persuasively. "We think to attend a wedding, but maybe not so safe. Also is not a good area for foreigners..."

"You'll have to try harder than that," I mutter.

"So, when it is darkness we visit local café, a boat on Lake Kaptai. You like it very much. Tomorrow we watch the sun rising. Okay?"

Anne Hamilton

"Why do we have to go when it's dark? So nobody will see me?"

"No. Only then is the best view and the best music."

"And the rest of the afternoon?"

"You take rest."

I sigh heavily and give in easily. "But not because I believe you," I warn Munnu. "Because it will take me more than sixty minutes to get out of this," I tug at the already dishevelled sari, its layers unwrapping like filo pastry. Munnu announces our decision, and the delight on our hosts' faces means there is no going back.

"But you have to tell them the truth," I urge Munnu.

"I talk later with Rana," he assures.

I consider attempting an explanation myself, something detailed and specific along the lines of "Me, him, no marry. Not husband and wife. Mistake." But somehow I know it will simply add to the confusion. It is not that I *mind* being married to Munnu, as it were. And telling barefaced lies to figures of authority is obviously fine as long as one gets away with it, but doing the same to friends is just not on. Then again, I don't want Munnu to lose face, even if he does deserve it, and he certainly will if I try to pre-empt him.

So, on the most beautiful of sunny days, in an exotic country where water laps at a lean-to boathouse on the shores of the largest artificial lake in the land, I lie on a daybed in a simple bamboo house feeling like *Alice Through the Looking Glass* where everything is back to front, and waiting for my comeuppance.

When night falls, Munnu, Rana, Shilpy, and I leave the house. Try as I might, I cannot view it as anything but clandestine. Rana lovingly wheels out his shiny, red motorcycle, almost carrying it over the bumpier parts of the lane lest a stray stone fly up and scratch its polished trim, and once at the main street, he revs up, climbs on with Shilpy riding in an expert side-saddle, and cautions Munnu and I to wait for a baby taxi.

We circumvent the town, the water almost constantly in sight. It is only a short ride—"to maximum safe area," says Munnu—before we see Rana, Shilpy in his shadow, waving to us from beneath a halo of white lights. A slatted bridge forms the entrance to a boardwalk, a wooden construction jutting out over the water to the so-called floating restaurant. Attached to the taut canopy are miniature fairy lights, their rainbow reflections glowing in the still water. Round tables dot the perimeter of the floor, and at the far end is an alcohol-free bar. As we choose a table at the water's edge, I have a sudden and unnerving picture of a trap door dropping me to a watery grave.

"It is a barge converted," Munnu clarifies, assuming I am gazing around with interest rather than locating emergency exits.

Pocket-sized laminated menus sport a translation of the Bangla script, but I cannot swear it is English: *soop, mutonn rise, dall, chick fingers, coffie*. Rana orders for us, a thin chicken and vegetable broth, lukewarm and watery but clearly made from fresh produce. Unusually, it is a leisurely meal, little pressure to eat up and get out, just low conversation, the spectacle of a lighted candle cake served for a family birthday celebration, and opportunity to get lost in the mesmerising mini waves under our feet. I try hard to emulate the relaxed postures of the others but jump when I see Rana's discreet gaze sweep with lighthouse regularity over the other patrons.

"He looks for young brothers to make your introduction," Munnu says unconvincingly.

We are sipping bowls of milky coffee, sucking at the froth with thoughtfully- provided straws, when Rana gives a routine glance, freezes, looks down, takes a gulp of his coffee and says something along the lines of "Don't look now, but a bunch of off-duty soldiers have just come in, and if they see Anne here this late at night without permission, we could all get thrown into gaol and our fingers and toes donated to medical science. On the count of three, leg it lads—and like, without drawing attention to yourselves might be best."

Suddenly deciding we are very cold, I copy Shilpy in hiding arms and head with my dupatta and stroll unhurriedly back up the gangplank. At the main road, Munnu expertly manhandles me onto the back of Rana's motorbike, and we roar through the comforting maze of unlit side streets, Munnu and Shilpy's baby taxi chugging in behind us. We could be filming a low budget action thriller, albeit with a dispiriting lack of James Bond's gadgets.

Munnu assures me when I see him again that we have not been followed and are quite safe, but that perhaps we will call off the sunrise tour just for my peace of mind and in case any of the neighbours *are* actually informers or terrorist spies. I consider the pros and cons of being taken by the police versus the rebels when Munnu says, "We eat and sleep in the underground room."

It is the icing on the cake.

With trepidation, I follow Munnu and Rana across the dark courtyard, down a steeply vertical and crumbling flight of steps half hidden behind the latrine and covered in overgrown ivy and tangled plant life, and push open a stable door.

It is semi-subterranean, a basement rather than underground but certainly far lower than the main house. Such proximity to the water suggests it spends half the year sub-aqua. There is a small anteroom, cell-like but large enough for a narrow bed, a collapsing dressing-table placed underneath a shuttered window, and a folding chair. The inner room *is* a double bed. There is no floor to stand on, just a step straight from the door way and up onto the patchwork quilt covering the soft sprung mattress.

From a single light bulb, a thin shaft illuminates the chill room and picks out the expected water line on dirty grey walls. Rana gropes beneath the coverlet and produces an old plastic cola bottle, half full of a clear liquid that is not quite water. From a pouch secreted in his wallet, he draws out a telling weed that is not quite tobacco, and three small oranges, presumably the real things, come from his trouser pockets.

"Party, party," says Rana.

The other two decide it is not etiquette to smoke dope in the presence of a lady, but that the lady could be permitted a taste of the intoxicating and illegal-but-everyone-turns-a-blind-eye liquor. One sip, heavily diluted, is enough to convince my oesophagus to go into melt down. Choking, I wave the glass away and watch even Rana, reasonably used to the tipple, sip it cautiously.

"Fire," he breathes. Literally. "Fire."

"For special occasion only," Munnu says. "Have some orange. It makes your tongue less burning."

Spurred on by the alcohol and my meaningful kicks, Munnu confesses our bogus marriage. Rana finds it hilarious, gives Munnu an admiring man-to-man punch and decides that my worldly wise ways are licence to ask questions about the high life in Europe and beyond. Since his mental image of the wild Western world is locked somewhere in Carnaby Street, free-love communes, and wearing flowers in your hair to San Francisco, I am destined to disappoint.

"Free drugs? Drink? Women? Available yes?" he implores.

"Available, yes. Free, not necessarily." I grapple with the semantics. Munnu is the inevitable middleman.

"Your country?"

I tell Rana that Ireland does not do badly on the alcohol front, but that he might want to set his sights on somewhere more generally liberal. "The Netherlands." I suggest. "Amsterdam might be a good start."

He listens with such concentration as if a quick trip to *Rangmati Travel* and a one-way ticket is a feasible option. "Girls. Friends?"

"He wants to know whether girls find him attractive in the West? Does he get girlfriends easily? Will there be enough...? This is enough, um...sex?"

I answer as best I can (must clock this up to tell Christine: more cultural exchange) without debating how much sex is enough. Rana draws the line at asking me to get him a visa, but only because comradely protocol demands that if anyone is to receive favours from me, Munnu is at the top of the pecking order, and Rana is but nibbling the crumbs.

"Thank you for your helping," Rana says formally.

Despite, or maybe in view of, our unmarried status, Rana has not grasped that Munnu and I do not wish to cuddle up privately under a single blanket. He looks incredulous, after all, Western women are famous for being faster than Concorde, and poor Munnu's macho standing takes a bit of a knock—he has to roll up a marijuana combination to deal with it.

On a point of honour, I am given the double bed and long into the night I hear Rana and Munnu giggling through the inner door. When I have to get up and fight my way through the natural obstacle course to the loo with only my trusty Maglite for company, I slip past them, curled up and deeply asleep.

I do not find it easy to get back to sleep, but strangely enough, it is not the thoughts of kidnap, hijack, being seized by the thought police, or romantically propositioned that keep me awake. I am consumed with curiosity: how did they get this bed into this room? And how will they get it out again when the rains come?

I spend the morning loitering around the house, my role as virtual prisoner still intact, whilst Rana drags Munnu off for an impromptu motorcycle-riding lesson. I keep falling over a little girl of about seven or eight with short, bobbed hair, and huge brown eyes who is scrubbing vegetables, stirring rice, and cleaning cooking pots. She sings along happily with Shilpy who attempts to teach her the rudiments of the harmonium. At first, I think she is another cousin but soon understand that she is the "maid," living here because her family could not afford her. She earns enough for her keep and to send a very small amount of money to them.

I eat a late breakfast a half an hour before lunch. Rana has found that the only bus to Chittagong centre leaves at 1 p.m. A further night here, they agree, is not prudent. "What happens when the security guard asks why I did not leave last night?" I ask between mouthfuls of mutton stew.

"They do not ask. The papers will be lost," Munnu prevaricates, but frowning slightly, he turns to Rana for advice.

"We tell that you are sick," Munnu lowers his voice and blushes. "We say you suffer the private ladies' problems in the stomach but that you do not share details with me. I say these things. You say you do not understand. They are too shamed to ask more. Okay?"

"What's another lie?" I shrug.

Rana accompanies us to the bus stop, and for a few harrowing moments, we are on display for the curious population of Rangmati. I suppose my rehearsing crying at will and clutching my stomach in agony is not particularly inconspicuous behaviour. Whenever the pavement reverberates, and we hear the whine of a gear change, we stand up hopefully. Multi-coloured heavy trucks wobble around the corner, pause, and offer us a ride. I nearly faint when I see an army truck trundle into view, and breathe again when I see that it is decommissioned and jammed with cattle in the back.

Eventually the bus arrives, and we are bundled into seats, bags crammed at our feet. It is like yesterday's vehicle but smaller and with no knee or elbow room. The windows are wide open, and Rana runs alongside us, shouting farewells. As we pick up speed, I look back and see him standing still in the middle of a dusty road, traffic going carefully around him. I feel a lump in my throat.

"He says," Munnu observes, "that he much appreciates it if you find him a European girl friend."

I sit with my head down, waiting—assuming that this casual driver does not drive us off the edge of the cliff face—for the bus to halt, the security forces to invade en masse, and drag me out to shoot me. It is meltingly hot, and every time I move I leave half my skin behind on the blistering plastic seats. I am so engrossed in peeling my arm from the windowsill that I barely register the slowing of the bus, and the thump of big boots making their way down the aisle. The teenage soldier, not his dedicated colleague of yesterday, looks briefly at me, asks which country I am from, nods, and goes on his way. We pass the *You are now leaving Rangmati. Congratulations on not being abducted and have a nice life* sign (or something like that; it's all in Bangla), and I feel a surge of anti-climax. No fainting, crying, or throwing up and pleading for mercy required after all.

23
Through Chittagong

The three-hour journey to Chittagong flies past, probably because it really is only three hours, and Munnu, swearing me to secrecy, entertains me with insider gossip from Khalia and SCI. I realise, as we swap stories about our families and friends, our plans and ambitions, that his English has improved tremendously, and that he is one of the few people with whom I have no need to choose my words or slow them down. Most amazingly, he knows when I am joking and when I am being sarcastic.

"This is because I spend so many weeks talking with you and Christine. The first days at Shanti Kendra, I am too shy to speak in front of my brothers. Now, I have much better English. When I translate for you, many times I do not have to think for the word. It is very good feeling."

"And my Bengali is still about six words," I say in disgust. "Mostly all food." I remember a long ago conversation with Christine. "My diary reads like an Enid Blyton story. It's my own fault."

"Is not true. You know many words, but like me, are very shy to use them. Also, all want to talk English with you. It is very different to talk with a foreigner than another Bangladeshi. Better for practice."

Stiltedly, in Bangla I practice asking Munnu his name, how he is, where he lives and his job. I listen to the answers and make my replies, ask for directions, the time, list the days of the week, and count to ten. I can also say, "I love you very much," which, as you can imagine, comes in extremely useful.

"Anne? Why you know this? Maybe Rakim says these words to you?" Munnu frowns.

"No," I say. "You know I haven't seen Rakim since the Trade Fair."

"He is not good boy for you. Anne?"

"Yes?"

"Maybe I love you? Do you think I love you?"

"No you don't," I say, light-hearted as possible. "You like being with me, and you like that everyone looks at us and wonders why we are together."

"Maybe this is little bit true," he yields.

"You need a nice Bengali wife." I tell him. "And I want an invitation to your wedding."

"Of course. But not for many years. There is Bachchu to marry first; he is already forty years. Then, is Mannu, who is five years younger."

He explains that tradition expects brothers to wed chronologically, although in extenuating circumstances, if, for example, the family finds a perfect girl and dowry for a younger sibling, that marriage could take place.

"And do you choose, or do your parents?" I ask.

"It can be either. Maybe my family knows somebody, and they introduce us to see if we like each other. Or maybe I meet a girl in Dhaka and take her and her parents home to visit."

After the outward tranquillity and silence of Rangmati, our arrival in the urban sprawl that is Chittagong City is jarring. Chittagong is the second largest city in Bangladesh with a population of only three million, slightly less than that of Ireland. In general, it is not unlike Dhaka, in the way that Liverpool is not unlike London. It has a more pleasant air. There is less pollution, better traffic control, and cooler, less humid weather. Probably because of the port—the busiest in the country—on one side, and the amount of through-traffic going east to the Hill Tracts and south to Cox's Bazaar, it feels less claustrophobic. It is possible to get out of the inner circle into relative countryside without excessive effort.

A rickshaw driver offers to take us to a hotel, and we climb in and calculate how much money we have to spend. Munnu has little to begin with, and I feel responsible for the financial aspects of the trip, but we have been handing out little brown envelopes faster than the average politician.

The rickshaw pulls up between a butcher shop and one selling loud hailers. The driver suggests that I remain in my seat whilst Munnu checks the availability of rooms.

"He will look after you," Munnu promises. "I go up two flights only—see that window up there? I watch for you."

"I think," I say with dignity, "someone who has survived abduction, murder, having bits chopped off, and has hoodwinked the police can sit alone in a rickshaw."

"Anne. You are so funny-type girl." Munnu laughs.

I sit complacently with my hand loosely on my bag, glaring in my best Hasina manner at anyone who comes too close. I have seen immense, burkha-clad women do this, and it always means they are given a wide berth. It does not work for skinny, pale, and dishevelled foreigners.

"Hey, hey." The rickshaw driver gets my attention and points up to the muddy building where Munnu and a stocky, dark man sporting huge aviator sunglasses are hanging out of the window trying to spot me through the crowds. Munnu points and his companion, presumably the hotel proprietor, squints before slowly and unmistakably shaking his head. I give a regal wave and my most beguiling smile, but his face does not soften. My self-esteem crumbles as I am turned away from a small tourist hotel in the back streets of Chittagong. I tell myself it is not personal. Often lodgings have a policy of refusing foreigners or women, or perhaps the hotelier thinks I'm an "exotic" prostitute. The gathering crowds understand the problem; they just have trouble verbalising it.

"No like," one young boy, climbing up on the wheel to get a better look at me, explains with engaging frankness. He, too, shakes his head. "No like. You."

"How can he not like me? He doesn't even know me." I slump back, tugging forward the rolled canopy to hide my unwanted face. Munnu climbs in beside me, calling instructions to the driver. I wait for the bad news, but he is grinning from ear to ear.

"I ask him for a room, and he says how many? I say two, and he asks where are the other people? I show him you wait here. He looks at you and he says, no room."

"Why is that so funny? What is the matter with me?"

"Nothing is matter. The man sees you and says 'she does not like my rooms.' I ask him to show me, but he says no. Again he says, 'she does not like it here.'"

The adamant innkeeper is determined that his premises are not suitable for the memsahib, but he does direct us to an alternative establishment run by his brother whom "she does like."

"It is perhaps that the brother's hotel is maximum expensive, and he knows you have money," says Munnu. "But is okay. People I saw there were strange people." He laughs again. "The man says your clothes are too *fitfaht*, and your face is too fragile."

So much for my indigenous cotton travelling dress and sinister scowl.

After a familiarisation trip around the city so comprehensive that I now qualify as a local, the rickshaw handler admits he has no idea of the location of the Residence Al-Amin, and he turns us over to a colleague to continue the quest. By virtue of yelling for help at various passers-by, we arrive in minutes and enter what appears to be a disused 1960s DSS block. Six flights up and still counting—I had better be on the approved guest list here—we finally go through a swing door marked "*Rec pt n*" and enter a lobby carpeted in swirling green. I plonk myself on a matching corduroy sofa two feet from an enormous tropical fish tank with a portable TV balanced on a plank on top of it. Behind a small counter, three men will decide our fate.

Munnu sits beside me and gives me the options in an undertone. "There is one room only. Two big beds divided by curtains. Clean sheets. Also private bathroom. No television. Fan only, no a/c. No mosquito net, but they spray. Married people only together, so you are my wife. We pay Tk350. Okay? Or we try another place?"

I compute the data, visualise the worst-case scenario of being ravaged during the night (by mosquitoes, not by Munnu), toss for it, and agree. One look at the stern bloke behind the desk, the loopy-looking "boy" beside him, and various other Hajji's who come from nowhere to silently stare, and I don't fancy having my own room any more.

"No wonder bureaucracy is gone mental in this country," I mutter to Munnu as he undertakes the slow and cumbersome paperwork required to check us in: His name in full, his father's name in full, his home address, his city address, his occupation, his age, his number of children. My name, my father's name, my husband's name (which again I have to ask Munnu how to spell and again, nobody seems to notice this discrepancy), my passport number, my reason for travel, my age which Munnu gallantly refuses to disclose. The clerks look me up and down like a heifer at the mart, ask an opinion from the resident chef and a passing blind beggar, and then write down "20 years." I love this place. The questioning continues. How Munnu and I met, where and why, and what is my shoe size and preferred skin care regime. I lose track after they want to know if we need a bolt on the bedroom door.

Ultimately, the rooms are only moderately prison-like despite the boy's knack of locating an unoccupied space by peering through a small glass square in the upper half of each metal door. When he finds one, we enter into a large, but only in length, room with one bed placed carefully behind the other. Each bed looks big enough to sleep about six people, although there is only about half an inch between the headboard of one and the bottom of the other. Just enough space, in fact, for a once-pink plastic shower curtain rigged up on a piece of string to be pulled across for privacy. There are two kitchen chairs and a washbasin against the remaining wall, a line of coat hooks, and an old metal stationery cupboard with three legs. A bolted door leads to a surprisingly spacious and tiled shower room and lavatory. Obviously, there is no shower curtain now, but in consolation there is a great selection of various sized buckets.

On close inspection, the patchy stains on the bed sheets smell like bleach, the reddish-brown ones on the walls are mosquito guts, and the black bits on the moth-eaten carpet are cigarette burns rather than rat droppings. Munnu politely offers to take the bed nearest the door; thus he will be on show when passing guests and staff gaze in through the peephole, and I may take the other one under the window—yes, our own window—as long as I do not mind him entering my space to get to the bathroom door. I graciously concur. We take the room.

No money changes hands. The boy does a quick inventory, and the room will be checked again as we leave. If we have managed to resist temptation to nick the ashtrays, chairs, and shower curtain, we pay the going rate. None of the previous guests have bothered to steal the bar of soap either; instead they have added to it their own donations of pubic hair.

"When do your other friends arrive?" the boy asks, chatty now that the moment for tipping is upon us.

He looks scandalised on hearing that we are the sole occupants. There is no two-person-two-bed philosophy in Bangladesh's budget hostels. Why waste hard-earned money when one could bring all one's friends? Indeed, it is likely that this *executive* room (courtesy of the privacy curtain) is usually shared by strangers. Potential guests are known to delay checking in until a group of them, probably all unknown to one another, congregate and pile into one shared room, thus yielding a great financial saving.

"Men only," says Munnu. "I do not think women do this unless they are family. Still, it is not so expensive here."

The boy vanishes to tell his colleagues about the weird people in Room 302, and I sink onto my bed whilst Munnu religiously unpacks—as he did in Rangmati—and hangs up his clothes.

"Anne. Maybe we take rest now. Later we eat."

"Fine."

All I want to do is sleep, confident that if I am attacked here, it will be random and by an average criminal, not by terrorists or the army. I change my clothes and must fall asleep straightaway. Moments later and from a long distance, I am woken by a whisper.

"Anne? Do you wake? It is Munnu."

"I'm awake," I say. "What's the time?"

It is dark outside. I've slept later than I thought.

"It is nine-thirty. We can go out for food, or I buy it and bring it back to you."

We decide to go out in half-an-hour. When I wake again, Munnu is making his way back from the bathroom, settling in his creaking bed.

"We sleep so long," he says. "Is too late for food. Midnight is gone."

"I hope you don't get weak from lack of rice," I say across the darkness.

"Anne. Would you like it if I make love to you now?" Munnu replies.

"No, thank you."

"Okay. Go to sleep now. In the morning I buy you eggs and paratha. Goodnight."

I lie awake for a while listening to the shouts in the corridor grow louder, jump when other residents fall against the door or turn the handle and begin, mistakenly I hope, to creep in. Munnu has a sixth sense for these occasions and growls viciously enough to receive a muted apology before telling me not to worry and go back to sleep. I obey.

I love this place. Love it. Like a ciné film, my mind runs through my adventures, my travels, my new friends, my horrors, and I realise for the first time since my arrival, I am truly at home in Bangladesh. I feel almost comfortable here. On this day, the 16th February, I have, in effect, fallen in love.

"Oh, would you ever listen to yourself? Cop on and stop being a sentimental old twit," I mutter out loud, grin to myself in the darkness, and dream spiritual dreams of fried eggs and roti.

Needless to say, in the morning, my moment of truth, of peace, of contentment is but a memory. I awake scratching frantically. My left shoulder, arm and entire back are covered in raised, angry, red lumps already irritated by my scraping nails and brewing horrible, infectious pus. Where there are miniscule gaps, the skin is black and blue with tender bruising from too many jostling rickshaws and buses.

Awkwardly I shower, and then cover myself with every cream, unguent, spray, and liquid I can find, swallow double the recommended dose of antihistamine, and pray for a plague of locusts or whatever is the appropriate member of the food chain to descend on the entire mosquito world.

"You look injured," Munnu says anxiously. "Do you like to visit the doctor? I can ask the boy? Already they wonder why we stay so long in the room."

I refuse. It is not necessary and anyway, I cannot face explaining to anyone why I disappeared into a dodgy hotel room at 3 p.m. one day and have not emerged until after eleven the following morning looking like a battered wife. I would probably be incarcerated for alleged disobedience towards my loving husband with the big fists. Or even worse, an enlightened judge would throw Munnu into gaol for assault, and I would be a deserted as well as abused wife.

"There is much to see here," Munnu tells me with the air of a seasoned traveller. "We may visit the Old City. There are Mosques and the Modern Ethnological Museum."

In all philistine honesty, I cannot be bothered. "I want to go to the seaside," I demand. "Now."

My timing cannot, for once, be faulted. There is a comfortable bus leaving for Cox's Bazaar in fifteen minutes, our seats still have springs, and there is room to shove my bag beneath the chair in front. Munnu buys a couple of newspapers to swat at annoying hawkers and beggars reaching up through the open windows or trekking down the aisle. One perspicacious elderly gentleman with a long grey beard and piercing eyes, covered from neck to toe in a white *djebella*, squats at Munnu's feet and explains earnestly why he alone of all the "mad men, old men and robbers" (his words) queuing behind him should receive a handout. It is an impressive spiel, even to someone with marginal Bangla. I expect him to produce projection charts and draw up a business plan demonstrating our investment terms. Munnu resorts to taking out his wallet and proving his lack of change.

"No problem, young sir," says the gentleman cordially as he whips out a substantial bundle of small denomination notes from deep inside his string vest. "Please, let me offer you change for a Tk10 note. Perhaps, if the sun is moving into Gemini—my astrological sign—even a Tk 20. Now my man, what do you say?"

I am so impressed by his resourcefulness and his cheek that I force Munnu to hand over a couple of *taka*. Sure enough, for a Tk 10 note, the beggar dutifully returns eight.

I am caught by surprise when, four hours later, the bus turns into the large, purpose-built bus station complete with proper parking bays, accurate signs, telephone booths, a shop, restaurant, waiting room, and toilets. There are a few buses pulling in and out, orderly people making their way onwards, and a neat line of rickshaws waiting for fares. And it is apparently in the middle of nowhere. I get out, stretch, gaze up and down the shining, melting, undulating tarmacadam road off which we have just pulled, and see nothing in either direction. There are green fields and palm trees on either side, but the road simply stretches forward and eventually disappears over the brow of a hill.

"This," says Munnu, "is the road to Cox's Bazaar, the—"

"—longest sea beach in the world," I join in. The place is never, ever mentioned without this postscript. "Yes. Buses must not go further because if they do, the rickshaw drivers will not make a living. This is a rule made by the thana—what you call the council, yes?"

Sniffing a fare, the rickshaw drivers abandon their neat row and vie to grab our bags. In seconds, a short-lived but vicious fight between two competitors sees us flying down the first hill, the young driver working up to full speed for the forthcoming incline. At first, I think the background jeering is good-natured ribbing directed at our man for winning the business, but turning round I see that a convoy of rickshaws are in hot pursuit, yelling and pointing, smiles turning to frowns as they get nearer. Picking up on the urgency, the rickshaw-*wallah* slows down to examine a rear wheel, which, buckling dangerously, appears about to fall off, thus launching us into the nearest ditch.

Reaching us first is the *wallah*'s sworn enemy of minutes ago. He claps our *wallah* on the back and offers the use of his own vehicle whilst he tends to the wheel repairs. We set off again.

"Why would he do that?" I ask. "Hasn't he just lost some money?"

"I think they work for the same boss. It does not much matter who gets the fare. Soon you see why the older man did not really want to drive us."

For a short while, maybe ten minutes, it is a long, straight road onto which the sun beats down relentlessly. We try pulling the roof forward, but this just serves to trap what little breeze there is and forces us into such close proximity, we are uncomfortably sticky from mutual perspiration. Munnu instructs me to double my *dupatta* over my head to avoid sunstroke.

"We are now having vacations," Munnu says. "Soon there is the sea, and we swim."

On either side of the road are a few houses with children playing or working in the small yards. Even the smallest of them carries a huge load of wood or sticks or a sack on his head. Shouts of hello and goodbye follow us as we alternately fly down the hills and struggle back up the incline. Regularly, our bare-chested rickshaw-*wallah* stops to mop his face with the edge of his *lunghi* and climbs down from the bicycle to pull us forward. Munnu gets off to ease the weight, but the *wallah* will not hear of me doing likewise.

It is, easy for me to say, a reasonably short-lived torment. Over the final hill and around a sloping bend, we catch a glimmer of an ocean barely discernible from the dazzling sky. We draw closer, watching the sun dance on the lazy waves, hear a distant, maybe imagined, lapping of water on sand, and the absolute silence of the open road grows into a busy village. When we turn to the left, the sea recedes behind half-built concrete shells interspersed with litter-strewn wasteland. Soon, a solitary guesthouse expands into three, four hotels and inns, and then the street is filled with places offering holiday accommodation.

Many of them are large, faded, and crumbling stucco buildings, some are newly-painted, modern apartment blocks, and others look deserted. All have familiar and uninspired English names: Sea Haven, Sea Point, Sea View ("Your special home in the sea"), Sunmoon, Sunny Days, Sunlight ("Your joys in sun is our delight"). Munnu says that when he was last here five years previously, none of these places existed. Accommodation was centred on the dirty, one-street village centre.

Under specific instructions to take us "somewhere clean that costs under Tk 500," the rickshaw-*wallah* indicates one or two establishments to Munnu, who declines them as being too far away, and eventually turns through neat gates into the small courtyard of the blue-trimmed, white facade of the *Zia Guesthouse*. Since it is sandwiched between the identical *Diamond Guesthouse* and *Zia Inn*, I assume that the *wallah*'s cousin/brother/uncle works here.

Greeted at the entrance, we are led into a tiny lobby and given the excellent news of vacant rooms at fair prices. This week prior to Eid is slack. Most patrons are the stragglers unable to afford prices of the high season, which begins immediately after the religious festival. The hotelier assumes we ask for two rooms believing them to be small. He is at great pains to inform us we are much mistaken. There will be plenty of space in one bedroom.

"He says," Munnu is instructed to tell me, his lips twitching, "that he is not the rough kind of businessman who defrauds innocent tourists to his country, particularly those who take trouble to find and marry good Bangladeshi men."

Oops. "Tell him that my religion forbids me from sharing a bedroom so early in our marriage. Tell him you, as my husband, must earn the privilege. Tell him you must come only by invitation," I say, smiling beatifically.

Munnu gives me a look, sceptical in the extreme, and says a couple of words, not, I imagine, those I have suggested.

"I tell him that girls from the West are strange."

238

Anne Hamilton

We are loaded down with bottled water, given a can of bug spray and a dusty roll of toilet paper ("special for the lady"), and then told, confidentially, that there is a roof terrace for special guests where we are welcome at any time. The porter carries our luggage, points out the lukewarm water switch, turns on the TV, and takes Munnu into the furthest room for a quiet word.

"He tells me that hard liquor is available," Munnu reports as the porter closes the door behind him. "I say not necessary. He finds it very strange that you do not drink alcohol, not even American beer. He is disappointed for us."

So disappointed in fact, that a couple of minutes later there is a tentative knock on the door, a discreet cough, and the porter is back for another urgent and low voiced, man-to-man conversation. I see Munnu accept three cigarettes even whilst shaking his head. The porter's face droops; he shrugs and vanishes.

"Marijuana," grins Munnu. "Drugs for our pleasure. I say no, but I buy cigarettes to make him happy."

"One, two, three, four…" I start to count.

"Anne. What do you do?"

"Before I get to one hundred, he will come back again. He won't give up until he thinks of something 'special' for us."

We are both giggling when the tap on the door comes. I wonder what has been thought up for our mental delight. Munnu cannot wait to tell me.

"This time he tells me he has movies. I say we are happy with the television, and he says they are special private movies. When I say no, he changes to magazines. Then he looks at me as if we are maximum unusual people. He urges us to go to the roof if we accept no other privilege."

"Here ten minutes and we're already offered booze, dope, blue movies, and dirty magazines," I muse. "What a den of iniquity. Do you think that 'going up to the roof' is a euphemism for an orgy or a gambling ring? I wonder if everyone gets this treatment?"

"It is especially because of you," Munnu says definitely.

Great. I'm not sure I like my apparent reputation. "I don't know. I bet if you were alone, he would be back to offer you a girl or two for 'company.'"

"Do you think so?" Munnu says wistfully, catches himself and puffs his chest out. "I am not that kind of boy," he protests. "Anne. Come. We are in Cox's Bazaar. The ocean is waiting."

239

24

A Bengali Honeymoon

Cox's Bazaar is possibly the one place in Bangladesh where I am not continually asked why I am here. It is obvious why I am here; like everyone else I will have come either to visit the sea beach or to spend my honeymoon. Every married woman I have met has been quick to show me photographs of a) the wedding and b) the honeymoon "swimming" at Cox's Bazaar. It is a rite of passage.

The shore is reputed to be eighteen kilometres long. It meets the horizon far beyond the scope of the naked eye and forms a watery border with Myanmar. Despite the construction viewed on the way in, the beach remains largely undeveloped. Munnu has heard that the few international tourists who visit compare it unfavourably with Goa, but neither he nor I can validate that fact.

The main road, the only road, to the central beach is a long, straight avenue with the seashore forming a T-junction at its head. Covered in a fine layer of windblown and gritty sand, either side is a clutter of cheap, wooden restaurants and tacky souvenir shacks selling hats, plastic beach toys, knee-length shorts and tent-like dresses, ice-cream, and photographic services. All are open to the street, their traders sitting outside smoking and drinking tea, handmade canopies offering some relief from the intense egg-yolk sun. They call out leisurely to every passing rickshaw, eye up the spending capacity of charabanc passengers, and watch this human traffic unload in the square parking lot at the edge of the strand.

Right on the beach is the outposts of the poorest traders. Some have formed makeshift stalls with discarded wooden planks and plastic awnings; others have their wares spread out carefully on blankets on the ground: sea shells and necklaces, tea towels, and cheap T-shirts.

The sand is hot and soft, and despite its dirty beige hue, is pleasantly clean given the general predilection for random littering. Nearer the water's edge is a row of multi-coloured umbrellas shading slatted, wooden sun loungers for hourly rent, each jealously guarded by its minder. Mobile carts piled with snacks, drinks, and cigarettes are pushed slowly between them. The ocean is a hybrid; neither the sparkling, cool, aquamarine of the Mediterranean nor the angry grey of the North Sea. The magnificent, white-tipped and random waves make a surfer's paradise—should the pastime develop here. At present, the most exotic water sport involves floating in black rubber inner tubes.

There is a respectable sprinkling of swimmers, mostly groups of men clad in shorts and singlets, *lunghi's* and shirts, ducking and diving and catching the waves. A little further down the strand, fewer females bathe, the majority being schoolgirls in blue and white sailor uniforms or young women in flowing *salwar kameezes*, fully dressed and soaked through. There is no sunbathing, no swimsuits, and the sun beds are solely for the safe repose of personal belongings whilst making the indispensable pilgrimage into the water.

An army of beach photographers tout for business. Everyone here is a tourist, many are day-trippers in large groups, and few of them own a camera. They crowd into the viewfinder, eager for a memento of the outing. Honeymooners pose self-consciously for romantic photographs under the setting sun.

The crowds are abundant at the heart of the beach, but a few hundred yards in either direction, they thin out and become visitors in ones and twos. The sand reverts to nature, its stretches empty and unfathomable. There is no development along the beachfront itself, simply row upon row of fir trees and beyond those, high in the hills, stands the lighthouse. Out at sea is a blank canvas with only the very occasional boat far on the horizon.

"Cox's Bazaar," says Munnu contentedly as we join the strollers. "Longest sea beach in the world. Anne, you like it?"

I love the warmth, the water, that indefinable and all too brief late afternoon light that draws over the uniqueness of this undeveloped place. It is captivating, alluring, and not a traditional paradise. Indeed, its attraction is that it *isn't* an international tourist haven. I attempt to get my feelings across to Munnu.

"It is good for those reasons," he agrees. "All Bangladeshis like Cox's Bazaar. But," he muses, "I like very much to see Australia, Bondai Beach. Very beautiful girls and very cool surfing."

I suggest that we, as travel companions, are less conspicuous here than in other places. We blend into the masses of other unchaperoned couples; fewer people are staring. Munnu smugly contradicts me.

"No. Still every person watches us. I like this. But," he cautions, "I think perhaps some people are not so friendly here. They are little bit more used to foreigners, and maybe the men look at you in a not nice way."

"So, my racy, Western reputation has preceded me, and a load of lecherous old men are waiting for me to rip off my clothes and go swimming in a tiny string bikini?"

Munnu makes some sense of this and grins. "Okay. I think you are happy. Also, I protect you."

"Might people think it is wrong for you and me to be here together?" I ask him. "I mean, if we really were married. What's the attitude to mixed-race couples?"

Munnu shrugs. "It depends on the people. Many are just interested because we are exceptional in Bangladesh. They wonder how we meet and what our families say. Some less educated think it is wrong. Also the very religious, but this is because you are not Muslim."

Maybe some of the glances I/we attract are more appraising than usual, but I do not notice any hostility or displeasure. We are stopped every three seconds for information or conversation. Complete strangers ask to have my photograph taken with them and reverently hand over their cameras for Munnu to oblige. I am slightly thrown by a new turn of events later on in the day when one excited bride lets go of her new husband's tightly-clutched hand, roots through her shoulder bag and presents me with paper and a pen.

"She is asking you for autograph," Munnu explains.

"You are joking? Does she think I'm someone famous?"

"I do not joke. She says you are first foreigner she sees in real life and please write down *To Raiza*."

Flustered, I oblige. I hope she is not too disappointed when she never reads my name in the credits of forthcoming Hollywood blockbusters. I mutter this to Munnu who is delighted.

"Enjoy this. You can pretend you are film star. Maybe Julia Roberts?" he suggests.

"Can I be Catherine Zeta-Jones?"

"I do not know her."

"Oh, I look exactly like her," I assure him.

He grins.

"Anne. I think you tease. You must stop now because more fans of you come for a signature."

The first couple have opened the floodgates, and I am inundated by requests for an autograph or a photograph: some greedy bodies even look for both. I flex my wrist to ease the cramped fingers and say a swift prayer of thanks that this has not happened previously.

"The professional photographers are very jealous. Maybe I make a deal for signed photographs of you and of us together?" is Munnu's enterprising idea.

"Don't even think of it."

Eventually, I do give in to the pressure to have my portrait taken. It is the only way to get rid of the persistent beach photographers who start to outnumber the autograph hunters. Munnu chooses one young lad with a large camera who enthusiastically wastes an entire film. He offers to waive the fee for the finished prints if he can exhibit them in his shop window. We tell him he may do that anyway, but we will buy our share for the going rate. He looks as if he has just been picked to play for Bangladesh in a Test Match and gloats at his colleagues who disperse good-naturedly, no doubt managing some unauthorised shots as they go.

"It must be a nightmare to be really properly famous," I observe.

"Me, I think it is maximum fun thing. Anne? Would you like to eat *chatpuri*?" Munnu asks as the crowd thins.

We buy steaming bowls from a stationary cart and splash out a few *taka* to hire a sun bed on which to sit and eat it with some sense of decorum. The all-enveloping parasol and fierce minder ensure that the worst of the crowds keep their distance, and when we emerge into half-darkness, the world has gained some semblance of normality. We find a rickshaw with only the usual, manageable entourage.

Before we can drive off, we hear a shout and see the *chatpuri* man jogging towards us. Munnu and he hold a brief but intense dialogue, the vendor grasping Munnu's shoulder like that of a long lost brother. I believe I see a glimmer of tears in his eyes.

"He thanks you for eating his *chatpuri*. Many, many of the people who took your autograph see you choose his cart, and they follow you to buy. For the first day ever, he sells all the food. He begs we come back and eat with him tomorrow for free. I say, maybe."

I nod and smile at the man, regretful that I have done absolutely nothing to deserve the accolades, but very glad that somebody has done well out of the afternoon's surreal quality. Munnu, far more able than me, is glowing from all the attention. But the *chatpuri* man has turned Munnu's mind to real food, and we stop at the roadside restaurant beside the gates to *Zia Guesthouse*.

Since it is early, only 10 p.m., Munnu figures we should also buy provisions to ward off post-midnight hunger pangs. This he does easily by remaining at the table and shouting an order across to the neighbouring store, delivered with alacrity by the assistant. Staggering under the bursting black plastic bags of bananas, biscuits, crisps, and cola, we pay paltry sums for outstanding service, reject the offer of an escort back to the guesthouse, and fall into Munnu's room to engage in the highly cultural activity of watching television—*Psycho 2* if my memory is correct. True to myself, I fall asleep before the first advertisements and am only roused at two o'clock by the efforts of Munnu wafting ripe fruit under my nose. He insists I join him in half a packet of sweet biscuits and some crisps, leaving the empties strewn across the floor.

"Slob," I accuse him.

"What is this 'slob?'" Munnu has antennae for an interesting word. He rolls it around his tongue and starts using it wherever possible. "This is good," says Munnu. "You teach me even more English. Maybe you will help me with an English essay?"

He is seeking a job lecturing in Computer Science at a highly esteemed, and therefore very expensive, Dhaka college. To get an interview, he has already applied in English and Bengali; now he must sit an examination in both languages and write an essay on the War of Liberation. If he is successful, he will then be granted a *viva* with the Board. There will be a shortlist, another interview, and only then, a candidate appointed. "I think maybe seventy applicants sit these exams," he says.

We pass a happy few minutes going through the relevant chapters of a dog-eared history text. I try to explain why such gems as *the Paki-army made tricks against a meatful butcher's son,* and *oh, such men and bastards made hay among the honour of the women* and other less-colourful phrases are strange to the native English speaker. We rephrase the paragraphs in such a way that a balance is struck between improving the syntax and grammar whilst not making it too precise.

"If we make it perfect, then maybe the examiners who write this book do not understand and I fail," says Munnu. He looks pensive.

"Are you nervous?"

"No," he says. "I wonder how I can write 'slob' in the essay."

When he offers a choice of more *Psycho* or MTV, I drag myself off to bed.

Fame is extremely tiring.

As dawn seeps through the partially drawn curtains less than four hours later, I awake and briefly consider watching the sunrise from my

VIP seat on the guesthouse roof. When I wake again, it is a quarter past ten and there is insistent knocking on the door. Resisting the urge to lie in bed and yell "*Ke?*" (Who / what is it?) as a true Bangladeshi would do, I hope the intruders will bugger off. They do not, and when the tapping becomes hammering, I scamper through the connecting door and enter discreetly into Munnu's adjoining room where he is snoring, spread-eagled across his bed, the interminable *Psycho* still going strong. It takes an age to shake him awake to get up and open my door. Which he does, calmly pausing for a cigarette on the way.

Deciding it is not decorous for a stranger to see me in my night attire, even if it is trousers and a sloppy shirt, I hurtle into the bathroom and thus have to skulk there running lots of unwarranted water whilst the bedroom floors are swept.

"Anne. You stop hiding now. The boy is gone." Munnu is leaning coolly on the veranda with studied nonchalance as I emerge.

"I wasn't hiding. I was taking a bath. And besides, there is a nest of ants under the mat," I say, a smokescreen.

"You were hiding. You are shy girl. But I trample the ants for you. Then we go to the sea."

We walk and walk along the relentless shore. Occasionally we pause to drink coconut milk. Hawkers galore carry fruit across their shoulders on bamboo sticks, their evil-looking knives splitting the shells deftly open. For namby-pamby types like me, they carry recycled straws in their vests; otherwise, it's a case of tipping the head back and downing a litre of liquid in one. It is custom to toss the empty shell on the ground for retrieval by the vendor ("Slob," notes Munnu, every time he sees someone do this) and to hand back the plastic straw, which he straightens out, spits on, and as good as new, returns it to nestle in the safety of his wiry chest hair to await the next customer. Seeing this in action, I drink, messily, straight from the coconut.

Periodically we are accosted by the few beggars and hawkers who anticipate rich pickings if they can be bothered to penetrate the milling autograph hunters. Naturally, I am a rich and soft touch, but to give to one apparently deserving widow is to create another clamouring faction. Nevertheless, it is impossible to ignore the thin little girl in the tattered sundress whose skinny wrists can barely support the shell necklaces she is selling, or the infant twins, hand in hand, who have a sticky bag of penny sweets remnants for sale.

"They say that they can eat only if we buy," Munnu tells me as we share out small amounts of taka, refuse the goods, and hope the money is indeed for them and their families, for food.

We pay a cursory visit to the Buddhist Monastery at the east end of the unremarkable town. There is a greater mix of Buddhist, Hindu, and Muslim here than in most parts of Bangladesh, the former partly due to the influence of Myanmar across the border. A faded, hand-written sign states in polyglot English that the monastery is a representation of Burmese architectural style and built in the nineteenth century.

"Okay," Munnu says after an infinitesimal pause, his duty done. "Now," he pauses, and then pulls out his trump card. "We swim."

During my time in Bangladesh I have seen, done, heard, even touched, and certainly smelled, many things that I once assumed beyond my means and comprehension. Some of the outwardly, most-ordinary experiences have verged on the surreal, less because they are intrinsically peculiar than because they are culturally so alien to me. One of the more unusual, yet pleasurable, has to be "swimming" in the sea at Cox's Bazaar.

In anticipation, I pull on my most flowing and least potentially see-through-when-wet *salwar kameez*. Munnu throws a towel around his shoulders, and we hail a rickshaw. At the edge of the water, we hire a sun bed for an hour, take off our shoes and judiciously, I remove my glasses. Public bathing is best done myopically. We wade, fully dressed into the shallow sea, wetting feet and ankles, the water level creeping up towards our knees. It has not occurred to me that even in the relative depths of winter, the water will be warm.

"Warm?" whimpers Munnu in his sweater and trousers. "It is so cold, I get sick."

We agree to differ, but it is definitely, pleasantly lukewarm. It is a sensuous, exotic feeling to stroll against the gentle pull of the sea, my sinuous overdress billowing out, the lower half soaked and clinging to my legs, the flimsy *dupatta* flying, curving out behind me in the breeze. It gives me temporary grace, and I drift along oblivious to any onlooker.

In fact, so far into a little world of my own am I that I fail to notice the sea is up to my waist and the upsurge is spraying my neck, face, hair. So instead of my once in a life time moment of elegance and glamour being recorded for posterity, the beach photographer achieves a series of action shots of me stumbling headfirst into something the size of a tidal wave, being hauled mercilessly upright by Munnu, and drenched and blinking blindly, spitting out salt water directly into the camera.

Anne Hamilton

"Shame this isn't a honeymoon," I observe, squeezing water from my hair-turned-rats' tails with one hand, and clinging onto Munnu's arm for dear life with the other. "The photos would be original."

We emerge to cups of hot, if somewhat suspect, coffee brewed from the flask of our sun-bed minder. My clothes are dry in no time, but Munnu's clothes, thicker and less suited to an improvised dip, remain damp and chill. His teeth chatter all the way back to the hotel. He shrugs philosophically.

"It must be done," he says. "It is point of honour to swim at Cox's Bazaar."

I contemplate how long before Bangladesh catches up with the rest of "civilisation" and some entrepreneur starts printing T-shirts with *"I went swimming at Cox's Bazaar"* emblazoned on the front. I am glad I got here first.

Touchingly aware of my ineptness in these matters, Munnu removes my wet clothes—not from my body, but from the heap on the bathroom floor where I have thrown them after changing, ("Slob," he says smugly)—and expertly rinses them through, wrings them out, and hangs them over the balcony.

"Let the dress drip dry," he orders. "If I squeeze the water from it, it damages the delicate sewing."

"Your mother must be so proud of you." I smile. I point out that his future wife will be a very lucky woman, and he proceeds to tell me that my husband is already a lucky man, and we have a mutually congratulatory moment ending in him inviting me and my entire family to his as yet non-existent wedding and me accepting graciously on their behalf.

We have walked the longest sea beach in the world, been swimming in the sea, and viewed the hotel's entire range of *Psycho* films at least once. It is time to head back to Dhaka.

We have no bus booked, but Munnu is confident that we will cruise the bus station and find something. I hope so because we are down to our last few hundred *taka*. Naturally, he grabs the last two tickets on the next convenient chair coach to Chittagong—Munnu could get a taxi on New Year's Eve night in Dublin, London and New York—and talks the driver into letting me board whilst he disappears into the crowd to forage for rations. I settle back, safe in the knowledge that we will be able to feed the bus in the event of a siege.

In the light of all the preparations for Eid, the journey takes far longer than anticipated. Not only has the traffic increased due to the number of travellers returning to their family units, but also every town, village, and hamlet is virtually impassable. Cows of all shapes and sizes are tethered at every available hitching post. At specially-erected cane fences, they stand in patient bovine lines; others are being led to market. Where there is no further room for cows, goats are squeezed in. Almost all are crowned with gaily-coloured flower wreaths or have equally bright garlands adorning their necks. It makes all the more poignant their sublime ignorance of the carnage coming their way.

The fate, or glory, depending on your religious persuasion, of these animals is to be slaughtered in celebration of Eid-ul-Azha, which is traditionally the day of sacrificing that which is dearest to you to commemorate the prophet Abraham's readiness to sacrifice his son to God. If one family cannot afford a whole animal, then a number of people, the local village or community, will join forces in buying one. Early on Eid morning, the animal is killed at some convenient place—the roadside for example—and the flesh divided into three parts and immediately distributed. It is shared amongst the poor who cannot afford meat, less-well-off relatives, friends, and the remaining immediate family. It is a solemn time, one of remembrance and redefinition of values, and, of course, the perfect excuse for both a jolly good get-together and eating far too much.

It is a logical arrangement that makes sense in modern times. The hungry will all eat. I tell myself this over and over again as the hundreds of comfortably fattened and placidly masticating animals stare me confidently in the face.

"Anne. I see you being sentimental. Stop," Munnu orders. "I promise the cow has a happy death. Somebody sits with her and pats her shoulder as she dies. Do you know," he adds conversationally, "cows scream when they are killed?"

"I'm not listening," I say. "Anyway, you're thinking of lobster."

At 5.40 p.m., a mere five and a half hours since we left Cox's Bazaar, we limp towards the bus station in Chittagong and find that every resident Muslim is doing likewise. Or trying to. Rumour circulates that all buses to all destinations are full. The weary tour companies may or may not put on extra vehicles. Bribes are no longer being accepted, and even the illegal touts have run out of tickets for barter. There is uproar. We cannot get near the terminal for desperate travellers swarming like disorientated ants whose leader has already been flattened in the rush. One wrong word could incite a riot. In fact, this might already be one. I am too far back to tell.

Anne Hamilton

The roar is deafening as people swap heart-wrenching and highly suspect sob stories as to why they have to get out of Chittagong ten minutes ago. They yell abuse at the impervious bus station staff and take a moment to curse this holy and wonderful religious festival which makes for annual pandemonium. The chaos seems somehow familiar, and then I remember. It is something we in the West call Christmas Spirit.

The call goes up of two empty buses to Dhaka. The crowd surges forward, and by dint of crawling through people's legs, knocking elderly widows out of the way, shouting the loudest, and unashamedly using me as collateral, Munnu manages to wangle magic tickets on a chair coach, a bus with partially-reclining seats. The crowd not going to Dhaka cheer his tenacity and slap him on the back with congratulations; those that are, glare balefully.

We have half an hour before the advertised departure of the relief bus, but Munnu trusts his fellow countrymen not one jot.

"They sell many more seats than the bus has," he predicts. "The driver will leave early, soon as it is full. You get on now. I bring tea."

In the overflow parking lot at the rear of the bus terminal, our bus is manned by a disgruntled crew who clearly have been bullied and cajoled into working this evening and are going to drive very fast and very erratically to make up for their inconvenience. I sit down and check that my seat reclines in the accepted manner—the point of a chair coach rather than an ordinary long-distance bus—as too often the lever is jammed, missing or holding the bus together and cannot be moved. There is nothing worse than having to remain bolt upright and pinned to a seat when the eighteen-stone businessman in front of you is fully reclined into your lap with a vertical view up your nostrils.

I am interrupted in trying to right myself from the prone position by a banging on the window. The glass is pulled open from the outside and a cup and saucer, loosely attached to an arm, hovers in mid air. I struggle up to see Munnu's surprised face a couple of feet below me.

"Anne. Do you take rest so soon? Here is tea." He boards with a large carton of cigarettes and a bunch of grapes suitable for mass hospital patient visitation.

"Is all I can get," he explains. "I think they are washed in clean water. If not, I pass the journey peeling them for you."

Repressing the urge to see if he actually would go this far, I eat a handful *au naturel,* indicating that I am now a bona fide temporary resident.

The estimated length of the journey from Chittagong to Dhaka on a "normal" day is five hours, for which the veteran traveller will read as six and a half or seven. A sortie by night, on the eve of the eve of Eid is anyone's guess. Two passengers at the back of the bus are running an informal book as to the time we will arrive. From the odds he is offered, I worry that Munnu's estimate of 4 a.m. is not ironic. I do not place a bet, being too busy wondering why two photographers are making their way down the aisle flashing at each seat in turn. After we have joined the others in being temporarily blinded by the industrial-sized camera, Munnu tells me it is a security measure.

"In case any passenger is robbed or hijacked. Or is a robber or hijacker. They are easily identified. This is routine on night buses where there might be slow travel."

"It didn't happen on the way to Chittagong," I remember.

"Very cheap bus. Chair coach passengers expect to be protected better."

As Munnu surmised, as soon as the bus is full and the driver and his assistant have amassed a further crowd of would-be travellers just outside the doors, there is a roar of the engine, a screech of gears, and we take off from the depot. The driver and his mate can hardly function for turning around to watch and laugh at the irate group of people running after us and impotently waving tickets through the cloud of exhaust fumes. But for the next two hours, the engine is more off than on. If the left-behind passengers had a mind, they could have caught us up in the manner of the hare and the tortoise. The sheer volume of traffic attempting to circumvent the tethered and wandering sacrificial beasts that are only semi-visible in the increasing darkness makes for a gold-standard traffic jam.

At 3.30 a.m. (not quite close enough to his original guestimate for Munnu to win the sweepstake—somebody else has estimated 3.15 a.m.) I am ringing the bell of Apartment 3B and hoping that the chirpy and off-key rendition of *Clementine* echoing around the silent building will not herald my having finally outstayed my welcome.

25

Week 12 - On the Feast of Eid

Friday, the eve of Eid Day, sees an influx of Hasina's relatives groaning under the weight of pre-Eid sweets and snacks. The bustle and flurry, the last minute errands and early preparations, are exactly those of Christmas. We must pay a final visit to Hasina's tailor who has the family's festive outfits in his possession. Hanan is already on holiday, and Mr Hoque has a seasonal golf competition, so the oft-absent Mithu, for once on an extended holiday from his beloved office, takes to the wheel. With it, he throws off his sedate civil servant demeanour and evolves into a five-foot-nothing turkey cock; his car is simply an extension of him. In appearance, Mithu's car, a prim Toyota Starlet, is a squeaky clean, washed-each-Sunday-morning-by-one-careful-owner mode of getting to one's destination at thirty miles an hour. If it were clothes, it would be nylon slacks and a polyester tank top. But with Mithu behind the wheel, it becomes tight leather jeans and a huge dangling medallion; it evolves into the Toyota Testosterone. At least there is safety as well as novelty in the relative emptiness of the main roads. Literally half the population of Dhaka has headed home to the villages, and the only busy places are the shopping centres where shell-shocked punters fight for last-minute bargains and snatch frozen beef cutlets from one another, having somehow forgotten to buy their share in a cow.

"It is like London. Like Harrods. Yes?" With her shopping done, Hasina beams benevolently around her, safe in the knowledge that her own household preparations are almost complete. "Shopping takes much longer than Marks & Spencer's at Marble Arch," she had said earlier in the day. "One more shop," she promises. "Meat for the freezer—in case there is not enough to share from the slaughtering tomorrow."

It is like seeing a road accident. The meat is hanging from canopy hooks attached to rusty scaffolding, and carcasses crowd the front of the stall like an obstacle course, and passing by without getting a slap

251

in the eye from a swaying piece of mutton flank is a laudable feat. Bloody off-cuts—skin, bone, offal, hairy ears, and glassy eyes—litter the floor. Hasina directs this dismemberment and supervises its stuffing into a jumbo-sized polythene bag or six.

It is heaven for the fat flies taking first pick of the goodies. Some settle on the hanging meat, valiantly swatted by a young boy with a witch's broom, but the majority indulge in an uninterrupted gastronomic experience feasting on the cut pieces, crawling languidly over the diced meat destined for the Hoque family deep freeze like a holiday maker at an all-inclusive who cannot resist temptation.

Three fine specimens have been so gluttonous as to die mid-mouthful and are gamely gouged out and flicked away before the butcher slings the meat into a bag. Let's revise that: two of them are gouged and flicked, the third I'm sure is now somewhere in a 5 kg bag ready to be marinated in yoghurt, herbs and spices, and roasted on the barbecue. Luckily, I don't have time to be sick. I am too morbidly fascinated by the hand of the man brandishing the knife. He has the tips of three fingers completely missing.

Maybe we're lucky to have only a dead fly in the bag. Though I do lay favourable odds that if Hasina got home to find three human digits in her meat bag, she would coolly calculate their weight and return to the maimed vendor to berate his carelessness and demand the extra meat owing. At the apartment block, we view the scenario from the other end of the scale.

"Come and see," Hasina says, crossing to the other side of the car park. In two of the empty bays, tethered to the concrete posts and lying on makeshift beds of straw, are two, dopey-eyed, creamy-beige cows, and a pint-size black goat.

"One is bought by the first floor, the other by the fifth floor. I do not know about the goat. I think it is a good luck gift to the customers for buying good and expensive animals. But," she adds, "bad luck for the goat."

"Where do all the animals go for slaughtering?" I ask, a vision of patient bovine queues outside sterile, purpose-built abattoirs being both bizarre and unlikely.

"They do not go anywhere," Hasina disapproves. "The butchers go to the animals, and they are killed right there. Right here," she adds, nodding at the three animals in front of us. "It is horrible."

I take in the spotless car park, the respectful yet tight security, the upmarket Gulshan residence, and try to imagine it converted to a blood-spattered slaughterhouse. Hasina expounds at length on the unpleasantness of seeing bits of newly dead animal everywhere.

Anne Hamilton

"We must leave here tomorrow before 9 a.m.," she decides as the lift ascends. "It is not nice to step through fresh and bleeding meat. Last year," she is indignant now, "the bottom of my sari, my new silk sari delivered only that morning, was soiled with blood. Ugh."

I know that there is little chance of us departing for Hasina's parents' home where we will spend Eid until mid-morning and resign myself to wading through rivers of gore and piles of quivering guts. Not to mention the sights I will encounter lying alongside the roads, fallen off the back of a lorry, or a passing offal cart.

Munnu and Bachchu phone from Takerhad to say "Happy Eid." I am inordinately pleased and feel native to be receiving calls from other parts of the country.

"Anne?" Munnu says. "I have surprise for you. Wait."

There is scuffling in the background, and then a ragged chorus of: "Anne! Happy Eid! Happy Returns!"

"Chapa, Asha, and Mary!" I shout, thrilled. "Happy Eid! Happy Eid all of you!"

"Happy Eid!" they echo before the line goes dead. "Happy Eid..."

Suez calls from his family home in Mymensingh, and Bonny, with Pavel and Rehana beside him, from his just around the corner from the SCI office. Borhan phones from his village. All offer last minute invitations to spend Eid, or at least a few days holiday afterwards with them. I even manage to get a phone card and speak to Christine in Sydney. She doesn't seem to mind very much that it's the middle of the night there.

Colouring my own dreams is the squealing, bleating, and mournful honking heralding the quick and "happy death" of the trio of animal sacrifices in the car park.

"At least people will eat tonight," I tell myself sternly on Eid morning.

Bely bangs on my door, her arms full of rich red and gold material, a heavy velvet dress, and silk trousers. She intimates she is going to dress me and that this gorgeous outfit is simply another of her cast-offs. I step into the deep ruby fabric, feel the weight of the fancy gold embroidery around the neckline, the sleeves, the hem, the softest brush of the silk pants. Bely decides my hair should be tied up and forces it into an untidy knot, securing it with my white shell clasp. As I glance in the mirror, the *salwar kameez* no longer appears strange to my eyes; I wear it easily, and it is only when I compare myself with the finesse of Hasina, Bely, and Mitali that I remember the impostor I am.

Hasina claps her hands and tells me how beautiful I look and summons Mr Hoque, resplendent in a white and gold Punjabi suit, to photograph me perched on the edge of a Victorian chaise longue with mock William Morris wallpaper in the background. My timid smile and gauche posture must be that of a shy debutante doing her first season—but with none of the coached poise.

"What do you think of my slippers, huh? You like them?" Mr Hoque holds out first one foot, and then the other for admiration. Bejewelled with coloured stones set in gold and hand-embroidered on white silk, they are props from the Arabian Nights. I almost expect the toes to curl up in a froth of magic tassels.

"Handmade in Pakistan," Mr Hoque boasts. "You cannot believe your eyes, hey?"

He wastes an unwarranted amount of film recording me from all possible angles, and then hands back the camera. "It is time to leave. Where is Mrs Hoque now? Always the women are late, so late."

Hasina is at the kitchen counter spooning cold sweetened rice pudding and sloppy vermicelli alternately into tiny glass dishes and her mouth. "Eat." She thrusts a bowl at me and another at her husband. "Try just a little. It might be that we wait for the meat to cook. You do not want to be hungry."

"Hungry? Bah." Mr Hoque pooh-poohs the very idea. "It is good to miss a meal sometimes. We eat too much food. Me, I have not been hungry since 1960. Yet still I eat, still you women make me eat," he says as he tucks in to breakfast, holds out his dish for more and more again. Hasina smiles and says not a word.

"Little bit more. Just little bit." She coaxes me to finish the gallon container.

"Now we must go. Come. Come." Mr Hoque bangs down the bowl, licks his lips and disappears to take his blood pressure.

Mitali rounds up her children, Oni and Fiona. Bely sticks close to Mithu, and we all wait for Hasina to direct travel operations.

"Now, Anne. You watch something very strange," Mr Hoque booms just before we leave the apartment. I assume he is speaking of the dismembered animals in the streets. But no. Hasina, laughing and unusually shy, kneels down in front of Mr Hoque, bows her head and touches both of his feet.

I agree that his jewelled sandals are magnificent—but that much?

"You will see this happening the whole day," Hasina explains the religious overtones as she struggles upright, balancing herself on her husband's impatient forearm. "It is a greeting, a tradition of respect from younger people to those who are older."

Anne Hamilton

"And I am the one who is older," mourns Mr Hoque. "Always she reminds me that I am the elder."

"As it should be, my husband." Hasina picks up her copious handbag and confirms the presence of her mobile phones. "Come," she says. "We visit."

Down in the car park, I cannot decide whether to avert my eyes or squint towards the temporary abattoir. Hasina recognises my dilemma.

"Anne, is okay. Most of the butchering is over."

A couple of industrious men with very large knives are dividing up a skinned and disembowelled carcass. A smaller, elderly man (the *mullah*—the priest—his head wear gives him away) is drinking a glass of tea and looking as if he should be elsewhere. Despite myself, I feel a bit cheated with the anti-climax of seeing a very scary movie that's not so scary after all.

It is not so once we reach the main road. Had Mithu been at the wheel, the sights would be passing in a hazy blur, but Mr Hoque's comparatively sedate transportation allows ample opportunity to drink in the scene.

Corpses in various stages of dismemberment litter the streets. Warm blood which has not yet clotted and congealed into crimson puddles runs in rivulets along the gutters, filling the cracks and slowly diluting pink as young boys throw cleansing buckets of cold water about the place. Heads, horns and skins strewn across the pavement are swept into tidy piles and the heaps look horribly like pantomime horse costumes, deflated and unreal and not yet brought to life by the actors.

Elsewhere, the chopping-up process is in full swing. Thickly-marbled steaks are laid out on rough sacking or torn plastic tarpaulins. The men and the boys—it is solely a male preserve—take it in turns to do both the physical labour and stand on the sidelines yelling out good-natured advice. Fleetingly I wonder about the public health risk of slaughtering animals in this public fashion. Whatever the rapidity and variable skill of the butcher, there is no taking away from the fact that the culling is by sweating volunteers fending off insects and dog life beneath the hot sun on a dirty and polluted roadside. It is how I imagine the Middle Ages in Europe.

The closer we get to Hasina's parents' house, located only a few miles across the city, the further the butchery has gone. When the brains, liver, and kidneys are neatly separated, the skinned heads stare sightlessly, just calling for an orange to be stuffed into their gaping, rictus mouths. Scavengers seize any opportunity to seek out these off-cuts. Mute and patient, tiny children and emaciated widows on their own pilgrimages loiter on the edge of the killing fields until beckoned forth to glean a few scraps of skin and bone. Mr Hoque swerves dangerously, letting out a bellow of laughter.

"Look at this, Anne." He peers over his shoulder towards me. "See Topsy and Tim—you know *Topsy and Tim* stories huh? Over there. See? With their prize."

I see two children who look barely old enough to be going to school, both with hair closely cropped, though one wears a torn dress and the other has a scrap of material acting as a *lunghi*. They hold open a green carrier bag, their faces turned gleefully to an older boy, a butcher's assistant, who laconically holds a bald cow's head, slippery between his palms. They chatter excitedly and the big boy, well aware of the momentous nature of the gift, teases them, pretends to offer it elsewhere. They howl in response. He grins and puts the thing carefully on the ground in front of them. He stands just close enough to ensure that the head is not snatched away by bigger and stronger contestants, and he watches the children whose faces become stern with concentration. Their puzzle is how to squeeze the big head— several times bigger than their own heads put together—into their small container. As we drive away, I crane backwards to see them painstakingly tearing the plastic, wrapping it carefully around the head, and, their little backs bent, they roll it like a punctured rugby ball protectively down the street.

The meat, due no doubt to what it represents, is handled carefully. As Mr Hoque steers the car down alleys growing narrower and narrower, he frequently pauses to skirt the obstacles. Eventually, in a back street near our destination, he slews the car across the road and parks crookedly.

"I think there will be no place in the car park." Hasina defends the necessity of having to walk further than is strictly necessary. "We wait here whilst I check." She fishes out the most convenient cell phone and dials her brother's number to get a full rundown on the progress of the cow killings.

"No," she sighs. "Some of the meat has gone upstairs but much is still being cut. We must walk to the apartments." She complains about the unprofessional work as we step into the morning sun. "They are so slow here. See how quickly the work was done in Gulshan? Always, my brother and his neighbours stop to drink tea and to talk. Last year they chewed *paan* whilst they chopped up the meat. I do not like this."

Mr Hoque rubs his hands together. "So we parade through the killing fields." He grins at me, quite aware that my blasé, seen-it-all stance is nothing but skin-deep bravado. "All in the name of religion," he says. "We eat the flesh and drink the blood," (I hope he is speaking metaphorically) "in its most fundamental form. Do not Christians do the same in a more sanitised way? What is the word the Catholic uses?"

And so, I pick up my skirts and, dressed in my borrowed best, I wade through knee-high carnage whilst discussing the rudiments of transubstantiation.

One of Hasina's brothers—let's call him Number 1—is in the thick of it with a rusty-coloured rope and a bucket of blood at his feet. His striped, blue and white vest looks as if he's the victim of an unstoppable nosebleed, his lunghi acting as a convenient cloth for wiping bloody hands. He and his fellows sit in party atmosphere around the animal, encouraged by shouts of children and women folk leaning over the balconies high above them. Each of the men pauses to greet us with an individual "Hello, how are you? Happy Eid." Like a cautious patient recovering from surgery, I tread gently and slowly, terrified I will slip and squash the holy sacrifice and face, if not the wrath of Allah, that of his disciples on earth *and* end up wallowing face first in raw and still warm flesh.

"Careful," Hasina warns me. "Do not step on the drips of blood. They are slippery and stick to your shoes."

Detritus on the stairs suggests that an incompetent murderer has committed his felonious act and hastened away without covering his tracks. Little drips of blood and scraps of fat are discernible on the walls and the steps, culminating in a small, child-high, sticky, red handprint on the door to the family apartment. In the large sitting room the ceiling fan is humming, the door to the balcony is open and the air feels cool and fresh.

Hasina tries to introduce me to those I haven't met, yelling above the din of welcome. "This is my youngest sister, and my niece...her husband...their children. My second sister...her daughter-in-law and baby. The two boys who are so shy...Meet my next brother, two more sisters, the butcher, the baker, candlestick maker..."

Never has there been a more viable arena for identification badges. Hasina's mother is a tiny, wrinkled woman with her hair pulled tightly back and a scarf over her head, lost in the immense depths of her armchair. She smiles in such a way it is clear from where Hasina and her siblings get their good looks. She is nodding and smiling at her attentive family, acknowledging their veneration as her bare feet are touched again and again. Occasionally, she is given a stray baby to hold, a fat and healthy babbling infant whose chubbiness enhances her frailty, her stick-like arms, and her liver-spotted hands. Hasina's father, receiving guests in twos and threes, spends much of the time in his bedroom, ostensibly praying but probably delighted to be protected from this frenetic crowd of people who claim to be relatives. In careful English, he thanks me for visiting his family. This reversal of gratitude is still unexpected. I assume I am in the position of privilege, and my resultant thanks are received courteously but often quizzically.

"It is the host's pleasure that you have honoured him," Hasina says.

At present the flat is a happily meat-free zone. As cooking has not yet begun, a brimming box of something akin to Turkish Delight is doing the rounds, and I am encouraged to fill my mouth until my cheeks are bursting.

"Put extra pieces in your pocket," Hasina urges. "We eat here later. First we visit my brothers. Come."

There is another flurry of feet kissing and knee grabbing which only the very old take with equanimity, the others showing varying degrees of embarrassment, attempting to laugh off the custom or play it down. I am offering up my own thanks that we are not eating so soon. It is barely eleven o'clock and the scenes en route have done little to whet my appetite.

In an adjoining wing of the block, in an apartment far smaller than his parents', Hasina's Brother Number 2 lives with his family. The three rooms are packed with old, as opposed to antique, furniture and indescribable knick-knacks of sentimental value.

"We do not have meat here either," Hasina warns me in a low voice. She looks anxious, and I wonder if I am inadvertently slavering, and the revolted fascination in my eyes is being misinterpreted as a rampant carnivore denied her immediate protein fix. "However," she continues. "There are sweets. On Eid day every home has snacks ready for visitors. It is especially rude not to offer food on this day."

And it would be equally impolite of the guest to demur.

In seconds the table is covered by great glass dishes of desserts: a sticky vermicelli pudding, wet and dry halva, coconut rice balls, and two large bottles of RC Cola. We all cram into the small dining-room which doubles as a bedroom, and shovel, slurp, and munch such that any passing alien would assume us given ten minutes to eat until the monsoon comes. A quick rinse of hands, and we pass to the next family apartment, that of (I think) Hasina's Sister Number 3 who has diverted from both the beef and the sweet tradition. I all but sink to my knees with a fervent hallelujah.

"Yes," confirms Hasina. "Instead she is serving kedgeree and chicken legs."

I can now empathise with a goose bred for foie gras.

"Keep plenty of room for the beef," advises Hasina, lest I forget. "This is why I give you only four chicken legs."

"Thank you," I say as she heaps spoons full onto my plate and takes double that for her own eager consumption. Seven or eight family members, Mithu, Bely, and Mitali amongst them, join us here, and we all sit around a large dining-table that has been dragged to the centre of the room. It becomes a regular meal, a scene played throughout the world on any high day or festival. As we nibble these aperitifs, Sister Number 3, squatting over a plastic cloth to protect the expensively patterned carpet, is methodically packing bite-size pieces of a skinned and boned dead cow into an array of recycled containers for her less well-off neighbours.

A full quarter of an hour passes, and the family gets edgy.

"So impatient," Mr Hoque says to me. "I am not in a hurry because I do not eat lunch. So much meat is bad for the health."

And I'm not in a hurry because I've had five breakfasts and a couple of roast chickens, I think ungratefully.

"Today only, do you see men in the kitchen," he continues. "They feel they have rights over the beef because it is they who have slaughtered it."

"They must see it is cooked perfectly," adds Brother Number 2, now in a spotless white Punjabi suit.

"But how would they know?" butts in Hasina. "No man, unless professional chef, knows about family meals."

"Right. Because too many women in the kitchen." Mr Hoque is determined to have the last word, and Hasina is reluctant to let him.

"I think this happens in UK too." Hasina looks to me. "And Ireland."

"The barbecue phenomenon," I say.

"What is this?"

I explain to her the seasonal male urge to don an apron and burn steaks over a charcoal grill.

"Yes, I see this," Hasina says delightedly. "But always it is cold…"

I will never find out if she is referring to the meat or the weather because with a cry of the Bengali equivalent of *ta-dah!* food borne on a wave of ceramic platters is brought to the dining table, as well as about eighteen dishes of beef still attached to great chunks of bone. There is rice, salad, and Sister Number 3's leftover chicken and kedgeree. For the first and last time, I see fully grown Bangladeshi men help themselves only sparingly to rice, barely three or four handfuls each. The order of the day is meat consumption. I spoon up a couple of lumps from the nearest bowl and attempt to slink back into the shouting, chewing, crunching, critical crowd. It is not that the food is unappetising. The rich smell of savoury gravy is fragrant and would be mouth-watering if I was even remotely peckish. Hasina sees me.

"Anne, you must try little bit more. You have only plain meat. Give me your plate. Give here." She holds out her hand and proceeds to describe the various dishes to me. "*This* beef has thin gravy only, but *this* one has a rich sauce and onions. *This* has extra chilli—I think a little too hot for you, so I give you extra of *this*, and some roti." She piles a half-dozen thin discs of bread on top of the steaming meat, and finds a chair where she can keep an eye on me whilst still yelling her opinions into the general melee. She is also feeding Fiona from her hand. The child opens her mouth like an obedient goldfish, but with no inhibitions over spitting out any morsel unpleasant to her taste buds.

"See what Mrs Hoque is doing?" her husband shouts towards me. "Feeding her like a baby. Bengali mothers never let children grow up, so always they stay dependant. In UK, Australia, USA this does not happen. Bangladeshi mothers. Bah."

The conversation, which until now I have been guestimating, is fast and furious. Suddenly it ceases and forty-five pairs of interested eyes, including assorted babies, are turned on me.

"Anne. Do you like? It is good, yes?"

"I never had anything like it before," I say honestly, knowing how good it would taste if I were hungry. "It is excellent."

Murmurs of approval all round. The silence continues.

"I will always remember Eid here with you," I say with feeling, appreciating more than I can say to the happy faces around me, these hospitable people who are treating me like one of their own. Smiles of pleasure and nods of encouragement fill me with the awful sense that I have begun a speech and am being expected to see it through to the bitter end. I rack my brains for suitable Bangla phrases. Luckily, someone chooses this moment to bring reverently forth the *pièce de resistance*, another two aromatic tureens of liver, smooth and slightly rubbery, and what appears to be mashed brown lentils flecked with fresh herbs. The liver disappears politely, similar to Westerners accepting the festive but much-reviled Brussels sprouts. The second dish is fallen upon with lip-smacking, finger-licking delight. Mr Hoque helps himself liberally.

"The real delicacy," he says with a beatific mouthful. "The brains of the cow. But," he warns me, "take only a small amount. It is very high with cholesterol."

"You warned me just in time," I say.

In the confused flurry of thanks and goodbyes, I definitely see strange faces. I am sure the company has somehow trebled in size. I would not be a bit surprised to hear that two marriages have occurred and at least three babies born in the last few hours.

With Hasina directing Mr Hoque from the front seat of the car, and Mitali, Fiona, me, and a couple of sisters in the back, we bounce down a poorly lit street clogged with covered and stationary rickshaws, haphazardly parked cars, and abandoned road mending equipment. Already, Mr Hoque has had to reverse three times for oncoming drivers even more stubborn than he. His nerves are frayed and not helped by the running commentary and inconsistent advice offered by his assorted female relatives. Out of nowhere an enormous, four-legged beast looms in the headlamps, and it is either this or the accompanying shrieks of the womenfolk that causes him to swerve violently. The car jerks, lurches sideways, and with an ominous clonk and tearing of metal, comes to a halt, tilted in such a way that suggests the back tyres have disappeared down a large hole. Mr Hoque revs the engine but the impotent wheels only spin and grind.

We all make a simultaneous attempt to get out, but the shift of our weight causes it to groan and sink some more. Scrambling out, Fiona starts to cry, everyone else starts to shout, and above all we hear the deep and astonished moo of an immense cow, her features now clear in the unnatural tilt of the lights. Mr Hoque is at the rear of the car inspecting the left wheel jammed deeply into a craterous pothole; the bumper and mud flaps scrape the ground, bent and twisted.

"All to miss the cow," yells Mr Hoque. "The cow! That cow should not be here! It should be dinner! Why was it not killed?"

He looks at the quickly gathering audience as if he really wants an answer. A rumble of voices offers advice (men) and sympathy (women) and a veritable horn-blowing traffic jam collects behind us. The animal in question, obviously terrified by her close encounter, supplements her plaintive mooing with a lavish emptying of her not-inconsiderable bowel. Fiona's wails turn into giggles, and Mr Hoque rants some more. Not even Hasina can get a word in.

"Who did not kill this cow, huh?" he demands rhetorically, looking as if he will happily correct the oversight right now and with his bare hands.

Fiona surpasses herself. "Maybe it is Hindu cow," she shouts, pleased with herself. "See? A Hindu cow. A Hindu cow is not killed for Eid." Reaction to her clever deduction being less than she would have hoped, she pulls on Mitali's sleeve. "Mama, I say maybe the cow is a Hindu cow..."

Mitali hushes her. "Maybe. But quiet now, papa is angry."

Fiona, mutinous, goes to investigate the damage and stands with her arms folded. "The car is stuck down a big hole," she clarifies for the intellectually challenged. "Is it broken forever?"

In fact, with a concerted heave from a gang of fit and obliging young men, the car is somehow hoisted out of its resting place and pronounced fit to continue the journey...which is completed in a very careful silence.

Back in the apartment, we change our finery for house clothes. Hasina throws down some plastic sheeting onto the kitchen floor, tips out two lots of meat—one share of the Gulshan car park massacre, the other a family gift—drags out a dusty "village" knife from a dark corner of the maids' bathroom, and prepares deep-freezable chops and steaks. Allowed to assist, we form an industrious cottage industry. I squish the meaty piles into see-through bags, Mitali labels them, and Bely (in between ministering to Mithu's needs) throws them into the groaning chest freezer. I will dream of raw meat for nights to come, the smell of it in my nostrils, picking scraps from the soles of my feet, scrubbing finger nails for ingrained slivers.

"We are finished," announces Hasina. "Parvin will cook this on her return." She glances towards the clock. "It is late. Anne, would like to eat a little bit now?"

26
Fantasy Kingdom

It is Day ninety-four in Bangladesh, the day after Eid, and Fantasy Kingdom is the new hotspot. The Hoque family and Hasina's extended relatives are taking a picnic.

Fantasy Kingdom is a theme park in the making. In Ashulia, beyond the urban sprawl of Dhaka where the residential areas peter out into a scattering of homesteads and partially-cleared sites for sale, there is a characterless tarmac road which might be European or American (save for the barrier to a toll road surrounded by rickshaws and painted trucks), at the end of which a far-sighted developer has a dream of a magical, pastel oasis, an embryonic Disneyland into which the excited middle classes will drag fractious offspring—and he will make a lot of money.

"Will Mickey Mouse be there?" asks Fiona suspiciously. "And the Donald Duck? Will there be a parade with mermaids?"

"There will be tears," Mitali says to me. "She has seen photographs of her cousins in Disney World in America. I think this place will be smaller."

From a distance, the complex is a cross between a superior garden centre and a Toys "R" Us superstore. Closer up, it is possible to spy half-built rides and attractions, all round-edged and smooth and half-painted in a medley of muted nursery colours. From the entrance, it seems as if a lot of weary travellers have come upon a marzipan and gingerbread house and have begun to dismantle and eat it. It is a project behind schedule and, loth to delay its grand opening to a less lucrative day, the park is open with half-price admission on production of coupons collected from a daily newspaper.

Fiona's young cynicism is easily dispelled. "It looks like a fairy tale castle." She talks in English for my benefit. "You see the cartoons? The animals on the roof. I do not know them, but they are pretty."

Hasina insists that, once beyond the turnstiles, we regroup for instructions. Mr Hoque listens momentarily, and then joins me in the

263

shade of a make-believe orange tree. "Jobs for the boys," he says, his business head on. "You know this phrase—jobs for the boys? But you do not know what Mrs Hoque is saying?"

She appears to be pointing out the two, over-wing emergency exits and the floor-level strip lighting that will guide us there in the event of power failure, but I've been on an aeroplane too many times. I think, not unusually, she might be talking about food. Mr Hoque enlightens me.

"Everything must have a coupon," he explains. "You like a drink or some food, so you bring your entry ticket to this counter." He gestures vaguely towards a semicircular bar counter behind us. Three bored-looking boys stand behind it. "Here they take your money and give you a coupon. Then you take this coupon to the drink stall—" He points out a mobile cart with an umbrella over the top "—where you exchange it for your choice. You see the problem?" He glares at me as if lecturing a junior accounts clerk in the art of high finance. "Inefficient use of resources. Duplication. Why do we not pay directly for the drink or the ice cream or the fish fingers? Huh?"

"Because," I say, the answer being obvious, "this is Bangladesh."

He roars. "Anne, I think you stay here too long. So let us try this system. We will buy ice cream."

Everyone pairs off in the way most likely to ensure a pleasant four or five hours. The teenagers need to demonstrate their superiority, their boredom with the childish attractions, and detach themselves from the embarrassment of family. They slope off behind the bike sheds to kick tin cans around and talk about MTV. The next generation, Mitali *et al* who are old enough to be comfortable acting like children, head straight for the Pirate Ship, a sort of swinging air-boat contraption that hovers in the wind before repeatedly plummeting to earth. They are beaten to it by five fleet-footed and rotund females shrouded in identical black cotton burkhas and huge, gold-rimmed Gucci sunglasses. All of them squirm and shriek through the ride, immediately get off, and stand in line for another turn.

The little ones are shipped off to a variety of dodgems, giant teacups, and a benevolent Ferris Wheel, their gloating mamas waving and calling as the bemused infants go round in circles. The men just disappear, probably to the car park, and everyone else wanders around enjoying the sun, the free day, and the bargain of half-price tickets. I attach myself to whichever group is in the marginal shade. For once, I almost blend into the crowd. Yes, people stop, stare and nudge their companions, but I am a one-hit wonder; far more interesting is the half-complete roller coaster, or the "ready soon" centrepiece: a log flume which promises, according to the billboards, to drench all riders in the "gentle crystal seas."

Desultory work goes on, that is to say the workmen lounge around with pencils behind their ears, drink Cokes, and knowledgably explain the aerodynamics of the roller coaster to gasping visitors.

"Auntie. Auntie," Fiona calls to me from standing point on a wooden bench, all the better to make herself heard. "I see people who look white like you."

The whole park turns to compare the facial features of the Australian architect, his assistant, and me. Fiona learns that these patient men do not know Christine and have not met her Aunt Bobby. They soften the blow by giving her a melting packet of M&Ms, and feel obliged to say a polite hello to me, someone with whom they have nothing in common but a skin colour.

"I wish the men were your brothers," Fiona says longingly. "They could come and live in our house like you."

Nobly, Hasina pretends not to hear this bright idea.

The sun is beating down, and I feel the blood drumming in my ears and the veins on the back of my hands thickening and pulsating with the heat. Today heralds *basanto*, one of the mini-seasons between the cold and monsoon times of year. It means, explains Hasina, that from today onwards, temperatures will noticeably increase.

"You are so pale, Anne." Hasina is concerned. "Why do you not get red in the sun? Are you sick?"

Fiona hears this and pats Hasina's arm. "Auntie is not sick," she explains. "She is pale because she has white skin."

"Do you have a fever?" Hasina continues.

"I don't think so," I insist, sure she has a thermometer—probably rectal—in the depths of her bag. I tell her that I find the glorious weather unexpected and that I must acclimatise.

"Hmm. I keep my eyes on you." She makes me drink a litre of warm water and eat an extra portion of the picnic fish fingers for the added protein. For the millionth time, I feel like a ten-year-old but take refuge in the fact that Hasina is mother to everyone.

"Maybe you are feeling homesick on this holiday?" Mitali joins in.

"Not at all," I say truthfully.

"Really? This is true?"

"Really." Home feels about a million miles away, a black-and-white parallel universe put on hold. I have always found it easy to be the one travelling compared with the one left behind. Of course I miss my husband, but we are both very self-sufficient, and since we met years ago in college, we have spent long periods apart. Still, in the face of

Mitali's scepticism, I do wonder if it should be this easy to slip between two lives.

I put the thought on hold for a cooler day.

About two hours before our intended departure, Hasina starts to reckon up who is lost, when they were last seen, and where. As if by some filial telepathy, the clan begin to congregate and soon there are enough of us to send out a search party for the latecomers. And then a second search party to seek out the first who fail to return with the original lost souls. There are more cell phones than at a Vodaphone convention. At one point, Hasina is having a telephone conversation with Sister Number 3 whom she berates for having slipped off home early. Actually, the sister tells her, "I am in the car. Look! You can see me waving!"

My flu-like symptoms increase throughout the evening, and I realise that my mouth is full of unexplained ulcers, painful when I eat. I try hard to convince Hasina that I will go without supper, and we compromise on a dish of frosty ice-cream. Whilst I dine royally, enjoying the numbness of my lips and throat, she sits quietly, shocked that I can survive on such feeble sustenance.

"Mithu is sick also," she thinks out loud.

That explains the groans from within his bedroom. With him and Bely ensconced therein, I had not liked to enquire.

"Yes. He has a fever and an itch." Nice. "I think he has too much sun today. You also. You must both take rest."

I spend the night tossing and turning with a mercurial fever, raging thirst, and an increasingly dry mouth and sore throat. Even worse, I've got Mithu's itch which, I subsequently find out, is from an infectious bite on his nose that spread to his forehead. What I thought was an ordinary pin-prick mosquito bite in the middle of my chin has mutated into a huge, red boil covered in a delightful spread of tiny blisters, and it itches like mad. Certainly, whatever was feasting on Mithu at Fantasy Kingdom seems to have had me for pudding.

I count out a triple starting dose of antibiotics, pull agonised faces as I attempt to swallow them, and significantly play down the symptoms in the company of my hosts, especially when I hear that Mithu is going immediately to the doctor.

"You are sure you are okay?" Mr Hoque says suspiciously to me. "Self-diagnosis can be a fatal mistake."

Prudently, I do not mention the self-medication and promise I will reconsider the doctor this evening. After an excruciating half hour gargling with warm salt water and application of a topical anaesthetic, both of which bring temporary relief, I announce my intention to visit the SCI office. Reluctantly, they let me go.

Post Eid, SCI is open and working to full capacity. That is, Bonny is behind the desk reading the newspaper, Suez is on the sofa reading his, Pavel is cranking up the computer, and Shahardot is tea monitor for the random staff and volunteers who wander in and out.

"We are sorry that the Srimangal Work Camp was postponed," Suez apologises. "It is good you visited anyway. Also, Cox's Bazaar, longest sea beach in the world. Is very fine place, yes?"

"We would like to make a programme for you," says Bonny. "We would like you to go to Savar today. Okay?"

"Okay. Great," I say. Physically, I'm not sure I'm up to it, but actually there is little chance the short trip will go ahead because some urgent business will definitely come up. Still, the sentiment is sincere.

Moni calls in, and then Bachchu, and Munnu arrives back in town for his job interview. None shows any sign of leaving and Shahardot runs around brewing more tea than could possibly be drunk at an AGM of the Women's Institute. Mid-afternoon, Suez apologises that he has no time to visit Savar today, but that Munnu is free to take me. I smile at the long-suffering Munnu.

"Have you time for this?" I ask him as we wait for a rickshaw. "Should you not be studying?" I remember the history essay.

He lights up a cigarette. "I finish for the day. It is my pleasure to take you, even if Suez does not say it is my duty as a volunteer."

"He said that?"

"Yes." Munnu grins. "I think they know that we are married."

"We are *what*?"

"Have you already forgotten the paper you sign in Rangmati, my shining Bengali wife?"

I snatch his precious cigarette and grind it under my heel. Munnu is nearly as astonished as the rickshaw-*wallah* who pulls up in front of us. "Anne. Why do you do this?"

"Because if I was your wife, I would not want you slowly to kill yourself with tobacco."

Munnu laughs. "It is good you care," he says, lighting another.

The young driver of the rickshaw giggles in bemused sympathy. His eyes follow the crushed cigarette, and I can see him thinking that Munnu would not have to put up with that kind of behaviour from a proper Bangladeshi girl.

The National Martyr's Monument is called *Sriti Saudha* and lies just outside the town of Savar, a few kilometres north of Dhaka. It is a fifty-foot high, tapering, concrete, triangle memorial in the shape of the Eiffel Tower. Dedicated to the victims of the 1971 War, the surrounding grassy platforms cover the mass, unmarked graves of the countless who died. It is a place of pilgrimage and a communal park, a convenient and pleasant place of patriotism suitable for a family day out. Temporary cafés and souvenir stalls line the perimeter, and the grounds are clean and well maintained. Little girls carry single red roses for sale, and the boys offer tin mugs of water. Two of them barter with Munnu. They will give him two cups of water for one cup of our cola. Munnu, soft-hearted to the last, refuses their water but carefully fills their mugs with Coke. They creep away as if they have liquid gold.

We make slow progress. Other visitors invariably stop us and ask Munnu for an explanation of me, and in seconds, an interested crowd has gathered. I say my few words of Bengali and get a standing ovation. Parents push their children forward to get a closer look. Those with cameras, fortunately for me a small percentage, request a picture of me beside their offspring, and I smile until I am weary and the light starts to fade. I often wonder how many of those polite and friendly Bangladeshis still have that commemorative photograph of their day in Savar when they met the foreign girl with the twisted mouth and the disfigured chin ("Anne. You exaggerate," scolds Munnu, "No person in SCI Office even noticed your problem.") who kept swallowing different coloured tablets. On how many metaphorical mantelpieces does my peculiar image still stand?

Mithu is undergoing blood tests for his illness. His visit to the family doctor, accompanied by his wife, his mother, and his sister, suggests an infection. I can hear his wails of anguish through the walls. On a visit to the bathroom, I peer briefly into his room and see him stretched out on the bed thumping his pillow, groaning with pain and Bely fondly wiping his brow with a cool sponge. Pain? *Pain?* If he had a stiff jaw and a mouth full of bleeding ulcers, *then* he would know what pain is! Still, I await his diagnosis with interest.

Guiltily, I cross my fingers and tell Hasina and Mr Hoque a white lie and say that I ate my lunch and dinner out. I know I am a teeny bit prone to exaggeration, but this time I am deliberately understating the torture when trying to open my mouth; it brings involuntary tears to my eyes. Mr Hoque is not convinced, and in desperation I consent to some more ice cream. Hasina hands me a two-litre tub of Mango Delight and a teaspoon.

"Finish it," she implores.

I face mission impossible. It would take an American to eat this much ice cream at one sitting. Fiona takes pity on me. Rooting in the container with sticky fingers, she takes a mouthful for herself, digs the spoon in and coaxes me to open my mouth. "Just a little, little bit, Auntie." In the end, we sneak the box back into the freezer when Hasina is watching television.

"We are going to a function at Sonargaon," Hasina, looking amazing, tells me. "I have left food in the fridge. Please eat it later."

Gratefully, I leave it there and go to bed.

I have finally sunk into blessed sleep when I hear the revellers return and sense Hasina's presence at my door. I am asleep I tell myself, fast, fast asleep, the pain is all gone. It works, and her footsteps recede, only to return in full force about five minutes later when she knocks and enters. Mr Hoque has deduced from an in-depth examination of the fridge that I have failed to eat. Would I like to do so now?

"Go away, and leave me alone to die," I screech—in my dream. Actually, I sit up and say, "No, thank you." I say it over and again, a battle of wills. I hear the same thing happen at Mithu's door and listen for a sharp retort.

"Go away, and leave me alone to die," he moans. Bely moans in sympathy.

But I do awake in far better humour. I never have been one for suffering in silence (although I understand this is a relative concept after watching Mithu's antics), but I feel benevolent this morning, probably something to do with the emergency Valium I overdosed on last night in a desperate attempt to force sleep. I glance at the clock and realise that Munnu will already be halfway through his English examination in prelude to the job interview. I cross my fingers and hope he is doing well.

Mithu returns from the doctor's surgery and is helped back into his sick bed. The driver is sent out for his life-saving medication.

"Anne, so interesting." Hasina comes to me in the bathroom and is all smiles, relieved that her son is going to get well and certain she can now identify my symptoms. "The doctor examines Mithu, the insect bite, and the infection, and he asks whether Mithu has bad ulcers in the mouth. He does not, but I tell the doctor about you, and it is the same infection. He says it is good that you take your antibiotic."

"What kind of infection?" I ask with interest.

Hasina frowns in concentration. "The doctor said so many things I try to remember." Her brow clears. "I know. You both have STD," she says pronouncing the initials carefully.

I choke on half the salt water I am swirling around my mouth and spew the remainder all over the bathroom floor. Hasina looks at me blankly, clearly unaware of what she is implying.

"It is okay," she says anxiously. "Just a virus infection. The herpes virus, which causes the shingles—yes? But it is not shingles this time. It comes from the insect bite."

"But Hasina," I say, thinking of Mithu as well as myself, I hope she has not called the bank and informed them that her son is suffering from a sexually transmitted disease. "It is not an STD. It can't be. Not if Mithu and I have the same thing, anyway."

"Why?" asks Hasina. "Do you know what exactly is STD?"

Delicately, I explain.

"Ohmigod," she says, putting her hands to her mouth. "That is wrong. I must apologise to you. Lucky I say it to nobody else. How can I be wrong? What does the doctor say?"

She is mortified, and I don't want to offend her by laughing out loud, even if the pain would let me. We sit down. She drinks a cup of herbal tea, and I pretend to do so. As far as I can gather, the GP must have said that the infection is an "insect-transmitted disease," and that Hasina, her fondness for medical terms tangled up with vaguely remembered English shorthand, has put two-and-two together and made twenty-two.

"It is a logical mistake," I reassure her.

"But so embarrassing." She begins to laugh.

"What joke?" asks Bely coming into the kitchen for a glass of iced water for the invalid. Neither of us reply. Somehow I do not think that her husband and I inadvertently sharing an STD would amuse Bely.

27

The Golden Bird and the Rocket

The final winter Work Camp I might have attended will not take place until after I leave the country. It is in Moudubi, deep in the Bay of Bengal, and requires a large time commitment. Summoned to the SCI office for a last evaluation, Hasina hails me a baby taxi and gives very detailed directions to the driver. When I arrive, I find the door is locked, and I do not understand the Bangla note taped to it. I scribble one of my own and shove it under the screen.

Empowered by my solo journey, I decide to take a walk around the National Assembly. As I stride along the shaded sidewalk in front of the building, ignoring the rickshaws-*wallahs* touting for business and the shopkeepers who offer me tea, I hear a persistent shout. Someone is calling my name.

"Anne! Anne! You wait!"

I turn around to see Munnu, cool and unruffled, jogging along the dusty pavement towards me. "Are you following me?"

"I call Hasina. She tells me you are at SCI. I say that it is closed today, and I rescue you." He pauses. "Anne. Do you know why I look for you?"

"The pleasure of my beautiful face? My inspirational company?"

"These things yes, but more important, your Sunderbans programme—"

"Wait," I interrupt, ashamed it had slipped my mind. "Your exam? How was it? I thought it would take all day?"

Munnu shrugs. "It was okay. Quite easy. I finish quickly, and they say they send me a letter in few days. I leave the room, and I feel good, so I think about you making a tour to the Sunderbans. You say you like to go there, yes? So I make a call to BIWTC. I find the paddle steamer to Mongla leaves Monday. It takes one day, then you get a tour into Sunderbans and return to Dhaka by bus. It takes maybe three days total."

"It sounds great. Thank you," I say inadequately.

The Bangladesh Inland Waterways Transport Company has a narrow, tiled entrance on a busy street in Motijheel, its ancient sign swinging above the main door. The house-like building is the usual higgledy-piggledy mass of tiny glass rooms on half-landings, and grim, open-plan offices along scruffy corridors. People sit at cleared desks surrounded by paper folders piled on the floor beside them. All of them look as if they have worked here for forty years and have grown grey and dusty with the furnishings. None of them appears particularly pleased to see a real, live customer.

"Tickets at the main desk downstairs," grunts one bored employee.

Munnu explains we have "an appointment," and we are grudgingly shown into a brown and cream cubbyhole with filthy frosted glass and a weary ceiling fan. The man behind the desk gestures us to sit and continues a brusque telephone call. He sounds as if he is arranging the watery execution of wayward commercial sailors. Munnu says he is telling his wife in Banani that "his boy" has collected the fish for the deep freeze and will be delivering it shortly.

Munnu begs a passage on the paddle-steamer and translates for me. "This man says the boat goes Monday at 6 p.m. It is overbooked, but this always happens after Eid. If the last people on the list have not reconfirmed their passage by 11 a.m. tomorrow, you take their place. Yes?"

"Yes," I say. "So we return tomorrow?"

"I return tomorrow. I make the arrangements, you give me the money—with little extra for...this man's trouble."

"Now?" I ask, beginning to undress.

"Not now. Tomorrow. He does not need proof you can pay. He sees you are wealthy foreigner." Optimistically, we emerge into the raucous, heat-filled afternoon. I am quickly wilting.

"You must go home before Hasina thinks you are hijacked," Munnu orders. "I travel with you so on the way you can give me money. I am sorry I must ask you for this, but it is more than I have."

"Don't apologise," I say. "Without you I would not have, or nearly have, the ticket."

"You will get it." Munnu promises, carefully averting his eyes as I grope around under my tunic to open the money-belt at my midriff. He waves me off at the main roundabout between the separate but neighbouring districts of Gulshan 1 and 2.

"I call tomorrow," he yells after me.

Anne Hamilton

True to his word, Munnu telephones just before midday. "Anne. I have your ticket," he says jubilantly. "I escort you to the boat. Do not argue."

No doubt he will also escort me back again when the boat fails to weigh anchor or whatever it is they do, but I am looking on the bright side. "Don't forget that I'll be at the Golden Bird Residence for Foreigners from tonight," I remind him. "It's next door to the Home for Distressed Gentlewomen," I add, but the joke is lost.

Hasina and Mr Hoque are leaving shortly for a vacation in Bangalore. With the house girls on their annual leave, the apartment will be closed up for the next couple of weeks, so I am moving to the hotel across the road.

"I wish you would stay with Mitali." Hasina purses her lips.

"You are so welcome," Mitali adds.

"You are very, very kind," I say. "But I've relied on you all long enough. And Mitali, you don't have space or time for me. I'll be fine. It's just one night now and maybe another when I return from the Sunderbans."

"Maybe you should stay with SCI people? With Rehana?" Hasina persists.

"No," says Mitali. "If she is across the road, I can check on her. Mohammadpur is too far away for me."

Running the risk of missing her plane, Hasina accompanies me to the hotel and checks that my room boasts all the facilities she has been promised. "I probably have more guests than they do," she says delightedly. "But sometimes this place is busy. Indian or Japanese college tours."

Through the wrought iron gates and the sliding glass doors is a reception area where a half dozen friendly and smart young men are lolling around. The manager and two nominated assistants have keys to rival a gaoler and an evangelical zeal to promote their empty guesthouse.

My room is huge, sparsely furnished with two double beds and a single, a television, sofa and table, a fridge, and *en suite* bathroom. For $20US, I get breakfast, lunch, dinner, laundry, all local phone calls and unlimited bottles of genuine bottled water.

Since this is probably the last time I will see Hasina, ("on this trip to Bangladesh, anyway," she says), I inarticulately seek out the words to tell her what she and her family have come to mean to me. I think she is finding the farewell as difficult as I am, and both of us jump up when her cell phone bleeps.

"Mrs Hoque? Where are you now? We miss the plane. Already you say goodbye to Anne six times. I come up." Mr Hoque crashes through the door and, with a final, bone-crushing hug for me, he drags Hasina off. I watch the car disappear up Road No. 125. I have little time to feel bereft. The hotel telephone rings. It is Mitali.

"Look out of the window," she commands. "Look to my apartment."

I push back the shutters, and there is Mitali with Fiona and Oni by her side standing on their balcony. We grin and wave like idiots, and the tableau breaks up only because I hear a knock at my door.

Hassan, one of the hotel managers, is loaded down with bottles of water.

"How many guests have you tonight?" I ask.

Hassan clears his throat. "One. You. It means special service for you."

The phone rings again. It is Munnu, checking I am all right. As I replace the receiver, Hassan knocks on the door once more. "Another call for you," he says. "Your SCI friend Suez checks you are fine. I take his number."

All this ringing and knocking is like a home from home. I wonder if Hasina has somehow engineered it. Clearly primed by her, Hassan returns to apologise for the lack of television or radio in the room and explains they have a central music system that is available to me through the ancient intercom. He tunes the erratically-piped music to a concert of Bengali songs, and my room is filled with the sound. Sentimental and full of agonising love and loss it may be, but it is also a treat after the constant Hindi film soundtracks. *Polligiti,* I learn, are more lively village songs, and *unchango* is classical music similar to that indigenous to India. The bamboo flute accompaniment is haunting.

After a while though, it is replaced by a tape of the popular modern singer, Shumana Huq, and the volume turned up. I expect the hotel staff have had enough of all that culture.

The next day, a rickshaw fights its way through the afternoon traffic and into Saderghat via the smelliest and most winding alley in the city. The source of the pong is chicken, thousands and thousands of furious, red-beaked, mangy-looking chickens. Stunned chickens crammed into crates, live chickens running free, pecking maize and each other, dead chickens strung together, plucked and being plucked by impervious stall holders. The squawking and squealing is deafening, so high pitched as to perforate the eardrum, and the smell so foul that even hardened Dhaka-ites press scarves and handkerchiefs to their faces. Severed heads twitch in the gutters, flies crawl over the discarded guts, and I mull over my misguided belief that eating chicken is marginally safer than beef.

The dockside is a seething mass of bodies like a crowd scene in a biblical epic: passengers, traders, beggars, officials, and crew members being hired and fired. Reluctant goats and cattle are dragged along the waterside and hefted into dangerously-tilting row boats, and crates of vegetables and baskets of fruit, sometimes two and three deep, are balanced atop the heads of old men and young boys. In the covered terminal building, travellers look as if they have been standing around waiting for days. Browbeaten and lost, they uselessly accost anyone in uniform.

Directions to the paddle steamer, indeed directions to anything, are scarce. Munnu and I are led on several wild goose chases before we reach Badam Tole, a pier only a kilometre or so away, where the large, white steamer spills into the berths either side of it, a benign giant dwarfing the smaller vessels.

The generic name for these BIWTC paddle-wheel steamers running between Dhaka and Khulna are the Rocket Ferries. They travel about four times per week and the total journey time can be as much as thirty hours. The estimated time of arrival of my boat in Khulna—if it leaves on time, if it leaves at all—is five o'clock tomorrow evening, a mere twenty-three hours away.

There are two decks to the squat boat. The front half of the weather-protected upper deck is, according to Munnu's translation of my ticket, reserved for first-class passengers and directly accessible from the cabins. We push our way through the alert hawkers and traders who wait for the smattering of rich Bengali tourists who are sailing, and are received by the purser who hurries us towards the higher level. I catch only the briefest of glimpses at the second- and deck-class areas. Here, travellers pay for either a narrow, wooden bunk or a space on the crowded floor. They bring their own bedding and food, and many are already staking their claim for the night. Most of them will disembark long before Khulna, in Chandpur or Barisal or one of the other smaller ports along the way. But some are here for the long haul.

Munnu sees me looking. "Do not think you should give one of these people your ticket and you travel second class," he warns me, grinning. "The captain would be horrified. He would insist you took his cabin. Too bad for the image."

He tells me that the crew on bigger boats are never averse to sleeping on the floor of the public areas and sub-letting their quarters to a passenger who has failed to secure a cabin. It might happen on the Rocket, but Munnu thinks it unlikely that the staff have anything but cramped bunks. We climb wrought iron steps and go inside to a central, white-panelled, fully-carpeted room complete with television, and a long sofa under the far end window where there are also doors to the balcony. A large, ornate ceiling fan hums overhead and a communal, white-clothed dining table runs the length of the area, and doors to the eight cabins open off from each side.

I am handed two keys, the first belonging to Cabin No. 1 nearest the front deck, the second for access to the two bathrooms shared between first class passengers. The cabin itself, though small, gives the impression of being bright and airy. The walls and wooden panelling is painted white. There is a narrow bunk against each wall, both made up with thin white sheets, reading lights, and individual fans above them. Clean net curtains blow gently at the large outside window, and these, along with the towels beside the washbasin and the bed linen, bear the faded blue Rocket Ferry emblem. Another door leads straight to a sheltered veranda, and beyond that is the outer deck dotted with wicker chairs and tables.

It is charming, like an elderly dowager who has seen better days but takes pride in making the most of the quality and elegance with which she was born. The simple yet refined furnishings and the surface are from a bygone era. I am reminded of Mr Habib's bungalow in the tea gardens of Srimangal.

"This is a fine boat," Munnu says wistfully, turning on the water supply, throwing open the doors, and testing one of the berths by stretching out with his arms crossed behind his head. He sighs and swings his legs to the floor. "Anne. There is one hour before you leave..."

I am hit by a brainstorm, an inspiration, a moment of madness.

"Come with me," I blurt out. "Why not? I have paid for a whole cabin." In effect, my ticket allows two and their children to travel. "And nobody is going to question you. I bet the purser assumes we're both travelling anyway."

Munnu demurs, but his face lights up like a little boy who has been offered a much coveted but unobtainable new toy. I want to hug him. I know he has never travelled on anything like the Rocket Ferry and for a long time in the future will not be able to spare the Tk 900 (about $45) it would cost him.

"I have no bag. Where do I sleep? Bachchu worries," he objects.

Anne Hamilton

"Buy a toothbrush in the market, telephone Bachchu and tell him you're helping a damsel in distress—again. He didn't object last time, did he?" I am brisk, pleased with my plan. "And," I add without a blush, "you can sleep in the other bed, or if not, I'm sure there is room in the lounge."

Munnu looks down. "This is all true. I very much want to go but..." he trails off.

"It doesn't matter that you have no money," I say. "I do. I want to give you this as a gift. You and your family have all given me something far more important than money. Besides," I am brutally honest, "I would like you to come. It will be more fun with a friend, especially one who speaks Bengali. I'm not really being generous, just selfish. Okay?"

"Anne. You really want me to accompany you?"

"I really do."

"I return in twenty minutes," he calls the words from over his shoulder.

Two seconds later when I go onto the veranda, he is already weaving his way back along the dockside. I lean on the rail, feel the breeze in the folds of my *salwar kameez*, and enjoy the mild pitching of the boat.

"*Ami bhuchi na*," I signal that I don't understand, laughing down as hawkers come to the edge of the boat, yell questions and offer up samples of their oranges, bananas, and snacks for my approval. One brave soul, encouraged by his mates, attempts to enter the boat but is refused by two of the crew. The trader argues, shrugs, and sells them a cut-price, brown paper bag of fruit instead.

The sky blends a pinkish hue; a jubilant Munnu returns and precisely at six o'clock. The engines are cranked up and shudder to life, groaning with the effort of shifting such bulk into the open water. Very quickly the clamour of the dock is replaced by the gentle hum and odd clank of the steamer's inner workings. We drag two chairs outside and are enveloped steadily by the night and by the peace of the open river. The lulling motion of the boat is conducive to just sitting, reflecting, and watching the world go by. We steam peacefully down the wide expanse of muddy water that dissects a green landscape of trees, shrubs, and the occasional cultivated field. Very soon there are few signs of life. The silence is accentuated by the space around us; even aboard ship there is only a handful of other passengers on the first class deck—all Bengali—consisting of a large family, two young couples, and a larger group, probably businessmen.

277

It is all the more shocking then, when the boat slows, sounds its horn and suddenly we are at the port of Chandpur. Still apparently in the middle of nowhere, there is a burst of noise and frenzied activity as people from the lower decks hurry to disembark and are forced to walk patiently in a single file track from the river's edge and up through the trees to a clearing which constitutes the port. More passengers take their place, provisions are loaded, and goods taken off. It is the briefest of interludes. In a blink we are back trundling through the water. A bearer discreetly whispers in Munnu's ear. Dinner, Bangladeshi or Western food, is served at our convenience in the cabin or salon.

"Do you think you can take food tonight?" asks Munnu, his way of telling me he is hungry.

We sit at the long dining table in the salon. The businessmen have already eaten, the family with their three young children and grandma are in mid-flow, and the two young couples have yet to leave the darkened deck.

"Probably they are on their honeymoons and think it is very sophisticated not to go to Chittagong," Munnu suggests.

Immediately we settle ourselves; one of the bearers sets out cutlery in front of us and places roti and water on the table. Ceremoniously he serves kedgeree and chicken, a dish of vegetables, and another of dhal.

"Anne. Do we use the forks and the knives?" Munnu whispers, his words directed to the tablecloth. "What do the other people do?"

My eyes sweep nonchalantly around the room.

"Nobody else has them," I report. The assorted company use their hands in the everyday way. "It must be especially for me."

"So, what do we do?" asks Munnu again.

"Use our hands," I decide. "And thank the bearer for the thought."

I pick at my food. It is fine, well prepared, and plentiful, but in the competition between pain from the loitering mouth ulcers and taste, pain wins by a whisker. Several times the bearer walks past, has an anxious word with his colleague, fetches another man from some undisclosed kitchen and finally bends to speak quietly to Munnu, who rapidly explains, receives an unconvinced nod, and turns to me.

"He is concerned that you..."

"...do not like the food," we finish in unison. "I wish I could wear a sign around my neck saying: 'Yes, I really do like the food, but there is so much of it, and anyway, my mouth hurts,'" I grumble.

"Maybe I make a speech to tell everyone?" Munnu suggests in mock seriousness. "I tap my glass with the spoon and clap my hands and say a toast. Yes?"

Anne Hamilton

"They wouldn't understand," I moan. "Refusing to eat is an alien concept to your average countryman. Agony in any quarter is not sufficient reason." I warm to my theme. It is a matter close to my heart, especially after the last few days. "If your bowels were liquefying after a consignment of poisonous fungi, or your stomach's being forcibly stapled for an obscure digestive complaint, you'd all groan whilst your lower intestines unravelled before your eyes. 'Just give me the *Flagyl* and I'll be fine. Where's my dinner?'"

Munnu hurriedly interrupts as I pause for breath. "Anne. You must say all of this again very slowly. I do not recognise some words. I think you tease the Bangladeshi appetite, yes?"

But I should not mock. In a country where food has been scarce and still is for many, and there is always a risk of shortage, why would anyone ever refuse a good meal? My punishment is having to describe to Munnu the concept of "liquefying bowels" whilst the diners slurp greenish-yellow, watery dhal.

Eventually, we leave the company around the large and blurred television screen and return to the grey plastic chairs outside my cabin. The air is warm, ("too cold," complains Munnu, rubbing goose-pimpled arms through his long-sleeved red sweater), the breeze just sufficient to keep the insect nightlife away.

"The quiet, the few people—it is very strange," wonders Munnu. "I was never with so minimum people. I think it is nice. For a little while."

Later, as I venture through the lounge, keys in hand and intent on grappling with the lavatory door—which is conveniently situated beyond the salon, turn right, down some steps, round a corner, and third on the left—I step carefully over such crew who have taken up their beds for the night. Top-to–tail and hip-to-hip, their bodies are stretched out on the floor, the sofa, the chairs, and under the dining-table. Nobody stirs as I tread on fingers, crush toes, trip over stray limbs and stick my feet in slack-jawed faces. I am unsure if they are truly, deeply, madly asleep or too polite to shout, "*Gerroff, you bugger*," to a paying guest. Soon, even the muffled chatter and occasional snatch of song floating up through the steerage decks ceases, and I easily drift off to sleep on the engine's monotonous hum.

My fleeting romantic notion of watching the sunrise, given that I was too damn lazy to do it in Cox's Bazaar, comes to nothing as the day dawns in a milky mist that hovers damp and tangible over the water. Instead, I am entertained by the honeymoon couples who monopolise the prow and bond over a *Titanic* impression. He, (of couple the first), instructs a crewman to wipe down the rails, she grips them earnestly, he comes up behind her, leans into her and they look, him unfocused and moody, she with a faint smile, out "to sea," and are photographed by the male of the second couple. They all swap places, and then, congratulating themselves, disappear smugly into breakfast.

"Ha!" I can imagine them saying over their eggs and toast, their choice of holiday vindicated: "That's one in the eye for the *Kumar's at No. 42*. All they have blown up over the mantelpiece is a picture of them swimming at Cox's Bazaar. So passé, don't you think?"

The day is passed skirting the Bay of Bengal, chugging back inland to ports no larger than a slip of land with a tin hut, continuing to Mongla, and ultimately to Khulna. At some point during the day, we ditch the idea of a tour of the Sunderbans as unfeasible. Time is simply too short.

"If we leave the boat in Mongla, we can take a day programme into Sunderbans tomorrow," Munnu suggests, studying the map. "Mongla is at the start of it, only five kilometres away. It is easy."

As opposed to Khulna which is actually fifty-odd kilometres further on, and the obvious point of entry when travelling by road. Of course, we might miss out on the delights of Khulna, Bangladesh's third city...but...

"We have to return there to get the bus back," shrugs Munnu, settling down for a snooze. "We have a few minutes free time. We see them then."

28
Week 13 - Into the Sunderbans

We sail into a natural harbour. To the left there appears to be a small yet self-sufficient village, on the right is Mongla, a larger and established town. We walk down the noisy gangway and blink in bewilderment at the sudden loss of peaceful calm. Amidst shouting and waving, heavily-laden passengers—most of whom, judging by their luggage, have relocated lock, stock, and barrel to Mongla—disembark from below stairs. Suddenly, we are spotted from a distance of two nautical miles. An enthusiastic and competitive band of Sunderbans tour guides descend upon us. Clearly there will be no problem renting a boat. In fact, there may well not be enough space on the water if there are this many people in the business.

The majority of the guides are young boys, all affably pitching their services, all amicable in their competitiveness. I wonder if, secretly, they all work for the same company.

"We have comfortable seats on two decks," boasts one boy.

"Comfortable—ho! You take our leftovers from the dump." His colleague digs him in the ribs and they have a conversation in raucous Bengali. "*We* have sunshades and cook the best food," he continues.

"Food you buy in my uncle's shop, yes. *I* will bring a live chicken and kill it right on the boat for your lunch. Very fresh," is another lad's selling point.

"So you say your own uncle's food is not fresh?" jeers the second boy again and is grabbed in a headlock for his trouble.

"I think these are messengers paid a few *paisas*. The big men run the firms in downtown Mongla." Munnu makes it sound as if we are entering the world of the Mafioso in inner city Chicago. "We choose one of them. I do not like the old fat man with the cigar. Too old and too fat."

Which is as good a way as any of (not) choosing someone, I suppose. I understand only fleeting snatches of the conversation, but Munnu is laughing so hard he can hardly conduct business. He fills me in later on when he does an accurate impression of the encounter. The boys nod politely in my direction but, quickly aware that I am not the leading force in this party, they exhaust their supply of English ("What is your country?" "How you like Bangladesh?" "You get me UK visa, yes?"), and return to completing a deal. One far-sighted young lad, called Gadji by the others, takes a calculated risk, leaves the scene for a couple of minutes and returns with bottles of juice and cigarettes, which he thrusts upon us "with no obligation" whilst whistling for a loitering rickshaw, piling on our bags, ushering us aboard, and telling us about his uncle's hotel.

"We go with him," decides Munnu, a *fait accompli*. "He takes us to a hotel, and then to his brother's office to arrange the boat tour." He nods the go-ahead, I nod meekly, and the boy nods approvingly, glad that the little lady—even if she is a fast Western girl—is doing as she is advised.

"Anne. Look to the Sunderbans," Munnu points out, and sure enough, just behind the freighters and other docked boats, of which there are a surprising number, is the start of the deep, green, dense jungle which defines the northernmost entrance to the Sunderbans.

We shoot down the dusty road at a hundred miles an hour, our new guide balancing on the side of the rickshaw and shouting information above the wind and the squealing tyres. Mongla, for all of its small-town feel, is a major port. The main street is directly off the docks and at once we are thrust into the hurly burly ambience of a village where everyone knows everyone else. There are the familiar restaurants and food stalls, barbers and loud hailer outlets, pharmacies and ceramic lavatory specialists, but in addition are the residential hotels, a taxi cab firm, telephone and fax offices. What I thought was a separate village across the water is actually an extension of Mongla although the only route from one side to the other is by way of a five-minute sailing. Munnu relays what he thinks I will find interesting, or what he can be bothered, from the running commentary in his left ear.

"He says many residents earn their living as ship crews. This makes Mongla less insulated—is this the word?—than some other places in Bangladesh. He says there are many smuggled goods in the market and that it is easy to buy alcohol. People do not even hide their drinking. I say we do not need anything, thank you," the good Muslim adds virtuously.

The Hotel Singapore is described in *Lonely Planet* as a "well marked two story building in the heart of town on the short lane leading to the ferry *ghat*." It also says that the rooms are reasonably clean but small: accurate on all counts. A balcony runs round the entire building on three levels with all the bedrooms opening off it. We take two on the top floor at the princely sum of Tk 140 (about $3USD). Behind each wooden door is a tiny, square room full of two beds, their hanging mosquito nets provide the only "curtains," and an old fashioned dressing table squeezed between them. The attached bathrooms are concrete boxes; stepping up to the squat toilet is literally (I imagine) like climbing onto a throne. Next door, I clearly hear the occupant clearing his throat and spitting as he bathes. I expect him to tap me on the shoulder and ask if I can please pass the soap.

Our cruise is negotiated down the street in the curtained-off booth comprising Sonag Enterprises and sealed with the aid of warm, syrupy mango juice. I sit and look intelligent whilst Munnu attempts a Hasina-type deal: a full-day tour aboard a private motorboat (sun canopy and comfortable chairs included), with three crew, lunch, a visit to the Forestry Department ("foreigners not usually permitted") and transport to the evening Khulna bus. It costs less than twenty dollars, and we leave at first light tomorrow morning.

The simple wooden boat is moored alone at the far end of the ghat. A bleary-eyed rickshaw-*wallah* is woken from his slumbers to drive us there whilst the boy, Gadji, travels alongside on his bicycle, the handlebars loaded with plastic bags and a box with air holes in the top wriggling ominously on the carrier.

Two other boys—it sounds patronising, but what else to call them? They are boys—lift onto the craft another box of food and one of crockery. A kerosene stove is waiting on the quay.

"If we get lost, we are easy to rescue," comments Munnu, referring to the bright pink canopy laced with white frills which, running from front to back, shades the full-length upper deck. Underneath is an enclosed area doubling as galley and rest quarters. The engine is like a large and unwieldy afterthought plonked at the rear.

"It reminds me of something," I think out loud, puzzled. The boat is a strange, squat shape, its height appearing almost too much for its length. Then it comes to me. "It looks exactly like a four- poster bed."

"Where is the toilet?" asks Munnu, ever mindful of my priorities and, by dint of clambering from top deck down one side and over the engine, it is possible to access an upended coffin containing a hole opening directly into the water below.

"Gadji says be careful not to put your foot down the toilet hole." Munnu translates the earnest advice. "One passenger does this and his leg got stuck and was dragged for many miles before it was noticed."

I resolve not to drink very much.

The upper deck is empty save for a rolled-up raffia mat, but as I make to sit on the floor, two plastic, grey stacking chairs appear up the steps and are followed by a card table, the green baize still partially intact. These are set carefully in the centre of the deck, and Munnu and I are invited to sit down whilst the engine judders and putters through a few false starts, shudders, and is coaxed (or rather, kicked) into life.

In contrast to the sleeping town, the river abounds with life. Small rowboats jammed with bodies are ferrying workers and traders from one side of Mongla to the other. There are cargo vessels pulling into port, their dark-skinned crews perched on wooden crates and sharing cigarettes before the heavy work begins. Makeshift canoes and curved fishing boats carefully negotiate the obstacle course of derelict industrial ships, their grey, gunmetal bulk now rusting, deserted, and half-sunk below the water line. Already warm, I welcome the slight sea breeze; Munnu huddles miserably into his sweater waiting for the sun to climb higher in the sky.

Gadji provides two oranges, two bananas, and a large bottle of cola. Laying them neatly on the table, he sits silently on the ground behind us and calls one of his mates to do likewise. The sound of my voice is suddenly loud in their presence, and I feel that any comment I make must be interesting, profound, and worthy of translation.

"Nice day," I say accordingly. "Nice boat."

"Very nice," agrees Munnu. "Nice oranges," he adds, peeling one and scoring it into quarters.

"Nice," smiles Gadji accepting the fruit. "Nice is good," he states. He turns to his colleague whose English is not adequate for such a philosophical and intellectual conversation and offers a quick rundown.

"Nice," the other boy enunciates. "Nice. *Shundur*," he confirms.

"*Shundur*," we chorus.

I search deep into my memory, a desperate attempt to move the conversation on. "*Ajker dinta...*" I start haltingly.

"*Ha, ha,*" the trio encourage me, hanging on my every word.

Encouraged, I continue my revelation. "*Ajker dinta kee shundur.*" I look around triumphantly and am greeted with a round of applause.

"*Ajker dinta kee shundur,*" we all agree. "What a lovely day."

284

Anne Hamilton

So overcome with the discussion that they decide to drown themselves or because there is some tricky piece of boat driving to do, the lads disappear head first over the side of the boat and land successfully—well, there is no splash—with a *whoop* on the lower deck.

We circumnavigate a small, oblong island that should surely sink beneath the jumble of tin shops and wooden houses, a tiny modern health centre dwarfed by an anti-AIDS poster campaign, and a school hut from which the children pour out, shouting and waving homemade flags. I have no time to ponder whether this is a daily event or laid on for our benefit because Gadji's face appears by my right foot to point out the dense, green forest ahead of us. Slicing the water into a dual carriageway is the outermost point of the Sunderbans, the world's largest littoral mangrove forest.

"What exactly is a mangrove?" I ask Munnu. "And are they always littoral?"

"Trees," he answers comprehensively. "I do not know what littoral means."

The inner forest is largely impenetrable by all but the tiniest vessels and the waterways are saltwater swamp, clogged with leaves and fallen trees. The Sunderbans are a UNESCO World Heritage site and a haven for birds and wildlife: humming birds to birds of prey, wild deer, monkeys, and every hour on the hour one of the boys pop up to say that he has definitely seen a Bengal tiger ready to pounce on a wayward crocodile. Then he adds *thatta korchi*: he is joking. Besides it's okay because the tigers in this vast reserve are not habitual man-eaters.

Hiron Point, the most southerly point of the Sunderbans, is at least eight hours away by boat and so far beyond our capabilities. As it is, we barely penetrate the edges of the forest, yet even here the sheer variety of trees is immense. They come almost to the edge of the water (hence the term "littoral"), are stopped only by a slip of muddy beach, smooth and slippery, and home to crocodiles during the rainy season.

At this point, a real writer writing a real journal would be able to list the trees, a brief but interesting description of their origins, lifespan and uses, possibly with footnotes and references to learned works. I groan out loud.

"Anne. What is the problem?" Munnu wakes up to ask me.

"I cannot name the trees. I don't recognise any of them."

"I help," he turns his chair to the side, puts his bare feet up on the rusting red rail and makes a scientific observation. "Tall thin trees," he suggests, "with big green leaves. Others with small leaves. Short, fat trees like a bush...Anne. Why do you not write this down?"

"Because you don't know the names either," I object.

"Yes. There—" he waves at a palm tree. "That is palm tree. And here, maybe this is...err...willow tree?"

In comparison, Gadji is a fount of knowledge. The giants are *goran* trees, which will grow between one and a half and three and a half metres tall, and the largest mangrove trees are a valuable source of fuel.

I settle for enjoying the view and the solitude. The Sunderbans are beautiful in their lush density, impressive in their enormity, but they do not have the magnificence of the traditional rainforest or a mountainous range. Their wonder is in being undisturbed, wild, completely given over to the elements. Settlers have been here for six centuries without that much change. Whilst I am selfishly pleased that I am seeing it now, the only noise being the intermittent coughing of the boat's innards, the only tourists, ourselves, I am delighted to learn that a 1903 achievement was brought about by my brother's namesake, the pioneer coloniser David Hamilton who established the oldest (still existing) co-operative society in India. He was also the first to print the one rupee note in the area, the start of local commerce, and he provided religious societies and dispensaries for the poor.

Good old Great-Great-Great Uncle David. We always wondered where he disappeared off to.

Occasionally, we come alongside a rowboat full of locals collecting fallen branches and dragging them precariously across their knees, or catch a glimpse of a larger vessel in the distance. In the centre of the river is another island community, a settlement of rugged and ramshackle dwellings, a selection of wooden boats bobbing in the water, and beyond them like protective talismans, large blue fishing nets circle the land. Fishermen and their children are expertly pulling in the blue tarpaulins and examining the catch. This habitat provides livelihoods for about 5,000 fishermen who must have permits and keep to a defined buffer zone. In April and May, the off-season, they supplement their income by collecting honeycomb. When our boat lurches, sputters, and the engine dies, they all look up with interest, call out advice and comment as we slowly drift. The peace is broken by shouts of the crew trying to both fathom the problem and keep us updated.

"The engine overheats," Munnu translates. "The boys wait for it to cool."

Anne Hamilton

Gadji takes the opportunity to brew tea, and Munnu and I speculate as to who will swim ashore to the ever-receding island if we remain permanently adrift.

"Is there a radio?" I ask.

"Anne," Munnu says patiently. "This is Bangladesh."

Marooned in the midst of a wide expanse of water, the sun's rays piercing the flimsy canopy above our heads, any breeze long gone, we quickly become an aquatic curiosity. Three little canoes paddle in convoy splashing their way towards us, and a shoal of worryingly-small children shade their bright eyes and beam upwards. "*Shaba shokale*. Good morning," they call out, giggling and perilously leaning forward for a better view. Munnu chats to them. Leaning over the side, he is caught up in their enthusiastic gesticulations and chatter.

"They bring a gift," he says. "Fish. Caught fresh today. They see us when we sail past and they think we like a fish for our lunch."

Barely are the words out of his mouth when he has to duck to avoid being brained by said species, three of which are thrown with enthusiasm in our vague direction.

"*Maach*," they confirm for me. "*Maach*." Fish.

"*Maach*," I agree. "*Donyabat*. Thank you." I look around for something to give in return, open the bag of oranges and toss them one at a time towards greedy hands. One little lad catches well enough for a profitable cricketing future. He leans back, arms out, catches the fruit in each hand and does an impromptu juggling routine.

Alerted by a shout from down below, the trio of canoes paddle safely out of harm's way as the boat's engine, sounding even more like a dubious, homemade generator coughs and hums into action. Soon, the little canoeists are pinpricks on the horizon, and we are entering the confines of Dhangmati Forestry Reserve and adjoining wildlife sanctuary.

It is impossible to moor the boat against the quay; rather it is anchored to one of a line of large rowboats that have cabins remarkably like a B&Q do-it-yourself shed, and we clamber from one to the other to reach bamboo steps onto dry land. Gadji ushers us down a sandy path bisecting the carefully-tended green grass and ending in a covered reception area. Here, a forest ranger is patiently shepherding a cluster of sweating and red-faced Bangladeshi businessmen, still clad with middle-aged and middle-class respectability in their shirts and ties. They disappear into the park proper, and Munnu and I are introduced to our own guide, a short, fat man with unbelievably shiny black shoes and white socks below his khaki uniform. Quick as a flash, I assume my nodding and smiling role as a Bengali wife, the only way I will gain access to the park at all, and without paying an extortionate contribution. "I'm happy to pay," I tell Munnu, who refuses to even countenance the possibility.

"It is not fair," he says. "It does not matter if you have more money. Making you pay more because you are a foreigner is a discrimination."

"Worse than me telling a lie?" I ask him.

There is, naturally a payback. Our guide determines that we are newly married and therefore will wants lots and lots of snapshots to show the folks back home. Accordingly, he commandeers my camera and makes us pose us for a series of "honeymoon" pictures whereby Munnu is half-way up a tree, and I am leaning on it looking adoringly up at him; the two of us standing arm-in-arm in a sun dappled, leafy glade; sitting back-to-back on the sandy ground...I would not be surprised if he demands film rights and puts all the photos together in some sort of montage to music with appropriate fade-ins and a circle of love hearts on the screen. I feel better when I recognise there is nothing personal about the photography. Up ahead, the guide with the Bengali businessmen is doing the same thing, albeit the shots are less arty. In fact, when the nine men see Munnu and me, they carefully dawdle to edge themselves into our shots, or gesture that I should tack myself onto theirs.

"They'll have trouble explaining this back at the office," I say.

In addition to all the trees carefully labelled in Bangla script, there is a special section of the reserve for the breeding of indigenous animals, namely, deer, monkeys, crocodiles, and snakes. Happily, in contrast with the experience of Dhaka Zoo, these all look content in their relative freedom and are eating the plentiful food with gusto, all except the crocodiles that slither in the mud looking mean. We have five peaceful minutes on the platform of a red and white striped watchtower.

"Anne. Do you see our boat?" Munnu tenses up.

Anxiously we see our little pink-canopied number sailing away without us—but no, they are simply moving out of the glare of the noonday sun to the other side of the waterway shaded by overhanging branches. A gradually-sinking dinghy is dispatched to collect us.

Back on the boat, I poke my nose into the makeshift galley and wish I had not. It is lunch preparation time, the floor is decorated with a pile of mixed vegetables leaning heavily towards the onion family, a cauldron of rice, and a dismembered chicken which, given the amount of blood around the place, put up a good fight. Skinned legs and thighs are in one pot, giblets and other innards are leaking over the deck, and the twitching, feathered head, lax beak and staring eyes, are a veritable fly trap. I scuttle up the ladder.

Munnu follows. "Slobs," he says cheerfully.

It is too hot to do anything now. Even Munnu is warm, and we stretch out the raffia mat and flop onto the floor much to the interest of our friends, the Bengali businessmen floating by in one of Noah's children. Gadji serves us lunch in such gargantuan quantities that it takes two of them to haul the dishes up the steps. There is much hilarity at my inability to eat little more than a hefty-sized hillock of rice and mouth-burningly spiced curries.

"He can eat 2kg of rice," Gadji says, pointing at one of the others who is doing a good impression of a vacuum cleaner. "Also, he eats maybe forty paratha."

I imagine this is poetic licence and sure enough—

"Not true," his colleague complains and goes on to clarify the situation. "I eat only thirty-six. Very small paratha, and this is on Eid day."

Fair enough. I probably ate the equivalent on Eid day too.

We laze our way through the afternoon, floating along shaded waterways, emerging into the glaring sun, sipping warm water, and hot cardamom tea. The boat is manoeuvred into nooks and crannies skirting the edge of the forest. The boys amuse themselves by shouting warnings of "danger" to the infrequent vessels coming our way and shrieking with laughter at the resultant alarmed faces.

When the sun begins to glow orange and drop slowly into the sky, we change course and head back to port. Doing their duty to the bitter end, the three boys accompany us off the boat in Mongla and lead us directly to a large tarmacked parking lot where buses, each in worse condition than the last, are filling rapidly.

"To Khulna," says Munnu.

29
Full Circle

Being a connoisseur of bus travel in the People's Republic of Bangladesh, I can clearly state that this is the worst experience to date. The equivalent of a service bus, it pauses every few hundred metres, whilst a hardy number of commuters squeeze their way on board, or hang onto the handle at the doorway.

The seats are narrow, upright benches that would be at home in a severe Presbyterian mission where penance is the name of the game. I share a cubic inch of space with a snotty-nosed child dribbling gruelly rice down his front and wiping his mouth on my *dupatta*. His fourteen cousins surround him. After about an hour and a half of suffering, we grind to a halt at the rear of a four-line traffic jam.

"Is this Khulna?" I ask Munnu, struggling to sit upright.

He enquires of the bus in general and is told, with broad grins and shrugging shoulders, that it is *almost* Khulna.

"Almost?"

"This is the line for the Rupsa ferry. We must take a five-minute crossing to reach the city. There is no bridge. It is necessary that we leave the bus. This is people only ferry. It will be little bit crowded."

We join the scrum to alight from the bus. I don't believe my feet actually touch the floor, such is the surge of the human wave. We grab the last two places beside a hungry goat and two burkha-clad females on the rear of a rickshaw van that weaves its way in and out of the mass of buses, cars, and trucks. It is dark and virtually impossible to see anything by the time we thrust ourselves onto the glorified raft. I am pressed against the body in front of me, another is pressing behind me, and I squeal loudly when I feel a deliberate pinch on my behind.

"Anne. What is it? What is your problem? A mosquito bites you?" Munnu asks, panicked.

"Somebody...some person behind me, pinched me on my bottom," I say incredulously. This is the first time anything like this has happened to me, and I am speechless, quite speechless and quite cross.

"They pinch you? Who? Who dares to pinch you? Show me the man. I kill him."

I look at Munnu, surprised at his reaction as my own. Gone is the pleasant, amiable, and patient friend; suddenly he is the irate protector.

"It's okay," I backtrack. "I don't know who it was. There are too many people. It didn't hurt, just shocked me."

"I find him," Munnu threatens, causing a rumble of discontent as he twists to glare behind him. "This is an insult."

It is nothing worse than on your average subway trip, far less intrusive in fact, and I almost wish I had kept quiet. Luckily, the ferry bangs heavily into something, and we all shoot forward and fall over like dominoes. The ferry comes to a shuddering stop. "Have we crashed?" I splutter, taking someone's foot out of my mouth.

"No. Here is the other side of the river. Very small."

"I've been in bigger baths." I start to agree when I feel another pinch. This time, I am quick to wriggle my arm behind my back and grab. It's not a very hard grab, and I cannot be sure I got the right person, but the sudden inhalation of breath at my right ear and the scurrying figure pushing past as we disembark, leaves me vindicated. I laugh.

"Anne. What is the joke?" Munnu demands.

"I grabbed the pincher," I say merrily. "No need for you to kill him."

Munnu is not amused. "I should punish the pincher," he grumbles. "I am here to look after you. I fail."

"Don't be a macho ass," I tell him. "You can look after me by finding a hotel, not killing an idiot groper."

"Macho ass," repeats Munnu. "Anne. Am I really a macho ass?"

It improves his humour no end. Preoccupied, he hails a rickshaw, ushers me on, and thinks a while. I can see the phrase "macho ass" vying for number one slot against "slob."

"I think in Bangladesh many men like to be macho ass," he concludes. "Anne. In your travelling diary, will you please write that I am red-hot sex god?"

Well, it will make a change to the endless bus journeys and meal times.

The rickshaw-*wallah* interrupts this cultural exchange with a hotel option. We are already through the centre of Khulna, smaller and more rural than downtown Chittagong, but with an unmistakable city atmosphere. We had tried a couple of mid-budget residences and found them full. Eventually we pull up outside a huge, five-storey grey building that screams functional and featureless. It looks like a down-at-heel city bank.

"I think there is room here," Munnu, the red-hot sex god, prophesies.

"If only because all the residents have killed themselves."

"Anne. Still you are very funny girl."

We enter the cavernous foyer of the empty Tiger Garden Hotel, mentioned ominously, I find thumbing through *Lonely Planet*, as the kind of place where "staff suggest to single male guests that they can 'arrange something' for them." The lone receptionist, behind his immense, dark wood counter, waves me to a threadbare chair and negotiates a price for rooms with and without t/v, a/c, w/c, v/d or whatever.

"Let's have it all," I suggest recklessly. "Televisions and air conditioning—why not? It is nearly the end of our trip."

The receptionist's face contorts. He looks as if all his birthdays have come at once, as if the general stereotype of crazy foreigners is correct, as if he wishes he had named a higher price, but particularly as if he knows that the rooms are actually all the same unfurnished shell, and he will now have to shove all this equipment into one. He certainly keeps us filling in forms long enough for the place to be redecorated.

Although it isn't. Upstairs, the long, empty corridors are in serious need of a lick of paint, the strip of carpet down the centre is a worn, dingy brown, and the even browner wooden doors are relics of an obsolete mental institution. Behind them though, the rooms are large, the bathrooms with fetching Barbie-pink suites and pedestal lavatories are even larger. The cockroaches crouched inside the air-conditioning units and behind the bed-heads are the largest of all. Even Munnu balks at crunching this many gerbil-sized insects underfoot, and the manager finds alternative accommodation down another corridor. I do, however, have a sneaking suspicion that he has actually lead us in a circle back to the same rooms, but slowly enough for a "boy" to de-roach them. It would be easy enough as there are no numbers on any of the doors.

Munnu leaves me to write my diary ("Remember: red-hot sex god. And if you write about the pincher, you must say that Bangladeshi men usually do not do this") whilst he vanishes to procure—guess what?—bus tickets and food. I am reluctant to let him out of my sight, convinced that he will never find his way out let alone back, and I urge him to leave a trail: string, breadcrumbs, cockroach carcasses.

Anne Hamilton

He returns quickly with the tickets, some curried eggs, and ice cream, which reminds me of a final piece of dietary advice for those intending to eat ice cream in Bangladesh: Igloo is vastly superior to Polar and much less runny when trying to scoop it up with your fingers, a hard-boiled egg, or on the edge of your toothbrush because your hotel doesn't run to spoons.

I wake early the next morning and remember that this is the last of my jaunts around Bangladesh. After a couple more days in Dhaka, I will be back on a plane...

I put it out of my head and wait whilst the room is checked over. As in Chittagong, paying up-front with cash requires that staff examine the vacated room to ensure the opportunistic guest has not nicked the television, slipped the coffee table into his briefcase, or ripped the headboard off the wall and blatantly walked out with it under his arm.

The bright and shiny blue bus is humming quietly right outside, and the other passenger already ensconced on the front seat and behind a newspaper. It is an air-conditioned bus, hence our lack of companions, but the only one for which we could get last-minute tickets. When the solicitous assistant has drawn the curtains across the tinted glass windows, it is like being in a limo, or a police van—or so I imagine, having never (yet) had the pleasure of either.

A couple of dozy hours later we pull into Jessore, into exactly the same bay from which we departed for the Mohinneycarty Work Camp all those lifetimes ago. I enjoy the feeling of familiarity, of recognition, and therefore, almost of belonging. It is enhanced when Munnu, outside to have a cigarette, knocks madly on the window. There, grinning beside him are Dr Musa, and Lite the pharmacist.

"Hello, Mrs Anne. Are you come to be my intern after all?" Dr Musa calls.

There is no time to stay the night, not even time to take tea, but still the two-minute reunion is a great finale.

Once again back in Dhaka, Munnu and I nearly have a fight.

Included in my original airfare is an overnight at the Sonargaon Hotel, which, along with the Sheraton, makes up Dhaka's five-star hotel accommodations. It is curiosity rather than any great need for luxury and pampering that draw me to checking in. How can a three hundred dollar room be so much better than one at Tk 140 (under $3 at the Hotel Singapore in Mongla) and even Tk 750 (about $12 at the Tiger Garden in Khulna)? It simply feels quite obscene. I intend to

293

take the room and steal as many miniature shampoos and embossed envelopes as I possibly can.

"You will come with me?" I say to Munnu, who is wary of this plan. We stand at the side of the main road shouting at each other above the noise of the traffic.

"I am not the right type of person to be in Sonargaon," he keeps saying. Each time he does, I get cross. I think he does it on purpose.

"What is the 'right type of person'?" I bully him. "You mean rich tourists?"

"Of course. It is fancy hotel. Very smart."

"If it's that fancy and that smart, then they will be polite and pleased to see you," I tell him. "If they're not, then we leave."

"I am very curious to see Sonargaon Hotel."

"Then let's go," I wheedle. "Before we choke on diesel fumes."

"We cannot arrive in rickshaw," Munnu decides. "There will be smart cars and limousines. We take taxi. You pay, rich girl."

There is something decadent about hiring an entire taxi for ourselves. We automatically gaze around to find others to share it, and realise that everyone who wants a taxi hails their own.

We slide onto the leather seats and the driver asks our destination. Munnu, a casual hand running through his hair, says "Sonargaon," as loftily as if he was born to it. He sits back and grins.

"Now don't tell me that you didn't enjoy that," I accuse.

"Maybe." He shrugs, still smiling, and then he lowers his voice. "What about my clothes?"

I look at them objectively: neat grey trousers, a striped white shirt still fresh and crisp, good shoes. Then I look at mine: a limp, cotton *salwar kameez* that appears to have been slept in, tatty sand-coloured sandals that have never been the same since the day Christine threw her dinner over them (don't ask), and my hair in an untidy knot. "You have to come," is all I say. "They won't let me in alone. I look like a vagrant."

"You look shining," he replies, gallant to the last. "I am proud to accompany you."

"Then just remember The Sonargaon is nothing but a big building with beds in it—just like all the other places we have stayed. It just has a bigger attitude."

The yellow taxicab sweeps into the curved drive of the grand, white hotel. A gardener is sweeping the driveway, the grounds are neat and well presented, and there is a concierge in a maroon uniform that clashes with the red carpet at the entrance. Bellboys are summoned by imperious patrons to load their Louis Vuitton cases onto gold-lacquered trolleys.

We pay an extortionate taxi fare whilst our luggage is lifted from the boot, nobody mentioning the red mud and dust of the Sunderbans which floats in a cloud and settles all over the floor. I nudge Munnu, and we try not to laugh as the enormous luggage carrier is borne off with only Mr Hoque's golf bag—the bag I have been using since Jessore when I realised my huge rucksack was only a liability—and Munnu's small briefcase.

"What do we do now?" asks Munnu.

"Exactly as Hasina would," I say. "March in as if we own the place."

The foyer is large and ornate, full of marble floors and sculpture, a tinkling fountain, the subdued clink of afternoon tea being served in the palm court, and the ubiquitous clocks showing the time in London, Hong Kong, and New York.

"Anne. I am the only Bangladeshi here who is not working." Munnu whispers to me as we wait behind a loud Indian family who need extra safety deposit boxes for their jewellery. "I feel everyone looks at me."

He is correct. There are Chinese faces, Japanese, Korean, Indian, even one American voice, but there is no Bangla being spoken, no Bengalis being checked in.

"Exactly how I have felt for the last three months." I tell him.

"It is a pleasure to have you here, ma'am, sir," welcomes the middle-aged and portly receptionist. "May I ask why you are visiting Bangladesh?"

"I am here to see my husband," I lie fluently and cheerfully. I might as well go the whole hog and see if I can get an upgrade into a palatial suite. It's a long shot but you never know. "But tomorrow I must leave, and he will stay behind until his visa is approved." I think about squeezing out a tear or two, but decide that would be dishonest.

There is a quick flurry of Bengali, during which I assume Munnu is backing up my story, and the receptionist turns back to me. "Madam, I have pleasure in making you a special rate. A large room with two king-size beds." He is too well bred to leer to my face, but I know he is doing it internally.

Self-consciously, we make our way through the ornate furnishings, the plush carpets, the chrome and gold-plated ornamentation, and into the carpeted elevators. The corridors are hushed with muted and inoffensive colour schemes, occasional tables and armchairs are set neatly into various alcoves en route.

"Where is the key?" Munnu asks when we finally arrive at Room 714.

I show him the electronic card that opens the door and activates the electricity, and I instruct him to turn on every lamp and appliance he can find as he incredulously tours the room. How can I describe the place? It is like any upmarket hotel chain anywhere, bland but comfortable with all the overpriced characterlessness required: pools, tennis courts, bars, restaurants. It is interesting to share the experience of the majority of foreigners and business people visiting Dhaka but to know, personally, what they are missing by staying here and realise that in their minds they are missing nothing at all. But very strongly I wish I was spending my last night in Bangladesh somewhere...well...Bangladeshi.

"Like a hotel in an American movie." Munnu is overwhelmed.

We spend a happy half-hour plundering the room of everything mobile, anything with the Sonargaon logo imprinted upon it, and anything small enough to fit into Munnu's bag without looking suspicious. He throws away his few clothes in order to fit them in.

We load the bottles of complimentary shower gel, shampoo, and moisturiser into his bag, along with the shower cap, sewing kit and—after using it—the shoe shine equipment, as well as all the stiff, cream stationery.

"How exactly are you going to explain all of this stuff?" I ask. "I can't imagine you going home to Bachchu or to your mother and saying, 'Yeah, just fancied a night in The Sonargaon. Have twelve little packets of soap and some matches as a souvenir.'"

Munnu shrugs happily. "I do not care. I think of something. They know I do not steal. Maybe I say a friend showed me the hotel. Maybe I say the truth. Nobody will believe me."

We flush the lavatory at random and pack the spare toilet rolls, waste copious amounts of hot water through the shower and out the bath, call for more towels, wear the robes over our clothes, turn on the hot towel rail and the trouser press. We run an impromptu trampoline competition on the two beds, each of which is larger in itself than the entire rooms in the Hotel Singapore, and then we flop down onto the cream leather sofa, put our feet on the sparkling glass coffee table (shoes still on) and Munnu flicks through the fifteen million satellite TV channels whilst I make a stack of phone calls to guest services to enquire about wake-up calls, airport shuttles, and to find out why the copy of the Bible is larger than that of the Qu'ran.

In all, we are thoroughly irresponsible and enjoy every second of it.

I telephone the SCI office but there is no answer thus scuppering my plans for goodbye visits.

"It is only 3 p.m.," Munnu says. "Keep trying. Would you like to take food now? Or..."

"Or watch the cricket?" I add for him as his eyes stray back to the screen. "You can do both!" I grin, brandishing the room service menu.

"My shoes do not cost as much as the New York-style cheesecake," Munnu marvels, pointing out the cheapest thing on the menu. He calculates that his whole outfit and mine put together are worth less than an eight-ounce beef burger and fries.

Throwing caution to the winds, we order a snack anyway. Munnu makes me do it. He is afraid that the operator will not understand Bengali. Twenty minutes later, a waiter attempts to wheel in a food cart the size of a small car. The man has all the concentration of somebody doing a supermarket grab with an out-of-control trolley except that he is doing it in slow motion. When he has created sufficient space to park the table, he crawls underneath and doubles its circumference by pushing up two large leaves. He motions me to perch on the sofa with my knees pulled up to my chin, and Munnu to sit cross-legged on the edge of the nearest bed, and with a final effort, he wedges the table between us and pulls out a couple of dishes of food from a metal cabinet hidden beneath the folds of the white damask tablecloth. Setting the dishes either side of the centrepiece, a plastic red rose standing stiffly in its vase, the waiter asks if he should return for the cart, and looks relieved, if sceptical, when we assure him that we'll leave it outside the door.

The whole charade takes twenty minutes, in another three we devour the ethnic chicken curry and wipe our mouths on the once pristine tablecloth. Then we reverse the obstacle course.

"I do this very careful in case I ever want a job here," Munnu informs me with a straight face. By dint of shoving and sheer, brute force, we eventually manage to eject the food trolley from the room.

"Why was that even harder than when it came in?" I wonder, hands on my hips examining the scrapes along the walls.

"I think," Munnu says, "we forget to put down the extensions before we move the table."

We go back into the room and tidy up the worst of the mess. We pause occasionally to listen to the muffled curses and exclamations of horror from the corridor and the crashes and bangs as things fall to the floor.

"I didn't think the trolley was blocking the whole hallway." I say. "Not enough to be a fire hazard or anything."

I again attempt several phone calls, but nobody is answering. Even when I call home to confirm I am on the verge of returning, the answering machine is on. I try Hasina's mobile but she is out of range in Bangalore.

"Maybe I should just go to SCI," I think out loud. "I'm sure someone will be there." I really want to say a final goodbye, not to mention the fact that my belongings, including my passport, are still cluttering up the office.

"I come with you," Munnu says.

"Do you want to take a rest first?" I ask.

"Okay. One hour only."

We flop on the beds.

"Anne." Munnu's voice echoes faintly across the abyss.

"Yes?"

"This is one hotel room. And I sleep further away from you now than my house in Khalia is to Chapa's."

Later on, we hit Dhaka in its rush hour glory for one last evening. Munnu tells the rickshaw driver to do a lap of honour to take in all the sights I have seen over the last few weeks: the university, National Gallery, Curzon Hall, Old Dhaka and the docks, Ahsan Munzil, Lalbagh Fort. I wonder at how familiar it has all become and try to balance it with that very first rickshaw ride in Shahardot's company. I want to stay longer, learn Bengali, learn to do things on my own, go back to Srimangal and be the teacher (Christine was interested in this job but decided, on balance, to try for more voluntary work in India), and visit Khalia with a little more self-confidence. We arrive in Mohammadpur and find there is nobody home. We bang pointlessly on the door.

"We take tea across the road and wait for Shahardot to return," Munnu suggests. "If he does not come in a short time, we go to the house of Pavel for the key."

"If all else fails we can shimmy up the drainpipe and climb onto the veranda. That door might be open." I squint upwards.

"Anne," says Munnu. "I do anything for you, but I won't do that." He pauses in thought. "Anne. I think this is a song. Which is it?"

Buckets of tea later, Moni pulls up in a baby taxi. We pay the driver to wait.

"Everyone is gone out," Moni says. "You are lucky that I come back for some papers."

"Do you know where my passport is?" I ask him.

"Right inside. Shahardot packed it in your bag for you."

I hope that its proximity to the front door is not commensurate with the SCI desire to move me on. Whilst Munnu hauls the luggage downstairs and loads it into the scooter, I leave Mr Hoque's golf bag, some meagre gifts, and a convoluted message for Hasina who will collect them later.

"Why do you not visit Pavel?" Moni suggests. "Maybe I come later."

Again, there is nobody home. It is an anti-climax. Having psyched myself up to say goodbye, it seems that everyone has already moved on without me, which of course is the nature of travel. A small part of me is relieved to circumvent the farewells. After all, I have been quite a nuisance to my hosts in general, if not (usually) on purpose. But I would like them to know how much their time and hospitality is appreciated.

"They are probably out celebrating my departure," I say gloomily, my mind flicking over the past weeks, desperate to find something I have done, achieved, left behind me for posterity.

"You learn that Bangladesh is not only about the starving babies," Munnu reminds me. "You show yourself to village people who have not seen white skin before. You help medical clinics. You dig roads. You become my best friend."

I sniffle. "How can I be down-hearted? I've met you and Christine and Hasina's family and everyone at SCI..."

"Anne. Do not cry. I wish to remember your shining face. And—"

"And the people across the road are watching and wondering why you are making me so upset."

The baby taxi is executing a forty-six-point turn when we spy Moni racing towards us with Bachchu beside him. They shout instructions. Munnu turns delightedly to me and says, "Pavel and Suez and Bonny are at National Assembly Park. They wait for us to meet them, and we take tea."

On the steps of the Parliament buildings, SCI are out in force. Rehana arrives with Farabia and Alvi, and we sit in an enormous circle in the middle of the grass, drinking tea and fending off hawkers. Suez even telephones Borhan, and he, proudly walking arm-in-arm with Shakila, along with his sister Fatima and a bag of wedding photographs, come down to join the throng. Being *Mrs* seems to suit Shakila who excitedly gets out the albums and tells Rehana all about her wedding day. Fatima reminds me of the prawn bhoona she made "by her own hand," and Borhan kindly circulates a photo of me stuffing it into my mouth—and missing. We make arrangements to meet in Ireland.

"It is like your first days," Suez reminds me. "Remember we all are here with you and with Christine?"

"The mosquitoes bite you badly," remembers Moni. "How is Christine? Does she mail you?"

"I was not here that day," Munnu mourns.

"I regret that you miss one new friend," Bachchu tells me. "SCI person in Rajoir—Mr Islam. He was in Dhaka on business but left us already. He must get back to his daughters. Do you remember Mr Islam? He remembers you."

I bet he does, I think. "What a shame to miss him," I say insincerely. "He was very—capable." It's the nearest grudging compliment I can spare.

"Does he also say how Shuna and Rokeya are being? Anne spends happy hours with these clever girls." Munnu looks innocently at his brother but cannot help sliding a grin in my direction.

"Oh, yes. Certainly, yes," Bachchu says in a very heartfelt manner. "Mr Islam says many things about them. Many things. I think that they must be very, very well. Very clever girls."

"All we need is Rakim to complete the circle." It is my turn to tease Munnu. "I never said goodbye to him."

"Rakim? Who is this person?" Munnu says loftily. "I must already forget this person who tries to offer you his heart but is not worth—"

"You did not complete our final evaluation form," interrupts Bonny with impeccable timing. "It does not matter, if you are happy with your programme here."

I take endless photographs, sign a couple of nonchalant autographs, and fade contentedly into the background. As the sun sets and the Bangladeshi flag is ceremoniously lowered, Bachchu, in his official capacity of National Secretary, raises his empty glass in a moving toast to SCI and its friends, staff, and volunteers worldwide.

Once more at the Sonargaon, the foyer is still dotted with foreigners looking rich and bored, and one repatriated Bangladeshi family with mounds of pristine suitcases just looking rich. In my room, housekeeping has replaced everything that Munnu is now selling on the black market.

Settling down to sleep, I feel extremely alone. When the telephone rings, I assume it is my wake-up call and wonder why it is so dark—my flight isn't till 10 a.m.

"Anne?" At five o'clock in the morning, Hasina's voice is bright and bubbly. "Where were you? I call you earlier. We ask the reception but they do not know about you. I want to say goodbye before tomorrow. I am so sorry to be away. I invite you to return and bring your husband. I like to meet this shadow-figure."

Anne Hamilton

We have a protracted conversation. I ask about Bangalore, she asks about the Sunderbans. We say goodbye, thank you, you're welcome, see you again, thank you, thank you, thank you, and then Mr Hoque comes on the line with some last minute advice.

"So, you fly tomorrow? Have you aspirin? You must take one aspirin to prevent the blood clots. I do this always. But for me, it is necessary because of the blood pressure, for you it is a precaution only. Good luck. We see you again when we visit Ireland. Wait—Mrs Hoque needs to speak to you again. Women! Bah! Always they are speaking on the telephone. I pay the bills. No wonder my blood pressure gets high..."

I hear his lamentations grow weaker as he hands over the phone and imagine him pacing the room.

"Anne? Now, you must be sure to eat breakfast in the hotel. Little bit, as food in the airport is snacks only. Nothing good there. You order room service and..."

I get up and dress, grinning broadly all the time. Never will I know what I did to deserve meeting such wonderful people.

30

The Last Day: The End of the Beginning

The airport is humming. Since so few people are allowed inside the terminal building, family farewells spill over lavishly into the humid forecourt. Unlike the excited enthusiasm of the *Arrivals* section that nonplussed me so many weeks ago, inside *Departures* there is an all-pervading sense of strain: the misery of those left behind, the knowledge of the distances to be travelled, and that it will be a long time before families and friends will be reunited given the unlikelihood of getting the documentation to visit a brother or son in their new country. Faces are anxious, and the shouting is louder than usual as people fight to be in the right place at the right time.

"Anne. How does this work?" Munnu looks around at the apparent lack of airline staff when we finally get to that torture otherwise known as Check-in.

There is a row of desks: Air India, Gulf Air, British Airways, Singapore Airlines, all deserted and closed, a small bank, and *bureau de change* which will open at midday, and little else. At the far end, snaking around a corner, I spy more desks and what appears to be a small cluster of people in front of them.

"Over there," I say and with difficulty we point the rusty and complaining luggage trolley to join a jostling, impatient, and mutinous crowd big enough to fill a half dozen 747s.

"This must be the place," I shout to Munnu across the noise. "Can you see a desk that says *Emirates*?"

By dint of jumping up and down, I make out the print on the handwritten signs taped up behind a row of distant counters: all *Emirates*, all unmanned. There is another crudely hand-made notice stating that the Dubai/London Heathrow flight will have a five-hour delay and thus checking-in procedures will begin later.

"So we go home and return in four hours," says Munnu, the virgin international traveller.

Dispelling his innocence, I explain the vagaries of air travel, and tell him that if we do that, some official is bound to whip away the signs two minutes after our departure and swap them for *Boarding Now* instructions. And that it is an unwritten airport rule that you have to join a long line and insist on checking in anyway.

"See?" I point at all the passengers arguing and tapping their feet in front of the desks. "I bet that in a few minutes, the airline staff will give in and start work."

"Twelve minutes," says Munnu, impressed as he watches *Emirates* staff take their seats and try not to shrink back in horror as the crowd bears down on them waving tickets and frantic passports. "Such panic even when the plane is very delayed," he marvels.

"Another unwritten airport law," I tell him.

For a while we stand in a line that is not a line, just a line of people attempting to decide which line they should be in. "If there is a Business Class queue, I should go to that," I finally admit to Munnu who jumps into the fray on my behalf.

"You should say earlier. It is a very short line," he says when he comes back a few minutes later. "But we have to push very hard because all the *not business* people want to use it, and the lady is very cross with them."

We squirm and heave and ignore howls of indignation as we viciously run over annoying people's feet with the trolley. Every now and then, Munnu snaps an authoritative, "Business," and the crowds unwillingly let us through, although not without a universal glance which says, "Riff-raff like you? What is the world coming to?" and makes them try even harder for an upgrade.

The smiling girl is friendly and helpful, speaks English and takes absolutely ages. As with the entire department, nothing is computerised and tickets are checked, seats allocated, cross-checks carried out, and baggage tagged, all by hand.

"Would you like your bag to go straight to Dublin?" she asks me.

"Not really," I say. "I'm stopping in Dubai."

"Oh? Oh, yes. I see now. I must start again as I check you to Dublin. Are you sure you want to stop in Dubai?"

"Yes, please."

"It is just that I never sent someone to Dublin from Dhaka," she says wistfully, and then ominously, "Does your bag have insurance?"

"Yes. But I really, really need it in Dubai," I say, in case she decides to send it to Dublin anyway for the thrill. "It contains urgent medical supplies without which I will die, and my descendants will sue everybody they can for lots of money."

It is the wrong thing to say.

"Excellent," she beams. "This is exciting."

Clearly, being a check-in agent in Dhaka lacks fulfilment. I am now resigned to the fact that my trusty, black(ish) rucksack will end up in Dubrovnik. "Well, at least that passed two hours," I say.

"Anne," says Munnu, "why have you guilt?"

What a question. Why do zebras have stripes? Why does the sun rise in the East? Why do birds suddenly appear...? "What do you mean?" I ask. "General guilt or something specific?"

Munnu looks rightly confused. "I mean, why do you not want to tell me you fly the business class?"

"Um, because I feel guilty," I confirm. "My brother knows I hate flying. He has a lot of air miles so he got me an upgrade with them."

"And you feel guilt because you fly this way to a very poor country like Bangladesh?" he verifies.

"Yes. Of course."

"You drink the champagne, sit in a big-ass seat with movies and restaurant food?"

"More or less. Do you think that is really awful? I bet SCI would be horrified."

Munnu grins. "I tease you. Of course it is not bad. If I have the opportunity, I do this also. All persons do. You think the beggars in Dhaka care whether you fly to Bangladesh in the front of the plane or the back?"

Or whether I fly here at all. Which puts me nicely in my place.

We park ourselves in two plastic chairs. Munnu is overjoyed to find a handful of famous people travelling, the members of a reasonably well-known Indian band sit beside us, and he joins in their conversation. The entourage pose for an illegal photograph and sign an autograph or two.

"Less fans than you have in Cox's Bazaar," Munnu notes.

Suddenly there is an announcement over the tannoy system which Munnu translates as my having to leave. We say a flurry of goodbyes—tearful in my case—and I load up my bags.

"But I don't want to go," I whine like child. "I want to stay here and take tea and go shopping with Hasina and on tours with you and sit in the SCI office and fill in evaluation forms and make Christine come back and..."

"Anne. You must go." Munnu propels me forward. "Also you must return soon."

At a sign that says *"Departures. Passengers Only,"* we face a serious security guard who wants to check my papers. He asks Munnu a couple of questions, grunts doubtfully and waves us both along.

"What did you say to him?"

"I tell him my blonde Bengali wife departs the country leaving me behind her," he grins. "He says I may come to the gate and wave to you."

Suddenly it is time to go, and I load Munnu down with messages for everyone I can think of. There is so much to say, and yet there is nothing. I take a step forward, and then one back. I suddenly think of something I have been meaning to ask Munnu for weeks, and I must know before I go.

"Munnu," I say. "What is calculus?"

He looks puzzled. "Calculus? I do not know. Why do you ask?"

"You must know," I persist. "You've told me a lot of stories and in many of them you start by saying, 'when I was in calculus...' Is it something in college?"

He looks at me for a moment, and then laughs out loud. "Not calculus," he explains. "*Cadet class*. I say 'when I am in cadet class.' It is a school that gives good education and also trains men for the Army. My mother sent me there, but I do not wish to be a military person. Cadet class," he repeats. "Make sure this is correct in your travelling diary."

"Yes, my diary," I say. "I will send it to you. But how should I finish it? What will I say so people know how I feel about Bangladesh?"

"Anne. Long ago in Khalia you tell me that you come to Bangladesh because you want to have your story to tell. Yes? And now you have this story."

I nod, touched that he remembers.

"So already you will have written everything. You just be simple."

Since he is right, it is only fitting that I give Munnu the last words.

He thinks carefully: "Say, 'I said goodbye, I got in the airplane, and went home. The End,'" he advises.

And this is what I do.

THE END

Epilogue

Hours later, I landed (with my luggage) in Dubai where the best thing and the worst thing was suddenly being invisible again.

A few days there were meant to be a bridge between Bangladesh and Ireland, a time to take stock and to acclimatise. It was more like having a foot in each place and being tugged in both directions until I was doing the splits. Every choice—food, clothes, company, entertainment—was a battle between Western and non-Western, and making the choice felt like dividing loyalties. I didn't want to get back to Ireland and let Bangladesh be nudged into a nostalgic interlude. Equally, I wasn't someone who had "gone native" who thought herself more Bangladeshi than the Bangladeshi nation.

Back home I appreciated *choice*: endless books to read without rationing oneself to a few pages each night, supermarkets so full of food that I could probably eat for a year without sitting down to the same thing twice, being able to talk about anything to anyone without the limitations of a language barrier, the unquestioning acceptance of a desire for privacy and personal space.

Of course, I thought long about the division between rich and poor nations: particularly every time I turned on a tap I remembered that *eighty per cent* of health problems in the developing world are caused by lack of clean water. Mostly though, I tried to paint a different picture of Bangladesh, one beyond the desperate poverty that demonstrates—trite as it sounds—people. Their needs and dreams really are the same everywhere.

In fact, I talked so much about the place that it wasn't too long before people started asking me when I would be going back. Now there was a thought...

It was three years later in 2005, ready to face a bowl of rice again and *fitfaht* in my favourite *salwar kameez*, that I popped my toothbrush and passport in my pocket and met Pavel in the grounds of Dhaka airport. We fought off a gang from an American charity who were

306

convinced I was their woman and wandered towards a taxi already hired and waiting down at the roundabout. It didn't actually go more than a few feet before breaking down, but the thought was there.

The main road from the airport, now a highway into the city, had been stripped of sidewalk encampments and temporary shelters. Had displaced persons been displaced again in a clean-up operation designed to ensure that visiting dignitaries should not be offended by unreasonable poverty and its trappings? The ban on unlicensed baby taxis saw the roads marginally less clogged and the fumes slightly less potent, although there was no getting away from that yellowish smog-fog. Rickshaw bells and car hooters were simultaneous in glorious discord, but *wallah*s were stopping—more or less—for the traffic lights in front of the brand new planetarium.

In her apartment, Rehana was as welcoming as ever, as were Farabia and Alvi, both all grown up. My subsequent reunion with Christine could have been staged in so far as it matched the original. Dozing familiarly, *smugly,* in bed some time beyond midnight, doors slammed, lights snapped on, and there was I moving over to make room beside me. Christine once again conjured a double-sized duvet and two pillows from her bag, but this time, we had brought the real necessities.

"You did remember the cell phone and the chocolate? Great, I've got the hairdryer and the Polaroid camera."

A few days later in Gulshan, Hasina and Mr Hoque paused in their entertaining of fifty visiting Rotarians to settle us into the otherwise empty Golden Bird Residence for Foreigners, where we renewed other old acquaintances: Mithu and Bely, with their baby daughter, Borhan and Shakila coincidentally—again—visiting from Ireland with their son. Mitali took us shopping in Boshundhara Garden City, surprisingly the newest, shiniest, and largest shopping centre in Southeast Asia, and where a box of imported crackers or a bar of Hershey's chocolate cost the equivalent of ten rickshaw journeys to get there to buy it.

At SCI, Bonny, Suez, and Moni efficiently staffed the office, though I'll pass over the moment when they took a collective look in my direction and said:

"Welcome back...Anne, is that you? You got fattie, much fattie."

"That's good," they hastened to add. "Maximum good, a Bengali compliment."

I decided to believe them implicitly.

SCI Bangladesh was distracted supporting other branches of the organisation in the aftermath of the recent tsunami with colleagues on standby to travel to Sri Lanka and Indonesia as required. After all, as Suez said, who better to do so, given the Bangladeshi experience of annual monsoon devastation?

Still, they found time to plan our programme, and with time to visit just one project, it was always going to be the Rajoir Work Camp—though Jessore, with their thriving voluntary health services, came a very close second choice.

We felt our way into night-time Khalia village, a much easier journey given the new, improved ferry's capacity to carry vehicles in the wake of a failed electricity supply that did nothing to dampen the greetings of Bachchu and Tapon and of Mannu, now the Winter Camp Leader. Aktar, they told us, was working in Dhaka, and Mary was studying there—we would see her at the weekend. Asha had a good job in Jessore district, but Chapa was comfortably present and she, too, had become a SCI camp leader.

It was a homecoming. Exhilarating, affirming, and the equivalent of indulgent aunts reminiscing over childhood quirks:

"Anne. Remember your Irish jig? Do it again. Remember when you took only three pieces of potato? Eat more. Remember you sang *Flared-Red-Jacket?* You broke the water jug? Broke the raffia? Nearly fell off the bamboo bridge? Met the mad Mrs Begum—"

"Be thankful that Asha's not here to remind you of the *monthly bleeding*," added Christine.

The changes in Khalia and Shanti Kendra were demonstrated in order of significance. Instant lemon tea on site proudly replaced the thick, milky *cha'* taken at the village tea stall. New masts made mobile phones and snow-free television reception abundant. Alongside an upsurge in hygiene and sanitation education—the focus of Chapa's job throughout the local villages—the prevalence of arsenic in the water was far more widely accepted and precautions duly being taken. The GUP hospital remained deserted amidst tentative plans to turn it into an agricultural college, and guess what? The elusive milk processing plant over in Takerhad had grown into a key national factory—and Bachchu made sure Christine and I took our long overdue tour.

We spent our time inside colleges and schools—no levelling of the playing field this year. In a makeshift room in Dhaka's old city, we had seen how a charity struggled to pay shifts of child labourers to attend maths and reading lessons a couple of times a week. In Rajoir's senior classrooms, we joined lessons and spoke English with the students. In staff rooms, we drank tea and spoke English with the teachers. In primary school buildings, crammed huts all too often requisitioned as sanctuary during summer floods, we watched "chalk and talk"—

Anne Hamilton

teaching by rote— in lieu of any other materials , and learned that female primary enrolment, now at eighty-three percent, had finally reached gender parity.

Everywhere those words *SCI, volunteer, Ireland* and *Australia* still formed a backing-track. We eased into the watching, the waiting, for people to arrive, for mosquitoes to bite, for work plans to be agreed ("maybe tomorrow") and comprehending only brief snatches of staccato Bangla. All around was that certain sniff in the air, of cooking oil and spices, grass and heat—elusive, wafting, familiar, evocative, the essence of Bangladesh.

And finally, what of Munnu? Well, Munnu wasn't there. Seven months earlier he had won the DV (Diversionary) Lottery 2004 that granted him a coveted visa to the USA. Perhaps it was that which balanced the changes and the timelessness of Bangladesh in my mind: Christine and me sitting with his family in Khalia and speaking on a mobile phone to Munnu in New York City.

Next time? Well, that will always be *when* rather than *if*. And in the meantime, I really am learning Bangla. Oh—and writing a book.

About Bhola's Children

Bhola's Children was registered as a UK charity (no. 1118345) in March 2007.

It was established to provide a permanent source of funding for the home and school for orphaned and disabled children at Bhola Garden which had been set up by Howlader Ali with assistance from an ad hoc group of individual donors.

The main aim of Bhola's Children is to provide accommodation, education and medical treatment for orphaned and disabled children on the island of Bhola.

The aim is to provide more than just funds. Many of the current donors take a close personal interest in the charity and seek to support Ali by keeping in regular touch by telephone/email and visiting the island. Europeans on Bhola are a rare sight and it is hugely appreciated when they make the effort to go there – the welcome is tremendous.

For more information go to www.bholaschildren.org

About the Author

Between her travels, Anne Hamilton currently lives in Scotland where she is working on a novel whilst studying for a PhD in Creative Writing at Glasgow University. Anne and her husband celebrated the birth of their first baby in August 2010.

Other Charity Titles by LL-Publications

The Great Right Hope: Book One of the Sid Tillsley Chronicles
ISBN 9781905091423

Mark Jackman donates 50% of ebook and 25% of print royalties to Zoe's Place - a hospice for terminally ill kids in Middlesbrough, and Alzheimers Trust UK, split equally between the two.

In northeast England, a monster has arisen. A vampire beast is stalking the Yorkshire moors, mutilating and destroying everything in its path. The vampire elders realise that the Firmamentum has cast its shadow on the world once more—a phenomenon which happens every few millennia where a human and a vampire are born ultimately powerful and destined to oppose each other...

Sid Tillsley is a forty-six-year-old benefit-fraudster from Middlesbrough. He's an overweight alcoholic, and also sexist, homophobic and a lazy git. But one thing sets him apart from his Northern brethren; he can kill vampires with a single punch.
http://www.ll-publications.com/horror.html

Coming Soon in Fall 2010
Oil and Water...and Other Things That Don't Mix
ISBN 9781905091850

The disaster facing the Gulf Coast has been on the minds of millions of people and the ladies of the She Writes™ - Southern Writers group expressed many feelings of anger, sadness, and disgust.

Fellow She Writes™ members Zetta Brown and Nicky Wheeler-Nicholson Brown decided that something needed to be done where people can put their talents together and make a difference. What better way than to produce an anthology where the proceeds will go where it is needed most?

Oil and Water...and Other Things That Don't Mix is a collection of twenty-nineworks centering on the theme of "Conflict...resolution optional,"written by men and women

100% of procedes raised will go direct to charities in communities directly affected by the oil spill.
http://www.ll-publications.com/oilandwater.html

About LL-Publications

LL- Publications is an independent publisher based in Scotland specializing in genre and literary titles in both print and ebook formats since 2003. Visit us at www.ll-publications.com

Also by LL-Publications

BARK! by Darrell Bain. ISBN 9781905091157

The hilarious tale of little Tonto, the dog who has to save the world from an accidental alien invasion!

"Tonto, a cross-eyed, ADHD affected little Weenie Dog with only one testicle is suddenly called upon to save the world from an alien invasion! Can he do the job? Well, perhaps, if a compulsively cursing alcoholic super-genius and his co-ed groupies combine forces with a cigar-chomping Italian from the pentagon and his air headed secretary. And of course they have to have help from Tonto's owners, who think politicians aren't much smarter than lizards. "This is a science fiction novel so insane it only begins to make sense when it's discovered that the aliens had a part in Tonto's conception to begin with!"

Included in **BARK!** is the autobiography of Darrell's own quirky little dog, Tonto, the inspiration behind **BARK!**

OOPS! By Darrell Bain. ISBN 9781905091720

Oops! is the third collection of stories by Darrell Bain. When Cupid and a Gremlin bump heads, the sparks fly in a rare fantasy story by the author. Others stories in the collection include *A Simple Idea*, an almost ludicrously simple method of eliminating corruption and idiocy from the political process, one that has been around for centuries but gone unrecognized. *Cure for an Ailing Alien* finds a nurse who must come up with a cure for an alien, one whose bodily processes are completely unknown. You'll be amazed at her cure! *Retribution* is the story of unexpected consequences when alien meets human. *Robyn's Rock* is partially based on a happening in the author's life during a walk with his granddaughter. There are many more stories in this collection, all written in the individual style that has kept Bain's readers coming back for more for the past twenty years. This a book to add to your collection, stories by a notable, multi-award winning author.

2009 Eppie Award-winning novel for Best Horror;

PIT-STOP by Ben Larken
ISBN 9781905091720126

LAST CHANCE AT REDEMPTION FOR THE NEXT MILLION YEARS.

Welcome to the Pit-Stop Grill, a roadside attraction along Arizona's Route 66 where travelers kick up their feet while sipping a nice cup of joe. It's a cool oasis in an unforgiving desert landscape. It's also the last stop on the road to Hell.

When ten people find themselves inside the eerie diner, unable to get out or remember how they arrived, all they know is what their waitress, Holly, tells them: a bus is coming. It will take them the rest of the way to a destination of unspeakable horrors. Led by highway patrolman, Officer Scott Alders, the group of strangers unite with a common goal-- escape. Each of them holds dark secrets, but personal demons are no match for the wraithlike bus driver who arrives bearing the nametag *RAMSEY*.

Driving an oily black bus with ghostly headlights and exhaust that smells of brimstone, Ramsey wastes no time picking them off one by one. As their number dwindles and the terror mounts, Scott Alders realizes it will take more than a police-issued sidearm to stop the evil that tracks them. But is there enough power in their battered spirits to combat a crimson-eyed driver with a schedule to keep? One thing is clear: you'll think twice before you make your next Pit-Stop.

"Ben Larken's *Pit-Stop* is a non-stop thrill ride from the beginning 'til the end. One of the best up-coming writers I have had the pleasure of reading in a long time. Right up there with King, Barker and Straub."
—*John Parker, Head: The Southern Horror Writers Association*

"*Pit-Stop* is an extraordinary horror/noir thriller. I can strongly recommend this book. It will shake your faith if you have one, make you wish you had faith otherwise."
—*Geoff Nelder, reviewer for Compulsive Reader and Café Doom*

The Hollows - Book 1: The Ticking by Ben Larken

ISBN 9781905091546

1949
A young girl is traumatized when she witnesses a grisly murder in the forest behind her home.

1999
A loving wife disappears in the middle of the night, leaving no trace of her whereabouts.

2009
Former detective David Alders rents an apartment at a typical complex; a quiet unassuming place nestled in the outskirts of Fort Worth called The Hollows.

David is at a dead end after ten maddening years searching for his vanished wife. With mounting bills and a daughter on the verge of college, he makes the only logical choice: sell the family home, get back to work, and take a cheap apartment. His daughter, Melanie, is secretly thrilled about the change hoping it means a fresh start for their withering family.
But The Hollows has other plans...
As a new community welcomes the Alders into its midst, elusive figures watch from the periphery, waiting for their moment. On the first night, a grotesque, burnt man seizes Melanie in her bed, spewing insane ramblings before disappearing into the darkness. She struggles to convince her father what happened was real, but David has his own problems.
Like the fact that he has just woke up in the wrong day.
Welcome to a tour through the dark underbelly of the last half-century where invisible hands take you by force to the demons of your past. Where you can find terror, time travel, and murder—all for one low monthly rent.

Welcome to... THE HOLLOWS.
Pray that the lease agreement expires before you do.

The Great Right Hope, by Mark Jackman

ISBN 9781905091423

"Even the best vampires need a good smack..."

In north-east England, a monster has arisen. A vampire beast is stalking the Yorkshire moors, mutilating and destroying everything in its path. The vampire elders realise that the Firmamentum has cast its shadow on the world once more—a phenomenon which happens every few millennia, where a human and a vampire are born ultimately powerful and destined to oppose each other...

Sid Tillsley is a forty-six year old benefit-fraudster from Middlesbrough. He's an overweight alcoholic, and also sexist, homophobic and a lazy git. But one thing sets him apart from his northern brethren; he can kill vampires with a single punch. Suddenly, and very reluctantly, Sid finds himself the centre of human and vampire attention. Some want to kill him, but others believe him to be the Bellator; the one to fight the vampire beast.

Murder isn't murder
If it's served with fries...

ORDINARY WORLD

by Tony McGuin
ISBN 9781905091133

"A modest proposal for the 21st century..."

This is the future.

Democratic institutions in the West have collapsed under the weight of the public's fear of terrorist attack. In uncertain times what people crave is the firm smack of fatherly dictatorship and the Church has stepped in to ensure a firm smack is exactly what the people get.

A world now betrothed to organized religion has nevertheless allowed big business to become even more debauched. GORDON A. GARGOYLE, owner of Recovered Unwanted Meat Deals, (RUM Deals) UK, a manufacturer of reprocessed meat run-off, has secured a concession to exploit the virgin market of producing burgers made from aborted babies. As far as Gargoyle is concerned, the only thing Jonathan Swift lacked was a slogan and a jingle.

Can anybody stop this? Well, with the seemingly random interventions of two desperate friends, a child-smitten romantic, the world's most feeble (and ginger) terrorist, a cancer-ridden devil dog, a curious little blue car and a mysteriously knowing Pub landlord, somebody may already have. Mornings are hateful. Afternoons are quite pleasant. It's just another day in an Ordinary World.

No ordinary book, ORDINARY WORLD is a refined taste of exquisite satire which takes a stab at a near future world gone mad...

A Human Reaction

by Peter Ashley
ISBN 9781905091720164

Earth is gripped in a devastating, post-apocalyptic final war that only one nation will be allowed to survive...

In his quest to bring a proud nation to its knees, Commander John Henson fails to destroy a seemingly insignificant enemy base, and in doing so is captured.

Lost: Commander John Henson, wanted for his lethal ability to obliterate the enemy compound of Fort Millawa, missing in action along with fellow soldier and lover, Salome.

Found: "Prisoner X" awakes to find himself a captive of Captain Rachel Dahan. He must now face what he has inadvertently found—a new perspective on the destructive conflict that has torn civilisation apart, and its impact on his very soul.

A Human Reaction finds a man suddenly no longer dedicated to his old life but struggling for a place in a new world.